Selected Letters of

Katherine Anne Porter

Selected Letters of

Katherine Anne Porter

CHRONICLES OF A MODERN WOMAN

Edited by Darlene Harbour Unrue

University Press of Mississippi / Jackson

www.upress.state.ms.us

The University Press of Mississippi is a member
of the Association of American University Presses.

First printing 2012

∞

Library of Congress Cataloging-in-Publication Data

Porter, Katherine Anne, 1890–1980.
[Correspondence. Selections]
Selected letters of Katherine Anne Porter : chronicles
of a modern woman / edited by Darlene Harbour Unrue.
p. cm.
Includes bibliographical references and index.
ISBN 978-1-61703-620-0 (cloth : alk. paper) —
ISBN 978-1-61703-621-7 (ebook) 1. Porter, Katherine Anne,
1890–1980—Correspondence. 2. Authors, American—
20th century—Correspondence. I. Unrue, Darlene
Harbour. II. Title.
PS3531.O752Z48 2012
813'.52—dc23
[B]   2011052326

British Library Cataloging-in-Publication Data available

For Jane

Contents

Editor's Note

When Isabel Bayley's long-awaited *Letters of Katherine Anne Porter* appeared in 1990, it was received enthusiastically but with a concurrent awareness that it must eventually be supplemented. Bayley's collection covers Porter's letter-writing life from 1930 through 1963 with an addendum of one 1964 letter and one 1966 letter. As George Hendrick, an early and respected Porter scholar, pointed out in a review of the Bayley edition in *Choice*, by 1930 Porter was forty years old, and her formative years, the period of experience that provided the sources for her highly acclaimed stories and novellas, lay behind her. "We need those early letters," he wrote. He might have added that letters from the last seventeen years of Porter's life, years in which she was evaluating her history, settling affairs and scores, and clarifying her aesthetic, were also needed to complete the personal record.

Because of the omissions, Bayley's edition does not approach a "life in letters." Indeed, the equivalent of a full biography was not her intention. A devoted friend to Porter for many years and her literary trustee from 1974 until her death in 1993, she selected thirty-three years of letters that collectively would be a "crown" for Katherine Anne Porter in her one-hundredth-birthday year by revealing the mind and spirit of a much-admired woman Bayley found largely absent in biographies that appeared in the aftermath of Porter's death in 1980.

With that specific aim, Bayley chose 271 postcards and letters for her collection, almost none of which, except the postcards, is presented in its entirety. Although the letters I have selected are half the number in Bayley's edition, they are complete, even when uncommonly long. I was guided in my selection primarily by my desire to present as much as possible of Porter's view of her moment in history.

The letters here have been transcribed literally, preserving Porter's misspellings, British spellings, and eccentric habits of punctuation, including her general avoidance of, or misuse of, apostrophes and the insertion of multiple points, dashes, or other typographical symbols that range from two to more than a dozen. There are no ellipses in these letters, a fact necessary to stress because the running points sometimes appear to represent editorial excisions. Anything in brackets is my own insertion. I silently corrected typographical errors, and I have not identified handwritten insertions as such in typed letters.

The following abbreviations in the headings describe the physical form of each letter:

AL	Autograph (handwritten by KAP) letter unsigned
ALS	Autograph (handwritten by KAP) letter signed
DALS	Dictated autograph (handwritten by someone else) letter signed
DTLS	Dictated typed letter signed
TL	Typed letter unsigned
TLS	Typed letter signed

The pages cited in each heading refer to the number of sides of pages on which the letter was written, regardless of size. The repository named refers to the location of the original letter. The following abbreviations indicate specific repositories:

BU	Mugar Memorial Library, Boston University, Boston MA
Columbia	Butler Library, Columbia University, New York City
Cornell	The Carl A. Kroch Library, Cornell University Library, Ithaca NY
Delaware	The University Library, University of Delaware, Newark DE
Harvard	The Houghton Library, Harvard University, Boston MA
HRHRC	Harry Ransom Humanities Research Center, University of Texas at Austin
Mississippi	Mississippi Department of Archives and History, Jackson MS
Newberry	The Newberry Library, Chicago IL
NYPL	The Berg Collection, The New York Public Library, New York City
Northwestern	University Library, Northwestern University, Evanston IL
Penn State	Fred Lewis Pattee Library, Pennsylvania State University, University Park PA
Princeton	Princeton University Libraries, Princeton NJ

Private	Privately owned
Stanford	The Green Library, Stanford University, Palo Alto CA
TSU	Texas State University, San Marcos TX
Vanderbilt	The Jean and Alexander Heard Library, Vanderbilt University, Nashville TN
VPI	Virginia Polytechnic Institute Libraries, Blacksburg VA
W&L	Leyburn Library, Washington and Lee University, Lexington VA
Washington	The University of Washington Libraries, Seattle WA
WSU	Washington State University Libraries, Pullman WA
Yale	The Beinecke Library, Yale University, New Haven CT

Abbreviations of the names of amanuenses:

gw	Virginia (Ginger) Woolley, University of Maryland student
wrw	William Raymond Wilkins, retired naval officer KAP hired as a personal assistant

Because of her varied experiences and numerous acquaintances and friends, Porter's letters are richly infused with names of people, events, and artistic works of all kinds. I have provided no notes for well-known names or those easily found online or in common reference works or current editions of standard collegiate dictionaries. For additional background beyond that provided in the chronology of Porter's life, the identification of recipients, and notes, the following bibliographies and biographical and critical studies are recommended:

Kathryn Hilt and Ruth M. Alvarez, *Katherine Anne Porter: An Annotated Bibliography* (1990); annotated bibliographies in issues of the *Newsletter of The Katherine Anne Porter Society* 1994– (http://www.lib.umd.edu/Guests/KAP/pubs.html); *Katherine Anne Porter: Conversations* [interviews with Porter] (1987), ed. Joan Givner; *"This Strange, Old World" and Other Book Reviews of Katherine Anne Porter* (1991), ed. Darlene Harbour Unrue; *Uncollected Early Prose of Katherine Anne Porter* (1993), ed. Alvarez and Thomas F. Walsh; *Katherine Anne Porter's Poetry* (1996), ed. Unrue; *Katherine Anne Porter Remembered* (2010), ed. Unrue.

Conversations with Katherine Anne Porter: Refugee from Indian Creek (1981), by Enrique Hank Lopez; *Katherine Anne Porter's Women: The Eye of Her Fiction* (1983), by Jane Krause DeMouy; *Truth and Vision in Katherine Anne Porter's Fiction* (1986), by Unrue; *Katherine Anne Porter* (1988), by George and Willene Hendrick; *Katherine Anne Porter: A Life* (rev. 1991), by

Givner; *Katherine Anne Porter and Mexico: The Illusion of Eden* (1992), by Walsh; *Katherine Anne Porter's Artistic Development: Primitivism, Traditionalism, and Totalitarianism* (1993), by Robert H. Brinkmeyer; *Katherine Anne Porter: A Sense of the Times* (1995), by Janis Stout; *The Ambivalent Art of Katherine Anne Porter* (2005), by Mary Titus; and *Katherine Anne Porter: The Life of an Artist* (2005), by Unrue.

In the course of preparing this edition I have become indebted to many persons. I am especially grateful to Patricia A. Steele, Dean of Libraries at the University of Maryland, College Park, and Beverly Lowry, cotrustees of the Katherine Anne Porter literary estate, for permission to publish all the letters in this collection and to Patricia Steele again for permission to publish those letters that are physically held in the Katherine Anne Porter Papers at the University of Maryland, College Park. From the beginning I have depended on archivist Beth Alvarez, also at the University of Maryland, College Park, whose efficiency and whose knowledge of the Porter archives are unparalleled. I wish to express particular appreciation for the encouragement of two persons who enthusiastically supported this project, as they did my previous Porter work: Harrison Paul Porter Jr. and the late Barbara Thompson Davis, trustee for the Katherine Anne Porter literary estate 1993–2010. I also wish to thank archivists at the following libraries for permission to print specific letters in their holdings: Mugar Memorial Library at Boston University; Columbia University Library; Cornell University Library; The Houghton Library at Harvard University; The Harry Ransom Humanities Research Center, University of Texas at Austin; The Newberry Library; The New York Public Library; Pennsylvania State University Libraries; The Green Library at Stanford University; Texas State University; Washington and Lee University; The University of Washington Library; Western Washington State University Library; and The Beinecke Library, Yale University. I owe special thanks to Susan Gilroy of the Harvard University Libraries.

I also wish to thank the University of Nevada for various kinds of institutional support for this specific project over the past five years, and I have greatly appreciated the aid of doctoral students Cynthia Bailin, Laura Powell, Karen Roop, and Conor Walsh.

And always, I'm grateful to my husband, John Unrue, whose support is immeasurable and whose contribution to my work continues to reside in his knowledge and wisdom.

Chronology of the
Life of Katherine Anne Porter

1890   Callie Russell [Katherine Anne] Porter born at Indian Creek, Texas, 15 May, the fourth child of Harrison Boone Porter (b. 1857) and Mary Alice Jones Porter (b. 1859), shortly after the death of the Porters' third child, Johnny. Her older siblings are Anna Gay Porter (b. 1886) and Harry Ray Porter (b. 1887).

1892   Mary Alice [Baby] Porter born 25 January; Mary Alice Jones Porter dies 20 March; Callie moves with father, brother, and two sisters to Hays County, Texas, to live with grandmother Catharine Ann Skaggs Porter.

1893–1901   Educated by governesses grandmother hires; attends public school in Kyle; attempts to write fiction; begins lifetime of voracious reading.

1901   Catharine Ann Skaggs Porter dies 2 October.

1902   Sets forth with father, brother, and sisters on several years of vagabondage and sporadic attendance at Texas public and parochial schools.

1903–1904   Attends convent school in New Orleans.

1904–1905   Informally changes name to "Katherine Porter" when brother, Harry Ray, changes his to "Harrison Paul Porter"; attends Thomas School in San Antonio for full academic year; performs in summer stock productions.

1906   Writes stories she sends to brother, Paul; marries John Henry
              Koontz 20 June in double ceremony with sister Gay, who
              marries Thomas H. Holloway.

1907–1911   Continues self-education and apprentice writing during
              miserable marriage; baptized into Roman Catholic Church;
              assumes baptismal names "Veronica" and "Maria."

1912–1913   First published work, an amateur poem, appears on the cover
              of a trade journal.

1914   Flees to Chicago; publishes an autobiographical feature story
              in newpaper; works briefly in movies; returns to Texas.

1915–1918   Divorces Koontz; legalizes name to "Katherine Porter"; begins
              to call herself "Katherine *Anne* Porter"; marries and divorces
              T. Otto Taskett; spends months in Texas hospitals with tuber-
              culosis; marries and divorces Carl Clinton von Pless; pub-
              lishes children's stories and articles in Texas newspapers.

1918–1919   In Denver, hospitalized briefly at a sanatorium; works as
              reporter for the *Rocky Mountain News*; fears violating the
              Sedition Act in World War I; nearly dies in influenza epi-
              demic; grieves over death of niece Mary Alice Holloway;
              moves to New York City; meets radical writers and Mexican
              artists.

1920–1921   Publishes three retold fairy tales; travels to Mexico; ghost-
              writes *My Chinese Marriage*; dabbles in revolution; writes for
              the English language section of *El Heraldo de México*; devel-
              ops anticlerical stance; falls under observation by American
              Military Intelligence; has love affair with Nicaraguan poet
              Salomón de la Selva that ends with abortion.

1921   In Fort Worth, Texas, works for the *Oil Journal*; writes shop-
              ping column for the *Fort Worth Record*; performs in Little
              Theater productions.

1922   Returns to New York; spends few months in Mexico to
              assemble popular arts show and produce accompanying

pamphlet; publishes first original adult story, "María Concepción."

1923   Returns to Mexico for few months to produce issue of *Survey Graphic*; publishes "The Martyr."

1924   Love affair with Francisco Aguilera leads to pregnancy; male child stillborn in December; publishes "Virgin Violeta."

1925–1927   Supports herself with freelance writing, editing, and book reviewing; undergoes removal of both ovaries after contracting gonorrhea from British lover Ernest Stock; protests the Sacco and Vanzetti executions in Boston; researches Mather family in Salem, Massachusetts, for biography of Cotton Mather; begins research into own ancestral history; publishes "He."

1928   Takes salaried position as copy editor at Macaulay; has brief love affair with Matthew Josephson; publishes "Rope" and "Magic."

1929   Lives in Bermuda for six months; publishes "The Jilting of Granny Weatherall" and "Theft."

1930–1931   Returns to Mexico for last extended sojourn; publishes "Flowering Judas" the story and *Flowering Judas* the book, a collection of six stories that establishes her critical reputation; meets Eugene Dove Pressly; visits the Hacienda Tetlapayac to watch Russian filmmaker Sergei Eisenstein work on *Que Viva México*.

1931   Receives Guggenheim Fellowship; makes voyage from Vera Cruz to Bremerhaven, Germany, with Pressly.

1932   Lives briefly in Berlin, Madrid, and Basel; settles in Paris; publishes "The Cracked Looking-Glass" and the nonfictional "Hacienda."

1933   Publishes *Katherine Anne Porter's French Song Book*; marries Pressly.

1934   Publishes "That Tree" and fictionalized *Hacienda*.

1935   Publishes "The Witness," "The Last Leaf," "The Grave," and
            "The Circus."

1936–1937   Returns to the United States; separates from Pressly; pub-
            lishes "The Old Order," "Noon Wine," and "Old Mortality";
            meets Albert Russel Erskine Jr.; begins college speaking and
            teaching.

1938   Divorces Pressly, marries Erskine; lives in Louisiana; pub-
            lishes "Pale Horse, Pale Rider"; receives second Guggenheim;
            speaks at writers' conferences.

1939   Publishes *Pale Horse, Pale Rider: Three Short Novels* to lauda-
            tory reviews; publishes "The Downward Path to Wisdom."

1940   Separates from Erskine; goes to artist colony Yaddo; publishes
            "A Day's Work."

1941   Buys farm South Hill, near Yaddo; publishes "The Leaning
            Tower" and "The Source"; speaks on radio programs; receives
            first Gold Medal for Literary Achievement from the Society
            for Libraries at New York University.

1942   Divorces Erskine; attends writers' conferences; grieves over
            death of father, Harrison Boone Porter; inducted into the
            National Institute of Arts and Letters.

1943   Travels to Mexico for the United States government as a kind
            of cultural ambassador.

1944   Moves to Washington, D.C., to serve as fellow at Library of
            Congress; begins to publish segments of her long novel-in-
            progress (*Ship of Fools*); publishes *The Leaning Tower and
            Other Stories* to enthusiastic reviews.

1945–1947   Works as scriptwriter in Hollywood; sells South Hill.

1948   Tours universities as lecturer and teacher in writing
            workshops.

1949   Accepts academic appointment at Stanford; receives first of
                many honorary degrees; moves to New York City.

1950–1952   Elected one of two vice presidents of the National Institute of
                Arts and Letters; attends the International Congress for Cultural
                Freedom in Paris; publishes essay collection *The Days Before*.

1953–1955   Fulfills academic appointment at the University of Michi-
                gan; makes appearances at other universities and art centers;
                travels to Belgium with Fulbright Fellowship but falls ill
                and returns to the U.S. after only a few months; leases house
                in Southbury, Connecticut; grieves over deaths of brother,
                Harrison Paul Porter, cousin Lily Cahill, friend George Platt
                Lynes, and editor Donald Brace; leaves Harcourt, Brace for
                Atlantic–Little, Brown.

1956   Attends Conference on the Arts and Exchange of Persons,
                Institute of International Education, New York City; contin-
                ues to speak on college campuses.

1957–1958   Works on long novel; publishes nonfiction; appears on televi-
                sion programs.

1958–1959   Accepts extensive speaking tour; fulfills semester appoint-
                ments at the University of Virginia and Washington and Lee;
                with Ford Foundation Grant settles in Washington, D. C.

1960–1961   Publishes "The Fig Tree" and "Holiday"; continues to speak
                at colleges and universities and to appear on television
                programs.

1962–1963   *Ship of Fools* published and becomes best seller; film rights
                sold; brief visit in Europe followed by year-long sojourn;
                returns to Washington, D. C.; inducted into the American
                Academy of Arts and Letters.

1964   Leases house at 3601 49th Street NW (Spring Valley) in D.C.

1965   *The Collected Stories* published; moves with editor Seymour
                Lawrence from Atlantic–Little, Brown to Knopf and then to
                Delacorte.

1966   *The Collected Stories* wins both the National Book Award and
        the Pulitzer Prize; donates papers and other possessions to
        the University of Maryland, College Park.

1967   Convenes the Katherine Anne Porter Foundation established
        to support young writers.

1968   The Katherine Anne Porter Room opens in McKeldin Library
        (later moved to Hornbake Library) at the University of Mary-
        land, College Park.

1969   Moves to a town house in College Park; sister Gay Porter
        Holloway dies.

1970   Publishes *The Collected Essays and Occasional Writings of
        Katherine Anne Porter*; moves to suite of apartments in Col-
        lege Park.

1971   Publishes "The Spivvleton Mystery."

1972   Receives Brandeis University Creative Arts Award; receives
        and returns Emerson and Thoreau Medal to the American
        Academy of Arts and Sciences to protest academy's refusal
        to acknowledge Ezra Pound's contributions to modern
        literature.

1973   The Katherine Anne Porter Foundation dissolved; sister Mary
        Alice (Baby) Porter Hillendahl dies.

1974   Reconciles with the Catholic Church.

1975   Accepts a medal from the American Academy of Arts and
        Letters.

1976   Returns to Indian Creek, Texas, for award at Howard Payne
        University in nearby Brownwood.

1977   Suffers first of several severe strokes; *The Never-Ending Wrong*
        published; ruled incompetent; Harrison Paul Porter Jr. is
        appointed guardian.

1977–1979   Health steadily declines.

1980   Moves to Carriage Hill Nursing Home, Silver Spring, Mary-
             land, in March; dies 18 September.

1981   Ashes buried at Lamar Graveyard, Indian Creek, Texas.

Introduction

Until she was thirty-nine years old, Katherine Anne Porter had an antipathy to letter writing, which she called a "subsidiary art." In 1965 she told an interviewer that her father had caused that aversion by criticizing her desire to be a fiction writer and wondering why she couldn't be content with writing interesting letters, as had the seventeenth-century noblewoman Madame de Sévigné. The letters Porter wrote until 1929, with the exception of some she wrote to lovers and a few directed to her family, were written mostly to convey information, with little regard to discretion or later usefulness, their common lack of literary eloquence a counter to her father's dismissal of her artistic ambitions. "I'm not much of a letter writer," she proudly told a lover in 1924. In 1929, however, when she was depending heavily on book reviewing for a livelihood, she reviewed *The Lost Art: Letters of Seven Famous Women* for the *New York Herald Tribune*, concluding that the art was "not so lost" after all and suddenly seeing the importance of letter writing. In addition to being silken threads of connection to friends and relatives, letters also could be records of thoughts, memories, feelings, past events recollected—all of which were notes for possible transformation into fiction. From then on, she was especially careful to make copies of her letters, carbon copies when carbon paper was available or typed copies when she had no carbon paper. She also asked persons to whom she had written in the past to return her letters to her. Some that contained information she wanted to keep secret she intended to burn or retype with the embarrassing parts excised; other would go into her file of notes that would provide the beginning points for stories or novellas.

While many of her letters were what she called "unpremeditated outpourings," others were carefully crafted in her pure prose because they had a public purpose or were gifts—small prose gems—sent to persons to whom she felt indebted. Most of her letters were social occasions, "conversations" she imagined she was having with the persons to whom she was writing, an attitude that helps explain her resistance to terminal punctuation and the fluidity of her voice that changes tone and subject from letter to letter, writing in phonetic dialect and using colloquialisms when she wanted to be witty.

She recognized the downside to letter writing in the extent to which she eventually indulged in it, sometimes writing more than a hundred letters in a given month, admitting that she was writing letters when she "should be working on that novel" or "gossiping" when she "should be writing" ("lotus eating," Glenway Wescott called it). But she also acknowledged the value of letters: they were "autobiography, in a pure sense" and even could contain "one's history." And if they were especially penetrating, as were those of W. B. Yeats, for example, they could be a "fine gloss" not only on her own art but also on "public history."

The present collection begins with a letter written in 1916 from a tuberculosis sanatorium in Dallas, Texas, the earliest available extant letter by Porter, and concludes with a 1979 letter she dictated to an unnamed Maryland nursing-home attendant, who wrote out by hand what she thought she heard in Porter's stroke-affected speech. Between those two, as sixty-four years of letters unfold, we find the chronicle of the life of Katherine Anne Porter personally, a twentieth-century woman searching for love from her family and others while she struggles to become the artist she is sure she can be. We also find a chronicle of the twentieth century as she observes it from her historical vantage point. She provides an insider's view of tuberculosis sanatoria; the influenza pandemic of 1918; the leftist community in Greenwich Village in the 1920s; the Mexican cultural revolution of the 1920s and early 1930s; the expatriate community in Paris in the 1930s; the rise of Nazism in Europe between the world wars; the Second World War; the cold war and its attendant suppression of civil liberties and competition for supremacy in space; Hollywood and the university circuit as havens for financially strapped writers in the 1940s and 1950s; the women's rights and civil rights movements; and the evolution and demise of literary modernism. She had a great deal to say about art and artists and revealed her firm belief in the obligation of the elder generation of artists to help the younger generation.

Katherine Anne Porter was a "modern" woman beyond the coincidence of living in the modern era. In a review she wrote of *Words for the Chisel* (1926), a collection of poems by her friend Genevieve Taggard, Porter objected to the label "feminist" that commonly was applied to Taggard. Arguing that such a term to describe a poet is "meaningless" (pointing to her already established opposition to the conflation of art and politics), Porter suggested "modern" as a better label for Taggard, because "she belongs to her time," "does not assume female poses merely pleasing to the eye," and is superbly "direct" in her "utterance."

On a personal level and in the sense she defined, Porter was surely modern. She defied most of the patriarchal mores of her Texas family, especially her father and brother, even though she never stopped seeking and yearning for their love and approval. But she was "modern" as a "modernist" artist, too, holding herself to the superb directness she admired in Taggard and others. She discovered the modernist aesthetic through William Butler Yeats, James Joyce, Ezra Pound, T. S. Eliot, Gertrude Stein, and Virginia Woolf (and behind them, Henry James) and was inspired by the intellectual challenges of Freud and Nietzsche.

Her letters reveal the extraordinary range of her reading and the works and writers she admired and those she disdained. She was in line with Eliot and Pound in her predilection for an "older" literature (Homer through the eighteenth century) that could be transformed into "new" literature and for classical concepts of control and purity of language. She was quick to disparage writers she considered effusive, verbose, unrestrained (she often named Walt Whitman and Thomas Wolfe as examples of that school).

By the mid-1930s she was friends with many important figures in the modernist movement and its ancillary agrarianism and New Criticism, and she was acquainted with, or had met, many others. Those with whom she did not have a close friendship she nevertheless admired for the aesthetic she shared with them. Her dismay at seeing the modernist shibboleths crumble before the replacement movement for which she had no name escalates, as her life fades and her own creative power evaporates.

The extraordinary value of Porter's letters lies in the span of subjects she addresses, the number of persons she observes, and especially in the artistic sharpness of her comments and descriptions. In her 1929 review of *The Lost Art* she speculated presciently on the value of the publication of letters by her and her contemporaries long after they had died: "Think of all the gayety," she wrote, "the brilliance, the passion, the political information, the tragic adventures of our days recorded minutely...." She could not have described her own more accurately.

Recipients

Francisco Aguilera (1900–1981): Chilean educator, writer, and poet. After earning an M.A. at Yale in the mid-1920s, he became director of secondary education in the Ministry of Education in Chile. He returned to the United States to teach at Yale in 1929 and later became specialist in Hispanic culture for the Library of Congress. He had a brief love affair with Katherine Anne Porter in 1923–1924, during which time she became pregnant with a child who was stillborn.

Carleton Beals (1893–1979): Educator, radical journalist, and prolific writer with a focus on Latin America. Founder of the English Preparatory Institute in Mexico City, he met Porter in 1921. She based her story "That Tree" (1934) on Beals and his wife, Lillian, and he was one of the models for Carlos in "Virgin Violeta" (1924). His nearly fifty books include *The Stones Awake: A Novel of Mexico* (1936), which Porter reviewed for the *New Republic*.

Gertrude Cahill Beitel (1881–1959): Well-read traveler and student of history and theater. She and her sister Lily Cahill (1885–1955), a successful film and Broadway actress, were admired by Porter for their beauty and ambition. Because Gertrude's and Lily's mother, Virginia Myers Cahill, Porter's second cousin, was an amateur genealogist, Porter liked to discuss with them the family history.

Janice Biala (1903–2000): Polish-American painter who lived with the British novelist Ford Madox Ford in the 1930s, when they became friends with Porter and her fourth husband, Eugene Dove Pressly. Highly regarded both in France and the United States for her affiliation with the New York school of abstract expressionism and for her contributions to modernism, she married the *New Yorker* cartoonist Daniel Alain Brustlein in 1942.

Margaret Grosvenor Hutchins Bishop (1898–1974): Minor poet and wife of the distinguished American writer John Peale Bishop (1892–1944). She became acquainted with many of the literary elite through her husband, who served as chief poetry reviewer for the *Nation* and was the author of poems, short stories, essays, and novels. John Peale Bishop died shortly after being appointed resident fellow at the Library of Congress in 1944, and Porter was selected to complete his term.

Harvey Breit (1909–1968): American poet, editor, reviewer, and playwright. A selection of columns he wrote for the *New York Times Book Review* based on his interviews with famous writers was published as *The Writer Observed* (1956). He was one among a number of younger writers Porter encouraged.

John Malcolm Brinnin (1916–1999): Poet, critic, biographer, and teacher. From 1949 to 1956 he was director of the Young Men's–Young Women's Hebrew Association Poetry Center in New York City, known for the high quality of its speaking series, which many times featured Porter. Becoming one of Porter's most treasured friends, he was asked by editor Seymour Lawrence to look after Porter when she was sequestered at a remote inn in Massachusetts finishing *Ship of Fools*. He published six volumes of poetry, three travelogues, and critical-biographical works on T. S. Eliot, Gertrude Stein, Truman Capote, William Carlos Williams, and Dylan Thomas.

Cleanth Brooks (1906–1994): Critic and professor. He was best known for his collaboration with Robert Penn Warren on the influential textbooks *Understanding Poetry* (1938) and *Understanding Fiction* (1947), both of which were significant in the rise of the New Criticism of the 1940s and 1950s. He and his wife, Edith Amy (Tinkum) Brooks, were Porter's close friends from their meeting in 1937 until her death.

Roger L. Brooks (1927–): President of Howard Payne University, in Brownwood, Texas, 1973–1979. Responsible for drawing Porter back to her homeland in 1976 for a visit to her birthplace at nearby Indian Creek, a celebration in honor of her eighty-sixth birthday, and an honorary degree, he was later vice president of Houston Baptist University and director of the Armstrong Browning Library at Baylor University in Waco, Texas.

Kenneth Burke (1897–1993): Literary, rhetorical, and aesthetic theorist, editor, musician, and critic. Like Porter, he was friends with Malcolm Cowley, Robert Penn Warren, Allen Tate, Caroline Gordon, and Marianne Moore.

Although early on he was influenced by Karl Marx, Sigmund Freud, and Friedrich Nietzsche, he later rejected the Marxist and Freudian schools of criticism that dominated the 1930s, a final political position with which Porter concurred.

Thomas Henry Carter (1931–1963): Editor, writer, and educator. While an undergraduate student at Washington and Lee, he helped found the literary magazine *Shenandoah*. The year after he met Porter he graduated and later became a professor of English at Patrick Henry Community College in Martinsville, Virginia. Two published volumes of his work are *Signs of the Times* (1963) and *Essays and Reviews* (1968).

Eleanor Clark: See Eleanor Clark Warren.

Walter Clemons (1930–1964): Writer and editor. A respected reviewer and critic, he held editorial positions at *Newsweek*, the *New York Times Book Review*, McGraw-Hill, and *Vanity Fair*. Although Porter admired his talent and encouraged him to continue writing short stories, he published only one book, "*The Poison Tree*" *and Other Stories* (1959). He was the recipient of the first award by the Katherine Anne Porter Foundation, which Porter established for the support and encouragement of young writers.

Monroe Fulkerson Cockrell (1884–1972): Texas-born banker, author, and genealogist. He is best known as vice president of Continental and Illinois National Bank and Trust Company of Chicago, Illinois, and as author of *The Early Cockrells in Missouri* (1966) and *Deep Depression Years* (1948). In the 1940s he began writing to authors whose works he admired, later publishing at his own expense several volumes of correspondence he titled *After Sundown*.

Malcolm Cowley (1898–1989): American literary critic, journalist, novelist, and poet. He interrupted his undergraduate studies at Harvard, where he eventually earned a B. A., to join the American Field Service in France during World War I. A chronicler of the postwar artistic communities in Greenwich Village and the Montparnasse Quarter of Paris, he was an assistant editor of the *New Republic* from 1929 through 1944. His best-known work is the autobiographical *Exile's Return* (1934). A supportive friend to Porter for many years, he argued with her over the role of politics in art and over his description of her as a "journalism woman" who chose Mexico for her place of exile rather than Paris.

Helen Rebecca (Becky) Edelman Crawford (1892–1972): Russian-born business manager of the Playwright's Theatre in Greenwich Village in the early 1920s. She and her husband, John Crawford (1895–1974), supported leftist writers and artists, including Porter, who finished "Flowering Judas" while boarding with them in the winter of 1929–1930.

Daniel Curley (1918–1989): Fiction writer, editor, and long-time professor at the University of Illinois, Urbana–Champaign. His collections of short fiction include *Living with Snakes* (1985), which won the Flannery O'Connor Award for Short Fiction. When he was editor of the literary magazine *Accent*, he published Porter's "Affectation of Praehiminicies" (1942), a chapter from her biography of Cotton Mather, her story "The Source" (1941), and "The Strangers" (1946), an excerpt from her novel-in-progress, *Ship of Fools*.

Albert Russel Erskine Jr. (1912–1993): Editor at New Directions, Doubleday, Doran, and Random House, where he was Robert Penn Warren's, Eudora Welty's, and William Faulkner's editor. Introduced to Porter by Allen Tate and Caroline Gordon, he became Porter's fifth husband in 1938. They divorced in 1942.

James Thomas Farrell (1904–1979): Irish-American fiction writer and journalist with a bent toward Trotskyist politics. His best-known work is the *Studs Lonigan Trilogy* (1932–1935), and he is most often praised by literary critics for his realistic portraits of the Chicago working class. He met Porter in Paris while he was publishing the three novels that constitute the *Trilogy*, and he corresponded with her sporadically over the subsequent decades. While she admired aspects of his realism, she objected to his conflation of art and politics.

William Cuthbert Faulkner (1897–1962): A major American writer and winner of the Nobel Prize for Literature (1949). Focusing for the most part on the social and psychological transitions in southern society that conveyed universal implication, he was an important contributor to the modernist movement and to the stream-of-consciousness strain within it. Porter admired his fiction and had fleeting contact with him in the 1950s.

Ford Madox Ford. See Ford Hermann Hueffer.

Caroline Ferguson Gordon (1895–1981): Kentucky-born writer and wife of Allen Tate (1899–1970) from 1925 until 1945. She met Porter in Greenwich

Village in the 1920s and became one of Porter's closest friends. Often identified with the Southern Agrarians, she published ten novels, including the
well-received *Penhally* (1931) and *Aleck Maury, Sportsman* (1934).

Charles William Goyen (1915–1983): Texas-born writer, editor, and teacher.
He met Porter in 1947 when she was working for Hollywood studios as a
scriptwriter, and they were friends and sometime-lovers through much of the
1950s. She considered him a promising young writer and provided encouragement as well as instruction. His published works include the novels *The
House of Breath* (1950), *Ghost and Flesh* (1952), *In a Farther Country* (1955),
and *Come, the Restorer* (1974).

Carl Henderson Griffin (1937–): Educator and critic. As a graduate student at the University of Florida, at both the master's and doctoral levels, he
focused on the works of Porter, first exploring the Christian symbolism in her
fiction and later narrowing his study to *Ship of Fools*. Several years after meeting Porter, he took a position with DeKalb Community College (now Georgia
Perimeter College), where he chaired the Humanities Department for many
years and helped found the literary magazine the *Chattahoochee Review*.

William Harlan Hale (1910–1974): American writer, editor, and journalist. A
graduate of Yale University, he was an editor at *Vanity Fair, Fortune*, and the
New Republic and a columnist for the *Washington Post*. His first book, *Chal-
lenge to Defeat: Goethe's World and Spengler's Century*, was published in 1932,
the year he was introduced to Katherine Anne Porter by Robert McAlmon.
He served in army intelligence during World War II and later published histories and a biography of Horace Greeley (1950).

Paul Hanna (1883–1925): Socialist journalist and editor. Correspondent for
the Federated Press, the *New York Call*, and the *London Daily Mail*, he was
sent to Mexico City early in 1921 by Ernest Gruening, editor of the *Nation*,
to do a set of articles on Mexico. With common acquaintances and interests,
Porter and Hanna became friends and corresponded for a few months.

Barbara Harrison. See Barbara Harrison Wescott.

Margaret C. Harvey (1896–1985): Journalist and advertising manager. A
reporter for the *Rocky Mountain News* in Denver when Porter was a reporter
there in 1918–1919, she maintained an interest in journalism even after she
moved on to positions in advertising. She was active in the Denver Press Club

and made significant contributions to Kathryn Adams Sexton's research for her M.A. thesis "Katherine Anne Porter's Years in Denver" (University of Colorado, 1961).

Josephine (Josie) Herbst (1892–1969): Novelist, essayist, and political activist. She met Katherine Anne Porter in Greenwich Village in the 1920s and formed a close friendship with her that lasted until 1948, when the friendship finally disintegrated over long-simmering disagreements about Gertrude Stein's importance in modern letters and about the relationship between politics and art.

John Herrmann (1900–1959): Fiction writer and political activist. He was married to Josephine Herbst from 1926 to 1934. While working for the New Deal administration of Franklin D. Roosevelt, he was a courier for the Ware Group, a covert organization within the Communist Party that delivered classified information to the Soviet Union. Having introduced Whittaker Chambers to Alger Hiss, he fled to Mexico when the House Un-American Activities Committee began hearings and the FBI launched its Hiss investigations.

Mary Alice (Baby) Porter Townsend Hillendahl (1892–1973): Youngest child of Harrison Boone Porter and Mary Alice Jones Porter. She married Herbert Lee Townsend in 1913 and in 1914 gave birth to a son, Breckenridge, after the death of Townsend. A nurse by training and a breeder of bulldogs, in 1916 she married Julius Arnold Hillendahl (1884–1954). Katherine Anne Porter always had a contentious relationship with her.

Anna Gay Porter Holloway (1885–1969): The firstborn child of Harrison Boone Porter and Mary Alice Jones Porter. She was Katherine Anne Porter's connection to the unremembered past, and she was the family member to whom Katherine Anne was closest and in whom she confided most. She married Thomas H. Holloway on June 20, 1906, in a double wedding with Katherine Anne and John Henry Koontz.

Ford Hermann Hueffer [Ford Madox Ford] (1873–1939): Influential British novelist, editor, critic, poet, and biographer. As founder of the *English Review* and editor of the *Transatlantic Review*, he was a primary force within the modernist movement. Porter met him through Caroline Gordon and Allen Tate in Greenwich Village in the 1920s and became close friends with him and his companion, Janice Biala, in the 1930s.

Erna Schlemmer Johns (1890–1975): Daughter of prosperous German immigrants and childhood neighbor of Porter. Her well-educated mother introduced Porter to the works of Russian writers and European painters, and Erna was the inspiration for Charles Upton's friend Kuno in Porter's "The Leaning Tower." She and Porter remained affectionate friends all their lives.

Matthew Josephson (1899–1978): Journalist, poet, editor, biographer, and historian. He met Porter at Macaulay and Company, where he became book review editor and she accepted a minor editorial position. They had a brief affair in the winter of 1928–1929. His numerous publications include the biographies *Zola and His Time* (1928) and *Jean-Jacques Rousseau* (1932) and his memoir *Life Among the Surrealists* (1962), which includes his account of Porter, to which she objected strenuously.

Otto Hermann Kahn (1867–1934): German-born banker, philanthropist, and author. As a patron of the arts, he supported such artists as Hart Crane, George Gershwin, and Arturo Toscanini, in addition to Porter. Among his many publications are *Let Us Reason Together* (1919) and *The Value of Art to the People* (1924).

Thomas S. Knight (1921–): West Virginia–born philosopher, educator, and author. Holding academic positions at Russell Sage College, Utica College of Syracuse University, and Adelphi University, he published *Charles Peirce: A Neglected Genius* (1965) and coauthored several works in the Great American Thinker Series.

Dayton Kohler (1907–1972): Virginia Polytechnic Institute professor, critic, and editor. Author of many articles, reviews, and books on modern American literature, he is best known for his contributions to numerous volumes of *Masterplots*.

Charlotte Laughlin (1951–): Texas-born educator. She was a young assistant professor at Howard Payne University in Brownwood, Texas, near Porter's birthplace at Indian Creek, when Porter arrived on the campus in 1976 to receive an honorary degree at commencement and to celebrate her eighty-sixth birthday. She visited Porter in College Park, Maryland, in the fall after their meeting.

Ludwig Lewisohn (1882–1955): German-born American critic, translator, and novelist. An opponent of American Jewish assimilation, he was among the founders of Brandeis University, where he taught until his death. His best-known works are the critical study *The Modern Drama* (1914) and the novel *The Island Within* (1928).

David Anthony Locher (1924–2010): Iowa-born poet and librarian. He met Porter at the University of Michigan in Ann Arbor in 1954 during her academic appointment and took some of her classes. They were friends for the rest of her life. He published several poems in tribute to her.

Robert Traill Spence Lowell IV (1917–1977): American poet, teacher, political activist, translator, and founder of the confessional poetry movement. He was Poet Laureate Consultant in Poetry to the Library of Congress 1947–1948, and he won the Pulitzer Prize twice, for *Lord Weary's Castle* in 1947 and for *The Dolphin* in 1974. Having met Porter in the 1930s through Caroline Gordon and his teacher Allen Tate, he had a reunion with her in 1952 when both of them were among the American representatives to the Congress for Cultural Freedom convening in Paris. He was the author of numerous collections of poetry.

George Platt Lynes (1907–1955): American fashion photographer. He met Porter in Paris in the 1930s through Glenway Wescott and Monroe Wheeler and remained her close friend until his death. When he was chief photographer for *Vogue* in Hollywood in the 1940s, Porter lived with him and a group of his other friends for a while. He made numerous glamorous photographs of her.

Russell Lynes (1910–1991): Author, editor, and art historian. The younger brother of George Platt Lynes, he was an editor at *Harper's* magazine from 1944 until 1967, during which time he published some of Porter's work and became her friend. Among his important books are *The Tastemakers* (1954), *Good Old Modern: An Intimate Portrait of the Museum of Modern Art* (1973), and *The Lively Audience: A Social History of the Visual and Performing Arts in America, 1890–1950* (1985).

Abby Mann [Abraham Goodman] (1927–2008): American scriptwriter and television producer. He wrote the play *Judgment at Nuremberg* (1959), a fictionalized account of the World War II trials of Nazi war criminals, and later adapted it as a screenplay for the 1961 motion picture directed by Stanley Kramer, which received an Academy Award for the best adapted screenplay. Collaborating again with Kramer, he wrote the screenplay for the motion picture *Ship of Fools* (1965), which was nominated for the Academy Award for the best adapted screenplay but lost to Robert Bolt's *Doctor Zhivago*.

Robert McAlmon (1895–1956): American writer and publisher. The founder of Contact Editions, he brought out Ernest Hemingway's first book, *Three*

Stories & Ten Poems (1923), William Carlos Williams's *Spring and All* (1923), and Gertrude Stein's *The Making of Americans* (1925), among many other modernist works. His own novels, volumes of poetry, collections of short stories, and memoirs appeared between 1921 and 1938. He met Porter in Greenwich Village in the 1920s.

Ignatius McGuire (1898–1963): Poet and medical librarian who held positions at Princeton University and with the United States Army and United States Navy. He met Porter in the summer of 1924 at the rented Connecticut farmhouse of mutual friends. Later he became friends with fellow librarian and poet David Locher, with whom he shared his memories of Porter.

Marianne Moore (1887–1972): American modernist poet, translator, essayist, and editor. When she met Porter in Paris in 1933, she already had published *Poems* (1921) and *Observations* (1924) and had served as editor of the *Dial* from 1925 to 1929. Her *Collected Poems* (1951) received the Pulitzer Prize, the National Book Award, and the Bollingen Prize.

William Maxwell Evarts Perkins (1884–1947): Journalist and renowned Scribner's editor who guided the publishing careers of F. Scott Fitzgerald, Ernest Hemingway, and Thomas Wolfe, among many others. He accepted for publication in *Scribner's Magazine* Porter's story "The Cracked Looking-Glass."

Harrison Paul Porter Jr. (1921–): Businessman, writer, and World War II veteran. Son of Porter's brother, Paul, he became well acquainted with "Aunt Katherine" in 1936 when he was a teenager and she recognized in him a kindred artistic spirit, which she nurtured through subsequent decades. In the last years of her life he was her court-appointed guardian.

Harrison Paul Porter Sr. (1887–1955): The second child of Harrison Boone Porter and Mary Alice Jones Porter. Christened Harry Ray Porter, he changed his name to Harrison Paul Porter in 1905 at the same time Katherine Anne dropped her birth name, Callie Russell Porter, and asked to be called "Katherine Porter." An oilman, he married Constance Eve Ingalls (1882–1971) in 1916.

Harrison Boone Porter (1857–1942): Father of Katherine Anne Porter. Educated at the Texas Military Institute, at College Station, Texas, and a member of the Travis Rifles, a home guard company dedicated to protecting the state from corrupt carpetbaggers in the post-Reconstruction period, he was a railroad man, farmer, salesman, and teacher. Well read in eighteenth-century literature and history, he was a rationalist and a skeptic who profoundly influenced his daughter Katherine Anne.

Ione Funchess Porter (1880–1953): Wife of Katherine Anne Porter's uncle Newell Porter (1864–1946). Born in Mississippi and exuding the air of a "southern belle," she was a glamorous inspiration to her nieces in their childhood and adolescence.

The Porter Family: Harrison Boone Porter, Anna Gay Porter Holloway, Harrison Paul Porter Sr., and Mary Alice Porter Hillendahl.

Cora Addison Posey (1869–1963): Indian Creek friend of Porter's parents. She idolized Alice Porter, from whom she took music lessons, and preserved Porter's parents' courtship letters given to her by Harrison Porter because they were too painful for him to read. Later she returned them to the Porter daughters. She remained a link to Porter's childhood.

Orville Prescott (1907–1996): Book critic, editor, and author. As daily book critic for the *New York Times* from 1942 to 1966, he reviewed numerous books, singling out more conventional narratives for his highest praise and judging such writers as William Faulkner, John Steinbeck, John Updike, J. D. Salinger, William Styron, and Vladmir Nabokov as "excessively overpraised" by other reviewers. He was the author of *The Five-Dollar Gold Piece* (1956), a memoir, and two books about the Italian Renaissance, *Princes of the Renaissance* (1969) and *Lords of Italy: Portraits from the Middle Ages* (1972).

Eugene Dove Pressly (1904–1979): Stenographer, translator, and American State Department and Treasury Department clerk. Fluent in several languages, he was a member of the United States Army from 1942 until 1945, after which he accepted additional military assignments in North Africa, France, Germany, Japan, and Mexico. He was Katherine Anne Porter's fourth husband (1933–1938).

Lucile Clayton Robinson (1897–1970): Reporter on the *Rocky Mountain News* when Porter was on the staff in 1918–1919. An admirer of Porter, she wrote to her after she saw *Flowering Judas* in 1931 and realized her old friend who was always considered "a writer's writer" had "made it."

Theodore Roethke (1908–1963): American Pulitzer Prize–winning poet and teacher. Influenced by W. H. Auden, he was encouraged by a number of other established writers, including poets and fiction writers such as Porter, who appreciated his compelling rhythms and images and universal themes. He held teaching positions at a variety of colleges and universities.

Raymond Roseliep (1917–1983): Ordained Catholic priest, academic, and poet renowned for his mastery of the English haiku. He was a graduate of Loras College, where he met David Locher, who introduced him to Porter, and he earned an M.A. from Catholic University of America and a Ph.D. from Notre Dame. He dedicated several poems to Porter.

Herbert Schaumann (1909–1982): A poet and a Nazi who defected from the German army and became a member of the U.S. Army during World War II. He met Porter in Washington, D.C., where he was stationed. Eventually a professor at the University of Maryland, College Park, he corresponded with Porter through the 1940s while she was working in Hollywood for movie studios.

Edward Greenfield Schwartz (c. 1926–2005): Scholar and critic. He began corresponding with Porter in the early 1950s when he was a doctoral student at Syracuse University and writing a dissertation on her works. He compiled an important annotated bibliography of her writings and published several seminal articles on her work, but she turned down his request to write her biography. He later was a professor at Purdue University.

Charles Shannon (1915–1986): Southern painter and teacher who achieved regional renown with his paintings that focused on African Americans. He helped finance New South, a cooperative venture in Montgomery, Alabama, that promoted the arts. A member of the United States military during World War II, he met Katherine Anne Porter in Washington, where they had a brief affair in 1944.

Grace Delafield Day Spier (1901–1980): Social activist and sister of Dorothy Day (1897–1980), primary force in the Catholic Worker movement. Active in the interfaith Fellowship of Reconciliation and supporter of Margaret Sanger, she became Porter's close friend in Greenwich Village in the 1920s and maintained an affectionate tie for many years. She and her husband, Franklin Spier, with whom she had three children, visited Porter in Bermuda in 1929.

Wallace Stegner (1909–1993): American writer, educator, and environmentalist. Known as the "Dean of Western Writers," he founded the Stanford Creative Writing Program after teaching appointments at the University of

Wisconsin and Harvard. His novel *Angle of Repose* won the Pulitzer Prize for Fiction in 1972 and his novel *The Spectator Bird* won the National Book Award in 1976. His many books of nonfiction include *The Sound of Mountain Water* (1969) and *On the Teaching of Creative Writing* (1988). Despite Porter's dissatisfaction with her Stanford teaching experience, she remained an admirer and friend of Stegner.

Herbert Steiner (1922–): A World War II soldier and aspiring writer who discovered Porter's fiction in the Armed Services edition sent to thousands of fighting men. He sought her out at Stanford to tell her how much he admired her and her work. He remained her adoring fan throughout her life.

Genevieve (Jed) Taggard (1894–1948): Poet, editor, and college teacher. She cofounded the journal the *Measure* (with Maxwell Anderson). She was one of Porter's most trusted confidants and most admired friends in the 1920s. The author of numerous books of poetry, such as *Words for the Chisel* (1926), which Porter reviewed, she was also the author of *The Life and Mind of Emily Dickinson* (1930).

Eleanor Ross Taylor (1920–): North Carolina poet and wife of the writer Peter Taylor. Her books of poetry include *Wilderness of Ladies* (1960), *Welcome Eumenides* (1972), and *New and Selected Poems* (1983).

Peter Hillsman Taylor (1917–1994): Novelist, short-story writer, playwright, poet, and teacher. At Southwestern (Rhodes College) he was a student of Allen Tate's, and at Louisiana State University he studied under Robert Penn Warren and Cleanth Brooks. From 1945 until his death he taught at colleges and universities throughout the United States, published numerous books, and received many prizes. His works include the novel *A Woman of Means* (1950) and the collections *Miss Leonora When Last Seen, and Fifteen Other Stories* (1963) and *The Oracle at Stoneleigh Court: Stories* (1993).

Julien Lon Tinkle (1906–1980): Author, literary critic, and professor. Educated at Southern Methodist University, the Sorbonne University of Paris, and Columbia University, he was president of the Texas Institute of Letters from 1949 to 1952 and long-time book editor of the *Dallas Morning News*. Among his best-known books are *The Alamo* (1960), *Miracle in Mexico: The Story of Juan Diego* (1965), and *An American Original: The Life of J. Frank Dobie* (1978).

Eleanor Phelps Clark Warren (1913–1996): Writer and editor. A supporter of leftist causes in the 1930s and 1940s, she married Robert Penn Warren in 1952. Her publications include the novel *Baldur's Gate* (1970) and three works of nonfiction, *Rome and a Villa* (1952), *Eyes, etc.* (1977), and *The Oysters of Locmariaquer* (1964), which won the National Book Award in 1965.

Robert Penn (Red) Warren (1905–1989): Kentucky-born poet, novelist, and critic. Associated with the Fugitive group of poets, the Southern Agrarians, and the New Criticism movement, he published many books of poetry, fiction, and nonfiction from 1929 until his last years. His best-known work is the novel *All the King's Men* (1946), which won the Pulitzer Prize in 1947. He also won Pulitzer Prizes in poetry in 1958 and 1979. Having earlier defended racial segregation, he later became a visible supporter of racial integration and in 1980 was awarded the Presidential Medal of Freedom by President Jimmy Carter. He and his wife, Eleanor Clark, were among Porter's closest friends until her death.

Eudora Welty (1909–2001): Novelist, short-story writer, photographer. Born in Jackson, Mississippi, she was educated at the Mississippi State College for Women (now Mississippi University for Women), the University of Wisconsin–Madison, and Columbia University. She worked for the Works Progress Administration as a photographer in the 1930s and published her first short story, "Death of a Traveling Salesman," in 1936. Her novel *The Optimist's Daughter* (1972) won the Pulitzer Prize in 1973, and in 1980 she was awarded the Presidential Medal of Freedom by President Jimmy Carter. Porter, who wrote the introduction to Welty's first book, *A Curtain of Green and Other Stories* (1941), was her advocate and friend from 1936 until her death.

Barbara Harrison Wescott (1904–1977): Publisher and philanthropist. Daughter of Francis Burton Harrison, governor of the Philippines during Woodrow Wilson's administration, she used her wealth to found with Monroe Wheeler the small publishing house Harrison of Paris. She befriended Porter and supported her work for many years. Porter dedicated *Ship of Fools* to her.

Glenway Wescott (1901–1987): American writer and member of the expatriate community that included Ernest Hemingway and Gertrude Stein. He and Porter admired one another's writing and were devoted friends for many years. His most highly praised works are the prize-winning novel

The Grandmothers (1927) and the best-selling wartime novel *Apartment in Athens* (1945).

Monroe Wheeler (1899–1988): Publisher and major force in the Museum of Modern Art in New York City. He met Porter in Paris in 1932, when he was friends with leading modern artists such as Picasso and Chagall. Joining forces with heiress Barbara Harrison (Wescott), he formed the small publishing house Harrison of Paris, which published Porter's *French Song-book* (1933) and *Hacienda* (1934). He was one of Porter's closest friends until her death.

Janet Loxley Lewis Winters (1899–1998): Novelist, poet, translator, and teacher. At the University of Chicago she was friends with Glenway Wescott and Yvor Winters (1900–1968), whom she married in 1926 and with whom she founded the literary magazine *Gyroscope*, where Porter's story "Theft" appeared in 1929. She was the author of several novels, including *A Narrative of Events Concerning the Johnson Family of St. Mary's* (1932) and *The Wife of Martin Guerre* (1941), and many volumes of poetry.

Morton Dauwen Zabel (1901–1964): Educator, editor, and author. A professor first at Loyola University and then the University of Chicago, he was widely respected for his book *Craft and Character: Texts, Method, and Vocation in Modern Fiction* (1957). Porter was one of his admirers.

Selected Letters of

Katherine Anne Porter

Part One

1916–1929

The most remarkable revelation in Katherine Anne Porter's earliest letters is her fierce belief in her artistic talent and eventual success. In 1916, while she was in the center of what she later described as her "ungodly struggle," with very little evidence to suggest she would achieve the celebrated status she eventually would reach, she praised an unnamed lover for his faith in her. "He believes I have the fibre of greatness and success, and never lets me forget it," she wrote her sister Gay. "You know," she said, "I have to be believed in." At that point in her life, twenty-six years old, penniless, with no formal education beyond the eighth grade, with two marriages and two divorces behind her, having suffered miscarriages and beatings from her first husband and still battling life-threatening illnesses—and with only a few negligible publications to her name—she was amazingly certain in her optimism.

By 1919, with her tuberculosis in abeyance, having survived influenza in the great pandemic of 1918, her faith in herself had not diminished. "I know well enough I am going to be a success in a very short while more," she wrote Gay. She was in fact close to ending her apprenticeship, built on voracious reading for many years, writing stories and poems since childhood, and the practical craft of newspaper work. "I shall write well someday—as well as any-body in America has ever written," she assured Gay. She saw her move to New York as necessary: "The time has come to do the work that will bring me to that stage."

In New York she met persons who would guide her through the 1920s and shape much of her artistic future. Among her new acquaintances were Mexican artists who convinced her to go to Mexico, to write and to observe the exciting cultural revolution taking place. Back and forth between Mexico and the United States between 1920 and 1923, she found her creative voice in her first original pieces of fiction, while she also "dabbled a bit at times" in the revolution. For the remainder of the decade she struggled to support herself with freelance writing and editing and continued to publish at well-spaced intervals more finely crafted stories.

Although she bravely declared in 1924, "I have arrived at such a serene sort of feeling about my work," there was nothing serene in her personal life. She moved from one love affair to another, experiencing the traumas of abortion and stillbirth and surgery that rendered her sterile. She recognized her romantic inclination that was at odds with her rationalistic art: "I have suffered a great deal from love," she wrote Gay, "or rather the impossibility of finding an adequate substitute for illusion." Her consolation was, in fact, her art, which had become a kind of religion. "Nothing is for life with me," she wrote, "except my preoccupation with writing. And that I did not choose. It merely remains, and I must suffer it." By the end of the decade, when she was approaching forty years of age, satisfied with the quality if not the quantity of her artistic work, she was able to affirm her earlier optimism: "The world grows to be a familiar place," she told Gay, "with no dark and terrifying corners, and no shocks and almost no strangeness."

To: Gay Porter Holloway TLS 2pp. Maryland

[Woodlawn Union Tubercular Hospital
South Lamar and Columbia Streets]
Dallas, Texas. December 21st, 1916.

Darling Old Dear:—

Mary[1] just called up and said there was a package from you to me at the office and Himself[2] is bringing her out to see me this afternoon, with the sheaves upon His nice arms. I am all a-tiptoe to see what manner of box it may be. Honey, I am hanging my head in shame that I am not giving you anything this Christmas but the dinky little things I am sending. I can't even get the package made up til after Christmas, as I do not get paid until today, and we are so busy making the tree out here at Woodlawn, I won't be able to finish getting your little things til Monday. But I am sure you understand.

It's great to play Santa Claus, Honey. Here is a little story the Dallas News Published (paid me $8.00 for it)[3] and so far the people have sent me $67.50 to spend for me babies. And of all the telephone calls and visits from people who make much of me. I have the real Christmas spirit, I tell you, seeing how fine folks are when you just once touch their hearts. Himself is so proud of me he can hardly see straight, and calls me the Good Fairy and Lady Santa Claus, and all such, and says I am quite the most talked of person in Dallas today, as every body is planning to send or give something to the Children .. Its going to be a happy Christmas. I weigh 120 pounds, if you please, as they feed me so outrageously out here, and I don't turn my hand except to teach the kiddies, and stay in bed nearly all the time. Of course, this week and the next I will be up most of the time, seeing after things, then after that I expect to go very quietly til Spring, when I will undoubtedly be well and strong, when the Dallas News has promised me a good job then.[4]

And then, Youngun, you know all this would be dust and ashes in my mouth if it wasn't for knowing that my Darling Old Dad and Sissers and my one goat of a bruvver are all getting along so fat and fine, making money and keeping well. If it wasn't for that I would want to die. But even if we can't be together this year, knowing that all of us have plenty and at least aren't worrying about money (any more than every body else is, anyhow) is all I need, at least, to make this heaven on earth.

Himself is giving me a beautiful warm robe, slippers to match, with electric bed pad to keep me warm, and a nice man has given me a gorgeous bottle of my favorite perfume, La Boheme. Your package is on the way, and so I am getting more Christmas than I deserve, certainly, seeing I am giving almost nothing. But you know I always have fame and glory and plenty to eat and wear, with no ready cash ever. That is, I do when I am lucky. And when I am not lucky, no one starves more unwillingly than I!

If only I might be there to decorate the tree for Mary Alice and Paul Porter.[5] But no such luck for now. I only solemnly promise this—that next year I shall help decorate their tree, and hope Breckenridge[6] and Dad will also be there to see it. I hope we will have a real reunion by that time. Some how I feel there will be another Paul Porter by then, as Alice says Paul and Connie[7] never write or visit any more, so I have my suspicions! I hope so, any how. This is a beautiful rambling sort of structure on the side of a hill with all sorts of wood and valleys around it—I can hardly wait for Spring to come, I know it will be so lovely out here. Open fires, and I sleep in blankets out in a long pavilion with the hot water bottle Himself gave me at my feet, and the down baby pillow Himself gave me at my head. So you see I am comfortable.

The Dear Heart has done everything for me, and we are immensely good friends. I mean we love one another very much, and its a strange affair, all told. But I am selfish, I guess, for its the kind that gives me everything, and takes nothing away; which looks to see if I am warm and well and fed and clothed and happy, and you know I never had a man love me like that. I have seen him only twice since I came here, but I write to him, and he calls me over telephone, but I am serene and go about my affairs, and nothing bothers me. He brings peace of mind and repose, which I have needed all my life. He believes I have the fibre of greatness and success, and never lets me forget it. You know I have to be believed in. Have met and become friends with the managing Editor of the News,[8] and expect something good to come of it. He has promised me a place as soon as I can take it. So you see, I am going to come out of this all right.

Well, I am talking about my self a lot, but I thought you might want to hear. Tell me all about your self and the two Darlings, what they do, and say and wear, and all about them. Will be sending you a new picture soon. Please have a good one taken of the babies and yourself, and send on. Please send me also one each of those pictures of Toosey taken at Longview. Some how they got out of my grip last Spring, and I have wanted one ever since. Don't forget.

A merry, Merry Christmas to you, My Blesseds. I am up a tree as to what will be acceptable to Toosey and Toddles,[9] but shall send them something to wear. I love you all extravagantly, and am happy as a june bug thinking what a fine Christmas you will have this year. Think of that nightmare two years ago! and be happier now.

With all my love and kisses, your very own,
Katherine Anne

To: Gay Porter Holloway ALS 8pp. Maryland

[Park View Hotel
Denver, Colorado]
Thursday Night .. [July 24, 1919]

Honey, your letter telling me of Little Mary Alice reached me today, nearly four days after Kuno's telegram[10] came saying our beloved Heart-Baby had been taken away.[11] Oh, my dear and dearest, you're having more than your share of bitterness in this world, and the whole desire of my heart now is to help you live over it somehow. I haven't a word to say except that I love you, my precious Sister; and you know I adored Mary Alice above all the other babies, as much as I love them.

It doesn't seem real that the wonderful hoped-and-prayed-for life has been snuffed out like a candle flame, and all that treasure of ours shut away from us ... don't know why we took it so for granted that the babies would all grow up, and have their day. . . . I can't say it is for the best, for I don't believe it. And my heart is so broken, I can do nothing yet except cry with you, Honey.

When you are able, please tell me a little about her—how long she was sick, and what she said. Oh, she was so heavenly-sweet, I have remembered every minute I ever saw her these past four days. And do you know, a strange thing happened, Sunday Night. I went to bed rather late, very restless and tired. And all at once I began to think of you—all of you—very strongly. Such a wave of homesickness and the wish to see you came over me, I cried until three o'clock. I made up my mind that if I still felt so in the morning I would go to Houston that day. And that day, about noon, the telegram came. I had a feeling that something had happened, but my mind fixed itself on Mary Alice senior, instead of the wee one.

Did you get my roses? I ordered two dozen little pale pink buds tied with silver ribbons, and had them telegraphed to you with a card "From Tante Katherine." I was very anxious they should be sent in time to help make a little bower for her, but I am not sure I got the address exactly.

Gay, it sounds futile, but I'm so glad you have the little boy—does he help any?

Day Later—I have been quite a while writing this letter. But words say so little when a calamity like this overtakes us. We can only grieve it out, after the manner of our kind.

Your letter, coming as it did after the telegram, was only a sad explanation of a mystery—I am trying not to think of our Blessed One as she must have been in the last days; I remember her as she was last year in Louisiana, in her blue dress and grey shoes, going across the bridge to the concert, with Lute[12] in tow. She was a beauty-loving little soul.

Maybe I shouldn't write to you like this. But I can't write at all, really. Because it is all a dream, my dear, and we are shadows. And one day there will be none of us left, either, and these bodies will be part of the Great Earth again.

I would like to feel that the part of us that dreams, and loves beauty, and hopes and strives for better and happier things, will live always, and find a lovelier, free-er place where we shall see all our lost ones again and do all our work again with a clearer understanding.

But I seem to have no conviction on the subject. I can only see that our sorrows come without warning, and our joys are brief. And the important thing seems to be courage. Without it we are beaten from the beginning. And you have always had your share of it, surely.

I love you, Darling brave, wonderful Sister and I wish I could be with you now. And I am glad you were all together in the first big loss to our little family. We are so few, we can't spare our darlings.

Baby Dear, or some of you, write me very soon. Love to all of you, My Dears, Dad and Gay and Little Boy Holloway, and Kuno and Baby and Breckenridge and Paul and Concha and wee Dorothy Ray.[13]

Ever and ever your own,
Katherine Anne

I shall visit the Queen of Heaven Orphanage in a few days and tell Mother Superior about Baby Mary Alice.

To: Gay Porter Holloway TLS 3pp. Maryland

Friday afternoon [September 17, 1919]. Rocky Mountain News [1720 Welton Street, Denver, Colorado].
Will Bring Mother's Picture with me.

Gay, Old Darling—I wish I could write you every day, my heart is with you so every minute. My work keeps me bowed under a great load, but I feel as if I had not a thought except about you and my ever to be beloved and remembered Baby.

Of course your letters bring me realization of what that loss actually means to us, but the tiny details of her life, and the little descriptions of her as she was at the latest day of her dear life give me also memory pictures to keep.

I grieve with you for her, and it does not seem at all possible that she has left us, and all those blessed hopes and dreams she represented are over and done with. I think I am nearest to you just now, old sweet, because indeed I did know what your hopes were, and how hard you struggled to give your Babies their rightful chance in the world. And tho I am over it all now, yet, like you, I would rather give up any one of the dear small Ones than to have them go thru the agonies of our forlorn childhood and terrible youth.

But it would never have been so with her, so long as you lived, I am sure. And she would never have dug into your heart so if she had not been beautiful loving and sensitive. I think both of us saw in her the shy souls of our own young years, and realized more than anybody her absolute need to be loved and surrounded with kindness. Oh, my dear, my heart is broken over that lost darling. I always had an idea that some time, maybe soon, I could have her with me for a while, and I know well enough I am going to be a success in a very short while more, and it was always in my mind that she should have, between us both, everything she needed for happiness when she grew a little older. I never said anything, because I have been seemingly such a failure, but I knew it was only my long preparation for fine work. And she was in my thoughts so much more than I can tell you now.

I think so much of her precious chin, cleft like a little apricot. She loved my story of how the Lord-of-All made that dimple with his thumb just before sending her out to you, while the angel held her up before Him by the nape of her neck.

I told her that story dozens of times when we were in Louisiana. She would come and lean against my bed, and say, "Now Tante, tell me about how I got my dimple!" And she would always laugh, and her eyes would shine, when I came to the part about the Lord-of-All touching her chin with the tip of his thumb, and saying, "Now!"

I wish you could come up here for a while, but honey, I am going to New York almost at once, and I wish to pass thru there and sail from Galveston in about three weeks. I thought of visiting with all of you for a few days, and then on to the next stage of my development. I've more than made good here—way more than made good, dear one, and they are offering me much more to stay. But I shall go now, and do better things. The time has come.

I shall write well some day—as well as anybody in America has ever written, and the time has come to do the work that will bring me to that stage.

I want very much to see all of you, and the dear babies. I wrote a letter to dad the other day, and I don't know what I did with it—whether I mailed it or not. I can't quite get all of your addresses straightened out, but if you see dad, ask him about the letter, and give him my best love.

I will write again several times maybe before I come, and will wire you when I leave.

All my love to my darling, brave, much tried sister. I cannot feel the religious urge as you do, but if you find a little comfort in it, I hope you come back to your childhood faith. Me, I can only say, be courageous. Be a soldier.

Your own loving
Katherine Anne

To: The Porter Family TLS 5pp. Maryland

Address me now, 17 Grove Street, New York City.
January 3, 1920

To my Bunch:

I write thus in a round robin because I have forgotten Baby's number, I don't know whether Gay is still in Livingston or not, and I prefer to send my screeds where at least one member of the family will be sure to receive them and send them around.

Gay angel child, your beautiful Christmas greenery made my room perfume-y and sweet for several days. It was nice to think of them being picked in the Texas woods, and I hope your own house was full of them. I didn't get any of that Christmas shopping done that I hoped for, for my life is a simple scramble for breath. I am as usual doing a dozen things, but this time all the things are productive, and leading to the same end. I have been transferred to the Select studio, publicity manager out there, which means that I spend three hours a day on subways, ferries, and street cars getting over into New Jersey to the studio. Once there, I live around on the stage, watching the players work, and write all the news of the picture making for the publicity office down town. It is a ghastly job, full of detail, a sort of sublimated reporter's work, but I shall keep it for so long as I need it. It is a responsible place, as the entire publicity department yowls all day long for news, and I am the sole source of information. I eat in a squalling bedlam of a café at the studio along with Olive Thomas, Elaine Hammerstein, Eugene O'Brien, and Owen Moore,[14] also stage hands, directors, "supers," and business managers, all so mixed up you can't tell one from T'other. Apparently it is an experiment in pure democracy, barring always the fact that the "star" of the day has her own corner table.

Christmas was a gay affair, as I went to an all-night party with a congenial crowd of artists, writers, and editors. We gave our little packages at Bessie

Beatty's (editor of McCall's)[15] and then went to mass down in Little Syria, and heard the Syrian version of the Roman ceremony. It was a weird thing. Afterward we went to a Syrian restaurant, and ate funny stuff, and danced, and drank Turkish coffee. We kept this up until the new wore off, and went back to Bessie's, I trotting thru the snow with a nice person whose first name was, I believe, Bill. Well, Bill and I ran races in the snow like two friendly puppies, finally picking up a tall Christmas tree lying by the side walk and dragging it home, where we stood it up in the hall, at five o'clock in the morning, with great ceremony.

By six thirty I was home in bed, but rose again at twelve, went to breakfast at another girl's, had egg nog and plum pudding later on some where else, and to another, tho shorter, party Christmas night.

At New Year's Eve Chappel[16] and I went to the country to a dear pair of artists—who are illustrating my stories, and beauties they are making—and spent a quiet time in their lovely house overlooking the Hudson river.[17] This is a beautiful country. I have been thru historic old Tarrytown-on-the-Hudson, and all over the Sleepy Hollow vicinity made famous by Washington Irving.

I have a contract for twelve fairy stories with Everyland a magazine for children here. I am doing the series from authentic legends of far countries—Kashmir, India, Persia, Eskimo Land, Iceland, and the first two are written. They begin in January and run thru the year, and are then to be made into a beautiful book, with Berta's illustrations. (Berta Hoerner is the artist girl, and Elmer Hader is her husband. They are wonderful folk, and I love them both.) Gay, I mean to dedicate the book to our Mary Alice Child, for she would have loved the stories, and I write them all with her in mind. I think to myself that Mary Alice would love it told this way, and then I write it as if I expected her to read them, as she could have done next year.

I am getting my house fixed up a little—it is eating me alive, that house, but I MUST have it. I suppose I have yammered about my purple furniture until you are all weary of it, but I must tell you once more how it looks. Think, I have been three months getting into the devilish place. But as it stands now, with the last thing bought irrevocably, my studio room is arranged thus—dull blue crash curtains, couch cover to match, piled up with pillows in vermilion, green, orange, rose, black and purple. The fireplace is black, and across the room, between two windows, stands a tall old fashioned black mirror, that reflects the fire. My desk, chair, a tall hall chair, and a drop leaf table are painted purple. A deep steamer chair is black with green cushions. The rug is dull blue, round woven fibre. The floor is black, and the walls are pure white. I have a tea table furnished with every color of pottery under heaven, blue, rose, gray, black, and, oh, my books are there, and I have two Holbein prints on the wall! There is a tiny dressing room, and a wee bath, and a kitchen the size of a closet, all fixed up in yellow crockery (the kitchen) and its a <u>plum</u> satisfactory house. The great lovely joke being, that, finished and done, the thing has cost me just $155, but it does seem as if I am forever buying something for it. But now a half dozen more things, and I am finished. And it is the sort of place I love. I don't like ready made furniture—I snooped around second hand shops and picked up funny looking things and painted them, and gosh, its grand! The wilder the place looks, the dearer it is to me!

I am writing on a special story for The World Outlook—by the touching title of Arithmetic on An Empty Stomach, being a bit of special pleading for hot soup to be surved to the poor kids in the east side schools, since they don't have enough to eat to make 'em efficient. God knows, I think the real solution is deeper than that, but hot soup is good for the misery of the moment, and as such, I'm for it.[18]

Arithmetic on any kind of stomach was always a sufficient curse to me. My real sentiment being that it ought to be abolished entirely.

Dad darling, as soon as I get going smoothly, I shall send you small gobs of coin regularly—that is to say, I hope I can send as much as $75 a month, anyhow. It may be a little less than that, and maybe more. But as long as I work and get along, there is not reason why you shouldn't share with me. The ineffable scoundrel who promised me great things in money has not yet come across nicely, and I'm too far away to protest effectually.[19] Seeing it was to be a free gift, I am probably a bit unreasonable, but in case that thing falls thru, I feel quite certain we can get along on our own. For tuppence I'd transplant you to a shack on the edge of the Hudson, where I hope to go in the summer, but you don't understand growing things in this climate as you do in your own, and I think a few acres in Texas would be about your style. And you'd be forever fighting with these damyankees, I know. But the more I think of it, I am convinced that it would be better for you to get about TWO acres right at the edge of Houston, on a good road, even if you had to pay as much as you would for five or six further out. This because you would be nearer the market for your honey and chicks, and would be nearer sociability with your fellow humans, too. I wish you would really look about, and see if this is feasible. A wee house would do at first, and maybe you could get it on payments, which I would keep up. If my writing keeps up nicely, there is no reason why we couldn't get it paid for gradually. I MEAN THIS, so look out for a place, and find out what it would take to start it all. And it would pay you a little the second year, wouldn't it? I know a woman who has made a snug fortune in bees in Colorado on two acres of land, and she has only had it four years. I know you must have certain equipment for chickens and bees, but you will have to find out about the cost, as my ignorance is profound on all such lore. I will simply do everything I can about money, and after this month I can send you a certain sum every month.

Let's do this, dad. It is entirely practible, I think. I'm more eager than you are to see the show started. I know things are high, but then, you can fix things and manage as I managed here for my house, and it suits one better when its done, I notice.

Paul, old honey, I am so very distressed to hear that your health is flopping a bit, when it looked as if you were pulling along in great shape. I don't care a hang about anything so long as my health holds, do you? Everything else waits on it, seems. Do try to get square again, and its you and me will make our blooming fortunes yet! Concha, your talented and promising infant shall have her gold bracelet soon as ever I get around to toddling to the shops to look. Shopping here is a discouraging thing. The town is miles and miles and miles of shops, until you get bluffed out entirely and don't go near any of them. I do remember how that blessed Dorothy Ray admired her ring when it was new—holding out her wee hand to gaze upon that lovely twinkling decoration on her finger.

Baby, I should write you a letter by yourself, honey, since you wrote such a newsy script to me, but this family note is so comprehensive, I want all of you to have all the news, so please write me again, anyhow, and tell me about yourself. All of you try to keep well, and tell me things as they happen. I am away off here, not exactly by myself, but just the same away from my own bunch. So don't forget me, kindly! Its a shame we can't make our lives near to each other, but Lord! I wish we had all left that country long ago, and gone where our luck was. I have found mine here, I think. If Gay were here, she could get a job at fifty dollars a week without half trying, and have a fuller life than she ever had. It is the city of opportunity, surely. And there seems to be room for everybody.

With all my love to my dears, Dad and Paul and Gay and Baby, the originals, you might say. With Connie, and Kuno, and Breckenridge, and the wee Holloway Boy and Dorothy Ray—a hundred kisses,

Katherine Anne

To: Gay Porter Holloway and Harrison Boone Porter TLS 5pp. Maryland

April 1, 1920

Darling Old Sister and Dad:

You all seem to have a genius for forming family combinations with Dad as the center.

The last time I heard from Baby—moons ago—she was all for having Dad with her in her grand, preposterously fine house, and got in a little pro- paganda against the farm idea, which is my dearest dream. . . . .

She seemed to indicate that Pater would have no earthly use for a farm, what with all the magnificence he would have in town. And the next thing I hear, Pater has retired to the sylvan simplicity of house keeping with you— and I can tell him from experience that it will invariably be simple and sylvan beyond description. I would give much to get a real line on you-all, and know for sure what you were doing and thinking. But I probably never will.

In the mails there came to me one day an impressive yellow document all over printing and handwriting indicating that I was now the proud possessor of three lots situated somewhere adjacent to Houston, on which I had paid $35 and had only $975 more to pay, after which they would be mine for keeps.

Now, who sent 'em? What shall I do with 'em? Who are they for? Is it a good thing? Dad, do you know anything about it? I know well enough I have NOT paid $35 on any lot any where, and what I want to know is this—shall I send the first payment? For God's sake enlighten me.

I myself think it would be a very nice thing, and you and Dad could run up a sort of shack on the lots, and have one of those happy homes that I have always read about and somehow have never chanced to run across in my travels.

What do you think of this plan?

Gay honey, I didn't send the rest of the money for the utterly simple rea- son that I didn't have it, and the devilish Woman's Home Companion hasn't sent my check yet, nor have they said one word about it. Authors for popular magazines have one devil of a time of it.

On the other hand, I am trying to get a ballet pantomime produced[20] and it takes everything. But I am getting a lot of good work done, just the same. About the wee bit I sent you, never think of it again. I spose you've forgotten all the times you came to my rescue. I probably owe you twice that amount.

I know spring must be a lovely time there. Here, we have no green leaves yet, but golden light and blue skies; April makes promises for May to keep.

I haven't sent you any copies of the little magazine because they are dev- ilish hard to get, the edition is exhausted immediately, but when the book comes out you shall all have a copy. They are very nice stories, really. And the illustrations are beautiful.

Gay, I believe you are shutting yourself away from a very lovely spiritual (or mental) experience by keeping on with spiritualism. . . . . . . I tell you honey—I have gone about a bit here, and have seen one or two of the best—and spiritualism is a superstition for darkened minds. It is the same as a belief in witch craft, and a personal devil. . . . . . It is not for enlightened people, or thinkers. And I tell you, emotion without intelligence is not worth anything.

And I want to tell you something else—if you will stop spiritualism, and forget all about the ugly and unworthy means resorted to by mediums to touch the dead again, Mary Alice will come back to you, suddenly, exquisitely, miraculously, and walk with you, and sit by you, and lean her little sleek yellow head on your arm as you read and sew. I know this is true, because she comes to me.

I would not for worlds deceive you, or tell you a thing I did not believe with all my heart to be true. . . . . understand me, I have seen nothing, heard nothing, touched nothing. But she is present, the tenderest and most beloved and happy presence surely ever any one could imagine. It is something quite definite. And it happened first about four weeks ago. I was walking down Fifth Avenue, and passed a window full of gay little spring frocks, some of them exactly made for her. And the windows were full of flowers, and the sun was shining.

I thought of her, as I always do when I see anything lovely with a fresh mind. And at once, she was there, not wee and chubby as when I saw her last, but tall and thin, with a little blue bonnet, I think. Any how, she slipped her hand into mine, and it was so real I tightened my hand together. And when we crossed the street, I reached for her again. . . . . . . it was very real. Not a touch, or a word, or a sight. Just an ineffable singing joy in me, and in her.

I have done my best to stop shedding tears over her. I used to sit and cry about her when I was alone. But that isn't the way. So later on, I was half asleep one night very late, when she came and lay down by me, and actually, I moved to make room for her. And again Sunday afternoon, I was sewing away on a blue robe lined with bright orange crepe, thinking how she loved bright colors, and at once she was there, at my elbow, and she leaned over, her head on my arm as I sewed. I just smiled, and went on sewing. But I knew there were two of us in that room.

Now that is all, except that she comes at times with varying degrees of nearness. And always at my right hand. And I did not seek it, deliberately would not, for I do think this cold blooded snatching after the spirits of the dead is revolting. . . . . . But I find it difficult to believe now that we do not have some sort of conscious spiritual existence after death, tho of course this sense of her presence might possibly be my own mind filling the gap left by her going.

I don't know. But I do know that if you will be easy and stop laboring to reach her, she will return to you. No matter what it is, it is a perpetual sweet happiness, and all of your own. I would hesitate to think that Mary Alice would prefer to reach her mother thru a hired ignorant woman who takes money for disturbing the souls of our loved people who in life would not have associated with them at all. If that sounds snobbish, I am sorry. But when Mary Alice comes back to you, never fear but that she will come direct, and in an unmistakable manner. Without a sound, or a touch, or a shadow. Get that firmly fixed in your mind. It will be within YOU, and nowhere else. She is altogether lovely, and that little heart leans toward you as she always did.

Strange, strange thing, Old Honey! But this is true to the last word, and told as simply as I can say it. Live in your own soul. Don't seek. Don't struggle. Nobody can help you one smallest trifle. Let it solve itself for you, in your way, which is uniquely your own, and which nobody can plan for you.

Now for other things. . . . . I hope you get settled comfortably, and have a happy summer. You didn't say what your job was. I wish you could come here and live. Any sort of person gets $50 a week. You could probably read proof on a magazine for that. And I know a book keeper and stenographer could get as much—or a private secretary.

Dad, I guess you will have that tumble down shack in Athlone covered with vines and spiders and honeysuckle and sparrows nests and cucumbers and poison ivy within the next week. Lord, how we do go back to the soil we sprang from as we grow up. I think all the time of a house in the country, a riot of old fashioned growing things all mixed up together. I should love to live here, but I can't imagine settling down in a country where figs and peaches and climbing roses don't flourish. On the other hand, I hate like the devil to think of the south again for a residence. So far as I can see, I am out of that country forever and a day. Here is where I can work, and where I can work, there I live.

Well, this isn't telling the world what a grand fine actor Charles Ray[21] is—nor yet is it getting a ballet in the style of Louis Thirteenth written. . . . . a versatile creature am I! I wish I didn't have to devour half my life to supply the other half with money to work with. But it is beyond help, so far as I can see.

Love to all of you, by name, in person, separately and in a lump! Write to me, all of you, and tell me the news. A hundred loves to my dears.

Katherine Anne
17 Grove Street

To: Gay Porter Holloway TLS 4pp. Maryland

July 4, 1920.

Dear Darling Sister:

I've been thinking all day that this time a year ago you were in Galveston with Mary Alice, and I remember her very plainly as you described her to me running along the sand in her little red bathing suit, her yellow hair shining in the sun.

And it doesn't seem at all real that all this year she has been away from us. For she is so living in our hearts. And I keep thinking that soon she will have her first birthday in eternal Life—I mean that she is eternally restored to the living earth, and is a part of the everlasting growing of the trees, and returning with the spring, and drinking in the rains.

Her silence wounds us but not her. She has her share in things we do not know, and whatever her portion is, it is good. I am sure we wouldn't grieve so. And yet my tears seem to be wrung out of my blood. I shouldn't remind you, maybe, knowing what your own heart must be now. But still I feel, too, that you might care to remember that I loved that ineffable lovely thing.

I remember her in little flashes—first as that tiny stormy baby two weeks old who cried enormous tears, her little funny cleft chin quivering with obscure, new felt emotions sown in her spirit before she was born. And then as a tiny little baby girl with a gallant little voice singing big tuneless tunes as she played in the yard alone that summer before Paul came. (I WILL call him Paul.) And the smile on her face, showing two wee teeth, and her blue eyes shining, as you trotted her on your knee one day. "Look at that face!" you said to me, turning her round from you as your feet patted on the floor playing "ride a cock horse." I looked, and saw something that never left me, and never will. And I am eternally grateful to you for turning her face to me at that very magic second.

And her startled, questioning, excited eyes that day I got on the train with you at Shreveport, to see you off, back to Dubach; I was to take a later train to Texas, but she being only three years old, did not know this. And she couldn't believe I wasn't going along with you.

And all the days in Louisiana........all the days there. Yet, remembered, it seems to have all happened in a flashing moment. It doesn't seem possible that we actually had her with us more than six years. And out of all that time, I can count the time I had with her almost by weeks. Or so it seems now.

Well, Beloved, we would have chosen otherwise if we could. Here is a song from "The Trojan Women" of Euripides that you will love:

"Even as the sound of a song,
Left by the way, but long
Remembered, a tune of tears
Falling where no man hears,
In the old house, as rain,
For things loved of yore:
But the dead hath lost his pain
    And weeps no more."

And here is the final chorus from the Bacchae:

There be many shapes of mystery,
And many things God makes to be,
    Past hope or fear.
And the end men looked for cometh not.
And a path us there where no man thought.
    So hath it fallen here.[22]

I am in a curious tangle of diverse work, with a dozen things on hand as ever. All of them interesting, all slow of doing and slower in paying, but worthwhile. My passports for Mexico went through without difficulty, only they closed the port of Vera Cruz on account of the plague, and I thought for a while I would go by land. But my ballets here have delayed me, and continue to do so, but they, I considered, are worth waiting to see through. Afterward, there will be Mexico. I only asked for six months, but the passport was given for a year. So that is convenient.

I am sending one passport photo. For Gay. I will have others finished and send one all around, as they are exactly like me. The best likeness I ever had made.

Am having curious experiences behind stage in New York theatres now, in connection with my ballet. The producer of a revue here is considering one, at great length, so I go at intervals to the theatre where he rehearses his company daily, and sit either on the stage or out front with him and several of the other scene and costume designers and composers, and talk. Lord, what strange folk do aspire to the career of the stage!

They come there for a hearing, sometimes bringing outlandish costumes, and they sing or they dance, and its ghastly enough to break your heart! I've sat through a half dozen afternoons of it, and I haven't heard more than two even passably good voices, and as for the dancers, they are legion and a perfect crescendo of dreadfulness.

How the manager can endure it without losing his mind I shall never know. And how they pick enough people for one show much less a hundred is another mystery to me.

I have a commission to write several interviews and a short biography of George Arliss,[23] the famous English actor who is coming over to make pictures of his two great roles, "The Devil" and "Disraeli." It should pay rather well, though I haven't talked terms yet. I think its an interesting opportunity.

In the midst of a general row of mixed work, I have written a twelve thousand word novelette, and am now so afflicted with nausea of it that I cannot bear to look at it, even for the purpose of correcting the manuscript. So it must wait a while to be done over. Thats the dreadful part of writing—once a thought is written down and read twice, it is old and insufferably stale to one, and all the heart is gone out of it.

Dad, about the money for the lot, God knows. I guess I am behind hand now. But I am strapped to the limit all the time, what with dentist's bills and doctor's bills for a curious rash on my hand, and current expenses, and the price of clothes. If I can turn out a ton of work I have in the next four weeks, I bid fair to have a little money. But how can I say?

Our relative, Lily Cahill, married Brandon Tynan, the actor, in St. Patrick's cathedral about a month ago.[24] They have been playing almost altogether in the same companies since "Joseph and His Brethren" in 1912, and I have always thought there was romance in it—you know my keen eye for romance! Lily was leading woman with Leo Ditrichstein, and Tynan was villain in the same play this season, "The Purple Mask." Lily has become a lovely, dignified creature of the "simpatica" type, far away from the dramatic actress she hoped to be, and showed promise of being. She is now merely graceful, very charming, delicately well bred, beautifully and conventionally dressed. A great number of nice things to be, certainly, but still not the ingredients of a powerful actress. I don't know whether she is disappointed or not. I started to look her up, but haven't. Maybe I shall, yet, sometime.

A long, long letter, when I really should be working, you dear distracting bunch. For I mean this for all of you.

How is Paul? Baby, what kind of work is it you are taking up? I should like to know. How is Kuno? I love all of you. How are the babies? Dad, I didn't forget your birthday, on June twenty eight. I remembered quite distinctly that you are getting to be a great big boy now. But I was so devilish broke I couldn't even send a telegram! Don't worry about me, for my mad luck holds, and the whole thing is abundantly worth while, filled with compensations that are wholly personal, the value of which cannot be measured, and would lose all in the telling.

Baby, are you still in your house? How goes Oil? How is that dear Breck-enridge? Does he remember me at all? How's that for Vanity? I wish my nev-vies an nieces to remember me!

Paul's infant must be a tall young debutante by now. She promised to be a pretty thing, too. Those nice little feet and hands. Tell them to 'ware, though. I once had wee narrow feet—when I was about eight years old. My respected parent used to amuse his leisure moments by telling me those same feet look like a jaybird's, and they probably did. They do yet. But they are strangely handsome when clothed and upon the highways, and that is the important thing. To be quite aboveboard about it, I have an incurable vanity in the mat-ter of footwear.

Goodbye, blessed ones, the lot of you. I shower my affections upon you. I wish you would say you love me now and then. You never do. Not right out, like that—I love you.

Tons of work waiting tomorrow. A kiss to each of you, on your noses and necks and scalp locks.

Ever and ever,
Katherine Anne
Seventeen Grove Street

To: Gay Porter Holloway TLS 8pp. Maryland

Address me: 20 Calle del Eliseo
Mexico City, D. F.
December 31, 1920.

Dear Darling:
Your letter could not have been more happily received at any time. And it touched the edges of events of which I would like to know more. My own life is a welter, so far as experiences are concerned, but I can not tell you how far I have come, or all that has happened to me on the way............If we could have dreamed, you and I, all those times we talked together, of how nearly I would achieve plain sight of the things I had set my heart upon, all those years would have been not so seemingly inutile and desolate.

My life is neither inutile or desolate, my dear one. It renews itself daily from enormous sources. This is a letter hastily written, in the midst of con-fusions and far too much work, as ever, but I wish you would share with me—oh, I do—of my many miracles, which I can only assure you of without telling you why they exist.

Life here is a continual marvel to the eye, and to the emotions. Politically, Mexico is amazingly primitive. I meet all the holders of the government reins, and the process of governing is naively literal. . . . . Later, I expect to be connected by a small thread to the affair, and now I dabble a bit at times, for it is very amusing.

I came here to write a book, as you know, fortified by letters from editors and publishers like Scribners and MacMillan, with an agreement with the United Press that I might write them a series of stories. Well—Here I began a little work for El Heraldo, once a good enough paper, now fallen into the hands of a very hungry politician bent only on standing in with the government and making money at the same time if possible.[25] I do book reviews and music reviews and fool political interviews. And it is all amazingly dull. When I grow tired, I quit a while, and they write me a note about it. Then I have a burst of energy an write a little every day.

Also, I am to teach elementary dancing and primary ballet in the brand new Institute of Social Sciences, a socialist school connected with the National University. It starts well, and in company with Roberto and Thorborg Haberman,[26] two radicals here, I am to write a revolutionary text book of English for use in our Institute. Nobody seems to realize elsewhere that a full fledged revolutionary government is in full swing here, with everybody from the President down a seething radical.

But another thing: THE MAGAZINE OF MEXICO has just been put upon its rather uncertain feet. It is a puking infant of the most helpless variety—it needs teeth, and starch in its knees, but it is my very own—that is to say, I am managing editor, and the first edition goes to press the middle of next week.[27] It is backed by a frightful set of rich American bankers who love oil and silver and coal and gold—love the very sound of those unctuous words, and can think of nothing else by day or by night, drunk or sober. They have got out a ghastly cover design which caused me a two days fit of nervous prostration but in three months I shall have it all my way or do a harmless, necessary murder. I really came here to do a wonderful Aztec ballet pantomime with the Mexican painter, Adolfo Best,[28] and we hope to open the National theater, which has been ten or twenty years building, next year, with this very spectacular affair. Wish us luck. In the meantime, here are the clippings which explain something of this.

I plan to fly over Popocatepetl[29] in a week or two with an American aviator, and we shall try to get some pictures of that restless monster belching forth his smoke and thunder. This is the first time Popo has smoked in more than a hundred years. The legend has it that when this occurs, Mexico is about to change dominions. I wonder. The Sleeping Woman—Ixtaccihuatl, the neigh-boring mountain, which has never even had a crater, is beginning to smoke also. You know we are ringed in with old volcanoes here, and I dreamed not long since that all of them spouted great fountains of flame and smoke, and that we were in the center of a wall of fire......... Ixtaccihuatl, the Sleeping Woman, is awakening.... I think there must have been a time when all these shadowed peaks cast stones and fire and lava upon cities..... I have dug out with my own hands skeletons and idols and pots and fragments of wall and roof many feet under ground, and all of them scorched and blackened.

This is a long letter about myself, but I write so little to any one—all my wonderful and dear friends in New York have not had a line from me.... Since I saw you, I have been working too hard and living too hard, to make any sort of record of it...... but I love all of you, I do love all of you terribly, and you are the very background and foundation of my life, which I cannot get away from, and which I would not get away from—if I lost any part of it, I would lose too much! I want very much to see you again, soon, and certainly I shall see you at least in time for June if you wish it, though maybe it would be bet-ter to send the money which the trip would cost. For I remember other births in your house, and they are among my personal tragedies.[30] If you can go to a hospital, in God's name do it, and now that I know six months in advance, may be I can help a little . . . I do not know, for I always disappoint you. So I shall not promise, and then it will be easier to do.

So the migratory Pablocito[31] has been in Alaska, and is back again, and loves Texas best. Extraordinary taste! Extraordinary Pablocito—one of my favorite human beings, really. Though he does not love me, and never did, and probably never shall, damn him. I am a victim of unrequited affection, as I have often pointed out to all of you.[32]

Honey, I must stop. The necessity of collecting a few hundred pesos from El Heraldo is upon me. . . . . One presents one bill for one's distinguished services, and with yells and shrieks and groans they pay within a week's time, though the effort plainly is death to them, no less. Mexicans are not in the least frivolous with their money.

There are thousands delicious things to tell you—of amazing contrasts and amusing situations. How one goes to a party at Chapultepec Castle[33] one afternoon and drinks tea and champagne with the President[34]—a former marauding general—and in no time at all attends the Lottery ticket sellers ball in company with the greatest labor Leader in Mexico[35]—and many oth-ers—and dances until two o'clock with one eyed men, and marvelous carbon colored Indians in scarlet blankets, who dance divinely—and one staggers home in the gray of the morning with vine leaves and confetti in one's hair. And goes that afternoon to a bull fight, and the next day to have tea with three rotund rich men who are clever enough, but smell offensively of money, and who wish to hold your hand, and be a father to you—or rather, three fathers. And I tell one of them I am handsomely supplied with a perfectly spiffing father, and a brother beside, and a lover into the bargain, and I can only be a "talking friend" to him. At which he sulks in his fat oil-magnate way, and I order my favorite dessert, which is frightfully expensive. He is putting his precious, altogether adored money into the magazine, and somehow thought perquisites of interest in the managing editor should be thrown in.

Eh, well. Can you get ASIA in your country? For my lovely Chinese story starts early in the year, and I want you to see it.[36] Just this minute got a note from the publisher, saying he was sorry I had been ill. I was, you know the first six weeks here—oh, flattened quite with a return of small hemorrhages, and I was late with my story, and held up their entire schedule, which should have made them my enemy for life. But no—they were charming and sympathetic—two qualities I dearly love in folk.

I believe that Pater must be suffering from writer's cramp. Not a line from him in years and years. Tell me these small, sordid details when you write next. Where is Baby and Kuno? How is his oil business? Where is Paul and Concha now? What is Paul doing? Where is Dad? Is he stopping with you? Have you your house done nicely now? Is your health good in these more than trying times of growing? How long before you will have to give up everything for the event?

I hope very much the baby will be a girl, and why don't you name her for me and Grandmother, as Mary Alice and Mother were remembered in our first Beloved One? Here is a very small poem I wrote with her in mind the first day after I came to Mexico. Every time I come to a new place, she becomes ineffably vivid to me for awhile—I have a curious and lovely consciousness of her, a heart wringing recollection of beauty that was for one moment only, and now strangely—oh strangely and woefully is not anywhere except in our thoughts of her.

It is quiet enough now in this house where she lay,
Watching the latticed window vines swaying in the sun;
Saying, "Oh, dearly, dearly I love the light of day,
And all the growing things that flower or run."

It is quiet enough now at window and on stairs,
And not again will she lift up her arms and smile and say,

"Oh, dearly do I love the dress the summer garden wears,
And dearly do I love the light of day!"
(November 5, 1920)

****

Christmas was a nice day of sorts—many things happened. I had dinner at the Haberman's—he is the one genuine Bolshevik in Mexico who is really helping to run things—in company with a beautiful bandit from Yucatan, Felipe Carrillo,[37] who is now a diputado—which means congressman—my beloved, a Russian woman who used to be a dancer in the Ballet Russe,[38] and that's all. I forgot to tell you—Felipe is the life long friend of the Hindu poet, Rabindranath Tagore,[39] and Tagore's book, "Gitanjali" is dedicated to him. The bandits are the most interesting and idealistic people in Mexico. I have met three of them, Soto y Gama,[40] who is now also diputado[41] of the left wing, rode his mountains with his gang for seven years with a copy of Karl Marx and the Bible in his pocket, and one sees him now sitting in the Camara—congress—sleek and handsome and reposeful, as Felipe describes him "muy simpatico, muy correcto"—very charming, very correct—as tho life had been quite simple for him always? Probably it has been—life is simple always to one with one idea.

Here is a story I must tell you, honey, then I will stop. Just before I left New York the editor of the magazine section of Hearst's New York American[42] asked me to call as they wanted to give me an assignment in Mexico. I wouldn't work for Hearst, not for any price, but I called to hear what was up. Here is the conversation exactly as I remember it—I mean the important parts:

Editor—"We want you to interview Pancho Villa[43] for us. What is he really doing now that he has a ranch of his own under government protection? Has he reformed?"

I—"He didn't need to reform. He always was a perfectly good revolutionist working for the peons. But he is making interesting experiments on his ranch, I think—I mean such experiments as paying his workers a living wage, and establishing schools for their children."

Ed—"Yes, I know that is what they are trying to tell us. I find it hard to swallow. Well, you can get help from the Mexican government in this, can't you?"

I—"What makes you think so?"

Ed—"I was told that you could. Why don't you manage it, and get us a corking story with pictures—you know what we want. Villa in all his glory, whiskers and guns if any, running his new show."

I—"What else do you want?"

Ed—"How do you mean?"

I—"Do you mean to tell me you will pay all my expenses to get just a simple color story for your Sunday magazine?"

Ed—"O, we'll syndicate it, and make a lot of money out of it. But naturally, the more sensational your story is, the better we would like it—Listen to me! If you get us a good story with pictures, we will pay you twenty five hundred dollars and expenses. If you get kidnapped, we'll raise it to three thousand. . . . . and of course, any price if you make an international affair of it!!!!"

Ah, ha! Well, I declined with thanks, and got out, and am going to write a book on bandits, but not for Hearst. And I am going to put that story in the very beginning of the book. Wait and see.

A funny sequel, though somewhat beside the mark. When I was talking over the Popocatapetl flight with the publisher of the Magazine of Mexico,[44] I told him this story in the course of talk. And a little later he said, "Alright Katherine Anne. Here is a bargain. If you make a good flight over the volcanoes and get pictures, we'll pay you such and such a sum. And of course, any price if you fall in!"

Well, Honey-darling and everybody in the family who may read this, you can see that life is very gay and absurd and full of work and foolish adventures.

I must stop talking along with you and get to my stories. I will send you copies of the Magazine. Adoring love to you.

Ever your,
Katherine Anne

Gay, keep this letter for me, as there are complete records in it which I shall probably never write again. I haven't time to copy it, and some of the material is important, I find.

To: Paul Hanna TL 4pp. Maryland

May 29, 1921. [20 Calle del Eliseo] Mexico City.

Dear Paul Hanna:

I was not offended.[45] Things happen so quickly here, I have not been able to record them. From one day to the next, events were monstrously out of proportion. I gave false values to everything. Now that they are finished, or nearly so, they are all dwindled to the true measures of their triviality. I can write of them now.

But the necessity for giving detail is gone. You probably are well enough acquainted with them. I went to Laredo some weeks since to examine this paltry business. I found the case against Retinger[46] had been dismissed in the Federal courts, and the Immigration authorities had taken turn to work a little mischief. It appears that Retinger will be deported to Poland—not a particular misfortune for him, I am given to understand.

It is a small part of our troubles here—we are having deportations, riots, arrests; an elaborately prepared comedy of respectability is being staged by the Mexican government with the American high politicians as directors. Mexico is to make a few comprehensive gestures suited to a nation of conservative temperament entirely without radical tendencies and recognition will follow at once. And though what will succeed this event is well known also, I cannot tell you anything more.

Haberman is in hiding, with the newspapers clamoring freely for his head. Most of the other foreign radicals have been met over the border, or have escaped to smaller cities. The Catholic clergy is taking on an activity usually called "sinister." They pull all their old wires, and all the bedraggled puppets dance with a great clatter. For the knowing ones, political tricks; rows between socialists and Catholics (happily marked by casualties on both sides) a beautifully organized press managed by skilled politicians—Pallavicina[47] at the head—. For the pelados,[48] the mouldy infallible device—a Virgin of Guadalupe has been seen to move; to shine miraculously in a darkened room: a poor fool of a woman in Puebla was thus favored by Almighty God. It is to be brought here—the priests properly insisting on a severe investigation carried on by themselves—and placed in an oratorio, where it will be shown to the faithful as proof that the great patroness of Mexico has set her face against "Bolshevism" as all radical activity is termed. Poor Virgin! To be Queen of heaven and chief ward heeler of earthly politics at the same time must tax the energies of even that versatile goddess.

Retinger's case is one ripple in this sea of intrigues. We raised his bail here, and immediately the authorities succeeded in setting it a few hundred pesos higher. This would go on indefinitely if we cared to continue the comedy. But Retinger decided it was best to stay in prison, to be deported, to let events follow each other logically; once free, he will go somewhere and quietly write a book. Isn't that the thing one does? Why bash oneself to pieces against circumstances when it is so easy to write a book?

He is, you know, accused of Bolshevism. A delightful bit of irony. The accusers know very well what they are doing. It is neither a case of Bolshevism, nor of passport irregularities.

As for your disclosures from New York: I know a great deal of the Gilbert Seldes[49] affair—I am acquainted with that dismal tale from five different angles, and for over a period of many years, beginning long before the time of Gilbert, you see. For he is not the central figure in all this, nor is Retinger.

I saw Gilbert only for a short while one summer in Colorado, and he seemed to me an incorruptible spirit involved in a situation he would never comprehend because of its rottenness. I may be wrong about Gilbert. About the situation I am not mistaken. It was my bad luck to witness a drama of petty intrigue, being drawn into the episode through a friend even more unlucky than I, and more involved because of her friendship for the other.[50] It is a long, complicated story I shall not fatigue you or myself with retelling.

But Gilbert has, I am sure, every reason to hate Retinger; he has erred a trifle on the side of ethics, I think, to choose the special moment of Retinger's disaster to tell his grievances. But this also is merely my personal interpretation of motives. Retinger has reason enough to do a little hating here and there on his own account. What else can I say? Between men, all extremes of bitter frankness are permissible. For me, I do not care to man the charge of felinity. Besides, I have made no emotional investment in this affair: I have been an unwilling observer of a sorry spectacle that would have revolted any casual eye witness. Of late, I have seen too much malice and petty treason— even my once boundless pity for fools has vanished.

Do I write too plainly? No doubt I do. For to write other than the barest commonplaces of acquaintanceship is to commit a fault of discretion......You know, of course, that I had known Retinger only a short while. You remember many distressing and amusing incidents of his career in Mexico. That he was a man bent on recovering from some recent disaster was only too apparent. I am able to form no further judgment of him. Probably the charges are true technically. How can I tell when I have no reason for faith in the integrity of the accuser?

I thought him singularly free from intellectual malice. Otherwise a lover of mysteries that did not mystify: a perverse sense of the dramatic: the flair for personal magnificence: a cult of self-worship that grew into astounding proportions. I have known these qualities in many people, distilled through many temperaments. He associated almost entirely with this type of mind. No wonder where or when they meet, they set to destroy one another with such ferocity. He has dramatised his adventures and himself until life is now only a fog in the midst of which he moves fevered with visions.

It is entertaining to watch at a distance. I feel an obscure resentment at having to take part, even remotely, in his curious pastimes. I prefer to choose my own disorders.

As for Gilbert, and his part in this, there is no hope for him so far as I can see. Not that it is of any importance. It is a typical episode of its kind, and the whole business is too wretched to write about.

Retinger will shortly be in Poland, unless the authorities finally decide to send him back to Mexico. The incident seems to be almost finished, with twelve weeks in prison for Retinger as the only visible change in any personal program; what might have been a small tragedy is rapidly assuming the proportions of enormous comedy, except to those for whom the taste of such laughter is bitter.

Letters are poor keepers of secrets, or I would tell you a great number of interesting things; I have luckily a variety of strangely assorted contacts; with the diplomats, with the revolutionists, with one or two governments officials, with a horrible group of interventionists who talk with a complete lack of restraint as to American plans here. I am making a story of these opposed forces; they blend fantastically. The one emotion in all of them is hatred for each other.

To: Harrison Boone Porter TLS 2pp. Maryland

61 Washington Square South
New York City.
July 27, 1922

Dear Darling Dad:

Things happen, don't they? Here I had struck New York, oh, so flat, I hadn't a penny nor a crust of bread, and was busily getting my stories written so a few checks would come hopping in. . . . when lo, presto! I was appointed by President Obregon to organize the Exhibition of Mexican Popular Arts in the United States. They wired me my fare and expenses ($800), and I dashed back to Mexico. There I found a tremendously interesting show going on. I studied and began writing the official monograph of the Exhibition, stayed there from April fifth to June 16, returned by boat, and here I am, getting ready for the very loveliest show you can imagine. It goes to Los Angeles first, so I shall skip to the coast in about three or four weeks more, to meet it there: I also have charge of a show for Diego Rivera,[51] the greatest living Mexican-Spanish painter, who is known all over Europe but not here. . . . and that will be pure glory only, but SUCH glory, dear dad!

I am writing for half a dozen magazines and newspapers at once: the stories will begin appearing in about two months more. It seems to me, dad honey, that my ten years of tussle are about to bear a little fruit. Getting started has been a terrific go, but now it seems to me that all I have to do is to work about three times as hard as ever I did, and I shall be alright!

Did you see my Mexican story in the July number of the Century maga-zine?[52] Let me know, and if you didn't I will send copies. I haven't any on hand this minute, and I want to mail this.

It seems curious to have an official appointment from a foreign govern-ment, when I went there in such a simple way to study their arts—inciden-tally, I learned a bit about politics; but I'm not writing any more after the Century story, for its too delicate a subject.

I have a lot of new pictures coming, really good ones this time, and I shall send them when they arrive. . . . . it may pain you to learn that I have turned completely frivolous, and now, your meanest child has hair black as it was in my cantankerous infancy, slews and slathers of black, black hair, nice and curly. Needless to say, it has been "cured" or restored, with black henna. This will interest that other painted woman of the family, Miss Mary Alice. I got tired of it gray.[53]

I wonder how you are all doing. Do write me a few of the hellish sordid particulars. I know they will be that. This family has a gift for trouble. . . . what I used to call "an instinct for misery." But I was pleased with Gay the last time, her state of mind was so perfect: and with Paul and Connie, because they seem so set on happiness and contentment with their Winkum-blinkum kids and the Ford.

I wish Baby could be well again. I think of her so much, especially of late she is on my thoughts almost too much. Tell me about yourself. . . . Dad, my life is so very full, I have arrived at such a serene sort of feeling about my work . . . I can do it, and that is settled. . . . well, I feel as if all the bother were well paid for.

Write me very soon. A kiss to you . . . I was on board ship on your birth-day June twenty eighth, just off the Bahama Islands. I remember that Gay had a birthday two days ago? My, but we're a grown up, dignified set, now!

Katherine Anne

To: Francisco Aguilera TLS 4pp. Maryland

[2025 Broadway
New York City]
n.d. [c. March 4, 1924]

Tuesday afternoon, late: and I wish you could see the sky! Smoky delicate greys with an ever-so-subtle wash of orange and rose. . . . I realise I had grown very sophisticated about sunsets. . I remember with a blush of shame that I once manufactured some graceless phrase about the cosmic banality of the moon . . . The dusty moth-eaten cleverness of one buried under a roof and not daring to look at a tree for fear of bursting into homesick weeping! . . . . Here, sitting on a brick roof at the head of Broadway, I am restored with one glimpse to the bosom of nature! . . . Today, it came over me, as I leaped mud puddles of melting snow across the long triangle of intersecting streets at my corner, that here, if ever I hoped to find it, was that hermit's cave in a desert which, you recall, we have discussed as the final Paradise of civilised minds.

For look you: In this one square, under this one roof, I did the following things: I had my <u>long</u> hair washed, and next door I bought thin grey stock-ings, and a box of face powder: One door up I bought a pair of black satin slippers and next door to that I left my bronze ones to be shined prettily. Around the corner, I entered a delicatessen and bought a slice of korned beef for Little Dig-dig,[54] and three oranges for myself. Two doors up I paused and asked them to send up and get my blouses to be washed, and left a suit with the tailor to be done over a trifle. At the bookshop I found a precious little old German collection of poetry, dated 1837. . . . I bought some pens and a typewriter ribbon. I didn't stop at the lingeries shop, nor the florist's, because I had no more money. I gazed longingly at almond patties in crystallized sugar in the candy shop, gave a passing indifferent glance at the automobile tires in the corner window, an impassioned one at the spring frocks. Noted that there was a sale on Palmolive soap at the drug store, entered my florid and rampant lobby, your letter was handed to me by the elevator person; Then when I shut my door, I am as silent and removed from the world as if I hung in air. . . .

It makes Hermitting so simple, and so pleasant, this having all the mechanism of supply shirring noiselessly beneath you, smoothing all the details of existence, while one sits upon the roof and meditates. . . . I need never leave this block again unless I wished to buy antique furniture, or go to the theatre.

Oh dear darling, Spring isn't late this year, but early. It is here now, and not only in my heart, but in the air. . . . For this one precious short spring, spring is enough for me, and my love and my joy are enough . . . It is a strange thing that I can love you so much, and have such happiness in it, when I know so well that you do not love me. . . . I believed (it is such an old superstition!) that unrequited love was true martyrdom . . . It is not. . . . The most bitter and tragic times of my life came when I was loved and could not love in turn. . . . I wouldn't be so cruel to you, my love . . you are free not to love me, but I am not free to love you if it troubles your heart. . . .

Nine O'clock.

It is not so painful as it would be if you loved life, but did not love me . . . for if I am to you only a small fragment of the vast unconscious cruelty of existence, that impersonalises it . . . If I feel lost, chilled a little, troubled with that hard pain that runs in the blood and searches out all the nerves from heart to fingertips, I have felt that pain for other things too . . . for the death of people I have loved. . . . . . you are alive, you are in the same world with me, if we will, we may see one another . . . Be deliberate, be cold, keep your "compromisos de antiguos contraidos"—irony, irony! You would be happier with me.

######

It is better for you to come here. You will like this place, it is so funny, and it is possible that N—goes to Boston at precisely that time you mention . . . Let it be then if you cannot come earlier. . . . A little later, could you go to the country for a week with me? But let us talk of that when the time comes.

These letters of mine. Surely you don't read them all at one sitting? You remember I told you that I never wrote letters. This is no longer true, strictly speaking.

Did you finish the poem beginning "La Musa de Verlaine . ." And wasn't it a little cruel to take my poem, "Una corona de espinas traiga Catalina," and invert it to comic uses? Or was it the deathly humour of that harsh realism that gives all beauty and affection to its natural destination, the dust?

———Goodnight, hijito mio; I love you.
Katherine Anne

> Lights on the river
> Are thin daggers.

The walls of houses
Have cutting edges at corners
Where the jagged teeth of iron railings
Keep guard over nothing.
Under my feet the stones,
And on my heart
The dark rain falling.
O, rain, be merciful.
Wash away the sharp edges of the world.
Crumble under my feet the stones of my desolations.

To: Genevieve Taggard TLS 2pp. NYPL

[2025 Broadway
New York City]
May 10, 1924.

About Midnight

    I was working along, Jedsie, in my solitude, going over old papers, notes and recollections from four years past, and found at last, after long search, this poem which I wrote two years ago in Mexico. It is very personal—all my poems are, all poetry is, all life is, but I love it very much, and want you to see it. . . . . It was written out of a definite mood communicated by a tremendous experience, and I think the title sufficiently explains it . . .[55]

    If you like it, print it. If not, darling, don't trouble. . . . . I expect you to be severe with me. . . . as you remember, on that time when you told me you could be cruel with me, because I am strong, I told you I liked that, because it fostered in me the illusion of strength. . . . . that was, and is, true. And so few truths last longer than a day! So you see, this is a very robust one.

Love and affections,
Katherine Anne

Write me a little letter to reach me on my birthday, May 15. I love my birthday, I was always so happy to have been born!

This Transfusion

You need not be afraid, I shall not wound
Your pride with my edged scorn,

Nor flagellate with my despairs
The surface of your heart:
For this my hate
Is not a lash, nor thorn
But a measureless, distilled
Vial of torment endlessly refilled.
And it shall fix upon your senses so,
Shall of your slakeless fibres be such part
As your wild blood shall mix within your veins
My hard, enduring pains,
Incorporate
With your immediate being.
And if your pulse should quicken, it shall be
To the sole desire of death, the ease of hell,
From this transfusion that was life of me.

K. A. P.

To: Gay Porter Holloway TLS 3pp. Maryland

North Windham, Connecticut.
July 21, 1924

Dear Darling Gay:
    Your letter was very much like you, and so I like it. I remember yesterday that you would have a birthday, probably before this reaches you, but I wanted to wish you luck, and happiness, too because its customary to wish for happiness, though nobody seems to know precisely what it is . . . I was thinking of Mary Alice all this month, too, and it doesn't seem possible that she has been gone for five eternal years. I never forget her for long at a time, and I never remember her without a bitter wrench of my heart . . . I loved that adorable tender and innocent baby . . . I think it was the one genuine lasting affection in me, for it outwears everything else, with a sort of freshness and gentleness that I never had for any one else in my life.
    She has come for me not altogether a child, and a lost child, but a very pure symbol of love, a small precious image, and I have buried my own childhood with her, and I feel sometimes that when I cry for her, I am crying over all the other lost things in my life, too. For she was the divine young victim who took upon her head all our dreams and visions, and went away into the wilderness . . . Children are the scapegoats of our love, Gay. To die young is

better, but the death of the children is the terrible part of the suffering which accumulates relentlessly upon those who live longer.

And yet, I know I haven't been altogether unhappy, and though I can't think of more than half-dozen days of my life that I would live over again, I am not so embittered about life that I can be sorry for having lived. So when I say it is better to die young, I am selfish again, with that selfishness we have in trying to determine what is, after all, the individual destiny. . . . It rests me, sometimes when I am doubly hard pressed, to think of that blessed child folded away quietly safely, forever, without a dream to disturb her. But she loved life, and she has been cheated out of it. And we have been cheated of her. And we must think of her with tears for the rest of our lives.

Tell me about your other babies: little Paul, or Harry, or whatever it was you finally decided to name him, must be a tall fine child by now. Is he good looking as ever? For he was a most beautiful baby. . . . The wee Lady Gay[56]—for such, I suppose, you are bound to dub her, is now a little past three years old. That's a delightful age, and I think you should send me some snapshots of her, with some of little brother too. And of yourself. I know you must have a camera. I charge you to send me forthwith some late snip-snaps of yourself, all the family, and the dog. I will swap even. I take an awful picture, as you know, but whatever they are, I will send them.

We—some friends and I[57]—have an old New England farmhouse in the deep country, a most delectable picture book sort of house in an old fashioned sentimental landscape full of little lanes bordered with old apple trees and ferns, thickets of wild berries, beautiful white wild flowers, little brooks—really, such a charming and delicate landscape, I love New England very much. I wish you could be here, for you would love it. I am convinced that the Eastern country is much nicer than the southern for country life, and you should save your pennies and invest a thousand dollars or so in a nice deserted farm here. If I didn't hope to go to live in Europe for a few years, next year I would try to get about twenty acres or so.

But I do not want to stop in one place for long at a time. Nothing is for life with me, dear sister, except my preoccupation with writing. And that I did not choose. It merely remains, and I must suffer it.

It seems to me I should add a few paragraphs on my love affairs, but they are fragmentary, playful or tragic as may be, and I nearly always believe them permanent for at least a week. So if I told you now I love some one for all my life, I should only be put to the necessity of explaining to you a little later that I was mistaken again, either in my feelings or in his. It is always one or the other, and sometimes both. I have suffered a great deal from love, or rather, the impossibility of finding an adequate substitute for illusion. . . .

Well, dear old child, I love you, and that's an affection that never fails me; and the steadfastness of your life has been a wonder to me. You have managed to give an impression of some thing whole and entire in your being, in spite of the most jumbled sort of existence it is possible to imagine, and you seem to have held to a dead center of calm somewhere in your innermost self, which certainly I haven't been able to do . . It seems to me I have been shattered and re-assembled over and over again, though each time I fly back to some magnet where my forces seem centered. But I can't hold it for long. And that, sweet old thing, is the sad secret of my life. . . .

Well, write me very soon. Give my love and affections to your husband and children. . . . I kiss you good night, and so to bed . . . cool as spring here, and the wind blowing through nice tree tops outside my window . . . I hope your summer isn't too hot . . . I am trying to get some writing done, but the country is so lovely I live outdoors most of the time.

Katherine Anne

To: Genevieve Taggard ALS 1p. New York Public Library

Windham, Connecticut, November 14, 1924
P O Box 13

Dear Jedsie—

Just how good—or bad!—a poem is "Requiescat," anyhow? And who is Burton E. Stevenson?[58] And what is his "Home Book of Verse"? Christ, what a title! For he writes and wants to put "Requiescat" in the new edition, and asks me my age, which I had fondly hoped had nothing to do with it. However, I kindly gave him the latest possible date on which I could possibly have been born, and said Thankee, Sir, for putting my nice lil poem into your dear little Fireside Wreath of Rhyme. Isn't fame a simple curse, what?

I have finished my story "Holiday" in a bath of bloody sweat, and am resting. . . . . . dear darlin', have you heard, out of the air, maybe, that I am going to have a baby about the middle of January? Now I've passed the danger period of losing it, I can't keep silent any longer. Write and tell me how mad I am.

Love and affections—
Katherine Anne

To: Genevieve Taggard ALS 2pp. NYPL

[New York City
c. December 11,1924]
Thursday—

Dear Jedsie: Your note came a few days ago. I should be happy to come up for Christmas—But I have had an illness, and I shan't be able to travel.

On December second my child was born prematurely and dead, and though I have never been in danger, still it is better in every way to be quiet.

I want very much to see you, dear darling Jedsie, please come and see me if you are here. Until after Christmas I shall be at the Dalletts—56 Charles Street—my baby was a boy. It was dead for half a day before it was born—

There seems to be nothing to say about it. My affections to Bob and Marcia–[59]

Thank you for writing me: I shall come to your home yet, and I hope it shall be soon.

With my faithful love—
Katherine Anne

To: Genevieve Taggard TLS 5pp. NYPL

[Merryall Valley, Connecticut]
This is Thursday. June 3, 1926

Jed

Bob was over calling you by telephone last night and I wanted to grab the receiver and speak to you also: After a wordless disappearance, Bob returned and gave me news of you. You were, he said, "all right." These are scant tidings. I hoped you would come back too for a few days anyhow.

All that fullness of green and bloom you promised have come true: I am perfectly happy .. never before so simply contented with what I have. Nothing happens, I will not let anything happen. I drowse, and refuse to be waked up. I read if I choose, or I lie on the grass and my sole uneasiness is a nest of wasps under the doorstep. They swarm out now and then over me. One of them stung Ernest.[60] I was glad it wasn't me!

I pick great pails full of dandelions to make wine: four gallons are in the brew. We'll have a bottle together for dinner next fall. I am not one who lets her cellar be raided by those heathen drinkers who think its quite alright if there's alcohol in it. It must be ripened wine or nothing.

Bob brought me good news that you mean for me to write a piece about Cummings for Measure. . . . The only thing I've had to write about in a long time. Send on the precious books, I'll begin at once. When do you want it?

Ernest gave me The Making of Americans[61] for my birthday, and carved me a little elephant paper cutter of soft pine. Cutting the leaves is half the battle of wading through. I find that admirable woman writes in a continual spiral, which is, as you know, the very form of the germ of life; it is not hard to read once you recognize that it is the spiral, and let your mind follow loosely relaxed—

"In this world where one hand washes the other" I find we have as always neighbors. The Grossenbacher's are so far pleasant, I have only the simplest dealings with them, a friendly indifference is the best insurance against complications. Jo and John[62] are delightfully haphazard and casual: John and Ernest built rival ships: Brittany fishing boat style, and we had races on the pond. The little boats were beautiful, with their coloured sails and nicely painted bodies, and both were sea worthy.

If the vast silence seeping from Bob's barn is any sort of true sign, then literature is well under way in that quarter. As for me, I am leaving writing to those that can do it, even the poor Herald Tribune is reduced to nagging me by telegram for reviews. But I mean to get off this batch of hack work, and then no more of this disgraceful occupation. I loved doing your book,[63] and one or two for the New Republic, and the Cummings job is precisely what I like doing. But every bore under God's heaven goes to Mexico and writes a dull book, and I get it from the Herald-Tribune. I shall quit playing Mexican expert. The fizz is all out of it.

Sweet chuck, in this placid nothingness you will read the history of my mind and heart at this ever-blessed moment. This room, your room, is full of lilacs and apple blossoms, in their presence one no more dares be cynical than before children: they know better and would shame me. Everything but the spring seems unnecessary, irrelevant, an intrusion. I wish you could come up here and lie on a grass bank for one week, with every nerve straightened out and rounded on the edges. Maybe I only wish for you what is the top of good fortune for me: you may not even want it, much less need it. But it being the best thing I can think of in this world, I can wish you nothing more.

We hear now that the house may go, you may give it up. This was well prepared for in advance, I am not surprised: all of us half-expected it. Grossenbacher says we may all stay on by the month as long as we like, there is no danger of a sale until spring. So anyhow, we shall harvest our gardens, and put up all the fruit we want, and that is Demeter's own plenty; Its a pity about this place going to some one else. I love it, and Ernest is pleased, but my poor Ernest is an architect, that is to say, a soul lost in contemplation of academic problems, and a house is not a house to him, but a mathematical arrangement and it seems that for entire purity, this house is now and then an inch or two off. . . . I know not where. However, this unevenness of scale does not prevent him from sleeping soundly, enjoying his food, and doing his block cuts; he is fat and brown, and I at least am brown. Darling, how good it was of you to let us have the house! That is the sum total of my feelings.

Now, its not a fair exchange, for you will have something live and kicking to tell me about your life in New York, but swap me tales of action for my drowsy subjective meanderings. Your days move at a visible rate, and I find it very exciting to see: Are you editing Measure now? What about a poem? Not that I have finished it, but when I do, will you read it?

Affections,
Katherine Anne

In Merryall
Post scriptum

If it were not that the garden must be weeded, the food baked and the dishes washed, the floors swept, and reviews written, and that my mind is uncontrollably not on these things, but set on a country too far away for any telescope to reach, I might mail my letters the day they were written. It must be four or five days now since I talked a word or two by telephone with you. Your voice sounded detached, far-away, Bob said you were in a rage of writing. Good for that! Here I find not the same sort of distraction that I knew in town, but nevertheless troublesome things that provide an excuse for my nervous inability to settle and grind. I have no alibi at all: I know that when the will to say your say is powerful enough, nothing so unimportant as human beings or circumstances can stop one for long. . . . I am full fed of the frustrated genius. I refuse to call myself such a poor thing. Somewhere in me the creative power is almost quenched, strangled speechless and I can't tell why. But it is in me, and nowhere else, that the trouble lies. That is why I lost hope, being denied the bright fantasy of blaming it on some one or something else.

Nevertheless, I am happy here in the exterior world, and now and then I get a grand interval of peace with myself: and write at top speed for a few hours: and in this way I am getting on with two short stories.

At the end of June or first of July I mean to be in New York for a few days, and hope to see you, and shall even share that very comfortable bed.... there is a downy one here, too, where I sleep such sleep as I have not known for years, between the windows where I get all the winds, and the green light from the full blooming horse chestnut tree.

I saw the second New Masses, better than the first maybe, but yet none so good. What makes them all so glassy-sharp, and ill humoured, and why do they write so very badly about everything? I still hope for some thing sound, simple, intelligent and warm from some one of them. But they are radical in the manner of the petty bourgeoisie convicted of the commonplace. That's only one way of being progressive, and I believe the least effective.

Jo began her book about two weeks ago, and read us about fifty pages last night: a good beginning, she has uncanny insight into the petty motives of drab starved people: she makes a sort of surface dissection of a very third rate little family dissolving under the strain of small town disgrace. Her style is plain and severe: she elects to write of something she knows too well and despises. Someday I hope we will find something in the life of this country we all know so well to love, and write about that. We will make better books.... have you read Tristram Shandy lately?

I have made a drawing of John, not very good, one of Ernest, tolerable, and one, very good, of a charming black cat who comes to visit, wearing white mittens, socks, and weskit. I have put him in my book plate which I cut in linoleum, and printed myself.

This letter must come to an end. Farewell in my best will. I watch the postman every day for the Cummings books! Does your book shop have magazines? If I sent a smallish check could they be mailed?

How much would these books cost?

Lucienne   Jules Romain
Death in Venice   Thomas Mann
Three Lives   Gertrude Stein
Confessions of St. Augustine (I have lost my copy I had for ten years!)
Life in Mexico, Madame Calderon de la Barca
Countess Martinengo Cesaresco's book on Sicilian Folk songs, I forget the exact title.

I should like the full set of Greek translations by H. D. and Richard Aldington, et al—but not at once. Can they be bought? I don't know if the supply is exhausted.

"Myro, a girl, shedding a child's tears,
Raised this little tomb to the locust that sang
in the seed-land:
And to the oak-dwelling cicada. Implacable Hades holds
their double song."

That's Anyte of Tegea you can see why I must have those translations!

Love—
K.A.

To: Carleton Beals TLS 2pp. BU

158 Waverly Place, New York
January 16, 1926

Dear Carleton:

Good luck for the New Year. Your card lacked an address but Kenneth[64] told me where to write you; E. E.[65] and I form a permanent Committee of Discussion on Ways and Means to Get Me To Mexico, and we have decided that your advice would be helpful.

Have you heard what became of the projected art exhibition that Morones expected to put on? I was to work with that affair. But nothing happened. Negotiations wilted on the stem, though I tended them faithfully for months.

This is no great misfortune, I would rather have something less air-tight, a simple job of work that would keep me in Mexico for at least two years; Mary Doherty[66] used to teach English in several suburban schools, and I could very well do the same. I used to teach dancing in the technical schools for girls, it was very amusing, and I am not so bad at it. You see my ambitions are modest, humanistic. I have prepared a series of lectures on American poets, and I think it might be arranged for me to give them there, quite aside from any regular work I might have. You don't need an assistant on Tass? I thought not. And yet you might consider it. Need I remind you that I am a demon newspaper person? Indeed, the job is the thing, I do as others do in Mexico, develope unexpected talents for curious chores; and willingly live in poverty for the mere sake of being there.

Advise me. But don't advise me to make newspaper connections here before I start. It is not so simple, the field is well covered on the regular assignments. Of course, I shall do a little free-lancing, one always does, but I wish for a native-born Mexican job of some sort, preferably one that will take me into the country, or suburbs . . . I have precisely three books planned, outlined, partially written, and whether they are ever finished depends on my being in Mexico for several years more.

You know, of course, that I prefer association with human beings rather than with the bourgeoisie; I would rather have a very little job with the sort of people I like than a very expensive, rich-off job I would have to do with cynicism. With these few previsions, let me know what you think of my chances. I know Spanish rather better than I did, I read and translate very well, though my speech stammers even yet. But that will cure itself with time.

Life—perhaps you know this—is not worth a damn here when one wishes to be in Mexico. So take a look around, and write me when you have time. . .

Give my remembrance to any one who asks for me, if you see Xavier[67] tell him it is I who can complain now of neglect. He definitely owes me a letter, and I am a harsh creditor.

Judging merely by dispatches, there appear to be some interesting complications on the way. But we will talk of this when I see you.

Faithfully yours,
Katherine Anne

To: Harrison Boone Porter TLS 4pp. Maryland

Salem, Massachusetts
February 16/28

Hello, Pop—

Here I bob up again, lean as a wolf for news. Gay remains the most talented reporter in the family, and throws me odd bits from time to time.

She tells me you have an Orange Grove in Magic Valley, and there's a row of words deserves to be in a poem.

Sister, in her funny way, remarks that she was certain I hadn't passed over, or I would have come back to ha'nt you all. I wish to say here and now, if I ever promised any such thing, I take it all back. I mean to do my walking in the flesh: and if my book is a success and I can collect car fare, I certainly do intend to walk in and haunt you nicely next summer.

I am working along on this book,[68] and am pretty sick of it. But its going to be very lively, and I'll send you the first copy when it comes out—and when I get home we'll have another family dinner, and I'll do the cooking. I am developed into a famous cook. I love to work all day at a spread, and then come out with a bouquet, and take a bow. Prima Donna cook, thats what I am.[69]

I have been studying and doing research into early American history here in the Essex Institute, and during those times I was too bored to read any more diaries of the Founding Fathers—and a hard-boiled lot THEY were—I amused myself looking through genealogical records—I found in the Tennessee and Kentucky books one item of interest . . . It was about John Porter, Captain of Infantry, from Woodford County, Kentucky, who was killed at the battle of Oak Ridge: He married a Sarah Whittsett of Tennessee and one of his sons married a Miss Blanton of Texas . . . Isn't this your Uncle John you used to tell about? The one who was buried in his friend's blanket?

I also found a lot about the Cadwalader Joneses of Virginia. Didn't you used to say this was my mother's family? I understood it to be so—. I looked up the Frosts, too, but could not find grandmother Carolina Frost, because I didn't know enough names to follow up . . . Tell me anything you remember about any of these people, with family names, and I would have some diversion tracing them out.

Strangely enough, the name Skaggs appears nowhere, though Grandmother always spoke of her father, Brigadier-General Abram Moredock Skaggs, and some one here from Kentucky told me there was an equestrian statue erected to him at the entrance of the Public Park in Louisville, I think. The genealogist here suggested that this name was a corruption of the Dutch Van Schaick—pronounced van Skake—and it sounds reasonable when you think of the way the forms of names changed in those days. No two persons of the same family ever spelled the family name alike. Note it was Skeggs and was so spelled in the Virginia Family—English origin, earliest notice about 1510.

Don't be nervous Dad, I am not taking up genealogy in a serious way, but I suppose my interest has some connection with my being so far away from my base, as it were, it is probably an obscure symptom of home-sickness. Cousin Jinny turned out to be the professional genealogist of the family, and one is enough.[70]

Tell me about your orange grove, that fascinates me. I hope to pull oranges off your trees as I used to steal the green peaches on the farm; the nicest memory I have is of that lovely orchard you made to take the place of the old one on the Carlton place, and don't I wish I might once more pull a ripe Indian-cling peach off one of those trees. . . . the Indian cling is still my favorite peach.

I hope you have good health: I continue as of old, neither sick nor well. I have to take care of my lungs, and I believe I was born tired. I know spring is the beautiful time in the south. I remember summer as a preparatory course for hell, and fall as a dead and bitterly ugly time, and winter was a mere long drawn out dying for me. But Spring was beautiful. I wish I could visit you in the spring.

It is almost here, and I still have a lot of work to do before I can move. So it will have to be late summer at best.

Think of it: last summer I never even saw a watermelon. Isn't that disgusting? But I went up to the country and took a very funny house, and raised all the golden bantam and country gentlemen corn I could hold . . . got even a little.

Now Pater darling, do write me a letter. I never forget you, but I have had so little good news of myself; I could never write except to say I was darned near starving, and thats no news at all . . . I don't in the least see how I have survived, but I have; I regret the time and energy I have lost trying to keep alive, that I might have put in on the work I love to do. But it simply could not happen, I couldn't make it happen. I have not an ounce of talent for making money.

Alas and alack. But the truth is, I haven't enough respect for money, and I don't find people interesting who devote their time to getting it . . . You have to love money better than anything else in order to make a lot of it, and I simply never could give up the things I liked to devote my time to something I cared so little about—so I have pretty doggoned near died for lack of a bone to gnaw at times. <u>Now</u> I do a little better. I hope you do also.

Write to me, and tell me all about yourself. Love and a big hug from–

Kinkyhead

P.S.
My hair is now long, and I do it up in a knot, and it doesn't look so wild.

To: Gay Porter Holloway TLS 5pp. Maryland

[Salem, Massachusetts]
March 5th, 1928

Dear Angel, got a letter from Dad in the morning and one from you this afternoon, so I laid off work and sat around reading the news.

It seemed I must burst if I didn't get the scrappy edges gathered together, and now I have 'em.

You sound cheerfuller and cheerfuller, darling, I believe with everybody else that TH was a sort of mortal disease to you, and until you were cured of him you couldn't possibly be cured of anything else. I discovered long ago that to fix your heart on one man was apt to be fatal. Though how I discovered it I don't know, for I could never, and cannot yet—fix on one for more than six months if so long. Yet I have been sincerely in love, and have had some terrible things happen. Now I too am fairly well settled in my mind, though I almost married Hidalgo, the famous Mexican caricaturist, about six months ago. He is a love, and a charming person: but I 'scaped out of that and came here, where I receive gloomy letters accusing me of various kinds of infidelity: physical, moral, spiritual, mental etc., and maybe its nearly all true. I cannot keep track of my feelings long enough to settle to anything. It is better to be alone, most of the time.

Ah your good coffee! I am still a fiend, and cigarettes are still the main part of my daily food. I would love to loll around and smoke and gossip until all hours. By the time I get there, you'll be up to the ears in the oil business, and be getting up by alarm clocks again. I hope not. I hope you never have to listen to an alarm again. I have a lazy woman's notion of Paradise, and a good part of it would be to lie around and drink coffee with you in some very sunny spot.

What you say about Baby and Jules is so funny, because Pop is SO annoyed that Jules spends a third of his income getting his suits pressed, or something of the sort. Pop says you are fat and efficient and sot in your ways and it won't do to cross you: that you are a good soldier and a gentleman? This seems such perfect praise I hurry to relay it on to you.

Well, maybe I didn't mean that El Dorado is a hole, but I stick to my story that it was: Oil is a great upbuilder, cars and pavements run after it! I was right about Mission, then, it is in that Brownsville country near the border, and I liked that place. I'll be glad to see it again. You mention the Chronicle, I remember Marcellus Foster[71] and his charming letter to the Red Cross about me when I was trying to go to France during the War: though what I wanted to go with the Red Cross for, I can't think now. I must have been out of my mind.

TH junior's letters are fine. I send them back to you because you might want to keep them. Such a boy! And he writes well, too. I think Missy Anna Gay ought to be snapped out of the convent and put in a modern child's school where they pay more attention to the child and less to piety. But that's merely my notion. She ought to be in some place where they let her model in clay and make things, and dance and try out her budding intelligence. I can't remember that I ever had a teacher who taught me anything. I had to dig it out in spite of them, and that's too hard a way.

Patsy sounds lovely, is her name Patricia by any chance?[72] I always thought Paul would end as a personality, since he began as one. He was always a schmart bye. The Porter men in this generation seem hell-bent on making money. The lack of it is indeed the root of all evil. It makes me feel rotten though for Dad to be so upset about his so-called financial failure. It takes a sort of money-sense to attract money, and if you're not born with it you can't. I used to be terribly troubled because none of us seemed to have it: but it isn't necessary to have millions, and after all, if you have a free head, you can manage somehow to make yourself comfortable in the world. I always thought Dad was simply swamped by four children he really didn't know what on earth to make of. Its a hard position for a man. Most of them would have, as he says, put them out to grass somewhere and worked it out by himself. I sometimes think it would have been better if he had, for now he would have money, and feel better about everything. As for me, I don't care if he never has any more than he needs for himself. I do want to feel that he is comfortable.

I haven't been writing much of late, only on this accursed book. Have two short stories out going the rounds, and one accepted by a magazine in Paris. My latest is very simple and short, a child story, called the Fig Tree, and very dimly it is about an episode of my own childhood. Don't do reviews and special articles anymore. Can't til this is off.

Lord, honey, wouldn't I love to gather around a coupla quarts of good tequila or mescal with you and Dad; one of the funniest episodes I remember in my whole life: I meant to write this to Dad and left it out, so I'll write it to you: was one time down in Texas at the Hillendahl farm, Dad, Baby and I went to a turnverein and drank all the beer we could hold, and toddled back through the woods very pie-eyed, and Dad was carrying the lantern and got mixed up in the branches of a freshly fallen tree. Well, when I remember Dad and the lantern going round and round in the tree top, I roar to this day. I was so busy falling in and out of gullies I hadn't time to laugh then all I wanted. There was one nice thing about Dad: after we grew up he never played the heavy father, and I can remember some very good times with him. Grandmother would have turned over in her grave, but just the same it is nicer to be chummy with your children.

TH's escapade was at least characteristic.[73] He must have stayed very young looking to have attracted an 18 year old girl. He is fifty or thereabouts, isn't he? That's not old by any means, but matrimonially speaking its certainly not so young, either. Here I am thirty eight and almost committed the nuisance of marrying a boy of twenty-six. He says I look twenty-eight, which is not true. I look thirty-eight, and don't try to deceive myself.

Oh that reminds me: what ever became of J.H. if you remember him at all. It seems so strange Gay that yesterday and the day before we were all young, and now, there's no blinking it, we are in early middle age. I can't think where the years are gone, now why I should be gray haired when I don't feel more than twenty-five. There is one charming thing about it: the world grows to be a familiar place, with no dark and terrifying corners, and no shocks and almost no strangeness. Things grow very clear and simple, so far as your personal life is concerned, and the mind grows firmer and clearer too. You can choose a little the things you want, and the rest you can examine and lay aside. Its very nice, really. I didn't think it would be.

Still I see the young girls who have arrived, without thinking, at twenty years to the point where it took me thirty to arrive at, simply because there was so much to overcome first—I mean this in personal philosophy—and I realise I was four jumps ahead of my generation, and should have been born fifteen years later to have been really comfortable in the world. Being a pioneer isn't my idea of a pastime.

Now Gay, I've simply got to stop. I wish I could see Anna Gay. I remember that darling squash of a creature, with that funny Gay-look that your babies always have, the spitting hissing images of their mammy, and how hurt her feelings were the night we left her in the hotel with the nurse-woman. Who is the mysterious Muz who annotated your letter, flinging, as t'were, the lie in your teeth when you wrote hard things about yourself? She sounds nice.

Darling, I remain a scrawn, I weigh about 108 in my galoshes, and the dread disease of age has attacked me i' the teeth. I'm having 'em fixed and fixed and FIXED, but Pop used to say, every damn time I bit into a hot biscuit or cracked a pecan, "Ah, ah, there go your teeth," and Time, or something, has borne him out. There they go, sure enough! He used to try to get us to use prepared chalk for a dentifrice, and the other day my dentist told me that, after all the fancy fixings, there was nothing better than plain prepared chalk and a little pure soap to scrub your teeth with. So Pop can get all chesty about the way he tried to bring us up. He was on the right track, poor dear, but we gave him no encouragement.

Well, I must get to work. Have a chapter to copy and correct. Drank two cups of coffee for dinner to keep awake, and now its nine and I'm sleepy already. Get up so very early to work in the morning while the place is quiet.

Bye Angel, send me another screed when you can, the sooner the better. Lord, I'm glad to hear you are having a rest. I'll join you in the summer.

Love and a hug,
Katherine Anne

To: Josephine Herbst TLS 3pp. Yale

May 5th—1928
561 Hudson Street
[New York, NY]

Well, Misz Herrmann, its good to know <u>somebody</u>'s gettin' her morphine regular, har har, because in this Dr. Caligari Cabin,[74] leave me tell you that even the nicotine supply runs out oftener than I like to think about:—but seriously, Josie, how do you expect to grow up to be a great big handsome girl with blue eyes and a lot of beaux, if you keep on flirting around with every sprig of poison ivy you meet? It'll stunt your growth, Josie.

Saw Miss Nimsie for a little while last night, (long while, I visited around at Becky's[75] til one o'clock, daylight saving time) and passed on the news about your mischance. It seems to me a little early in the season, but I know nothing of that plague, and evidently it has no closed season. I hope you are getting better, and I wonder if there is any way of rooting it out at the Grist Mill estate. You can't go on having this happen every spring. Spring, as you know well, was designed for better things.

Joan threw a large literary tea, borrowing Liza's house for it, for Margery Latimer on account of her novel.[76] It was one of these intimate sardine tin affairs, with big and little fish swimming nobly in gin cocktails, and if I ever go to another one I deserve to be hanged as an incorrigible fool. And if I ever give one may I be berled in erl. Thank God you're in the country and maybe they won't give you one. Lucky Misz Grist Mill.

Carolyn and Allen are settled here, happy happy to breathe without orders, and they set off to the country to visit the newly wedded Jim Rorty, with Nancy between them, all three beaming and fresh and free.[77] A pretty sight if ever I see one. Allen's tea came off in regular order also, with everybody drunk and putting his or her tongue out at everybody else: you know the charming atmosphere of good will and good manners that animates the artistic life of this vast cultural metropolis.

I think the book is selling, the reviews have been helpful, hardly a dissenting word, which is an author's idea of Paradise . . .

Me, I cook a little, and wash a few dishes, and mend my rags, and lick my sores and copy on Mather. . . . with a review or two for the check's sake. No life, no life at all, but I can't think of any other I'd prefer, so I suppose I'm happy.

Darling, I suppose you're right when you insist on hate being a more powerful and effective motivation than love; but like love, hate should be entertained only by powerful and effective minds: otherwise it is mere malice and a putrid little version of it even so: I'm thinking of Margy's wretched little book, in which she pursues her little victims with hat pins, and a garden hose spouting noble words. It simply will NOT do, I'm supposed to write something pretty about it. I will not. (Alas, as I read the above, I find that I have said something that must go in the review—about hate, etc. Pawdon muh. Professional reviewing has that corrupting effect.) Its hard enough to say clearly what needs to be said, if this filthy atmosphere is ever to be cleansed even a little. I don't want the job, reviewing is low work, and there's no excuse for doing it unless the poor hack gives at least an honest opinion. Nobody respects any body else's opinion, why should they, aren't they all geniuses? and the only unscared critic I know is Allen: but as for me, God forbid I should praise anything to my own inner shame. Its odd how they lead you up to an author at tea, cocktail in hand, with a charming air of saying—"Now, give this little girl—or boy—a great big hand!" And even I am so stampeded I dare not smile humanly upon a critic for fear of some one accusing me of vamping him for a favorable notice. No, angel, this is no place in which to sprout the green tendrils of your imagination. Better away to almost anywhere.

Writing you a letter, Josie, is no work at all. I must be at my tardy labors. When your poor body of this death has cast off its grave clothes, come forth like Lazarus and gimme a word.

I want to hear about the Grist Mill, now it is May there must be all sorts of things to watch, and I wish I could be there to watch them with you. Now and again I see Eddie,[78] a solid supporter of yours from start to finish, every line you write him he considers no less than a classic, he passes them around and we all make whoopee, because he is right, they are classic. Tell Mister Onion Farm Herrmann my affections remain fixed where they were, if he knows what I mean, and many ladies inquire after him tenderly.

As for the gentlemen, Misz Pomona, there's no countin' 'em any more. Nevertheless, you do well to set your higher aspirations on something less perishable, like the stone barn. And I wish I had one to lean on in my numerous crises.

Love and remembrance, write me news.
Katherine Anne

Say hello to Mister Coffey, and did Mrs. Gummidge arrive in order? She was a wild cat when she left this house. Della has the fourth one, Miss Mickey McCluskey, there's Theophilus here with me, and Weedlums with the Tate's until yesterday, when he disappeared off the roof and did not return. Enormous distress on part of everyone but Allen, who has stopped caring, if he ever did.

To: Gay Porter Holloway TLS 4pp. Maryland

September first, 1928
Note new address: 49 West 53rd Street, New York City

Dear Darling:

Pater wrote me about the first of June that you were to meet him in Houston, and attend the Democratic Convention (What a show that must have been. I heard the nomination on the radio.) I remembered it would be Dad's birthday on the twenty-eighth. I sent him a photograph, having nothing else to send. It must have surprised him greatly, for I have not had a word from him since. Nor from you, though I believe I owe you a letter, if we must git formal.

Now of course, I've lost your address, but I feel you must be a prominent citizeness in your neck of the woods, so I'll just send it care the Postmaster. UnDOUBTedly he knows Miz Holloway, the big insurance woman.

I was up in the country, in Pennsylvania, for five weeks, and gained a little, and rested up, and did a little work, so returned ready for the fall. By some accident I found this apartment, and now I am in the very heart of New York, I who have lived so long down town I believed I could never be contented anywhere else. I liked the old graceful houses, and the crooked streets. Here it is strange, with the houses of the enormously rich elbowing those houses that once were homes of the rich and are now apartment houses where even I can afford to dwell. The Elevated trains and the squalor of Sixth Avenue on the west, and the smug glories of Fifth Avenue on the east. Noisy and pretentious. But live here I must because this is a comfortable and cheap apartment, and very pretty.

My book is even yet not finished, I do have such a tussle to make ends meet that I spend nearly all my strength and time doing magazine and editing work, so there's very little time and strength left over for my own work. But that's a common thing with writers, and so I only speak of it to let you know why I do not come through sooner with the things I am living to do. When I look back I cannot tell you why or how I have survived. Yet I am here, and not too badly off.

I have a story in a book of stories and novel-fragments to come out this fall. The American Caravan. You will probably see it in the book shops. Also a very short tale, "Magic" in Transition, a magazine published in Paris. The Outlook has taken an article, and next Sunday I have a review of Gertrude Stein's book in the Herald Tribune. If only to God I can get through this book and be free really to work at my own stuff, I shall never complain of these bitter years. There seems to be always a little help somewhere, never quite enough for freedom, but enough to keep me alive. So you see, you may be justified yet in your belief that I shall be rich, though that was never part of my plan, and has nothing whatever to do with the things I really want.

You were telling me of some plan or offer you had, I suppose by now you are at your new work. Darling, when I think I have had a long struggle, I have only to remember you, and I feel as if my splintery plank had been a bed of roses. I hope by now you are more comfortable. I was always ease loving, but for years I slept on a hard bed and ate less than I wanted from choice. That's all very well. Asceticism is no virtue in itself, and yet if you choose to live the muscular life it can be done very charmingly. Its when you don't choose any longer, but must lie on your plank sick or well with aching bones, that hardship has no shadow of virtue in it, but only useless and wasteful suffering. Now I want a down pillow, and so I mean to have it.

I finally succeeded in wringing a letter and a snap shot out of Baby, but that's all. She's no letter-writer, and yet I remember how brilliantly and imaginatively she used to talk. In the picture she looked beautiful but very worn, and I think she has never learned how to take care of herself. Dad, bless him, seems as infatuated with her as ever, he wrote delightfully about her.

In July I meant to write you but it was too bitter and I could not. I know there is a difference in our feelings, and yours demanded some sort of consolation for you to survive at all: whereas I have been stubbornly rebellious and will not accept any; every year I swear to myself I will not remember any more, and yet the whole summer is a gradual approach to that terrible anniversary, and afterward I think almost constantly of that beloved child, and with the same bitterness and frustration that I felt from the first. Nothing can take the place of her living in this world; even if I could communicate with her I would not. I loved her so much I never loved anyone else by comparison. And I know that my feeling for her was little beside your own. I wish, my darling, there was some way of forgetting.

You must talk about yourself when you answer, and do, if you have any, send me some little pictures; if you haven't, then rush out in the sunshine and get somebody to snap you "as is." I think you must be very impressive with all that heft, and how did you do it? Baby is a hank and I am a bone. But it lurks somewhere in the blood. Remember tremendous Aunt Liza Myers,[79] and the perfectly redundant cousin Keziah Some-body-or-other who once visited us? From Kentucky. Well, I suppose you've followed that line. I want badly to see how you look.

Its half past one in the morning, and all very quiet for the moment. I love sitting up all night and sleeping till noon, the night belongs to me. If you will believe it, I think of you more and more often, and it struck me as strange that you never had any idea of coming to New York, even for a short visit. After all, boats leave New Orleans and Galveston every week, and land very nicely over here in Brooklyn. Couldn't you save up your round trip fare and drop in for a couple of weeks? You'd love it. You don't need clothes. Just enough to get here on, and then you could buy a dress and hat if you liked. Clothes are cheaper here than anywhere else in the country, and prettier.

I've often wondered why I was the only member of the clan who can't keep still. Almost everybody takes a trip one time or another, but not MY family. No sir. They stay put. Why? Think about this a week and it won't seem so wild.

Hope I have better luck persuading you than I did trying to get Baby to Mexico. She simply never even answered the letter. That's what she thinks of travel.

Good night, honey. Let me hear quickly. Tell me news, and how you feel, and all about you.

Love and affections,
Katherine Anne

To: Rebecca Crawford TLS 4pp. Maryland

["Sunnyside"
Bailey's Bay, Bermuda]
Monday night. March 11, 1929

My darling Becky,
New York was windy, dusty, sharp, and everybody's noses were blue and pinched, when I went on board the Avon. All the passengers wore flowers and looked cheerful, though slightly mildewed, and the friends who came to see them off had no flowers, and looked glum and positively gangrened. The band played, British sailors rushed around saying, "'nkyew!" and "Eaoh!" and I staggered to my cabin where I lay in a coma until four o'clock the next after noon. It was a very rough night, so I've been told. I wasn't sea-sick, anyhow not the wommicking kind. I just lay half-conscious, too damned tired to believe that I should ever rise again.

Well angel, I DID rise again, wobbled upstairs into the bar, took a whiskey soda—twenty five cents!—and wobbled out on deck, where I was tucked into a rug and lay there in a coma until six. I wobbled back to the bar, took a whiskey soda, and suddenly, as if by miracle, I bucked up enormously, went straight into the dining room and ate a tremendous dinner. I then went to bed, slept all night, had coffee, and was out roaring around the deck before breakfast. The day was heavy blue, sunny, calm ... about noon islands began to rise out of the sea, the Avon edged straight up to the dock at two o'clock, the band played, and the slightly mildewed human cargo from New York began to crawl off, pinning on its now-faded flowers, and being waved at by sunburned persons lined up along the dock. Victorias bursting with fat vacationists rolled by on the coral paved streets, hundreds of persons in all conditions of life paddled around on bicycles, negroes lolled around looking as if they had not only time and Bermuda, but all eternity and heaven for their playgrounds. . . . I thought, here is a plan I know by heart, I can live and be happy. So I crawled off with my faded flowers, gathered my baggage, got into a victoria and drove six miles into the country along the coral roads, low white-washed walls, palms, oleanders in full bloom morning glories, cedars, nasturtiums—what a dull catalogue of what beautiful things. Sunnyside was sitting by the road, a low white tropical house. I marched in calling, "Thorborg!" and who should rise up to meet me but Thorborg, Basil, Della Day, and Franklin Spier![80] They were not expecting me until Monday. Della and Franklin are stopping across the bay.

Well, I am settled in the east wing with two big rooms all my own, my papers are scattered out so that I feel settled, and having settled, I go across the road and lie flat and watch the sea change from pale green to cobalt blue and pale lavendar ... All ready I am a little sunburned; I eat and sleep.

My head is troublesome, but I feel it improving. I was never so calm in all my life, it is as if everything were washed away that had troubled me, I can draw a full breath and begin to make some sort of orderly plan.

This is my first letter, and I meant to write it yesterday to catch this morning's boat. I saw her moving out toward New York this morning, and for the first time in years I saw a ship leaving without a terrible feeling that I was being left behind. Please tell me about yourself when you write, for of course now I wish you were all here: Mary Jane[81] especially would love it. Say what they please about dangers from the tetanus germ, I never saw more healthy thriving children than these, born and reared here.

Here, Becky, I shall find everything I have ever needed: and you'll see whether the work is not done! You remember the plan we talked of before I left: if it happens, I am given a free year, I choose to spend it here. Here I shall finish Thieves' Market[82] and get out a book of short stories.

I wish I could see you and I wish you could see how things are here. . . Later I'll send snapshots of the place. It is heavenly beautiful. My affections to Hedwig, to John, to Mary Jane, to Bill . . .[83]

With my love,
Katherine Anne

Friday.

I just heard that the Fort Victoria sails this afternoon, so one more word!

It might be entertaining? to tell you how I feel, what I think, and so on: but it seems more important (and you have a novelist in your family who will probably bear me out in this) to tell you what I DO, and the feelings and thoughts will somehow come to the surface of themselves.

Well: this household was in a state of beautiful excitement last evening, with everybody rushing and uttering soft round cries of joy. It was the second evening of the new moon, and perched upon one horn there sat a tiny star, equal in brilliance, equally self possessed. None of us had ever seen this. It was the event of the day.

Yesterday morning I walked three miles on the white road, around the bay, to have lunch with Delafield and Franklin. We scrambled up to the high point of the rocks overlooking the sea, took snapshots of each other, lay in the sun, were happy to be together. They both look marvellously well, its a pity they go tomorrow. Two weeks more and they would both be well.

It is now about half past eight in the morning, and my work table is set between two windows facing east, with sun and soft salt air and not so far away the shining sea. . . . I have my books and manuscripts all arranged, so the minute I feel rested, to work for me! Here I can take my vacation as I work, for all I needed was light and air to be well. I go to bed about nine o'clock and get up about seven thirty. All ready this seems a perfectly natural routine.

Tell Hedwig that I have worn the sweater every minute since I got here, it is impossible to think what I should have done without it.

Darling, I look over this letter, and I see plainly that contentment has no history. There are a lot of things, very practical, I want to write about, but I'll do it later. There seems to be so much time. I have got it in the back of my mind that you and Mary Jane are coming to Bermuda for a spell! Do you suppose that is merely a dream? I hope not. I'll tell you minutely all about the place, the way of living, the food, and so on, so you can decide about it, so soon as I discover everything for myself.

I am writing to all the doctors who examined me, especially to Doctor Baron for the X-ray plates, as there is an excellent dentist here who looks after Thorborg, and if anything is wrong I can have it attended to here. Also tell Hedwig not to jump too hard on nice Dr. Carpenter, who might well have been deceived by my rattling chest, and if he hadn't scared the very Devil out of me, I wouldn't be here! I almost feel grateful to him, even if I did put in some pretty soggy days on his account.

As for you, Becky, I am confounded. Where shall you be repaid for what you have done? Such virtue (in the good old Roman sense) as yours must— shall—have some reward other than its own existence. THAT will take some thinking about, too.

Good bye for the moment. I hear breakfast coming on. I made myself coffee early, but Basil really runs things in the morning, and shortly we shall sit on a porch in the east sun and eat such breakfast knickknacks as bananas and cream, herring and boiled potatoes etc. . . .

Love and affections,
Katherine Anne

To: Matthew Josephson TLS 3pp. Yale

["Sunnyside"
Bailey's Bay, Bermuda]
Friday night, March 16th I think, 1929 [March 15]

Matthew, I meant to write, indeed, I have tried to write, but it was not possible. Now I think I may simply try to answer your letters, I do not even know if I can do that. You will have to forgive this, I need time to recover.

Yes, I looked for you even to the last minute. Yes, I received your radio. It troubled me horribly, as everything has troubled me for it seemed a great while. I was distressed about the sickness of Eric,[84] I feared you might be over-taken by disaster in that child, I feared this, but I feared also for him because children die in great terror and bewilderment: I have seen them die. If any-thing happens to your children, you will never be whole again. I was troubled too by the immediate past that took on so suddenly the features of an old memory, full of the senseless, reasonless cruelty of—maybe!—a natural phe-nomenon imperfectly understood. It is quite possible that everything that has happened is natural, inevitable, that I am merely perverted in my notions of love, of human relationships; why do you reproach yourself for not being with me when you were "having a perfectly good time" somewhere else? It seems to me the whole art of life is to know your preferences, be certain where your interest lies, to recognize your love, to admit your true feelings and follow the true bent of your mind. . . . . I fail lamentably in all these, how can I reproach you if you fail too? Yet after a long time, it was made very clear to me that you were set on destruction where I was concerned. It was painful, even now it is mysterious and painful. Why were you so? I believe even now when you speak of your special feeling for me. I speak of mine for you still without shame, I know how I feel, I love you. You are afraid of that word, but I am not. You have nothing to lose by that word in me. You should know this by now.

You must not think I might hate you. Why should I? When you wound me you wound yourself, I could not possibly wish to wound you again. And there are so many bonds between us, it is wasteful, it is stupid, to wear them away with caprices, to test them with such pointless trials of strength.

You said in one of your latest letters that you could not promise me candour. I promise you only an attempt at candour, for the complications of my feelings, my thoughts, about you are endless. It is better, isn't it, to fix on one or two verities and (as you were demanding of the artists not so long ago) to "chew on them for dear life?"

Can you not then admit frankly that you are a man involved in ambitious projects, torn between many desires, drawn in a hundred directions by conflicts between your emotions and your intellectual convictions, arrived at by God knows what paths of reasoning. . . . ? I can understand all that. There are many things in you I cannot hope, nor even wish to know, they are not my affair, I have so many affairs of my own that require my energies—but I ask you not to be arrogant with me, look again at me, you will see a human being entirely friendly, entirely devoted to you, full of concern for you; Ah, Matthew, my darling, why have you been so devious with a woman there was no need to deceive?

All this time, you see, when you have been treating me quite as if you were somehow involved in a situation with a woman who would behave like a mistress, or a wife, to whom you must explain, crookedly, your motives, apologize for your neglect—did you neglect me? I am not your wife nor your mistress—I have been waiting for you to come awake, carry yourself as a friend toward me . . . Now maybe distance will do for us what nearness could not. Did you really believe that I had so many people around me merely because you did not come often? Matthew, I have always been besieged by people whom I bore with somehow. That is a grave flaw in my character, that I cannot defend myself effectively from attack by idle and wasteful people. You know that when you really wished to see me we managed it successfully. Will you please not say such things? For you cannot possibly believe them. And you cannot expect me to believe them.

For the first time since I have known you, I dared to read again all your letters, and when I came to that mysterious break, that sudden change, that occurred during the trip to Chicago, I thought "something occurred here, at this moment, the motives will probably always be a mystery to me . . . maybe even they are a mystery to him. But so it happened, and it is this that is real." Even so I may be deceived again. It may have been a part of that plan you have always in your mind. Policy. Tactics. . . . . Well, my dear, you were my invisible companion on the boat, even here you seem nearby, alive. If I have vanished from you, still I brought you with me. You are the one human being towards whom I could wish to turn with entire confidence. But that is a child-ish dream. Forgive me.

Katherine Anne

When I write again, I will tell you about how brown I am getting, how soft the sky, how brilliant the sun . . . how comfortable the hammocks! I am a beachcomber, no more . . . you sit on a park bench, please, and keep me com-pany. I have no toothpicks, not even last week's newspaper. Otherwise, I am a cheerful social pariah, without ambitions, prospects, or desires.

Also I want to write about the Transition business. And many other things.

To: Delafield Day Spier TLS 5pp. Maryland

["Sunnyside"
Bailey's Bay, Bermuda]
[Spring 1929]

Delafield darling:
As for naming your child, if it comes a boy I don't see how you could do better than David. That is a fine name. Deborah is lovely, too, but I don't think it is quite so impressive as David. How do you pronounce it, Déborah, or Debórah? For I never knew any one with the name, but it looks lovely in print.

Myself, I meant to name my child Miranda, which is my very favorite name for a girl: it appears that I shall have to adopt one for the sole purpose of knowing a child named Miranda, for no one else seems to want it. I love all kinds of gentle names, like flowers: Susanna, Malvina, Miranda, Lucy, Gabriela. As for letting the poor innocent name itself, the thought does credit to Franklin's generous modern attitude toward parenthood: BUT! I don't know about boys, but when I was young I knew a little girl whose parents allowed her to name herself. When she was four years old, she named herself Begonia Bell. The parents bore with this, and at seven she changed it to Violet Gwendolyn, and again at eleven she re-christened herself Olive Patricia, and around fourteen or fifteen she decided to be plain unvarnished Betty: and all the time her bewildered parents were calling her Baby.

I watched this drama unfold throughout the years, and I decided then it is better to tag 'em early and let them get used to it. Me, I was baptized Katherine Anne Maria Veronica Russell Porter, and I can't see that I was ever any the worse for it. At least I had a possible choice left to me. Suppose I had decided—or rather, they had—to call me Maria Veronica. I might have been a totally different sort of person. But I doubt it strongly.

I ask you again: is there anything you want me to bring you from Bermuda? Anything you would trust me to select? French and English baby gear is cheaper here than there, and they do know how to get the little devils up nicely.

I sent a pale yellow raffia bonnet to Becky's baby, I kept seeing her in it, in my mind's eye, and Becky says she looks lovely in it. But yours will be far above such vanities for some time to come, a large, wooly, ear-muffish arrangement will be his headgear this winter I suppose. I imagine you will be over-whelmed with gifts in the shape of blankets, flannel shirts, socks and belly-bands. WHAT could I find that would be suitable, becoming, useful, without forgetting the decorative possibilities, and that won't be just another of those things? But I imagine many persons are beginning to ask themselves that question. Ha! I just thought of something. You probably won't get more than twenty of 'em. Wait and see.

Matthew named his new one Carl Philip Emmanuel, which is very grand.

You'll be happy to hear that I had, on the same boat with your letter, the dummy of the Devil Take Cotton Mather, and the binding is very nice, a decent clerical black with pale orange lettering, but the jacket is beyond all words blatant and vulgar, and I hate it: it misrepresents the book, and I think they should have sent it to me before they had it made. They must have surmised I wouldn't like it. They quoted chapter headings I wrote describing the book two years ago, and misquoted a lot of them, and indeed, the whole thing looks like a circus poster. Now what does one do in such a case? I don't take the book solemnly, but it is not cheaply sensational, I wrote it as well and as simply as I could, and if it is no good, why, then I have written a bad book, that's all, and must bear the horrid consequences. But I did not, unless I am most terribly mistaken, write a noisy vulgar one. So I just hope the reader will hastily remove the dust jacket and throw it in the wastebasket. Its a very expensive book, I think: $4.00, and the print is nothing particular, and they have done a lot of fancy things to the lettering, such as pushing in a lot of Old-English script here and there in the title, and in the dedication it looks damned odd to see Becky Edelson's good German-Jewish name sitting up in prayer-book type.

I suppose all this is none of my affair, I'm to look after the writing only, but I don't like it just the same.

It was thoughtful of you to send me the New Masses, I was surprised to see that Mike[85] considers me a writer, but I was happy in a low, villainous way to see somebody kick the stuffing out of Floyd Dell.[86] I didn't see the papers comments on the argument, and I wish I had. I never see a newspaper.

My prejudice against F.D. is really founded, I love to flatter myself, on a certain principle of rejection in my mind. Certainly it can't be personal, for I never saw him but twice. The first time, I had been in New York for five days, and this was the fall of 1919. I was at Rose Wilder Lane's[87] flat in King Street. I came in frozen with wet feet and rushed for the fireplace. A blonde young man was standing there and I said with fatuous gratitude—"God, how I love fire!" And he said, "Oh, well, its entirely a matter of one's complexes, you know—" and Rose came up and said: "K.A. this is Floyd Dell."

Four years ago I was at a party at Alex Gumberg's[88] and Floyd was spread out on a couch talking to a girl, and I drifted by and overheard him say: "But where SSSSex is concerned, we haven't come out of the Cave yet!" and I thought: "Why should we? A nice, dark cave. . . ."

But there! And I'm afraid its true that these two casual contacts kind of prejudiced me agin him. . . . . .

There is this about Mike: He sticks to his guns, and he mortally is learning how to write. I get tired of the whole confusion, but I prefer Mike to Floyd by a long jump, and Virginia Woolf to either. Neurotic Budgewudge that I am.

I want to ask a deep question. What in hell is a Bourgeiouse: I never know how to spell it, so I give you a good selection, and you can fix it up yourself—? It appears to be something that everybody else is except oneself. Now f'rinstance, I don't in the least consider myself a—you know what—yet I have been called that behind my back, and to my long-suffering face. And I think I know plenty of 'em; I do smile at Natalie, for example, with a jorjus superiority, for who was it had paint and rugs and wicker furniture and new floors at Caligari? Not us, certainly. Who first complained of insects? I ask you. And what is her whole ambition but to be a dressmaker, the most middle class of ambitions. For who will be her clients? Certainly not the proletariat. And not me, for I can't afford to dress proletariat style. I have to buy my clothes on Fourteenth street along with the other workers, where I can git covered up for $7.98. And as for Woodstock, I was there once, and of all the piffling, middle class, Budgewudgery I ever ran into, that won the sweepstakes. And I know people like Armando Zegri,[89] for one, who go there in the summer. The air is positively unbreathable! Etc, etc.

Darling, I'd give my head—in its present condition, no gift, for I have sinusitis again, and it lowers the mind, let me tell you!—to hear a little music of the kind I love, and to see some nice fresh new paintings, and to see a few persons that I want badly to see, and all that. Yesterday, I broke my rule of enclosure, (maintaining strictly the other three of poverty, chastity and obedience) and went with a very nice Mrs. Wharton from Philadelphia and a very nice Mr. Tuseau of New Orleans, for a long swim, a picnic supper on the rocks, and afterward in the early twilight, we set out in a grand big speed boat and tore out about ten miles into the Atlantic. I didn't get in until after ten o'clock, but was so refreshed I worked until nearly one, baking bread the meanwhile. Beautiful bread, and a very clean copy of chapter 18. When I come home will you let me bake you some bread? I just learned here, from Anna the maid, and it is my pride!

The Peggy-Malcolm[90] household sounds a triumph of domestic economy. Here, I've been experimenting with the Elijah-Raven motif,[91] and it comes in beautifully. If a little boy shows up with fish, why, we have fish, and if he doesn't, we don't. The same with everything else. I take what God sends to my door, and the meals come around approximately on time, because the time is when they come around, if that is all clear. In the morning, I get up at five or six IF I didn't sit up too late the night before. If I did, I get up about nine. I make myself three lovely cups of coffee, and I wander around in the dewy garden while I drink it, rambling in now and then to fill the cup. Then if I have oranges I take orange juice, and if I don't, I eat bananas, or if no bananas, a pawpaw, and if nothing, why then, nothing. After a while if I feel like it I eat bread and butter, or mush and milk. Then I go to work. Around two o'clock the maid comes up and invites me to come down and see what she has pulled together for lunch. Its apt to be almost anything, like cabbage and cucumbers, with a piece of good wholesome fish, or a slice of bacon, and a mango. I swallow it gratefully, come up and lie down for a siesta, get up at four, take a cold bath, a cup of tea, and go to work. About ten or eleven at night I go down and raid the icebox. Well, in God's name, who could have dreamed that housekeeping could be so simple? I shall never be afraid of it again. I see now how it can be stripped to the gears and made to work for you, instead of you working your head off for it. And I'm getting fat on it. I weigh 120 pounds.

Dorothy's[92] job sounds delightful: delightful for her spirit in it. She is growing a real religious! I shouldn't be surprised to see her end in a convent. . . . In the meantime, what about her "No Continuing City"?[93] If she isn't doing anything about it, I will, if she gives me permission, write to Ray Everitt at Harcourt Brace about it. I can do this because they have asked me to come to them when I am finished with Horace Liveright. That's pretty of them to express it that way, for indeed, a little more, and Horace will be finished with me. I didn't mention this to them. Please tell Dorothy. I did manage to recommend a novel and get it accepted at Coward-McCann's, at last. And I want Dorothy's book to be published. Do remember, honey . .

Love and affection to Franklin, and to you . . . write me again.

Katherine Anne

To: Josephine Herbst TLS 7pp. Yale

May 21st, 1929
Hilgrove, Bailey's Bay, Bermuda

Dear Misz Herrmann: In my imagination I have chased your infernal flivver on the first lap of your campaign til I'm out of breath. I don't actually know that you're gone yet: it may not be a flivver: you may be going by train part of the way: but I keep thinking of Carolyn and Allen getting away with hullabaloos in a cloud of dust: I'm sure you do it much more orderly, Mrs. H: I suspect thermos bottles and neatly packed suitcases, cigarette lighters and an emergency case among your equipment. But how can I know anything at this distance unless I'm told? So gimme a description of yourself on the road.

Funny: I ought to take in a newspaper or something. I went to Hamilton the other day for the first time since April 18, I think, and there saw a Mercury and in it a piece by Traverse Clements, name I don't recall having heard until your letter: and in the World I noted that THAT play, Carnival, had come in, run four weeks and closed again, and until now I have not had a line from my collaborator such as he is, nor a penny.[94] Then I picked up a Dial and saw where somebody roasted hell out of my poor dear darling Matthew for sumpin he didn't do. For no matter how justly you may sock him for his critical thises-and-thats, he did write a gorgeous book on Zola, and this fiend in human form says not! These two latter items made me feel that p'raps it is just as well I don't keep up with all the news.

The last I heard from the Daily Racket (Gabbler, Gobbler, Rumpus, Rocket, Rucas, Fracas) was that it was going to get itself printed in Paris.[95] I call that running away.

It isn't as if they couldn't get it printed here. I mean, there: U.S.A. Its not so seditious as all that.

Darling, I've got a book too. Honest to God. It leaves here hot or cold on the first of June. I don't know anything about it. I can't bear to read it, and I wish I'd never started it, even now that its finished I can't get warmed up to it any more. Its taken too long, there have been too many breaks in it. My copying and editing simply degenerated into a plastering job, trying to conceal the cracks. I should have written it red-hot in the mood I was in at first. But I'll say this: its got everything in somehow, and it has got some lively moments....

I envied you till I turned fairly green, "tingling as you finished it off ..." that is the way it should be. I'm crazy to see it, and this time I'll try to get advance proofs so they won't hurry me up so on the review....

So far, part of your prophecy is right: I'm gaining, I weigh 114 pounds, which is heavy-weight trim for me, I am freckled like a guinea egg, but sunburned so they don't show—Much. And I have red cheeks. . . . but no lover. No lover. Imagine. . . . And I can't imagine ever finding another, and since I celebrated a certain birthday a few days since, I say to myself, "Misz Porter, its time you settled down to that life of chastity long overdue before you're fo'ced. . . ." God knows, a woman can't be thirty-five—not THESE parlous days,—and keep the tender heart and the merry old illusions. I am really— not this minute, for at present I'm very happy, but there's a future, Misz Herrmann!—I am really, then, in one hell of a quandary. Do I want to drift into old age and go to the poor house alone? Not by half.

On the other hand: Do I want to take on some human being, go through all the struggle and hell-raising that it takes to get even a little settled, and spend the rest of my gala days few as they are at that sort of thing?

NO.

Well then: Do I want to go on as I have, having affairs of varying degrees of intensity and time, full of upsets, miseries and confusions, and some little joy, and at the end throw it all over and be left with an impression of having just got out of a hurricane with my life in my hand?

The answer is as above.

Then what DO I want?

Answer: I'd like to write two novels and go to Europe: or the other way about.

Also I'd like to have a little money for occasional boat fare.

That seems to be as far as I've got. These are the fruits of solitary contemplation about what I really want in the world, and God knows I surmised it before I left to be a hermit.

So I think I'll just keep on working and let it go at that.

I know what I do want: a lot of books. I'm covetous about books. I dream of getting stacks of books exactly the kind I want: all the beautiful grand books I haven't read, and want: all I have read, and want to read again. I want a mess of books. And I'm gonna have 'em.

Your news about Madame Gummidge de la Tato is very inspiring. I have here a prosperous yellow and white hellion who opens the screen when he goes in and out, sits up and tucks in his fore arms like a kangaroo when alarmed, goes when the doors are locked and he can't get out and pee-pee with exquisite precision down the bath tub plug. Not a drop goes amiss. He hides behind a bush when we take walks, and leaps out saying "prrrp!" and sits by me when I eat, partaking lightly of such knicknacks as ripe pear, tomatoes, cheese cake, banana, string beans, and Nestle's chocolate. I don't give him much, the merest nibbles: and not all these at once, but its no fault of his he doesn't live on 'em.

Believe it or not. I really at last have such a cat.

Well, I wish an itinerary through America included Bermuda, and you'd drop by on your way back. . . . I'd love seeing you, and there's no prospect of my getting back for many months . . . that is, unless my money runs out. But there's the advance, thank God. I have the place until January.

OOOOOOH! Josie, I almost forgot something important. Can you make bread, I mean with yeast cake and all? A woman comes here to cook and do the housework, and so one day I went down and hauled off and watched her while she baked. The next baking day I did the work and she directed. And the third I made bread! Great big puffy sweetsmelling fresh bread that simply enchanted me. I had always thought it was perfectly impossible to do. It isn't.

Otherwise I keep out of the kitchen and far from the broom and completely off the ironing board, because I can't do it and do anything else. You know how mortal hard I take my housework. But this isn't really criminal luxury, for she does it all for three dollars a week.

Good bye Angel. My love to John who praised me so sweetly. I am only a weak woman and I need a little approval occasionally.

Hot as hell here, but now cooling toward evening. I'm going to have some tea outside and go back to work. Love to you–

Katherine Anne

If Liza[96] isn't too loaded down, I will send you a packet of herbs by her hand. I believe there is a law or something against it, but will see what can be done about that.

K.A.

Also a Madonna brandy bottle.

Part Two

1930–1939

In her fortieth year Katherine Anne Porter was "launched" with the appearance of her first book, *Flowering Judas*, a collection of six stories Harcourt, Brace published in a limited edition that was so highly acclaimed by reviewers that her position in American letters was established. Leaving Mexico on the strength of a Guggenheim Fellowship and sailing to Europe, where she remained for six years, signaled the new phase of her career, which all along had been hindered by money worries. The year before she received news of the Guggenheim award, she explained her "special problem" to Otto Kahn: "[F]inancial security," she wrote, "is supposed to come with growing reputation, but unhappily, unless one makes some sort of compromise, it does not always follow."

Money would continue to be a problem during the Depression, but it was slightly alleviated by her steady publications throughout the thirties. After three years in Paris, Porter married Eugene Pressly, who had made the trip from Mexico with her and found a position in the American embassy. The two of them moved in and out of apartments leased by Ford Madox Ford, Allen Tate and Caroline Gordon, and Ezra Pound. She forged new and enduring friendships with Monroe Wheeler, Barbara Harrison, Glenway Wescott, George Platt Lynes, Sylvia Beach, and Adrienne Monnier, comfortable in the wide community of expatriate writers and artists and finally becoming the celebrated cook she disingenuously had told her father she was in the 1920s.

By the time she returned to the United States in 1937 to more or less settle for good, she had published some of her most significant fiction, and "Pale Horse, Pale Rider" was nearly complete. And after futile attempts to write a long novel since the early 1920s, she was beginning to see that what she thought was a novella-in-progress was turning into a long novel. With her return she also acknowledged that her marriage to Pressly was essentially over.

In 1938 Porter divorced Pressly and married Albert Russel Erskine Jr. While she worked on the long novel—titled variously "Promised Land," "The Land that Is Nowhere," and "No Safe Harbor" before it would be called "Ship of Fools"—she slipped into the college and university circuit of writing workshops and speaking engagements that would modestly sustain her financially for a long time. Her friendship with Caroline Gordon and Allen Tate was as strong as ever, and through them she became friends with Cleanth and Tinkum Brooks and Robert Penn Warren, concurring in part with their agrarian and new critical aesthetics.

The decade came to a close for Porter on a high note—the publication in 1939 of *Pale Horse, Pale Rider: Three Short Novels*, which included "Noon Wine" and "Old Mortality" in addition to the title story. The reviews were again glowing, and the book went into its third printing within six weeks. "I hardly believe it," Porter reported to Caroline Gordon. But the pleasure of her achievement was darkened by concerns about the war in Europe, which she had watched evolve throughout the decade, and what she already suspected was the failure of her fifth and last marriage. She had not "dwindled into a wife," as she fearfully prophesied to Caroline Gordon.

To: Otto Kahn TLS 1p. Princeton

74 Orange Street, Brooklyn, New York
[c. March 11, 1930]

My dear Mr. Kahn:

My friend Delafield Day gave me seventy-five dollars which you were so good as to send me, and I think you might be surprised to know how much I needed it, and how much immediate help it was.

When Miss Day told me she had asked you for an interview for my sake, I was immensely hopeful that this long painful apprenticeship to prose literature was about to end, and that I should be set free for my serious work. My poverty is quiet absolute in a way that you might not understand, since it is true I am rather better known than is usual for one who has been unable to devote any real time to her work. I have survived really on the immense moral support and encouragement given me from sources that I respect: and literally by the charity of friends who cannot, and yet do, afford it. It is not possible to continue in this way, and I give my time and energies to a literal day by day labour of writing fugitive articles and reviews, and even this kind of work is not of the kind acceptable to popular magazines which pay well. My serious work is also published in such magazines as transition, the New Masses, the Hound & Horn, and for the most part given away. It is rather a special problem, because financial security is supposed to come with growing reputation, but unhappily, unless one makes some sort of compromise, it does not always follow.

I have work in hand, a glorious promise, but simply not enough money to live on until the work is finished. My biography of Cotton Mather, which embraces a study of early American religion and politics, has been for three years in preparation. It will be published in the late fall—if I am enabled to devote myself to it—and there can be no financial returns on it for many months later. A small, very beautiful, limited edition of my short stories is also to be published, on which my royalties will be precisely $120. My novel, which I planned four years ago, has for a background the very significant Mexican Revolution of 1920–22, and will require at least a year's work.

It is this necessary year that I ask you to give me, or it seems that my struggles must continue until the whole creative edge of my mind shall be spent in it. I wish you would consent to see me, allow me to answer your questions, to show you some part of my work. And please accept my thanks for your present help. I cannot say it came at a specially critical moment, for my whole existence is a mere series of them, economically speaking: but it was a very blessed relief, and provides me with a short breathing spell.

Sincerely yours,
Katherine Anne Porter

To: Malcolm Cowley TLS 2pp. Newberry

Apartado 2075, Mexico, D F
June 17, 1930

Dear Malcolm:

You know that whatever little retouching you did of the Kay Boyle review[1] was perfectly all right; it showed up so prettily I was half-persuaded I had done it all myself! I wanted to think so, anyway. I'm sorry you had the trouble with it, and next time I'll try to organize it so it can stand without working over.

I suppose you would send me other books if you thought I could get them done. If you haven't given away Carleton Beals' book, "Mexican Maze," let me review it. There have been several books on Mexico I might have done fairly well by. Except that none of them have been worth long reviews. I will just do a short one on this if it turns out to be that kind of book. I can read a copy of it here and do the review, and not wait on the review copy, which takes so long in the mail. Let me know.

Something else: you know, I suppose, that a sudden shift has taken place here, with Cabrera[2] exiled—I saw the N. R. editorial on this and approved it hearty—and two Calles[3] men suddenly "resigned" from their office (you know the internal meaning of those verbs to resign, to suicide, and to accident, as used here) one of them being Moisés.[4] It all happened last week and suddenly. I have Cabrera's statement published here, and can translate it for you, or write the story, together with the uneasy changes surrounding it, if you like . . . In fact, would you like one of my political articles? I've published only two—one in the century magazine years ago, and one in the Freeman, I think in 1922. I promise not to write as an authority on Mexico, nor apologist, nor propagandist, nor enemy, but as an observer putting two and two together in the probable but distant hope of getting four out of it. Let me know if you would like this, and so help me God I'll do it quick and keep within the word limit. Dear Malcolm, I know my little failings. I've had them pointed out to me often enough. Only I do pray you, if I write the article, give me my head to make what comment I please. I'm frightfully tired of discreet soft soap . . . But the N.R. is beginning to be a place where a man—or woman, I hope—can speak his mind. Those pieces by Edmund Wilson make me feel like seizing my typewriter and putting down a few words.[5]

Let me tell you two Mexican jokes: First an old one at the time of Obregon's presidential campaign, when the "Sonora Government"[6] was at top form. Two peones were passing by the National Palace where some repairs were being made, and the whole place was surrounded by scaffolding rather like the beginnings of a crate. "What are they doing to the Palace?" asked the first peon. "God knows," said the other, "but I suppose they're packing it up to send it to Sonora."

Second joke. New. And a fact. The president[7] is nicknamed the Mule, and is known as Calles' man. Lately Calles won several prizes on his cattle and horses at a fair. And somebody you know here said to him, "It's a pity you didn't enter your Mule from Chapultepec . . certainly the finest in Mexico."

Heigho, we're a merry race!

I suppose I'll see Moisés only once more before he goes to his hacienda, and then he announces he is going to Guatamala to study Indian life there. Last week he planned to go to Rochester, to the Mayo Brothers for treatment, (he has been ill and looks badly, a little better now) but this is off. By the time he comes back I'll be gone. I must be out of here by September, my identification card says so. I let it lapse, stupidly, and Moisés wrote a note for me, and it was quite allright if I left in September, the extension I asked for. I suppose I could have it extended further, but I don't want to. Europe and Guggenheim Fellowships are calling.

Eugene Jolas[8] came, suddenly showed up one afternoon. He had been robbed of his clothes at the Guatamala border, arrived with very little money, and sat agonized for eleven days waiting for a check to go through, too proud to come anigh his friends for aid. He was a little racked and torn therefore, inclined to quit Mexico without a backward look. He is a delightful person, I think. Hart[9] came over, and we were all most dismally drunk, with a slight passage at arms—of course—between Crane and Jolas before the evening was over. Jolas relapsed into a German accent and accused Hart of schneakingg out on him in a certain situation but vaguely described and long since past, in Paris. Otherwise the evening went off very well.

Next day he went up to Taxco to stay with Natalie Scott[10] whom he knew in New Orleans, and has not returned. Meant to work on a novel. Said he was reviving transition in the fall, but this time a fairly conservative magazine of philosophy and criticism. Felt that his revolution of the word had been much misunderstood. I said, yes, but hadn't he expected that? It seems he had not. I liked him immensely.

####

Kay Boyle wrote me a letter like a streak of friendly lightning, and a touch of rain, inviting me to visit her in Nice. I mean to go. Seems we have been a mutual admiration society all this long time, without mentioning it to each other.

###

Peggy[11] writes she is coming to Mexico in July, and we are looking forward to her. She says you are getting out your book of essays, dear Malcolm, do give me one. And I wish you would do me a great favor. Ask the New Republic bookshop to send me "Axel's Wheel" and "Savage Messiah,"[12] and let me pay for them when they come. I can't any longer do without those books, I can't send a check in dollars, and the post office will let me pay for them in pesos.

This letter seems to have all sorts of things in it. I hope for a quick answer, with news. I should like to see New York again for the sake of the people in it—three or four persons. Give Sue and Bill my love.[13]

Katherine Anne

To: Maxwell Perkins TLS 1p. Princeton

Calle Ernesto Pugibet 78, Mexico, D F
July 3, 1930

Maxwell Perkins, Esq.,
Charles Scribner's Sons, Publishers,
Fifth Avenue at 48th Street,
New York City.

My dear Mr. Perkins:
In the silent company of several thousand others, no doubt, I am working away on a story for your contest. It can't come to much more than 15,000 words the way it is working itself out now, and I might prune it to a little less if it needs it, though I should hate to disqualify it on the grounds of length. I may call it "The Cracked Mirror" or "Saint Martin's Summer," or something quite different if a better title occurs. I suppose it is a love story. "There's love in it, anyhow," as Rosaleen the heroine decides, near the finish.

You may find a copy of the Gyroscope with young Holt's[14] story in it, if you write to Yvor Winters, Box 286, Route 1, Palo Alto, California. I had the complete file of four numbers, which I valued, but they have disappeared, alas, or I should send the story on to you.

I'm glad to see Josephine Herbst's stories coming on. I've liked her work seriously for several years. Did she show you her fine one called "I Hear You, Mr. and Mrs. Smith?" But I suppose by now she has several new ones even better.

Janet Lewis (wife of Yvor Winters) is worth watching, and there is a man named John Crawford, at 78 Orange Street, Brooklyn, who has a novel called "The Return Through The Passage" that it seems to me you might like to read. I like reading it about three times!

Very sincerely yours,
Katherine Anne Porter

To: Kenneth Burke TLS 2pp. Penn State

Calle Ernesto Pugibet 78, Mexico, D F
July 20, 1930

Dear Kenneth:
 Would you lend me your name as sponsor when I apply for a Fellowship in the Guggenheim Foundation? It is a very devil of a makeshift, not at all my idea of a happy solution of my problem, but still I shall try it. I suppose every one approaches the idea with the same mixture of hopefulness, pessimism, apology—apology to oneself, I mean. It is a last resort.

 You may know that I have no degrees, no academic honours whatever, no education, in fact. This may hinder me, though I understand that the Committee provides somewhat for this condition by relaxing the rules in favor of Creative Writers! I may slip through. By the time the appointments are made, I shall have enough work to show to justify your sponsorship in part, I hope, and enough health to work rather better than I am working now.

 This resting and getting well business is a clammy bore, enough to kill you, really! But oh, Pragmatism, how it works. I do improve, no doubt at all; it seems reasonable to make plans and I make them. When I first came here, I was happy enough for a few days, then fell into a horrible distress of mind, and felt I could not possibly live here: and when that passed, the happiness was gone for good, but I saw it was quite possible to stay and finish what I came for. So I have tied some furniture around my neck, and made myself morally responsible for the existence of a very merry-hearted little Indian girl, and filled a half-ton desk with manuscripts, and so have made bolting an impossibility in my present somewhat reduced state. How often have I jeered at those who did the same, calling them names. Now no more. I shan't move again unless I get the Fellowship!

This country is now being flooded with an abominable, treacly, oily gooey mess of Political Good Will, you have simply to shake the professional good-willers out of your hair when you come in from a walk, Morrow, Ivy Lee, Chandler, Herring,[15] and his one hundred eighty-nine trippers, each with a ring in his or her nose, are all, all here. It is Herring's boast that he taught the Mexicans the virtue of debate from a platform. There was a time when Mexican political enemies would not appear on the same program. But they have learned how from the Americans, and can perform astounding feats at seeing all sides of a question. There will be less shooting and more lying, and the graft must now be split half a dozen ways more, with the Americans superintending the split. This will be that. The trippers are being led around by their nose-rings, seeing Mexico.

"Obregon! fué presidente,

General, y buen ranchero!"

Better general than president and better ranchman than either, and they celebrated his death-day yesterday with classical dances and speeches about Progress before the trippers. . . . Orders were out before the recent deputy elections that any man caught carrying firearms on election day would be arrested on sight. A good business man then announced that he had invented and was manufacturing in quantity a deadly weapon of wood, in club form adorned with steel spikes, suitable for the election-day wear of a gentleman. The Governor and the chief of police then issued orders prohibiting the use of these gadgets, also. Election day passed like a dream of spring, with only a few stabbings and cuttings here and there. Alas, they had clean forgot to prohibit the use of knives!

I believe this is an indiscreet letter. But I do want to tell you little things that you might not read in the newspapers!

Do you come near the end of the Declamations,[16] and when will they be published as a book? I was sorry not to see you again, and I hope you will write to me.

Katherine Anne

To: Caroline Gordon TLS 7pp. Princeton

Ernesto Pugibet 78, Mexico D F
January, Twelfth Night [6], 1931

Dearest Caroline:
    "The Ice House" is a noble tale. I, too, go around reading it to people. I do like your stories! They are full of light, and very firm and sure. And your conversation—no one who has not tried it can imagine what it takes to get people in stories to talk like that. Don't let your aunt get YOU to any psychologist. Let her go herself, and leave you alone.
    Your story began the Christmas spirit, and a telegraph from Peggy and Malcolm helped a great deal, and that was all the Christmas spirit there was, until tonight. On the 16th of December the Posadas begin. Families gather in their houses, arm themselves with lighted candles, and form a procession, with a favored child going ahead carrying the Pilgrims: little painted clay figures of Mary, mounted on a burro, Joseph, and an Angel. Mary and Joseph wear hats, and the angel formal heavenly dress. The procession moves around the patio, singing at the top of its lungs. Then half of the people go inside and close the door, and the other half stand outside with the Pilgrims, and ask for shelter. (Posada) The argument goes on for about twenty five stanzas, in a very old and charming tune, the ones inside refusing to take the strangers in, the ones outside insisting. Finally the wanderers announce that Mary, Queen of Heaven, and Joseph, and an angel to boot, are being turned away, and the others sing joyfully, "Why, Mary, how could we know it was you? Come right in!" (a very free translation) and the two halves join again, and howl their heads off as they march around the patio. Then they have a party, and break a piñata, (a large clay jar covered with colored paper in various shapes) which hangs from a beam. And every one is showered with nuts and candy and little gifts. This goes on for nine nights, until Christmas Eve, when the Posada ends with a little manger being set up, and arranged with kneeling beasts and angels and shepherds, and everybody goes to midnight Mass. Then when the children wake up in the morning, they find Mary and Joseph comfortably settled, and the Child in a manger full of moss and hay. Its very charming, but there are no presents, yet. Only the servants get a little gold piece each, (the traditional coin was called an aguinaldo) so this is Aguinaldo Day, and this in memory of the inn servant who helped Mary to bring forth the Child-God. (El Niño-Dios.) Then there are festivities every day and every night until Twelfth Night, when the Three Kings arrive at the manger, bringing gifts in which all the children share. There is no Santa Claus whatever. This Spanish

tradition is completely different from the Teutonic one. I know that Twelfth Night was very important in England until at least the sixteenth century, and I wonder if the Northern legend did not take hold afterward. I think this way of celebrating Christmas is in the very oldest Catholic tradition of the Latin countries, and that Saint Nicholas is the survival of an ancient Norse god cult.... I don't really know, but it sounds reasonable. I watched from my roof the neighborhood holding posadas in their patios. Today my Teodora brought her little two year old niece, and I gave her a present, and she gave me one, and I gave Teodora a present, and Teodora came tonight bringing the traditional Twelfth Night bread, called rosca, a dry sweet bread made in a ring, full of fruit, and a tiny porcelain Christ-Baby concealed in it for you to break a tooth on. So Christmas is over, and a very pretty spectacle it was but I never really felt it was Christmas until tonight, though I set up a very creditable manger on the twenty fourth. I am going to save it very carefully for Nancy's Christmas next year. There are little clay burros and bulls, kneeling, and lambs and dogs and chickens and even a rabbit, and shepherds and hermits and all.

But: and this is back to your story so full of Christmas spirit! I know two persons here, a man and a woman, whom I like, and they are the only two persons in Mexico I really care to see.[17] They seem quite satisfactory until Christmas, and then! Here, you see, everybody burns fireworks at Christmas, as we do at home. Its a Latin custom, seems. The heavens have been noisy with rockets since the sixteenth, and tonight they are ablaze. But these two admirable persons are yankees from Pennsylvania and Missouri, and they hooted at the idea of fireworks. Fireworks at Christmas! Wait, they said, until the fourth of July. I said, I had never lit even a firecracker on the fourth of July and I wouldn't think of beginning now. They said, Thats the time for fireworks. Who ever heard of fireworks at Christmas? I said, Vicksburg fell on the fourth of July, and that's all that date means to me. They said—and so on and on.

So I bought three roman candles and went up on my roof with Teodora and fired them off.

I paraphrased Saint Augustine: "It maketh a difference whence cometh a man's joy."[18] It does make a difference where you were born! Christmas without fireworks is not, for me, Christmas. So I mean at last to live where I can enjoy them at the proper season.

You should know better than to ask me a question. This, darling, is the way Christmas is in Mexico.

###

Anyhow, I was revenged on my Yankee friends. One at a time, I read them your story. They hated like the devil to do it, but they broke down and admitted it was finely done.

I treasure your recommendation, and sent a copy to Kenneth Durant, who is sick. I think it will help him to a recovery. Its a positive fact that the incidents you relate are symbolically, if not factually, true. For not three months ago at a party I suddenly kicked Carleton Beals on the shins, something I have been longing to do for eight years, and I wish I had done it on my first impulse.

While Liza[19] was here, she spent the first few days bedeviling me to stop smoking, explaining that all my wrinkles and grey hairs were caused by this devastating habit. Then she suddenly began smoking violently herself, and I heard no more of that. But years and years of lecturing from various friends had finally its awful effect, and about two weeks ago, I stopped. The day your letter arrived. Let me explain. I stopped at bedtime the night before, saying firmly I would not smoke the next day, or indeed, ever again. So I lay in bed reading until eleven o'clock, smoking with a heavy heart. It was my last night of comfortable happiness, lying in bed, smoking and reading. I faced a hellish desert of years of discretion and dull careful living. Could it be that, at thirty six, I was getting old, crippled, rheumatic and blind? Would I be eating milk toast next? How long must it be before I buy false teeth? Was this, in short, the end? It seemed so. I shed five or six tears. (I mean it.) Then I took one last loving smoke, and crumpled up the empty package, and fell asleep very miserable. The next morning Teodora brought me your letter with the coffee. When I got to the paragraph about smoking, I gave Teodora fifty centavos and said, "Bring me two packages of Monte Carlo and a lot of matches." And five minutes later I was smoking. This is the whole history of my reform. I love cigarettes and wine and rare broiled beefsteaks, and other poisonous substances, and they agree with me wonderfully. It isn't as if I had a bad heart; I have a 200 horse power heart. Its only my lungs and I'm tired of humoring them.

The Flowering Judas copy came safely, and I knew you had a review copy, so I didn't send you one. You had written that Allen would do a review, remember?

Speaking of hearts, its a shame Sally Wood[20] can't come here, but many persons suffer with hearts in this altitude. New Mexico, I believe, is pretty high too. I should think she would need a lowish, warmish, restful place, near the sea. Why not Charleston? Not that thats a seaport, but isn't it warm there in winter? Asheville? But I suppose that's too expensive. My grandmother's sisters used to go to White Sulphur Springs for their blessed healths. I shouldn't think she would like the gritty, dusty, hotness of most parts of New Mexico. I abominate dust storms above all kinds of weather. They're just beginning here.

Did your Christmas party come off, with the United Brethren of the New Confederacy[21] drowning their differences in eggnog? I hope so. The movement is too tender for schisms, yet. Tell them for God's sake to hold together until they get a tradition of unity established. Then they can fight as much as they please. "I'LL TAKE MY STAND"[22] is a very seriously good book. I rather kept wishing they'd be a little more belligerent, but was delighted to see so much plain speaking with so much composure. I preferred Allen's and Ransom's and Andrew's and Stark Young's, surely four most different pieces and points of view, not only for their styles, but for the ground they covered. Its a fine start towards something, if internal dissensions don't run them aground. I wish I might hear the debate at Chattanooga. I wish I might have been there for Christmas, in fact I wish I were there and not here.

Tell me this, darling: Is it a fact that those cabins are livable if one wanted to move in and keep house?[23] Could I push two together and put on a lean-to? Because if I don't get the Guggenheim scholarship I still have my allowance until the fall, and Perkins has asked for anything I might do, and Stringfellow Barr[24] asked for an article, and the New Republic has taken one and will take three more, and I expect to make my own living if the Guggenheim fails. But it must be a simple way of living . . . So I thought I'd come to Tennessee and live in those cabins until my fortunes mend. I have enough furniture for several cabins, and little by little I expect to ease out into a larger house with an acre of my own. What do you think? Or now that you have lived in the community, do you think it would scandalize any one if I attempted to live like that? If so, I won't. Do you suppose if I scraped up money enough for a first payment, I could find a house at a reasonable price? Elizabeth Roberts[25] seemed to think I might in Kentucky. From where you are now sitting as you read this, how far is it to Kentucky, seat of at least half my ancestors? I thought it might be rather fun to go back to Kentucky and meet five or six hundred cousins. From what I gather, the woods are still full of Porters and Rheas and Wards and Boones and so ons. To say nothing of the Skaggses. Skaggs? I don't believe there is such a name. But never say that to a Skaggs.

It comes to this, that if I don't go to Europe this year, I probably can't go until 1933, and so I might as well settle, once for all. Tell me what you think of the cabin idea. I like it, myself, but there may be local mores against it. Don't let me make a mistake. If I come south, I mean to live there as a member of the community and not as a stranger. Here in Mexico I live pretty formally too. Only in New York do I feel as though it doesn't greatly matter how I live, it will be understood by enough persons you like to make it simple and not outlandish. But you will know what to tell me.....I couldn't do it in Louisiana without consequences, or the place has changed. I remember very well why I left the south, but maybe by now the atmosphere has changed a little—or maybe we are strong enough to change ourselves...I don't know. Once I simply smothered in the atmosphere of traditionalism and formalism, I ran from it....I think it would be better if everybody could run for a while, and then come back strong enough to defend oneself against the deadening things, and to love again the living elements. Its not natural to live forever away from one's roots....I have no intention of doing it. But I have no intention either of not thinking what I please, nor of conforming where conformity would cramp and annoy me. What I want is a few acres of land and a house of my own in the country. I think I can manage to get along very well with this. Give my Nancy my endless love and tell her not to forget me. If Andrew is back tell him I am going to write, and that was a grand letter. Allen's TO WHOM IT MAY CONCERN notice confirmed again one thing said about my work: that I wrote out of something that must be inherent in me, for I was not in the least aware of what I was doing. That is to say, I did not write consciously as a southerner, but yet wrote AS one....his review was beyond all my hopes magnificent.

   Will you believe that I am on my sixth Bach prelude, and am tottering through a Scarlatti Capriccio? Paul Higgins[26] gave me three lessons a week for six weeks, taught me my notes, how to read somewhat, hastily knocked the principles of harmony into my resistant head, gave me three books of scales to run, the preludes of Chopin, Bach, and a miscellany of music by Scarlatti, started me off in the third year of music, and left me to my fate. He has gone to New York, but I sit two hours a day at the piano—at first much more, but two hours I find enough for a day—and I get so much happiness out of it. I wish I had begun ten years ago when I first wished to. It is like beginning to write: you start in a vast thick fog and slowly work your way outward.... It is very comforting to discover that principles work almost infallibly, good music never betrays you, the pattern is there, and works itself out mathematically. When I can afford it, I shall take lessons again. I want to play William Byrd and Henry Purcell and Frescobaldi and the early Flemish composers. I love Chopin in the Preludes if you play him by a strict pattern, as if he wrote in the 17th century, and don't smear him all over the keyboard. I said this to Paul, and he played me a few preludes that sounded exactly right...

Darling, this must end. . . . Do you realize that we knew each other for really only a very short time, and have spent the rest of the time writing letters to each other? This too must end. Give my love to Allen.

Katherine Anne

If I get the Fellowship, I want to visit you in August—Will that be allright?

To: Lucile Clayton Robinson TLS 5pp. Maryland

Ernesto Pugibet 78, Mexico D F
January 10, 1931

Dear Lucile:

Your voice out of the past was instantly familiar, for I remember you as well as you do me: at the time you knew me, and until I went to New York in the fall of 1919, I was almost automatic and unconscious, for you probably remember that I had almost died, and it had cut my life in two, so that I was not then the same, and was never again the same. The spirit and energy that appeared to you supernatural was in fact just that. I have not the slightest idea how I did it, nor precisely why, but I am beginning to see a little what I must have known in my bones then, you might say: that the latter time would be better than the first, if only I would consent to survive and see it.

But even so, through this cloud in which I moved, and I saw you and Buck very clearly. You were both darlings, and I knew you were up against a battle too, but you were so young and charming and really very wise children. I used to remember you both and hope you were as happy as you deserved to be. Buck had all kinds of fine qualities, and the two of you together was a perfect combination. And then too, you were so dashingly good looking, very! There are other impressions that I can't seem to get down on paper, except the one of youth at its very clearest and best and fullest, as if you could grow into anything, could do anything you pleased out of that fountain of certainty which is youth. I do regret Buck. I resent death which takes away such a person, and leaves the earth simply maggoty with dull cheap mediocrity.

Your own history sounds as if you'd had a pretty good scrap on your hands and had somehow won it. My own small victories are always temporary, provisional, very relative. My history doesn't seem to have so much shape as yours. When I went to New York I got a job doing moving picture publicity for Selznick; I earned $125 a week and in a year had saved enough—what with ghost writing on the side—to take me to Mexico, where I stayed for a year and a half and somehow got all tangled up in the Revolution, knew almost everybody in it and was fearfully converted to Mexican Art—the natural antithesis to Mexican Revolution, which doesn't seem to get anywhere, while the Art really does know its way about. If you were in California eight years ago you may remember a big exhibition which was staged, I think in Los Angeles. I was appointed by President Obregon as the American organizer and wrote the monograph for it, helped to collect it, arranged to have it open in New York, and then Mexican politics got in its awful work, and it was sent to California instead, where after being shown it was sold for expenses. That ended my official connection with Mexico. Since then I have been its most cantankerous friend and implacable critic. I went back to New York and started the banal career of all determined writers: I did editing jobs, book reviews, and starved in basements and attics. How many letters I have had recently from old friends who remember me starving in attics and basements! But somehow I knew all sorts of people, went all sorts of places, and had a pretty good time. I wrote a few stories and gave them away mostly to small magazines who printed the kind of stuff I liked, and then got a contract with Liveright to do a biography of Cotton Mather—My own damned notion, so it serves me right—and since then for four mortal years I worked in the Public Library at New York, Salem, and Boston, off and on, without money, world without end, doing that book. It isn't finished yet. I laid it aside this year and am working on a novel which Harcourt Brace will publish next fall. Hastily last December we pulled my stories together and rushed them into print, a limited edition because the publisher was really afraid I wouldn't sell, and not for any snobbism of my own, which I hope you understood. I think its indecent exploitation to make people pay 3, 4, even 5 dollars for a book made to sell at $2.50, and this is my last limited edition.

Then in the spring I blew up for the third time with tb and was sent away here. I live very comfortably and cheaply in a bare Mexican house, with an Indian woman to cook and clean, and mostly I stay in bed, or sit at the typewriter biting my thumbs and cursing. Such is the life of a modestly successful author. From time to time have had some one of the masculine order to weep on—that is, I might have wept on them if I hadn't mostly fought with them. But I have been lucky with friendships, not with love. Men seem to be of two kinds when they get near me: they wish to gnaw my bones clean, or they hang around my neck, get underfoot, and are in every possible way a curse and an obstruction. This isn't bitterness: for a while I was astonished, and then rather relieved to know there was no man I need ever take seriously again, nor allow to interfere with my life. I like men very well, But they are at their best distributed around the landscape in the role of faithful friend. Several that I came dangerously near marrying are now well married to someone else, and a good thing, too. I like them just as well, better, because they [are] much pleasanter in the form of human beings than as lovers. This is not to say that I did not fall frightfully in love, and don't regret it. There was nothing to stop us except temperamental differences, and we put in two years of tooth and nail battle which I now remember rather cheerfully. But I think it taught me something! This about exhausts the subject. But you had the right idea about me in this regard. Men appear to think I was something on a platter to be eaten with radishes. I sometimes wonder if that isn't their ordinary version of love, but other women are more adept at reversing the process.... If it must be one way or another naturally I prefer to do the eating. But I'd rather it wasn't that way at all.

As to Hollywood, ten years ago Hunt Stromberg[27] wired me to come out and join his scenario department (he had been with Selznick when I was) and I rejected the idea with something like horror, which hurt his feelings, and I haven't heard from him since. Several good friends of mine went there on the grounds that they would only work a little while, enough to make some money so they could then return to their own serious work, and they are there yet, wallowing in wealth, totally unable to cut down expenses and go back to the necessary simple living if they want to do their own work ... I am but human even as they, I love every kind of luxury and ease, I have a passion for dress that, in poverty, took for a time the inverted form of almost disgraceful shabbiness: If I could not have my dresses by Chanel and LeLong and hats by Suzanne Talbot I might as well get my wardrobe from the Salvation Army—and I almost did! So, I resisted the temptation to go out there and make money. I still feel I was right. Twice in my life I have resisted money because it didn't come on my terms, and I still don't see what else I could have done .. In the end, I think I shall be comfortable from my books, and even so, write only exactly what I choose to write .. That, Lucile, will be a triumph.

Park French![28] What a ghost of a word! I hadn't thought of him in years upon years. John O'Brien was, I thought, working on a newspaper in New York several years ago. Do you remember Sonya Mischell the Pianist? Mrs. Vanderbilt—which one I don't know[29]—sent her to Munich, I think it was, to study, she came back and gave a concert, but somehow did not do well, and was teaching in New York when I saw her last. I liked her. I can't think what kept her from being a happily successful artist. She had all sorts of good gifts.

There should be others we know in common, but I can't think of any just this minute. It was lovely of you to write me, I am very happy to know you read the book, and found something in it. Its only a beginning and represents my scattered difficult years from 1924 to 30. There were ten stories in all, but they chose only these six. There is another in O'Brien's Best Short Stories of 1930.[30]

When you feel like it, write. I am happy to hear from you. Give my interested good wishes to your husband, who sounds like a charming person.

Katherine Anne Porter

To: Kenneth Burke TLS 1p. Penn State

Apartado 2075, Mexico, D F
March 20, 1931

Dear Kenneth:

Cheerful news came from the Guggenheim Foundation people the other day, and I am now a Fellow. My gratitude for your part in it, we won in this lottery! I am just ingrate enough to be peeved over the fall of copper, along with our other severe falls of the year past, which cut my stipend from $2500 to $2,000, because of my being an "unmarried Fellow," as they explained. I was immensely pleased to think that if I had had a husband, the Foundation would have helped me take him to Europe; this is a very enlightened attitude on the one hand, but disconcerting, on the other, to the unwed who already have penalties enough.

Your article (rejoinder to Wilson) on boring from within the conventional citadels warmed my heart; incorrigible and unconvinced to the last ditch you are, and may you never go back on this state of mind.[31]

I have moved to a suburb[32] and have a long skinny house with a ragged garden and a small orchard full of debris and fruit trees and a swimming tank which leaks, and all at once I find myself leading a domestic life, with three chickens and two turkeys, a kitten, a puppy, and my cook Teodora who brought along her mother, a grand ancient who says, "Valgame Dios!"[33] in a long chant over every smallest household accident. She sleeps on a straw mat and eats fried beans for breakfast, and is an example of fortitude and uncompromising adherence to the principles of her being and the traditions of her race. She greets me in the morning with "God be with you!" and says at night, "Sleep with the Angels!" and means it from her heart. God sends the rain, according to her, and God willed that she should have rheumatism, and it was God who decided that she should forget her beans and let them burn. I put up a good fight, but still I have an uneasy sense of being under the eye of a capricious Overseer who is likely to play almost any kind of trick on me at any moment. I live entirely among such people; they have only feelings, no hope at all; a resignation to poverty, to being tired every day, to looking forward only to sleep, to being thankful if they are sure of food for tomorrow. There are fifteen millions of beings just like this, here, in this country, and they have for weapons a sense of comedy like poison-tipped arrows, malice and humility, and a love of death. They are so in love with the thought of death it makes them happy to talk about it. When it comes to them they make no resistance whatever. If any one tries to tell you about the "Indian Revolution" spit in his eye for me. . . . . Some day if you would like to hear it I will tell you something about this "Indian Revolution."

The novel goes along. I am waiting to see your "Declamations" made into a book.

Katherine Anne

To: Harrison Boone Porter TLS 3pp. Maryland

Apartado 2075, Mexico, D F
June 26, 1931

Dear Dad:
Your letter last night. I am disappointed about the European trip, but I suppose your reasons are good enough. I was thinking, too, what a rackety-cackety time this family always has about money, wondering if we would any of us ever recover from our peculiar despair of poverty, that chained feeling we have that we have no money, can never by any chance get any, and can't move hand or foot until we do get some. . . . . I know this, I have such a hatred and contempt of most of the ways of making money, I dislike and won't associate with people who have only their money to recommend them, and in spite of the fact that I have accomplished quite a lot of things in the face of actual starvation, it is really time for me to think of the future in a more particular way. Whatever I hope to have in this world depends simply on whether or no I can write books: and to write for money is a pretty poor and sad way to make it. So long ago I have made up my mind to poverty and a certain distinction as an artist. I don't believe a six weeks trip to Europe would cost you a $1000 or anything near it. Good God, I have to go and live there a year on just twice that sum!

The Fellowship stipend is arranged more or less this way: subject to each Fellow's need. The ordinary amount is $2500 but in this year of depression Copper is collapsed with the rest, and the Guggenheim Billions would not stand the additional $50,000 dollars for the regular Fellowship. I am supposed to travel and live on $2000. How one does it I don't know, but I suppose I can add to it by writing an occasional article or story. I have asked for mine in four installments of $500 each, and on the first I am supposed to get to Europe and hang on by my teeth for three months . . I shall make one effort to get them to give me $250 for the first trip, but it is very uncertain whether they will. Half a dozen magazines have asked me for stories, and among them Scribner's pays the best, so I have been working on a story to send them, but the damn thing doesn't come off.

My allowance from the rich-off person[34] stopped in May, which was the time set for it, but the relief of that one year has done wonders to put me on my feet and restore my balance. I am still thin and jumpy, after having got almost fat for a few months, but my general state of health is so much better I am hardly recognizable. For a long time I had to struggle against the very strong temptation just to fold my hands and curl up my toes and quit the whole devilish nuisance of life and struggle. I never had such an almost uncontrollable impulse to blow out my brains and call it a good day's work. But as my health was restored a little and the grind eased up—thanks to that angel of a friend—I could collect my scrambled mind enough to tell myself that that was a very ugly self-pity and I ought to be ashamed of myself. Accordingly I was ashamed of myself and began to recover. . . . Now I am in a healthy mood of resistance and energy. I work as much as I can and don't spend my spare hours beating myself over the head because I am not working.

This garden is heaven on earth this morning. The rainy season is upon us, and for a week at a time we have dark soggy weather, the very walls of the house soaked and drooping. Then one morning the skies are clear, the sun comes up warm from the very edge of the morning, and the colors and smells and feel of the washed air are as near Paradise as I ever hope to come. All the flowers, roses and heliotrope, honeysuckle and geranium, floripundio and Spanish jasmine, lilies and Sweet-by-night bloom afresh and the orchard is full of figs and alligator pears and apples. . . . . The mulberries and apricots are past, the peaches and pears yet to come. Having all this country space, I decided to raise a few animals. So I have fourteen little turkeys ten days old, and four little chickens. I had eighteen turkeys to begin, but they variously got drowned in the pool, squashed in the hen house doors, and two died of the mysterious ailment which the Indians call "Hit by the air." Evidently when anything gets hit by the air its all up. Its their name for any kind of sickness they don't understand. I had also a lovely little goat, but he hanged himself in a rose vine when he lost his footing on the rock pile. The cat had kittens. I have three charming ducks. No doubt about it, this modified country life is very pleasant. I don't expect to find anything like it in Europe. But I am not really looking for it. There, I shall live in a cheap hotel and devote my time to writing. This year was as much for convalescence as for anything else.

About my coming to Galveston, there is still time for me to see whether I am going to be able to finish and sell my story, or an article or so. If I do, I shall be able to come by Galveston on my own. You can imagine that I will not allow you to spend a penny on such an enterprise. If you spend any money on travel, let it be your own. IF the Foundation will advance me what I ask, and IF I finish the story, I would then make up the difference on my Fellowship stipend, and could go to Galveston, and on to Mission or Houston for a few days. I suppose then I could sail from New Orleans to some port in Germany—or does one have to go on to New York? I plan to leave here about the last week in August, as my permit to remain in this country expires on September 1st. I would leave at once except that my lease on this house ends on that date too.

The political situation here seems to be shaping up for some kind of little crash, but then it always is, so we won't go into that.

I write a few disjoined stanzas, and then read a little in your letter, and find I am not answering all your questions . . . No, the Fellows are not all driven aboard one ship like a mess of prize cattle and herded into Europe at once. . . . . We are eased in one by one, at whatever date we wish to go. Most of those appointed to Mexico were here within two weeks after the announcements, and some of the ones for Europe are gone already, but there will be several to go in the fall. I know four of them and two are good friends, so it will be very nice seeing them there. One former acquaintance, Hart Crane the poet, came here, and took a house just around the corner. He is mad as a hatter, and never sober, and I am waked in the night with him bawling like a bull calf at the door for help, about twice a week. He has gone out to a low cantina, got boisterously drunk, has been arrested by the police, who now want him to give them money not to take him to jail. He never has a penny in his pocket at these times, having spent it all for liquor, so half a dozen times I have gone down and given the policemen three pesos to let him go. The next day or two Hart shows up repentant, pays back the money, and the whole thing repeats itself. So the last two times I just didn't go to the door, but let them take him off to jail. I keep the garden gate locked so he can't get in, and refuse to see him, because his conduct when he is drunk, and his language, are not pretty, and I mean to snub him formally from this time out. He takes it very hard, climbs up on my roof and gets into conversation with my cook, but never succeeds in seeing me.

I did not know him very well in New York, and thank God for that.

If you're not going to Europe with me, I mean to go first to Germany and then to Russia, for a look at the two most promising and hard-driven countries in Europe, and then look for a pleasant climate in which to live. I would stay in Moscow except that there is no room now, and the winters are so frightful I probably couldn't survive there. I have, and have had for twelve years a sympathy for Russia, but I want to see for myself what is really going on there. I doubt if ever I can be a real communist, but am what Trotsky defined as a "Fellowtraveller." Daddy, there's a very grand new book out by a good friend of mine, Andrew Lytle of Tennessee, called "Bedford Forrest And His Critter Company." I wish you would get it, for you would like it, I believe. . . . Andrew contributed to a book of essays by the Southern Agrarian crowd last year called, "I'll Take My Stand." Of the twelve contributors, six are friends of mine, but Andrew's piece, "The Hind Tit, a Defense of the Plain People," was the most amusing. Ask Gay to get you these out of the public Library. Andrew is a throw-back, and whoops her up for the Old South. I told him I'd heard of the war being fought over again at intervals in those parts, and had even listened to some of it in my time, but I never saw it fit over round by round, charge by charge, volley by volley, until I read his Bedford Forrest. I have a deep sentimental feeling about it all,—near communist that I am—and am torn between a feeling that its all perfectly useless and a wish that it were not. Between the Old South, or even the New One, and Russia there's a long, long way to go. Let's see whether or not I make it.

This is growing into a very long dull letter. Darling, do what you think best about foreign travel; I expect you not to put in danger any of your future for such a little jaunt. After all, to what end? It would be fun only if you could afford it without worry. Its true, I know nothing yet of the miseries of the old, but believe me, I can give you first hand data on the miseries of youth. I look back on my life with astonishment, being unable to remember anything but unhappiness, misery and hardship, frustration and struggle, but on this foundation I won through to something, even though now I am unable to tell you precisely what. You are quite right to prepare as well as you can for a tranquil old age. . . . Already I am wondering what I shall do when the time comes. But I think I'll follow your example and get myself a few acres in the country; and dig in with a piano, the study of languages and an interest in farming. Be, in fact, an old fashioned southern country lady. . . . But who knows? I may stay in Europe, though I greatly doubt it. I have at least half a dozen good novels to do before that time comes.

I'll let you know whatever happens. Be very sure I don't mean to go away without seeing you. . . . . Its just that I don't quite see yet how I will manage it.

Love to Gay, and to Breckenridge if he is still there. Tell him I practise on the piano two hours every day, and am playing Bach and Scarlatti and the French and English music of the 17th and 18th centuries, and that I hope he will keep on with his music and never let it go. And when I come we will talk about it and I want to hear him and T. H. junior play on their piccolos and cornets, which always seemed to me perfectly impossible instruments to play on, so they must be pretty darn good if they can get music out of them.

Love and affection,
Katherine Anne

To: Harrison Boone Porter TLS 3pp. Maryland

[Letterhead:
Norddeutscher Lloyd Bremen
An Bord des D. „Werra"]
[August 31, 1931]

Dear Dad:
Three days out and nearing Havana. I wrote some letters yesterday, saying two days out, and nearing, etc, but it seems I was wrong. Today at lunch they brought around identification cards for landing at Cuba, so we must be not far off.

All the last days I kept thinking there should have been some way of getting over to see you, but I could think of nothing that would not straiten me so financially that my whole first four months in Europe would have to be spent writing at reviews to make a living, and it hardly seemed reasonable to go to Europe for that. The time seems very short at best, and we have all wasted too much time worrying about money. I mean to come through once for all to the place where I can devote my energies to something else than trying to connect with enough food to barely live. So we shall see each other soon and under a happier star.

The last days were a scramble, in spite of my determination to take it all calmly. A daily visit to the doctor, taking shots of something in the arm— strychnine and something else to make blood and settle nerves. This took hours, for I lived out of town. Then packing, trying to sell out my few sticks of furniture, give away my cats and dog, finishing up last minute reviews, with people wandering around the place at random, it was a holy mess and I shall never take another house until I have my own for good and all. There were all sorts of false starts: my letter of credit was mixed with some one else's, and I couldn't lay hands on it until two days before time to go. Then I got notice that the "Werra" was stuck on a sand bank in Tampico and would probably be very late in sailing from Vera Cruz . . . All came out well, and then in Vera Cruz a terrific storm came up, and the elevator shaft of the hotel was struck by lightning just twenty feet from my room, which dazed me and made me good and sick the next day: the storm burst like a bomb in my face, but I knew at once I wasn't hit, for if I had been, I should never have seen it. One might as well be killed as scared to death—isn't that an old Texas saying?

At long last I went on board at four o'clock in the afternoon, and so far the voyage is heavenly. Gorgeously hot and moist, after the tension and cold of the altitudes. I eat and sleep, and write a few letters and shall keep on writing them to be sent at every port until my whole forty six unanswered letters are disposed of. This is a very small boat, seems to me, for such a long voyage, but we stop at Havana, Tenerife, Southampton, and then Bremen. From Bremen I go up to Berlin for about two weeks or a little more, then to Paris, and down to Nice. I expect to settle there, or nearby. Probably in Villefranche, but I really cannot tell yet.

Dad, darling, I have discovered something which really makes me sick. This very boat came up to Tampico around the first days of August, went back to <u>Houston</u>, and left there only a few days ago—about ten. If I had known that, I could have flown over to Brownsville and then gone to Houston, and sailed on this boat. The fare would have been almost the same, and I might have wangled the one way ticket on the plane . . . Didn't you know that boats to Europe come through Houston, of all places? I did not, and kept looking for one to sail from Galveston . . . Not finding any, I gave it up as being too complicated to attempt. . . . Imagine it. I wish I had written to Gay, she might have known about it. If I had got there, I might have persuaded you to buy a ticket and come on. It would not have cost much more than the trip to Mexico you projected in the spring. About five hundred dollars for a fine trip. But you gave excellent reasons for staying at home and I think myself there are always good ones . . . When I come back I'm going to try to buy myself a farm house in Pennsylvania or some eastern state and dig in for life. . . . I must have at least a place to leave my books and stuff when I'm travelling. This thing of pulling up by the roots every time one takes a trip is too upsetting.

This little ship is steady as a—I can't think of any comparison: but she goes straight and smooth, and doesn't think she's a porpoise in disguise as most ships I've gone on seem to think . . . There are flying fish and sunshine and deep blue, blue water. How I do love a ship! And it gives me a lovely feeling of happiness to be going where I have so much wished to be.... One thing certain, I'll not go back to Mexico for anything. I'm tired of that troubled, troublesome country, and now its over run with tourists and Good Willers and Culture-hounds and Chamber of Commerce and Rotary persons, and one might as well be in any God-forsaken American town full of Go-getters. By the way, oughtn't that Rancho Bonita be properly El Rancho Bonito? It has something to do with the adjective always following the gender of the noun, or something of the sort. It looked odd, I thought. Mary Austin made the same mistake in one of her new books, mentioning El Rancho Antigua.....[35]

I wanted badly to see your orange grove, I hope it keeps thriving and prospering; By the latest, I'll be there in October, 1933. That's a short time. I left New York May, 1930—nearly a year and a half ago, and it seems like day before yesterday.... Time goes too quickly, that's one of its great faults.

Gay sent me some charming snap shots of the children, hers and Baby's, but I never hear anything from Paul, or of him, except an occasional smack at Connie in one of your letters; or Gay's ... I gather—and wouldn't I be foolish not to? that that was not such a good match for Paul. Yet it seems to hang on, produce young, and so it must be something near what they both want. If Connie is not very intelligent, why, a great majority of women are not, and most men are not mental giants, I've found. An intelligent person is rare, and you shouldn't be angry with Connie for that....

After this profound and intelligent remark, I think I'll go in the bar and have a whiskey-soda—to your health, my darling, and long life, and prosperity, and a near meeting for us.

...... Those are asterisks, representing whiskey-soda being guzzled joyfully.... My present well-being, snatched so precariously out of the air, reminds me again that I leave a troubled world and go to one more troubled. Mexico is in ferment, Cuba is, or was lately, under martial law, Spain is going like a spinning-jinny, and Germany on the verge of famine ... Southampton seems to be the only peaceful port we shall touch, but that's because England always muddles through dumbly, ferment is slower and quieter in those people; as for our own country, the rich and the upper middle class are quite content to see millions starving around them and do nothing, and I have very little hopes that the starving ones will really do anything by way of protest ... It is because even the most wretched soul has in his heart a nasty little idea that if he hangs on long enough, he'll get rich too, and then to hell with it ... So he doesn't dare to do anything that might upset the present system and spoil that chance he foolishly thinks he has to get into the white collar class also.... I may be wrong, but it appears like that to me from here ...

Instead of cheering me up, my liquor has made me very mad at the social system ... So I shall stop and make a few notes on the Mexican government which I need for my novel.... Goodbye, honey, love and affection. When you see the others, remind them of me, too. And write me care Guaranty Trust, 4, Place de la Concorde, Paris, France..... I shall let my mail accumulate there and pick it up as I go through .. meantime I will be dropping notes at ports along the way. With my love.

I do wish we might have seen each other ...

Katherine Anne

To: Malcolm Cowley TLS 2pp. Newberry

Berlin, September 25, 1931
Care American Consulate-General, Bellevuestrasse 8,

Dear Malcolm:
For the moment, I am settled permanently in a stuffy little hotel, the Thüringer Hof, on Hedemanstrasse, near enough to all sorts of things, but not noisy, for a city.... The tale of how I landed here when I was firmly on my way to the south of Italy through Paris is simple enough: Only a North German Lloyd tramp steamer was leaving Vera Cruz at the very time I had to leave, or go through a long rigmarole of having my Mexican permit extended. So we got German visas, and decided on Berlin. Our boat rambled all over the world for twenty-seven days, past Cuba, the Caribbean Islands, Tenerife, the coast of Africa, two ports in Spain, and even stopped at Bologne, when the captain was swearing all the way he would not stop there, on to Southampton, and so up the muddy Weser to Bremen; we tore our hair at all the ports where we could have left that boat if the agent had not deceived us, leading us into having only a German visa to start out with.

I had wanted to come to Berlin, but not just yet. We are here, and I am well finished with travel for the time being. Living is very cheap here, this hotel has steam heat, and I am collecting odds and ends of wool garments against the cold. It is enlivening to be in a city once more, and easier to stay indoors and work a little. I wrote the first draft of a short story on the boat, and in these two days have finished it up and have begun a poem. The manuscript of the novel is still packed away, but it will come out in a few days ...

The second day, I went to a bookshop and ordered Mrs. Woolf's novel,[36] so it will be here by Monday at least. I will send on that review quickly. The

Paris mail has been sent for, and I am watching for the New Republic for my Chase review . . .[37] There was more I could have said, maybe more explicitly, but it seemed useless. It is no good wasting critical energy on worthless books. The best of it was published in the N. R. and his whole idea was worth that series of articles, and no more.

Here I feel the atmosphere of great poverty, strain, and thrift, with prices for food counted in odd pfennigs, great numbers of men in early middle age with scarred, mended heads, glass eyes, artificial legs and arms: but few beggars; and the street women who come out after ten o'clock at night are very fresh-faced and young and well-dressed . . . I have not seen anything but the center of town, from Unter den Linden down to Belle-Alliance Platz, and round about. I am badly dressed but so is almost everyone. I am not expected to be rich, and that is very comfortable for me, because I am tired of never having enough to live on. There is a night life, and cabarets, and a few French shops, but I need not feel I am missing the tone of the place if I never go near them . . Last night in a little restaurant we were eating our tremendous plates of red cabbage and meat and potatoes, when a whining sour voice drooled out of the radio:

"It maaaaakes me feeeeel so bloo

When you saaaaay adew!"

The waiter explained that it was a famous American jazz orchestra broadcasting from a cabaret nearby, and gave us the address, certain that we were going there at once.

When I grow afraid of the cold, I take comfort that four million persons are living here through this winter, and so will I. Now I want only to get some work done, and here is as good a place as any, and now is the time.

Did you see Eugene Jolas? I wish to see him once more at least, to tell him the story of what happened when I went to see Gottfried Benn,[38] carrying Eugene's letter. . . . It was funny and I will tell you sometime when I am not so hurried . . . Well, he speaks only French and German, and I speak only Spanish and English, so that is enough of a plot . . . It was only that I went in serious hopes of saying something I wished to say, and of hearing him say certain things I had been told he would say in a particularly interesting manner . . . We were happy to see each other in four languages, not one of which matched, then we drank coffee and made helpless gestures at each other, and were both pretty exhausted at the end of half an hour . . . When he spoke French I could understand, but could not answer, and that was even worse . .

1st moral: Never present letters of Introduction.

2nd moral: Never go to Europe without a working knowledge of French.

Do you have any friends here? Tell me their names, but no letters! Only if I should happen to run across them. That is much better.

I had a letter from Peggy full of woes such as can happen in Mexico: the one that made the most lasting impression on us both was that she sat on a freshly painted toilet, got a green ring on her little behind, and as the bathroom heater is out of repair, she must wait for time to repair the disaster . .

The surface of this place is all a welter of feather beds, over-stuffed furniture, men and women shaped like something by Albrecht Dürer, great masses of sculpture full of senseless energy without direction, hanging dangerously off every cornice and facade—streets like burnished iron and great platters of cheap harsh food. But later I may be able to tell you about the new houses, and the new music and painting, even the literature . . . one will be a clew to the other.

Give me news of yourself, remember me to anyone who asks of me. I hope now really to be able to send you some small sketches of the kind you asked for. There are many waiting to be done.

Love,
Katherine Anne

To: Eugene Dove Pressly TLS 4pp. WWSU

Three o'clock, Tuesday, November 3 [1931], Berlin, at 39 Bambergerstrasse, Berlin, at that piled up desk, with a fine streak of sunlight across it!

Darling, the first day we have not seen together was the loveliest to look at and feel there has been since we came here, and surely one of the most miserable I have spent anywhere for a long time. Did I see your face change at the last second as I ran along beside the train? Or was it because I was getting ready to weep? why must I cry so much? It's horrible to shed tears in the street, mopping with a wet handkerchief; and a humiliated red-eyed slinking along with a feeling that there is really no place to go, no place at all.

I went on to the book shop and sat in the nice back room on the big stool and looked at books for two hours, and bought a Hound & Horn—there's another, imagine, and Peggy the wretch not sending my mail!—and then went over to Zuntz's and got coffee, and bought a handkerchief and walked home very slowly, and am just here this fifteen minutes, and bawling again like a calf, because everything came out so badly for us and we really did this because there was nothing else we could think of to do, and I DON'T like it![39]

I've been trying to follow you along, thinking what you might be doing, what you might be thinking and feeling, and I simply do not believe it is possible to stay here without you. I love you so much, you darling, and I have such a rotten conscience about my despairs and my habit of worry and my irritable nerves, but I depend on you entirely to love me anyhow, for you know my heart, and you know I love you.

Its no good trying to write now. I could die thinking how hard it was to be happy together, not for anything in us, or our feelings, but because of the fantastic things that happen to make us unable to live in the moment we have, because of the petty and horrible and cankering worry about money. I think we manage badly, too, worse than most people, and we must think of something to have life simpler, and get something we really want for the little money we have, instead of spending it all barely to live and not even doing that very well! But I tell you this: it was better to come here together as we did, and I am glad of it, and we can certainly manage it so this separation won't be for long: though even now it is too long. It is better for you to be in Spain than in Mexico, my angel. I'm going to settle in and work, and we'll be together again sooner than we dare to hope for just now. And of course we'll feel better in a little while, but this is a dreadful day! I'm going to wear through it, and write you some more tomorrow.

Few minutes later. I just remember that I copied a poem from Robert Graves' book to send you. I'm going to get the book in a few days I hope.
[Porter here quotes poem "Flying Crooked," by Robert Graves.][40]

This has something to do with us, but I can't quite put it together in my mind just now.
Thursday morning.

I hope you sent me a feelthy postcard from Paris saying, "Wish you were here." Yesterday was a day of pure recklessness. I went to the bank and drew two hundred and some odd marks, added them to what I had already, paid Mrs. Reichl[41] her thirty three marks, then went out and bought a beautiful pink corset, a set of pinkish wool unnerware, a boosting-halter that would do your eyes good, two pairs of silk stockings, a black purse which I decorated with my big silver pin, a lumly pair of shoes, black with snakeskin, just what I wanted, four beautiful linen handkerchiefs, a pair of oh, God, how swell black gloves with white streaks on the cuffs, in short went quite mad, forgot to eat all day long, went to the book shop and got Graves' poems, came home, sat down among my plunder and read until midnight, meantime finishing off that whole bottle of hard liquor, and so to bed without knowing how I got there. This morning I had breakfast at eight, a bath, and sat smugly down to my typewriter and worked until now, nearly noon. When the wish to write you got me down, darling, and so I will wait until after lunch to work again. You'll be pleased to know I still have 120 marks, (even the teacher is paid[42]) and all my clothes, and can't think how I did it, because everything I bought is very good and very pretty. I still haven't a hat, but that's not a thing to be taken lightly. I'll take a whole day for that some time soon. Having got all my stuff and my two dresses, I still automatically rise and assume the blue jersey, I can't accustom myself to clothes any more.

Yesterday morning I woke up thinking My Blubbety Blub is in Paris: This morning I woke up thinking, Now My Angel is in Madrid; I can let go now and feel that you are no longer tired and bored on a hard bench, or not eating enough, and all the other things that made me so uncomfortable. There's no use even talking about the way I feel about your being gone, but the web doesn't seem broken, we are still together in some odd way.

####This is a hellish typewriter, isn't it? I was going to strike off a few symbols denoting a change of topic, but its too much for me. No letter has come for you yet, but we need not begin to worry for some time. I had a long letter from Malcolm yesterday, taking everything I wrote to him about the Sacred Cow, like a dove. In fact, the most friendly and confidential letter I ever had from him; and at the end he said to let him know what reviews I wished to write, and to send them anything I had on hand, because he was very anxious to print things for me and so find me a little extra money. He wrote about Peggy, too, and explained his side of it, poor lamb, as if he had committed some terrible crime in falling in love with a pretty, healthy, young woman. I blame him only for not having known his mind and having a little more courage several years ago. Its hard on Peggy now, entirely too hard, but I can't think what she expected. Most women have a kind of blind vanity and self-love that won't allow them to see anything straight, and Peggy has more of it than any other two women I know. Ah, darling, in the end, whatever it is, I hope we behave better than that to each other.

No, I won't talk about ends. My feeling about all this is, that we have done all that we could and it didn't work so well, and now we're trying something else, and we're going to have our life together someway, and very near the way we want it. I love you entirely, I don't give a hang for any other man on earth, I want to live near you, and I'm following this idea happily. If we work, we'll be together again. So Here's to work this minute. By May first there must be a novel. And sooner if I can do it. A kiss, many kisses, honey, to make up for that measly smack we exchanged at the station. How funny, I thought afterward, that we had not kissed each other at the house, nor in the taxicab, nor in the station. Just one little last kiss. But for me, I know I was so miserable and in such a tension I never even thought of kissing. It would have been nothing at all suitable to say what I felt.

Please, darling, write me everything that has happened to you, I shall be hanging on the postman's visits more than ever . . .

Love and love and more love to you,
Katherine Anne

To: William Harlan Hale ALS 2pp. Maryland

[Letterhead:
Hotel Malherbe
11, Rue de Vaugirard
(Près du Luxembourg)
Paris-VIe]
[February 14, 1932]

And you and you, Bill my dear, why are you not in Paris, or I in Berlin, or both of us in London, or anything but this? Its been too long, I have been writing six lines of a note and destroying it every day, because I could never finish any of them. Now—it is Friday night, eleven o'clock, and at eight tomorrow morning I leave for Madrid—I shall be twelve hours in Biarritz—why are you not in Biarritz?—where will you be by then?

It has gone like this—Jimmie's Bar, The Dome, The Select—to see Emma Goldman[43]—Le Coupole—and so on around once for each—a day with Jolas and his Maria:[44] a day with Ford Madox Ford and his newest wife[45]—a visit to Sylvia Beach,[46] who received your regards with pleasure, and tea with Caresse Crosby,[47] who praised you more than I intend to tell you: and who asked my advice about selecting Bob's stories,[48] which I did in a cautious if eeny meeny miny mo kind of style—

To the Cluny museum to see old mss of music—to the Louvre to see Italian "Primitives" (we'll talk about those quotation marks some day, if you like) to the Quay where I squandered my patrimony on a beautiful map of America 1631—(not rare!) a visit to Sainte Chapelle, and to Notre Dame where I lighted a candle to your long life and happiness—and to the Caveau Rouge des Obliettes to hear the old songs: And it seems I have the job of translating them (to be sung); a project of Monroe Wheeler, if you are acquainted with him—I am not. Ford arranged it. They will pay me not well, but I love doing it, and it will be a book—

To the dressmaker, for a lovely <u>red</u> dress. Yes, I know what your Mr. (Doctor) Spengler says about red.[49] It is a childish, a barbaric, a woman's color. Your Dr. Spengler may go jump in the lake. You should see my dress!

To a Bal Musette on Ash Wednesday. To the Baths of Julian the Apostate, where passed a parade of 'Camelots du Roi'[50] surrounded by policemen to protect them from the Pacifists, who shoot them on sight, I was told—

And more of everything. <u>Why</u> were you not here?

It has been a violent change from life in Berlin until that Saturday night, and now it is Lent; on with the old familiar hair shirt and to vainglory of joy!

It does seem as though every minute brings me nearer to a weddin', or why should I go to Spain? What can I say except that, if I seem vague, it is because I mean so certainly to stand by it once it is done: and I dare any man or woman not to tremble in his or her boots at such a resolve!

I remember you very happily. I wish I had not to go so soon!

With my love—
Katherine Anne

To: Caroline Gordon TLS 4pp. Princeton

Bâle, Switzerland
June 16, 1932 ..

Dear Caroline, I did leave 32 Rue de Vaugirard about two weeks ago and came here to visit Gene, who has, bless God, a job in the Foreign Service, one of these appointments for life with a gradually rising wage and the prospect of being shifted from Embassy to Consulate to Embassy and back again, from Siam to Turkey to London to Neuve Laredo, Texas. . . . He has already been moved from Madrid to here in three months, and it appears the next stop is London. So I may as well prepare to be a wanderer on the face of the earth. I like Bâle. It sits along the Rhine looking like something by Albrecht Dürer. Its full of associations that I like: my favorite portrait painter Holbein lived here, and before him his father Hans the elder, and his uncle Abrosius, who was no mean painter himself. Erasmus of Rotterdam, in his later time lived here; and the row of little houses built by Crusaders on their way to the Holy Sepulchre, or coming back, still stand just across the river, still occupied, with smoke coming out of the chimneys, red geraniums on the window sill, and cats asleep on the porch ledge. I don't know why a house like this, built just ninety years before Columbus discovered America, is so much more impressive to me than a cathedral built at the same time. But so it is. We go to choral concerts at the Münster, built in 1100, and hear Bach Contatas: You will say that one might find more and better antiquities in Paris. But not such really Gothic ones, with the fire still going on the hearth. Where would I hear a Bach duet, a beautiful song if ever I heard one: "Gott, ach Gott, verlass die Deinen nimmermehr!" the voices flying like swallows to the very peaks of the pointed arches, but in a little place, where I would hear of it in time, and have the right mood to listen?

Still do I love Paris with a hopeless love, hopeless because except my luck changes, I shall not see it more than once a year. The apartment is empty, but I told the concierge I was coming back in two weeks, and it appears that in four I may even go back. I left a few little things there, and I want to make certain it is cleaned and the linen counted and the gas bills are paid, etc, before I give it up entirely ... About your Paris visit I was thinking this: My plans too are unsettled. We may go to London about the latter part of July, though it is not certain. In that case, I will just come back to Paris to see you. You will stay in Ford's apartment, won't you? They are giving it up in October, Janice wrote me. But until then it's open at least. If we don't go to London, why don't you, and Allen and Nancy, in your Ford, just come to Bâle for a visit? We live in a small hotel overlooking the river, not expensive. There are lovely walking and boat trips to be made, we can pop over into Germany and go through the Black Forest. Gene and I walk every week end; last week to an old Schloss on the edge of the Black Forest. A road by the river, where we stopped and waded when we liked: and rested on a mound of new hay outside the castle wall, in the sun, and it was all very pleasant. You may be tired of such country amuse-ments by now; Paris with aperitifs and streets may be what you would like. I can like Paris at any season. So let me know if you can't come to Bâle and I'll be back to Paris to join you ...

Here I am utterly alone. I see Gene in the evenings, but from waking up until six o'clock I am alone, with nothing to do, no one to see, I have not spoken to a soul for two weeks except Gene. The days are lovely, the river runs so steadily it settles my nerves, and little by little I have got out all my manuscripts and began very tentatively to experiment with writing again. I have about thirty short stories, and two novels, all in the first ragged stages of notes and occasional full paragraphs; the main novel is not even half done. . . . But I am not so hopeless about it as I once was ... Ford asked me how the novel was getting on, in Paris, and I said, I was snagged on it. Couldn't seem to get over certain problems. He said if I would show it to him he would help me work it out. I said, that with all the gratitude possible, I felt I simply had to work it out myself. He rejoined that I was the only writer of any gifts that he knew who had not sooner or later come to him for advice. "But you'll come to it," he added, very firmly. I didn't go on to explain that I could NOT come to it, for the reason that I would rather die with my novel unwritten than not to work it out, inch by inch, word by word, problem by problem, <u>for myself</u>! So I told him what was only the simple truth, that I had read his critical estimates and reviews of the Novel, and had found them helpful. . . . . But I thought again how really, he is almost the last of the old order of Men of Letters, and he has come to the time when, in the old way, he should have a School, a set of disciples and adherents, and I suppose he really wants such things. . . I hope that one day, I don't expect it soon if ever, I shall know one-fifth as much about <u>making</u> a novel as he does . . .

The Paris newspapers carried one set of dispatches about Hart's suicide. Tactfully, not a soul had written me a line about it. You know that kind of tact! But of all people, Monroe Wheeler had heard some details somewhere; that it took place at noon, that Hart dived from the middle of the upper deck . . . When he was drunk in Mixcoac he used to threaten to jump off the roof, but would always reconsider, saying it was not high enough. But he gave me some damned moments. Sometimes the circumstances of a man's death will change, or re-compose, the facts of his life: set them in another light, add some meaning you could not find before. So it may be with Hart's death to many persons who knew him. But I think not for me . . It was not his "pace" that proved too much for me. It was simply that he revealed himself to me, in every relation of life, as so indescribably swinish that I was utterly sickened and alienated, and that for good and all, without regard to any further accidents of life or death. . . . . About a month before they sailed, I had a long letter from Peggy,[51] telling me they were in Taxco together, living a normal life, though they did not expect any of their friends to believe it: and that I must forgive Hart, take her word that he had not meant to do as he had done towards me. Both of them seemed determined to think it was Hart's homosexuality that I hated, and nothing could be more absurd than this. If this had been so, I should have never have even begun a friendship with him. It is true that he put the cap sheaf on my long and painful experience with perverted people: the one element of a great talent aside, he was like any other pervert. My own feelings were fearfully mixed: for he was pitiable, and he should not have been. It outraged me that deliberately he would exploit a sense of pity in me, then behave with intolerable insolence, going on, with increasing drunkenness, to a sheerly beastly exhibition of malice that was childish without the right to be, almost comic in the way it overshot it's mark, and yet quite unpardonable for its deliberate intention. And then a day of the most appalling, embarassing apologies; and in everything, the melodrama and hollow attitudinizing, the fixed idea, of the insane. At the last, I could almost believe he was insane, but there was always some point at which he gave himself away, and I could see that, even in his most drunken times, he really knew quite well what he as doing and saying . . . It was all very terrible, and I regret it, but I do not regret his death. I think it was well done.

I did not answer Peggy's letter, and have not heard since. She wrote that they were both such practical livers of life, they were getting along beautifully and both had found what they wanted. It will be a great thing for Peggy, proving as it does that she is the widow of a better poet than Malcolm. She was very embittered against him, gradually working herself out of shock into a healthy fury. I like Peggy. She's a good out-and-outer. I tried several times to write to her, but the whole situation seemed so ridiculous I could not think of anything to say that even remotely touched it and yet preserve a shadow of gravity.

You didn't send the Angel Flores item,[52] but it doesn't matter, because if I could get anything ready for it, it would be a miracle, and I don't expect one. I really envy the Winters family their energy, absorption, the way they can keep multiform interests all going side by side at top speed . . . Its a gift.

Where do you think you'll be, for good, in Europe? I suppose almost anywhere. I've seen Berlin, and I've seen Madrid, and I've seen Paris, and I've seen Bâle: and I've lost Berlin, and I've lost Madrid, and I've lost Paris, and I've got a hankering to leave this place before long. I started out on a kind of parody of a song of Kipling's, but it didn't hold. . . . I ran into an old friend, but from old times, really, Sonya Mischell, a pianist, in Paris. She had just given a concert, and was on her way with a crowd of friends to Mallorca to the Chopin Festival. My idea of music is not Chopin: but I was thinking of going to Mallorca anyhow. The Spanish composers were going to be there, De Falla among them, and all the crowd were going to stay at George Copeland's house;[53] and I was invited to come on. I would have too, except that I cannot, never could, get ready to go anywhere on only two days notice. So I stayed away. Echoes floated back that it was all too heavenly and I was silly to have missed it . . .

In Berlin my chest blew up and the doctor told me I had a new infection about four months old. So went into the cure there, and about got it down. In Paris I went to the Hospital and had a thorough test: X-rays, blood test, every possible test, and the doctors said everything was null. That the lungs were badly scarred but no active work going on at all. But to make forever certain, they inoculated a guinea pig for me, and in about two weeks more I shall have a final report. If the guinea pig is still in good health, why, so am I. It sounds like suggestive magic of some kind . . . But it really looks as if I shall be able to forget the damned lung business once for all. I know I feel better than I have for years upon years. Its such a relief to be able to walk all day and climb hills and swim as far as I like without thinking maybe something is giving way inside . . . I'm going to get breeches and ride horseback. Gene and I are planning to do a lot of canoeing. I hope the job will leave us here until the summer is over, anyhow. I send a small snapshot taken at the Zoo, just to show you how fat I am.

I suppose Nancy knows all about Zoos, but I'd love her to see this one, or better, the Paris one where we could ride the elephant. Here, the animals are the tamest I ever saw; a double humped camel with a nose like feathery velvet tries in the most friendly way to swallow your hand with a piece of grass, and a large serious minded pelican, but near sighted, mistook Gene's green necktie for a piece of spinach and tried hard to haul it off of him. While I was bending over to feed one goat another goat almost got my straw hat, and the baby elephant is too hound lazy to take peanuts with his trunk, but opens his mouth wide so you can toss in a handful at a time. This is for Nancy. I hope we'll go to the Zoo some day and we'll even make photographs of the baby lions and bears.

It would be fine if I got the Scribner prize, but I don't expect it. And I wish to God those blurb writers would stop calling me one of the younger generation. Just because they never heard of me is no sign I wasn't alive all this time. If they could see me once they'd change their tune . . . I'm getting pretty sensitive about it, who never paid any attention to the years before. I have protested in writing, that youth was no career for me even when I had it, and it certainly is not going to be one now. But its no good. . . . I'm going to send another for the next contest, if there is one . . . I have several long stories planned. Five of them would make a largish book . . .

What's your next novel going to be about? I'd think—if I didn't know better—you'd feel twice as confident with this *Penhally*[54] back of you. Except that every beginning is a new venture; nothing one did before seems to help much, though I suppose it does really in some mysterious way.

Love
Katherine Anne

Ca' 'line, I have a bitter complaint to make. I have no picture of you at all, and you did not send me one of those lovely ones published on the book jacket. Why not?

K. A.

To: John Herrmann TLS 3pp. HRHRC

Basel, Schweiz, August 3, 1932

Dear Mr. Champion:

(For I insist that fight was no draw, I don't give a damn what the referees say) I had a letter from Mrs. Josy Fortune telling me about it, and the Scribner's came yesterday confirming all. . . .[55] Congratulations no end, and you should have had it all. I say this after reading both stories: and I had no previous grudges against Mr. Wolfe to influence me. I never read "Look Homeward, Angel," though many people had raved and told me it was oh, what a book! It may be, but Bascom and Delia Hawke have thrown me off, I'll never read it now, I fear . . . Not that I don't think he had two good characters there, and the material for good stories. But, oh, that messy, affected tricky style, that false fat "gusto" the critics have been wallowing in! It is not for me, I'm afraid. I'm always a little wary when anybody is called Rabelaisian. I like Rabelais too well to have him diluted with such feeble pee-pee. . . . . I'm happy you got half the prize at least for all kinds of reasons. First, because you should have got it, that's flat. And second because you spiked so nearly and sweetly the little game Scribner's was trying to put over . . . After I saw the blurb they gave him, I realized that I was sitting in a game where the other fellows were wearing aces up their sleeves . . . Of course, they were going to get him for their list, and naturally they were going to advertise him, and what better way than to give him the prize? And when I saw the lousy lot of stuff they were running every month, I was ashamed of being seen in such company. . . . They weren't going to print any story they thought could possibly give Wolfe a real run for his money . . . I didn't expect a prize—naturally, I had a forlorn hope—but (a) in these parlous times they were certainly not going to give any such sum of coin to any female. (b) I am already booked with Harcourt and they couldn't publish my next book anyhow. (c) They don't like my work, not really. I had the devil of a time wiggling in, and I kept on because I needed the money. (d) Rosaleen I think is a pretty good story, but it is not prizewinning caliber . . . and so on . . . So I was never even in the running. But I was simply outraged at the way they were going to put Wolfe through by hook or by crook. . . . Well, Josy told me how the judges put a stop to that. . . . And was your little friend pleased! God, it was the best news I've had for many a day.

"The Big Short Trip" is a grand story. It is put together like one of poor old Sam MacHenry's fine watches. (It occurs to me they probably will think of that) The technical part of the job (don't let me make you weary. I am always astonished when some one tells me what a swell job of technique I've made on a story, because I don't know the first thing about it. What IS technique? I believe in it, and I know it when I see it, but I don't know how its done, even when I do it myself.) is a knock-out. The grand energetic start of that hope-illusioned man, that worn-out faithful old horse about to drop in the harness, and he doesn't know it, and then the gradual wearing down of his spirits, his utter dumb oxness about the real condition of the country he lives in and has travelled over for a generation, the way he takes his death-blow from his son, everything is done so gradually and so perfectly, I couldn't see a false note anywhere. As for the feeling of the whole thing, it is simply ghastly, enough to scare you, it is so true a picture of the average man, the average good decent business man who really believes that everything is all right just the way it is, all he has to do is work hard and pile up a little money and then he has earned a vacation, and has done his whole duty in the world. The style is clean and firm as if you'd whittled it out in good sound wood. I have thought sometimes, in some of your stuff, that you cut things a little too close: but I don't know. After a dose of Mr. Thomas Wolfe's prescription, I take it back . . . There are all kinds of things in your story. The Russian motive, that starts at the beginning as just a little threat, a little underground murmur, and rises to a roar when he sits trying to read his son's letter—that's effective; you made that point perfectly. I could go on: the gradual change in his feelings from the time he deliberately oversells his old customer—not from malice, but because he really thinks he should combat this hard times attitude—to the last, when he himself suggests to the buyer that maybe he'd better cut the order a little: that was a good detail.

And the way he goes looking for a little companionship, lonely as a lost dog and hardly aware of it: first, telling everybody he is quitting the road, thinking they would rejoice with him: and finding that he'd better not speak of it, because it either got him into parties he didn't want or caused jealousy in the men that couldn't quit yet: and then again, trying to find someone who could console him for the loss of his son, for that was what it amounted to: really, the whole thing ends by getting under one's skin . . . You should have had all the prize. The story is too good for Scribner's anyhow, and that's a fact . . . I have a small particular hunch that Edmund Wilson was a great stumbling block to their plans, God bless him. I've liked and admired him for years and think he is a marvel, with his straight intelligence and his perfect honesty. I believe he was the one who held out. He can hold out, everybody knows that; he was one of my sponsors for the Guggenheim fellowship, and I have a feeling that you've got a strong arm when he is on your side . . .

Josy says you want to go back to Russia, maybe next year. You remember, maybe, that for years I was simply on the verge of going over and trying to become a party member: it seems to me we used to argue about it a little, I mean about the artist's side of that question, and I haven't overcome it yet, but I haven't been to Russia, either. And I worked for Communists for quite a while, in Mexico, and a little in New York, and I saw things that gave me sinkings in the pit of the stomach, and put me off somewhat. So I decided to wait and go to Russia, and see for myself, really see, and study, and take the training and the discipline exactly as it is handed out, before I took a step. I left one way of life, a way very strictly marked out and ordered with only one end in view, because I was unable to accept it all without reservations and so live and act freely within that boundary: it is terribly important to me not to take again a step that implies a life-allegiance to a fixed rule, and then be unable to go through with it because of honest doubt......I have several friends in Russia now, men and women, who are party members, and, as they describe themselves, good bureaucrats, because they have very important party jobs, and they are as silent on any of the things I really wish to know as if they had descended into the grave, and come back without any word.... It has been and is a great question with me. I know this, I am against what we have now: it has been almost instinctive, for I can reason myself into something like complacence for a few minutes: then something happens: a strike, a riot, anything at all, and instantly, like a machine, my mind snaps into its proper frame, I know where I stand without any argument or the shadow of hesitation.... But can I be a Communist? I mean by this a working party member, for I refuse to think of any kind of compromise ... Well, can I? For I must be sure....

This goes on pretty steadily, and has, and will, until it is settled somehow ... I hope you make quicker work of it, and come to some conclusion that will mean something. That is what I want: if I do it, it must mean something and I must be willing to stand by all the consequences.....I know that lately the news out of Russia, and by this I mean the party propaganda, the talk of enemies—has upset me. I know how to deal with enemy propaganda, but what can I do with the party bulletins? But Josy says both of you may come to Europe soon, and if you do, we'll have long discussions, I hope, and thrash the question out a little ...

I am living here quietly and very happily, taking long walks in the Black Forest; this past week-end we had two days and a half, and went up to the Feldsee, and from there to Lake Titisee, and so on to the Schluchsee, and down to Saint Blasiem ... The country is beautiful and sweet and very fruitful looking, and all South Germany seems so peaceful. But in almost every town we ran into Hitler meetings, and all along the roads were scattered the Hitler swastika in white paper, and Hitler placards: and today I read that Hitler is about ready to demand Nazi rule ... I can well believe it. All last winter Berlin was in a furore, but the Nazis were gaining steadily ... I think the time is coming when we shall all have to make a choice, and take one side or the other. I know where I shall go, but I do not want to wait for a crisis ...

Dear John, I'm going to cut short or you'll never wade through one of my mss. I'm boiling with enthusiasm about your good luck, it was overdue, and now it has come. I hope you'll be able to use the money exactly as you like, and get just what you want with it so far as money can buy it ... Anyhow, you've got the satisfaction of having done a good job, and believe me, money won't buy that!

With my love,
Katherine Anne

I haven't been able till now to get near what I have been trying to say about your story: that it is the most appalling portrait of spiritual bankruptcy I have almost ever seen: and not just an individual bankruptcy, but of a whole class of society. And hopelessly so, because it is past the time where a new idea or hope might fill them with life again: they're afraid of a new idea and they don't want a new hope ...

To: Harrison Boone Porter TLS 3pp. Maryland

[Hôtel Savoy
30 rue de Vaugirard
Paris VI, France]
March 22, 1933
Paris.

Dear Dad:
By now you have my news, and yesterday came your letter, with a note from Gay saying you had been sick ... She thought it must have been serious because you had a doctor, and knowing you so well, you'd never be so impulsive except for good reason ... I hope it is past now, and what happened to you? Gay, of course, forgot to say, if she hadn't already forgotten to ask ... Do let me know.

Your notes on Grandfather I have already copied off and put in the folder where I keep your letters. This year I am to be in the "Best Short Stories" collection again (edited by O'Brien) and also in a kind of biographical encyclopedia called "Living Authors". . anyhow they wrote and asked for a new photograph and such personal notes as I might care to give them . . . I wish I could earn enough money with this modest fame to get me a boat ticket home, I do. I can't eat newspaper notices . . . You remember the story in Scribner's last spring—"The Cracked Mirror"[56] It is that O'Brien will republish; I remember you said you liked it . .

The best news I've had out of your abject country is that, at last, somebody is going to be sensible and allow beer and wine again. So when I do come, I'll really be able to bring you that suit case full of sherry and cognac I promised . . . You should have had your good wine and beer all this time. You wouldn't have got sick, I'm certain . . .

Gay writes that Paul and Connie brought the new grandson down to see you.[57] Says he is too beautiful for words, blue eyes and black hair: then adds that he has mismatched ears and a birth mark on his tummy. He'd better be darned beautiful to overcome these drawbacks . . . I remember little Paul as being the handsomest small one I ever saw, and I hope this fellow is not going to be outdone. I wish they had named him Harrison Boone, for you, but I suppose both sides of the family have to be considered . . . Believe it or not, I don't even know the name of the third one—a girl, I think. My God, you are all so vague in these important matters . . .

Gay writes also that she is taking a cut in salary and a lay-off or what the Foreign Service calls "a vacation without pay" and so is Gene. He's been reduced ten percent and one month's vacation, but we'll survive, just the same . . . We've found a small furnished flat, very pleasant, and very cheap, and are moving in on the first of April. Things may get better next year or they may not, but at any rate, we are assured of a basic living, and anything I may make from writing will be just so much edge on the show. We are going to get along like two puppies in a basket—we always have been perfect friends—and are planning for a happy life . . . Its lucky for us the kind of happiness we want does not depend on money. There must be a little, but a great deal is not important.

Dad, I have thought a great deal, for the past few years, on the particularly lonely life you must have had all this time, and I have wished many times that you might have found some intelligent pleasant woman that you could have cared for, and who would have made a liveable life for you . . But I suppose it is not really possible to love truly more than once, and if one dies young, the other is simply left. . . . I had such a horrible experience in my first marriage, and was so criminally wronged in it, it took me years to recover from the shock. I never really found any man who would do for me, until now. I think you would like Gene: he is so sensible and intelligent and altogether decent, he hasn't, himself, any idea how nice he is. Just naturally, quietly a fine fellow

and no nonsense. If I can't live happily with him, I give up: there's no use trying. He is precisely the man for me.

Did I tell you some one here is translating my stories into French, and I
suppose next year or sooner they will be brought out by a French publishing
house. Also, I believe, they're going to be published again in England. . . . I've
never been satisfied with that limited edition business, I think it is a cheat, not
only to people who would have liked the book, but to me. My whole aim is to
have more readers, and I have no use for the snobbery of limited editions . . .
But the publisher was after a certain kind of publicity for me, and I suppose
he got it . . . I tell you all these details because I think you are really interested
to know how I am getting along. I'll probably never be a best seller or rich by
writing, but I believe you will be more pleased to have me have another kind
of reputation: that of being a really good sound artist, and what little reputation I have earned is based on that and nothing else . . . It is what I want, and
nothing else would give me any happiness at all.

I find, as I get older, that I want to get down to bedrock reality about
everything: in ways of living and feeling and thinking and working, I never
had any use for fake or pretension in either art or life, but I was often deceived
and took fake things for the real ones. That is well past, I know exactly what is
for me and what is not, and I pay no attention to all kinds of things I once was
led to think important . . . Its a very calm and easy way of being, but it did not
come easily: I have earned all of it.

Two Days Later. . . . . Friday. . . . .

Yesterday was Mi-Carême—Mid-Lent—a holiday, so Gene and I went
out to the Bois de Vincennes to the Zoo, and afterwards to the woods to dig
up little violet plants. We found some Jack-in-the-pulpits, and brought them
home with plenty of earth and root and set them out in a green pot, and I
expect them to grow up and bloom. Also long strands of ivy, which grows
nicely in a box . . . Its absurd to think I've always wanted to live in the country,
and grow huge gardens, and must now look forward to watering pot-plants.
But so it is. One stays where one's living is, I suppose, and learns to like it. Of
all places I know, I like Paris best and can live here more simply and with
less trouble than anywhere else . . . STILL, I WOULD like a little house in the
country, where I could keep the kind of animals and birds I like: ducks, and
a certain kind of Chinese chicken I have seen here: white, with their feathers
ruffled the wrong way, and down like geese underneath the feathers, and brilliant blue and purple combs. . and some pheasants and goats and a couple of
deer and perfectly round black pigs. I do love pigs. I keep thinking something
will happen to us that we can do this and have these things, but it is not reasonable, the way things are . . .

Then too, in this country, one could never raise cape jessamines and black figs, and I can't imagine having a place where one couldn't grow such things. So I suppose I'll just keep on day-dreaming and enjoy my country house more than if I really had it. . . .

All this thought of the country comes of having spent an afternoon in a very small, carefully pruned forest; and the sun is shining today, which doesn't always happen here . . . I must get to work. I'm trying to finish up the notes to my translation of the old French songs I started last year, as the publishers are anxious to bring it out . . . So maybe in a few weeks I can send you one. Its really lovely: Some of the songs are as early as 1180, one at least dated 1250, and so on down to the late 17th century . . Get Gay or one of the boys to play the melodies for you. They're sweet as little bird songs . . It will be a beautiful book, too: a famous printer[58] is setting it up, and the music is all hand written, in the old style, and it is illustrated, and bound handsomely—or will be, and sells for tons of money, but I have already had and spent my piffling wages out of it . . . The author simply cannot get any money for work: all the others have got twice as much as I have, and I really have done the work. Without my translations there wouldn't be a book at all . . . Just the same, it is a good job and I'm pretty proud of it . .

Honey, I think my news has about given out. Send this letter around to your little set of serpent's teeth, as I shan't be up to writing another. This really answers Gay's letter as well: or so I hope. By now she has had one—meant also for you—telling about the wedding and sending a clipping . . The newspapers got the biographical details from the official papers, where I always give my birthplace as Indian Creek, and they put you down as living there yet, but such little errors are always part of newspaper items. It doesn't matter; but you haven't seen that place for at least thirty five years, have you? And I always give my legal residence as being Mission, Texas, a place I think I never saw at all . . . You have to say something, and I always felt that my headquarters were wherever you were . . .

I mean to look up that General Fitzjohn Porter: he sounds like a very nice relative to have on the family bush . . . I told you, didn't I, long ago, that I found mention of the young Captain—or Lieutenant, but I think it was Captain—John Porter, killed at the battle of Mansfield, or Bayou La Fourche, in an old book of Genealogy in the Essex Library at Salem, Massachusetts—and all the rest of our family bush no doubt if I had known a few key names to go by . . . Don't think I've gone mad on genealogy, for I haven't, but I do think it is good to know a little where you came from and what kind of background you have. Its a part of my study of human character, my own character and nature included . . . In that study all sorts of details are important . . . Also, living in a foreign country has caused me to turn back a little to my own origins, I don't want to feel uprooted and exiled; I do have a foundation of my own, and mean to repose myself firmly upon it . . . I don't want to make of it something it is not, I am completely competent to live by my own blood and traditions, and the more I know of them the more at home I feel in the world . . .

Well, my darling, this seems to be going on and on . . . I'll write again very soon . . Do let me know how your health is, what your illness was about, and for heaven's sake take care of yourself . . Try to eat properly and don't expose yourself to weather changes. As soon as it is permitted, I'll send you a dozen bottles of good red wine. I shan't wait to bring them. Its the best and most pleasant tonic on earth. I drink two glasses of wine at lunch and dinner and simply couldn't do without it . . . I should think all this time you might have been making your own. But you shouldn't put sugar and such things in it: just plain, pure fermented grape juice is what you need . . . I wish you had a barrel of it . . .

My own health is even and good, and my whole once-wrecked nervous system seems to be righting itself nicely . . . Love and kisses from your child,

Katherine Anne

To: Ione Funchess Porter TLS 3pp. Maryland

Care Guaranty Trust Company
4, Place de la Concord, Paris, France
n.d. [c. May–June, 1933]

Dear Tante Ione:
I didn't send you a line with the announcement of the Song-book because I really didn't know whether it would reach you or not. Gay is vague beyond words about all such things as addresses, dates, and so on. Now I have seen your handwriting—Gay sent me your letter in which you said such pretty things about me when I was a child—I feel you really are somewhere and even have a box number. Before that I could think of you only as floating in air somewhere. You are a dear to remember me so gently: I believe I was an awful child and the devil of a nuisance to all: but you were, for me, something to live up to. I had a natural taste for luxury, and your rustly silk petticoats and rings and fine hair and perfume and wee elegant feet and hands simply made a life-long impression on me. I think of you always as a nineteen year old girl. You should have been always that. I remember "breaking in" a pair of

kid slippers with terrific heels for you: stumping around the house in a proud agony. They were too small for me.

Every generation seems to turn out a roamer, and I was that in mine. Life keeps on whistling me further and further from my starting place, but I keep a firm family-cord that I can wind back to it at any time. I have lived in New York and Mexico and Berlin and Madrid and Switzerland and now Paris. It doesn't matter much. One can write anywhere. I never wanted to do anything else, and its a good profession. You carry it under your bonnet, and a portable typewriter is all the equipment, so I travel light. I picked up a husband or two here and there, but they did not wear well. And this spring in Paris I did finally marry again.

You wouldn't recognize me now. I have almost white hair, and am too matronly for words. I send a little snapshot made in Switzerland last summer. Also a small picture of my adorable Gene. He is ten years younger than I am, but he belongs to my generation somehow: maybe I am a chronological misfit, for I am more at home with his turn of mind and point of view than I am with persons of my own age. So thats all settled.

This year I mean really to go home for a visit. First I must finish a biography which has been too long on the way, another book of short stories, and then I shall just go and loll in the bosom of my preposterous family for quite a spell. We haven't seen each other for nearly twelve years. Gay's tall girl Anna Gay was a squashy pigeon six months old when I saw her for the first time, and the last until now, as it turned out.

Spring is Beautiful everywhere, isn't it, but in Paris it seems to me especially lovely. Everything buds out so gently, in a soft mist, with little bursts of pale clear sunshine, and the whole city is so lovely; the nicest city ever I saw altogether. I suppose we shall stay on for a few years, since Gene has a job in the Embassy here, and unless we ask to be transferred somewhere else, Paris may just become our dwelling place. There are worse places to settle down in.

Gay sent me your copy of the famous Tree. Wotta family! Respectable, salt of the earth, too honest for their own good: I suppose the Irish branch went from England and Wraxhill Abbey Warwickshire, probably with Cromwell, and so we, too, get in to the mob of eight hundred million souls who claim Norman descent from some adventurer or other who came over with William the Conk. Simple faith, Mrs. Porter, is for most of us no substitute at all for Norman blood. You surely do remember that silly remark of Tennyson's that

Kind hearts are more than coronets,
And simple faith than Norman blood.

Nonsense.... We're all Normans together and not a kind heart in a ton of us. Or
so we hope. The ancestor I'm really fond of is Daniel Boone. Or you know who
I mean. And so we really started in Pennsylvania, for our two main branches
are from there. Well, well, after all this yammer about our grand old southern
blood ... I'm beginning to be able to account for a great deal in my own mind
and character that somehow couldn't be made to fit in with what I had been
taught were our origins ... Pennsylvania, of course. I spent a summer in that
state and fell in love with it. I know now why. It is really my native state. Gene
also comes from there, of English Quaker and Scotch Presbyterian blood. No
wonder we get alone like a house afire. And our birthdays are in May, his the
twelfth, mine the fifteenth. There you are. Everything can be accounted for.

I should love to know all kinds of things about you and Uncle Newell.
What business is he in? Economics rule our lives to an extent I wouldn't have
believed possible. We live on next to nothing at all, because neither authorship
nor Foreign Service are get-rich-quick schemes. But we live happily and busily. How is your health, which is all-important. What do you do to amuse your-
selves? We go now and then to the Bal Tabarin and see the Can-can danced
very handsomely, and four times a year, roughly speaking, we do up the town,
lolloping from bar to bar until we wobble home at dawn after having been to
Les Halles markets to watch the vegetable trains come in and eat onion soup.
We walk in the Bois de Boulogne on Sunday mornings and sit on cafe terraces
for beer late in the afternoon; once in a blue moon we take in a special moving picture of some sort, but it has to be special because I hate 'em anyhow.
We live in an apartment the size of a roomy bird-cage on the top floor of an
old house, looking over a beautiful convent garden which was certainly here
in 1551, according to an old map I have. I have become a really fine cook, and
so we eat like gourmets, or gourmands, or just plain gluttons if you like, and
we drink good Burgundy and various kinds of likker; Gene translates books
and short stories from the French in his odd moments, I write perpetually on
a dozen things at once and now and then finish something. So it goes. So far
as I can see, this is life.

Of course there are literary teas from time to time, but I keep away from
them as much as I can. Social life is not for me, I'm too selfish to waste my
precious time on anything I don't care for. What time I have for playing goes
literally to the piano. I finally got around to studying music, which I always
loved and needed, and what a pleasure it is....

I hadn't the faintest notion of turning out all this monologue when I
began, but you know I always loved to talk, and to listen again, so you must
write me news and gossip and stories about yourself; its the nearest substitute
for that conversation that we may never have together.

You mention Lou Bunton and Joe and Lady, and I wonder too what became of Uncle Asbury's children, Kitty and Leslie and Horace.. Cousin Lily Cahill, the actress, was in Paris this fall, but I did not see her. She just passed through on her way to the Riviera. Her picture in the paper here was young looking and beautiful.

I would send you a copy of the Song-book, but it is a limited edition, there aren't enough to go around, and the same was true of my Flowering Judas. But this year I shall have regular editions of my books, and Flowering Judas is to be reprinted, and then my family connection is to have copies of the works of its sole living author, whether it likes it or not ..

Love and many affectionate remembrances to you both, from your niece,
Katherine Anne

Permanent address: better use it because we're going to America for two months soon, and a letter will always be forwarded:
    Mrs. Eugene Pressly
    Guaranty Trust Company
    4, Place de la Concorde, Paris, France

To: Janice Biala and Ford Madox Ford TLS 2pp. Cornell

[32 rue de Vaugirard
Paris VI, France]
Monday, October 9, 1933

Dears:
Gene, at the office, is supposed to be writing to you also. It was getting our habit to wonder Janice about you, what with no checks and all.[59] As for us, we have been making plans, yesterday we decided that come hell come high water we would get to Toulon for Christmas. From this distance it looks altogether probable and easy. We have come through the dark tunnel and have arrived at a sort of modified Fiddlers' Green, and we have two months in which to gather a little bundle of francs for holiday joy .. We'll get there in time to prepare for Christmas Eve, and stay over a while, and by then I hope you will be able to come back with us as you said you might.
So that's settled, barring acts of God.
I'm fed up with putting off living for the sake of surviving. Fed up pretty quickly, for I never did it before in my whole life. But then, I was fed up living

on the edge of a crater, too, and this little time of retirement has restored my taste. My motto has always been, Not by bread alone: device, Grasshopper rampant, singing in the sunshine. To become the wise and improvident ant is not possible for me, not for more than a little while anyhow . . . But I'm glad we did it, for once. Once is plenty.

Gene bought a book the other day, and I bought a box of face powder and a little bottle of perfume from Molinard, my very favorite perfume maker, and we felt so rich-off and lush about it. Glenway and Monroe took us to the Ópera Comique—Le Près aux Clercs, if it isn't spelt all wrong, very tunish little work, and we're asking them to the Caveaux to listen to all those old songs over again. These things don't cost much but they cost something, and I shan't get my black velvet scrap made into a beret until next month but who cares? Hats are never becoming to me anyhow, and Malaga grapes are sour.

Harcourt Brace is going to publish Cotton Mather first, before the novel. It is le desperation on his part, I suppose, he probably wants to see <u>something</u> for his advance three years ago, and I am most happy to hand him this.[60] They are disentangling me from Liveright ruin in some way, I don't even ask how. . . . A chapter from this book, called "A Bright Particular Faith, A. D. 1700" will be published in the December Hound & Horn, along with Gene's translation of "The Foolish Virgins" by Adrienne . . . A kind of family number it will be. Nice, I think.

Mr. and Mrs. Philippe Soupault[61] have finished their translation of "Flowering Judas." It turns out that Philippe seems really to have done most of the work, but Madame signs it because there seems to be, or have I misunderstood? A prejudice against a man translating a woman's writings. Something beneath their male dignity, I take it. To hell with their dignity. The least one could say for me is that I am a better writer than Soupoult . . . It is to be published, I am not sure where, but I gather, in Europe. I have not seen the translation yet, though they keep promising to show me.

Henry Allen Moe[62] dropped in for an evening on his way through to somewhere not long ago and we drank a little framboise and talked politics. Not a word about art or Guggenheimers. Gene and he grew very animated and happy, predicting by infallible portents the total ruin and damnation of just everything. It was a cheerful evening.

Gertrude Stein's biography of herself by Alice B Toklas[63]—or Alice B's biography of Gertrude by Gertrude Stein—is creating a monstrous furor. She—G.S.—swings a mean little axe, by all accounts: I haven't read it yet. What I hear of it, Ford, reminds me of something you once wrote about Henry James: how, when he was angry, he forgot his convolutions of phrase and hesitations and spoke out in straight brutal English . .[64] G. S. seems to make herself all too clear when she is smacking her disciples and rivals.

It would seem that a little bell goes jingle, jingle in Alice B. whenever she sets eyes on a true genius. This bell has rung only three times in her life, once each for Gertrude Stein, Picasso, and Alfred Whitehead.[65] But G. S. appears to have a bell that goes off like an alarm clock at the most inopportune times, judging by her choice of genius—she prefers Scott Fitzgerald to Hemingway, and Carl van Vechten[66] to either, it seems. I don't mind this, for I don't prefer any of them. Its her taste in comic strips that has destroyed my faith in her: She thinks the Katzen jammer Kids are supreme works of art, and seems never to have known Krazy Kat or the immortal Pa Perkins . . .[67] This is where we parted such company as we had kept—onesided as it may have been, for I appear to be the only living person who has really read her works in toto— once for all and ever . . .

Janice, you spoke of five francs for the postage on the manuscript . . Did you mean the five francs on the check, or did you enclose currency? for it didn't arrive. Better not try to keep up with the accounts, I can't. Gene is keeping it all straight. About every fifth check we owe you charges, for it comes each time to something over four francs. As for the manuscript money, let it wait, and don't think about it. In any case, don't try sending currency. It simply is not safe.

Love and affections to you both . . .

Katherine Anne

Next morning. I can't quite place Delteil,[68] but it is a name I know from somewhere. .

Next to selling a picture outright, praise from the right person is the most heartening thing to an artist . . . Sometimes, I know from experience, praise from some one you trust is better than being accepted by an editor, for one just naturally distrusts 99 editors out of a hundred, and why not? Only, one has a passion to be read by the people one wants to be read by, and how can this happen unless one is published? So with painting. . . . You should have a show, and something written about you by some one not a fool. How to manage this? I haven't the faintest notion . . . This may be a vocational prejudice, but I think most criticism of painting is more beside the point than literary criticism, even. Further than this I cannot go in disparagement.

Glenway and Monroe came in for tea, and they had been reading already a copy of "It Was the Nightinghale"—said they would have brought it but thought we must have a copy. We haven't. Is one coming on, or shall we order it? I'm dithering to see it . . . as if I had not read it twice already . . .

Tea. I have some delicious tea given me to try, by a friend. <u>What</u> tea. I know now I haven't cared for tea because I hadn't tasted exactly the right kind. This is beyond description fragrant and rich and mild. When you come back you shall have quarts of it. Its a dark China tea with its own little white flowers in it. No jasmine or other exotic whatnots. Gene and I lap it up with huge slices of fresh bread, little dark round loaves from the bakery down the street which makes the best bread I ever ate, and we eat it still so warm the butter melts on it. A new prospect of sensual joy has opened before me, I am now a tea drinker. . . .

The song book is coming out in two weeks. I'll send you one. The weather here has been simply enchanting for weeks—well, for months really, always changing a little, but always lovely. I never saw a fall come on so gently, really summer turning very slowly into winter as fall should do. . . It spirits me up no end. I must get back to work. Write soon.

K. A. P.

To: Josephine Herbst TLS 7pp. Yale

October 16, 1933
166 Boulevard Montparnasse, Paris XIV

Josie darling: Its completely impossible to believe I wrote you last May, but I realize it is so and that all this time I have been waiting for something to happen about that review . . . I will tell all, and you're to keep your shirt on and not do a thing about it until I let you know the end. I know my Josie's inflammable nature, and I'm furious too, but determined to keep calm and hew to the line until a few chips fly, anyhow. I wrote instantly to the Hound & Horn and asked to review your book[69] as being precisely the new kind of American novel the Hound & Horn was (supposedly) looking for, it being not only the best American novel I could remember, but as good a book as I ever swung an eye over . . So the editor wrote—this before your book was in the shops—that they had already chosen their novels for review for <u>this year</u>, and regrettably yours was not among them . . . So then I wrote and asked how they picked their books until they had seen them. And so then Mr. Kirstein[70] showed up here and I asked him again and he said it was a matter of space. . . . So I wrote to the New Republic and got no answer not even unto this day. I didn't write to the Herald Tribune because Caroline Gordon asked me last February not to ask there, as she meant to review your book for them. Did she?

So then: When Gertrude Stein's book came out, or a little before as usual I wrote to the Hound & Horn and asked to review it . . . meaning to haul in your book by the nap of the neck, in my bawling out Gertrude for her damned pretentiousness about American literature, or indeed any other kind, by picking out Fitzgerald et al, and never having heard of John or Grace Lumpkin etc etc . . . And Kirstein wrote back a very friendly letter saying he had given this book for review last spring, and was there anything else I wanted to do for them? So I wrote at once, yes, I wanted to review your book, "Pity Is Not Enough . . ." This was only a week or ten days ago, so I am waiting for an answer. And if you like, I shall write and ask him why he doesn't ask you for stories, as you are the best, etc, etc, you know what I shall say, and if you're willing to take their piffling pay, print the Man of Steel or Iron or whatever there. . . .

So darling, say nothing to him or to the New Republic, let's be as politic as they are for once . . . I really don't know, Josie, whether its a matter of the gempmun trying to hold us gals down, or what . . . Kirstein is friendly beyond words, asks for stuff, asks me who I think should be published, and all that, and yet makes his plan without including some of the only books fit to read . . . I don't think its malice, I think it is a matter of spots before the eyes and a touch of deafness and more than a touch of dumbness. . . . . About the New Republic I am not so sure; so far as I am concerned, there is the matter of the Stuart Chase review, which certainly damaged our relations at least on my side . . Then I didn't come through at all with a review they gave me of Virginia Woolf's novel, "Waves." This didn't help my credit any, I feel pretty certain, and why should it? But why in God's name they should snub your book, you a member of their group in as far as you could be a member of any group. I mean, certainly a political sympathiser, and certainly a damned sight straighter on points than they are, all in all—this I cannot understand . . .

And again, with that set, towards me, there may be some sort of hangover of the Hart Crane episode . . . Let them think anything they like, I shan't explain or tell anything any more. . . . They all behave with a, to me, incomprehensible lack of foothold on any firm point of view. They write one sort of thing and do another, profess a belief not at all in harmony with their mode of life, and what can I make of this? Its true I am too far away, I do not any more really know what is going on, but I feel from the hints I get that there is something wrong in their divisions and categories. . . . . I noticed Malcolm, in an argument with Macleish, said he was unable to divide himself up into categories, poet, editor, human being, etc, and if this were true, it would be very fine. But is it?

I shan't go on with this, because you will know what I mean without more words. But I shall do a review of your book for the Hound & Horn yet, and

though it won't be a regular review, it will be a kind of essay, God save us, that
is, a piece in which I can spread out a little and take in some territory around
your work, as well as your work itself . . . I <u>shall</u> do this, and young Lincoln
might as well make up his mind . . .

He took a chapter from Cotton Mather, it will be published in December
. . . Also a translation by my Gene of a short story by Adrienne Monnier, to
appear in the same number . . . And though he does not know it now, he is
going to print a short story by you and a review of your novel by me. . . . . . Now
let's wait and see if I am just bragging . .

I hope you get your Hitler pamphlet done. Did I ever tell you that while
in Berlin I met von Goering[71] at a dinner? There were present some bright
young First and Second Secretaries from the British Embassy, two conservative members of Parliament who had flown from England that day for this
meeting with Hitler and Goering, Louis Graveure[72] the opera singer who was
once bald as an egg and now appears with a flooriant growth of tan colored
hair that to save your neck you cannot tell from real. It really appears to be
growing from his dome, which I believe is manifestly impossible—but anyhow, with my frivolous mind, I am off the track . . Well, Goering and I got
along so well that we left the party and went to a cabaret, not alone, you understand, accompanied by his combination body-guard and secretary,[73] and sat
there and talked. He was very softened and sentimental about his wife, who
had died about a month before, and wanted to talk about women; with that
extraordinary warmth and tenderness that only a certain kind of German
can have for women, I do believe; He was as attractive a man as I ever met, sat
there openly holding my hand and stroking it and telling me that I was too
beautiful and sensitive to be about the world by myself, and that, in being an
artist, I must not forget to be a woman, and more of the sort of thing that usually one puts one's tongue out at most disrespectfully, and would you believe
that I actually felt sympathetic to him because he was so obviously talking out
his heart about his wife, whom he had really adored . . . I was dying to get off
the subject and get a little political talk, but it was no good. I said, "The whole
trouble with me as artist and as human being is that I have always been too
much a woman." This delighted him and he kissed me, smack, smack, right
then and there, or shall I say, here and there? At long last, he began to tell me
that he and Hitler were going to make world history within the next half-year,
and remarked merely in passing that the Jews were the ruin of Germany, and
that when the Hitler regime was established there would not be left a Jew in
Germany with any economic or political or cultural power. I said, "How do
you dare cut away suddenly so much of your life? Cut off such a channel of
richness?" And he said "Oh, naturally, it will be painful at first, but it will be

like rooting up old trees to let the new forest grow ..." I said I believed it would do damage that could never be repaired. He said, They must learn to be good Germans or they must go ....(Needless to say he did <u>not</u> tell me he was going to set the Reichstag on fire.)

That was about all. He took me home and embraced me like a big bear at the door, and when my Wirtin[74] learned that I had met her idols and that von Goering's car had stopped at her door, she almost fainted and after that the house was mine . . I think unless you had been there then—I went to Communist meetings and to Hitler meetings—you could not imagine what a hold Hitler and Goering had on the suffocated middle-classes—the white collar clerks and the oppressed landladies and the little grocery shop keepers and the waiters ...They were all his, and it was like watching a Methodist camp meeting—those Hitler rallies. And God, how they adored their soldiers and policemen, and how they hated Jews, and how blind and ignorant they were; I never had just known exactly this kind of people before, I suppose they're alike everywhere, but in Germany I talked to them all over because they were so anxious to talk, and because they were so preponderant in a majority—they were so anxious about their house linen and their bits of furniture and how they strained to keep up appearances and how frightened they were because they were about to slip into the proletarian class. If they couldn't keep plush on their chairs and mended white linen on their tables, they were lost and swamped . . . Hitler would save all this for them . . It was very sad and painful. The women, even the little milliner who made me a hat or two, cried all the time ... I never saw women cry so much ...Once I went in to buy a pair of gloves in a very decent little shop, and when I could not find what I wanted, the girl burst into tears. . . . The milliner wept when I decided I simply could not afford a certain hat. "Oh God," she said, "How everybody is so poor now!" My landlady, a beautiful Viennese woman like a fine little China figure, fifty years old and with skin and hair like roses and spun silver, sat on the floor looking at pictures of herself in her Paris clothes and driving her lovely horses, and wept ... I thought, I know all about poverty and hunger and how it dulls and thwarts you, but it was never the important thing with me, there was always something else, and this is what it means when there IS nothing else . . And still I think they cried not because they had lost their money but because the country had been defeated. Any man who would promise them that they would be a nation again could have them outright at the price of a few little promises.... Hitler got them ... Its an outrage ...And its no good blaming them for their leader, when you see how Roosevelt has put it over on millions.... with a few promises ...

There is frightful excitement here now over the Germans leaving the Geneva conferences . . . But the French press is being most wonderfully sensible and calm, and Hitler made a very conciliatory speech directed towards France . . . It would seem that England is to be the goat this time. Both France and Germany seem to want to blame England for something or other. . . . I have just enough patriotism left to hope we shall not again be the goat . . .

Now darling, how did I get off on all this? But I think you may be interested . . . I hope that the United States is really going to recognise Russia . . Next thing, you'll hear of us settled at Moscow, if that happens . .

What kind of material did you get about the children? Jewish children or just anti-Hitler children, or what is worse, Hitler children? I am prepared for any horror. The stories of the concentration camps that filter in here are beyond anything I have heard yet . . .

The news about the Mather book is that Harcourt and Curtis Brown between them have made some sort of arrangement with the new firm that seems to be setting up on Liveright's remains. I know little about it, and that Harcourt will take over the book. I am working again on it. . Its no good boasting about how damned much work it has taken to get three things into the book: First, historical exactitude: 2: a true study of Mather's temperament: 3: to make it read so easily no one will be tempted to doubt what I am telling them . . . Well, and a 4th: to have it really interesting . . .

A bale of gratitude for your good words, Miz Grist Mill. Believe me, they help! I really think it is a good book, I have put my back into it and no mistake. . . . The reason I haven't tried to market it anywhere else is because the damned thing has not been finished. But this winter will see it through, blessed be . . . I have a bibliography of seven hundred titles—three hundred added since I left Salem in 1928! Yes mam, I know my subject from the marrow bones out . . .

I wish to God I were in Pennsylvania or somewhere in the south to help the farmers fight . . . You know, when the war got into that territory, my hackles began really to rise. That's something I can understand. I've been wondering how long it would take those men to turn and fight . . . That horrible patience is of course part of the nature of them . . . they wait on the rain and the sun and the seed in the earth, they have to be patient and long suffering and heavy burdened at best, I mean, even if markets were good and transportation arranged decently, and everything done properly, still their work is hard and endless and depends on so many forces outside their own efforts . . weevils and blights and droughts and floods that come with the suddenness of lightning . . . It is this I think that gives them their awful resignation and fatalism, and it is this they have to fight in themselves first, before they can conquer the hostile perverted world that <u>will not let itself be fed</u>! I am in perpetual amazement that from the very beginning of history, the rulers

have tried endlessly to crush the people that produce the food for the world
... Why is this? When this question is answered, and not until it is answered,
shall we begin to get somewhere.... UNTIL THE RULERS CONSENT TO
ALLOWING HUMAN BEINGS AND WORKING BEASTS ENOUGH TO
EAT, they may as well not talk their bloody nonsense about good government
to me. . . . . . There is every year of this world enough food produced to feed
every living creature in it. And every year millions starve and other millions
exist half starved. . . . . I want this changed, and it is the only revolution in
which I take the slightest interest.... and I don't really care by <u>what</u> means, so
they are <u>effective</u>!

Well, darling, I didn't start out to write a pamphlet myself ... But I think I
may end up doing one. I hope they have good hardy leaders who know all the
practical details; I mean a good tactician, who can meet play with counter-
play ... The farmers are hampered by a lack of economic and political education. They have had to stick too close to their plowing and planting . .

Your raising money for the farm leader just reminds me that I owe you
five dollars. . . I will send it positively on the first of November when we get
our hands on dollars ... If I can I will add a couple of dollars for Bentzley's
wife . .[75] If I win in the lottery I'll send some more . . We got our already piffling wages cut just one fourth, but they may be restored intact on the first.
We are just living along, watching pennies, but we have got our standards of
living chewed down to within our means, and it is not so bad, because rent
is cheap and you know I am a good cook, and Gene is the Spirit of First Aid
in the Housework incarnate, God give him long life, and so we get along so
damned cheerfully I almost have a guilty conscience to be happy in this quite
abominable world ...

He is simply one of those rich natures that seems to be able to get all its own
jobs done and have plenty of time and strength left over to put a shoulder to the
wheel of the other fellows chore also, and then plenty of time and spirit still to
enjoy himself in his quiet way, and rest if he gets tired. . I try, in my thwarted and
misguided maternal instincts, to mother him now and again, and he runs from
it like the devil was after him. He seems to want to mother me, and I am one of
those feeble souls that can take that sort of thing when I can get it . . We both
love Paris so much that just being here is something, and we do occasionally get
out and pleasure ourselves a little, though neither of us have been in a cafe even
for an aperitif for months, and we don't miss it . . Philippe Soupoult and his wife
have translated two of my stories—Granny and Flowering Judas, and they are
to be published here. Glenway Wescott and Monroe Wheeler have got my song
book off the press, and I am going over there this afternoon to sign 695 copies of
the damned thing ... I am sending you a prospectus, but it doesn't mean a thing.

I am sending you a copy the minute its really bound and ready. It is simply a heavenly beautiful piece of printing: and the songs are good too..... if I did pick them and translate them ..

Well, at last I have a name sake, though it hasn't been announced to me by the parents... Maybe they meant another Katherine Anne ... I hope not ... Why, I would give Mr. Pearce any details if he asked for them, but how could I know there was any curiosity about me? About that, I wonder. Nothing could be less dramatic than my life, long may it continue! I work better than ever I did, which might not be saying much, I am beyond words happily married, and you know there is nothing duller than that, for any one except the two concerned....

Ford Madox Ford dedicated his last book "It Was The Nightingale" to Gene, first because he's terribly fond of Gene and second because Gene helped him with his manuscript, and there is a letter to Gene in the first pages, in which I figure inconspicuously. Ford, with his gift for exaggeration, makes it appear, to Gene's infinite embarassment, that my lil husbing is at least an ambassador. Well, he is just precisely secretary to the Third First Secretary, and won't pass his examinations for diplomacy until next year, when maybe he'll be something else. Who knows and who cares? What we wanted was a job and a living and we have it.

Just the same it was like you to be discreet about publicity and all that, and you just keep it up ... I don't much believe in all this personal touch system between author and public. I do love a private life, and I should like the public to read my work. That is all they need to know about me, or any other author ... I have been reading all the wonderful flood of personal memoirs around poor Lawrence, a perfect, shameless hyena feast if ever I saw one ... Every scummy little parasite that ever touched his poor defenseless life is telling all about it ... Between them they have about managed to ruin him. He may really have been the perverse little beast they make him out, but its a poor service to do a man they all professed to adore ... It makes you doubt him a little that he so let himself be surrounded by these people, either corpses or vampires all, it seems to me by their own testimony, all except Aldous Huxley and Catherine Carswell, who after all are the only real talents among them ...[76]

But that Mabel Luhan, that Brett, that John Middleton Murry,[77] and who else? Their books stink. Thats the only word I can find for them. And I can't see why Frieda Lawrence[78] doesn't just take an axe to the lot of them, if she really is the virago and shrew they all tried to make her out ... I would write a piece about it saying what I think if it wouldn't get me into such filthy company .. And the best thing is to let them die of their own inanition after they have drained out of themselves all the life they had derived from him ...

Well, youngun, this must end . . . I have it on my mind that I have not written for God knows when to the few people I really care for—Becky, for the first, and one or two others. It is morning, getting fallish and chill, but a little gray sunlight. I must straighten up the house and get ready for the afternoon's endeavors—did you ever sign your own name 695 times handrunning? Of course you didn't, what a silly question, and I don't know any one else who ever did, and it sounds a little nightmarish to me, but I'm going to see what its like. . .

Ah, well, Josy, I do have one regret. That I couldn't get the little money to pay down on that hill-house, which was of all the houses the one I really wanted, and so Gene and I would have come there to live some time or other, for we mean to manage somehow, diplomacy or not to live at last in America, Pennsylvania for choice—he was born there—or New York State or Connecticut. Will all the old stone houses be gone, do you think? I suppose so, or so expensive we could never afford one. So we'll not worry until the time comes . .

Now do haul off and write me at respectable length; take this as a model for size. . . . Give my love to Mister Rooted-in-the-Serl, and tell him he'll have to do double duty since I am not there in the Farmers' War . .

Don't say or do anything rash about the Hound & Horn hesitating about your review, they'll print one yet. . . . .

With all my love and affection. I gave your book to Philippe Soupoult, who was all het up about it. Westcott has it now; Sylvia Beach says it goes and comes regularly from her lending library. It will spread about, I'm not really worried over that. But I have something to say about it and I have no idea of being choked off . .

Ever your'n
Katherine Anne

What about translation? I know you've been translated into Russian, but French? Shall I speak to Soupoult? He might be interested for himself or know someone who could make a good job of it—

Darling, you know well you're more than welcome to use any way you like anything I ever wrote you about your work, or that I ever wrote to anybody else, if you like. I wish I could write more and better . . . I wish you would apply for a Guggenheim whatnot and take me for a sponsor . . . I just finished recommending some one else whose work I like, but my God, it doesn't compare with yours . . . So why shouldn't you have that $2000? And there is now a limited number for study in the United States, if you feel you must stay on your native hills and dales, and I can think of a lot worse places to be! Try it, Youngun. Let's see what happens . . .

October 19—

I've started a long short story. Something new. I'll send you a copy when its done . . .

When I read this letter over I realized I had set down a lot of things I had not written before for my own record, so I copied it off for my general file, letterbook, journal, etc . . . Can you imagine? I never did that before. But I wanted to remember: and that's why its going away late. I may write about farmers and Goering yet!

Love and affections
K. A.
Miz Montparnasse

To: Barbara Harrison Wescott TLS 2pp. Maryland

166 Boulevard Monteparnasse,
Paris XIV, June 30, 1934

Dear Barbara:

This is the only copy of HACIENDA corrected properly enough for you to read and get some notion of how it will be in print. I really wished for you to wait for proofs, but that may be some time off, and I am too anxious for you to see it.

Since it was finished, I have done nothing but work on the biography, hoping to have it all over with by the time I meet you in Salzburg; I am so looking forward to that, I cannot think of having it even a little marred by tiresome, unfinished work. I had very good news of you from Monroe, but that was long since. The cure must be going on, I hope, I hope! Monroe said you would need your riding boots and some other things for Hungary, and I am to bring them, so surely that must mean you have, or will have, finished for good with Davos. Let me know when and where I am to pick up the suitcase, and if there are any kinds of affairs you want attended to here that I am capable of looking after for you, do tell me what they are. There must be something, and I should love doing them.

Just now, I have seen Thunder over Mexico, Sinclair's version of Eisenstein's film, Que Viva México.[79] A dull spoiled affair, full of the most stupid evasions, cut to ribbons and fitted together again and in all the wrong ways. I regret all the fine ideas and all the work that was thrown away in that business. I don't wonder that Tissé, Alexandrov and Eisenstein (alias Stepanov, Andreyev, and Uspensky)[80] were tearing their own ears off with rage and frustration.

Such pleasure as I could take in it, beyond the photography, which nothing can spoil—was childishly personal; recognising all the people in it, even the burros and dogs: and all the scenes; and knowing that I had them all in a story of my own, too ...

July 10th:

Barbara darling, its no good trying to write. I put this letter aside for one day, and look! So I shall wait to see you. I hope your memoirs are getting on better than this biography.... Do you remember Robert Graves' quotation at the beginning of his memoirs?

"The science of geography
Is different from biography:
Geography is about maps,
Biography is about chaps."[81]

And have you read Henry James' <u>A Small Boy and Others</u>-?[82] I'll bring it along if you like. No use to say I will mail it. That might mean next year . . I had never seen it, and it is one of the most interesting personal records I ever read.

All the "faults" his critics saw in James, I am happy to find he saw first in himself. His inability to participate in any scene: and his choice of England as a dwelling place, two points around which his commentators revolve like moths around a lamp, were just precisely natural for him. After reading his memoirs, it is very clear that almost no man—or let's say man of letters—ever followed his own bent and desire more simply than James did. I don't quite know why this pleases me so much, except maybe I am weary of the whole theory of frustration as motive power of artists. I think that, more than any other kind of person, artists manage to live the kind of life they want, no matter how odd their choices may appear to onlookers.....

####

I hope your father is perfectly well now. Monroe told me the operation was difficult but successful ...

With my love, Katherine Anne

To: Caroline Gordon TLS 5pp. Princeton

[Imprinted: 70 bis rue Notre-Dame des Champs VI]
First Day of Spring [21 March]. 1935

Dear dear Caroline:

Your letter just came, on what is always the most important day of the year for me: for six weeks at least I'll be in a complete dither of senseless joy and why? Merely because its spring. It happens every year, and keeps on happening, though you'd think I'd be settling down about it. It has nothing to do with my personal fortune, my health, my happiness: it is simply a gayety of the heart related to the season, depending on the weather, an end in itself; It is quite enough just to be alive; I wish my mother could know how one child of hers at least, blesses her name.

Your long letter was so welcome, quite like your old way of writing. Just surviving has been so almost-impossible for all of us, I think we have had no energies left over for keeping up amenities. Things have braced up a little for us: I think our act of madness in taking this house brought us good luck. The house is good luck in itself. You are right, all the things you name are at this number . . . You know how it is, I've only lived in this enclosure three months so I haven't seen a soul except the concierge, but several persons have written about the place and seem to have pleasant memories of it.

We have the small house and garden with an atelier facing the house. Just now our lilac trees and a little cherry tree are budding and beautifully, yesterday we got out the green garden chairs and table and the big yellow and white garden umbrella, and had our lunch in the sunshine, and we're going to eat out from now on, unless it rains . . . Last evening we ate out again, with our own little terrasse café, and drank a whole bottle of Reisling 1929 by way of aperitif and celebration. Oh, its too damned bad you're not here. We could have such a merry time. Gene loves the place so its impossible to drag him out even to a moving picture; you know he never was much of a gadabout; so the other night I suddenly struck and said, "I'm good and tired of cooking, we haven't been out for food since we came here, just what do you mean never inviting me out?" He looked consciencesmitten, and said, "Well there isn't any restaurant we can afford where we can get as good food as we have at home." I was touched and flattered by this, but held out firmly. So we broke down and went to Delaborde's on the Quai Malaquai, and there ate the best duckling with orange and the most delicious trimmings, and had a bottle of beautiful wine, and came home in a taxi, and I felt as if I had been on a wild night out . . That's how quietly we live now.

I didn't see all the reviews of your book,[83] just three or four scattered here and there in the more decent sort of review places, and they were all not only good, but intelligent, I thought, and I was pleased with them for you. . . . I don't know what the run of the mill was like, but I imagine as stupid and cheerless as usual. Since then I have got the book for myself, and I think it is magnificent. . . . That fellow who said it read as if there was no straining after style was quite right, dear Caroline. It reads as if a gentleman of the old south who knows not only Latin and Greek but English, had sat down and written his memories in the first words and phrases that came handily, and the kind that came handily would naturally have this sure, slightly formal and balanced rhythm. Well, I do know at least what it takes, and you have really succeeded. Its fine masculine prose, and why shouldn't it be, you writing with the sound of your father's voice, all the voices of your fore-fathers, in your ears. It's odd in a way how our development runs along neck to neck. I have come to the time when I simply must take my own advice and sprawl. I began it, a very discreet sprawl indeed, when I started the long stories. The one I am trying to finish now is called Pale Horse and Pale Rider, and it should be about twenty thousand words, but the editors keep calling for some more five thousand word "perfect" stories. Well, its just possible I can't write any more "perfect" stories . . . But that is their worry, not mine. I've got to have more room, and I'm making it. . . . About this magazine, I hope it comes off well, in spite of what I consider a plot against us, writers of fiction . . . This is the second magazine to announce policy of no fiction, and the other, The Needle and Magnet, or is it Cat and Fiddle, or can it even be the Cock and Bull—you know, the one that takes the place of the Bitch and Bugle, announced not only a blacklist on fiction but I take it, no prose to speak of except critical essays . . .[84] Its their business. . . . positively. Such announcements arouse me to a frenzy of indifference.

Yes I know, I'm being vulgar, and enjoying it. But oh, you do know how I hate tight little cliques, and manifestoes, and ex cathedra announcements, such as "The Revolution is just around the corner," or "There is no work of importance being done at present except in the departments of poetry and criticism." I beg leave to differ with both of these and all similar formulas. And when I differ I differ and I mean to do something drastic about it . . .

That Revolution talk reminds me—but I must have told you this long ago—about how, when I first went to New York, 1919 to 1920, I fell in with a crowd just back from Russia, and heard every day of my life that the Revolution was not merely just around the corner, it was camping on our doorsteps waiting the precisely right moment to blow us up . . So I went to the country for three weeks and drank milk and swam in a creek and picked blackberries and talked crops and other basic things of life with country men and women, and came back and met it may have been Mike Gold in the street and the first word I heard was Revolution, so I said vaguely, "Oh, yes, whatever became of that Revolution?" and was rewarded with such a look of contempt and hatred as made me fear I had really started one . . .

That was really nearly fifteen years ago, God help us all, how we sail through time . .

So if they expect to have it this summer they'd better get a move on. . . . I feel about that as a wise woman once said to me in regard to something else which I can't remember, "The thing itself is quite alright, but I can't endure the talk about it."

Here of course, everybody talks war. Germany having re-armed openly at last—having been re-arming semi-secretly since 1920, has thrown the French into a quiet hysteria. Of course, France started it, as she has started every row she has had with Germany since the Franks went to Germany and the Gauls stayed in France. . . . (that's pretty synthesized history, but you'll allow for details) by getting nervous over the skimpy crop of war time babies who will shortly be ready for military service, and raising the term to two years . . . This smoked Germany out in a hurry, and so while Italy, France, England and maybe Russia and maybe America are talking of ganging up on Germany, the French newspapers are being bitter and trying to blame it on England who seems to have kept up trade relations and no better with Germany than any one else, and who was inclined to be merciful in the debt question: and England of course is blaming America, but you know how it is: in the end, they will gang up. Poland's attitude is just Polish: the Poles have announced they don't care what country Germany goes to war with, just so it isn't Poland. . . . .

And so everybody talks war, war, and we sit here feeling as secure as medieval Thieves in sanctuary at Notre-Dame; but last night there was a great roar and flurry of airplanes over Paris, and Gene said, "do you suppose they're Germans?" I said, "What about that underground defense on the border that is supposed to shoot an impassable curtain of fire and bullets straight into the air higher than planes can rise?" For such is the fantastic popular belief. Gene said, "The only thing we really know about it is that it cost a million francs an inch to construct." And it probably won't work, whatever it is supposed to do. So let's wait and see . . .

Just the same, the day after Germany's announcement, the German team came over and beat the French at Soccer, and the town was stuffed with French soldiery and gorgeous enormous red German busses, which had brought thousands of Germans to the show. The game went off nicely, but the whole day was stiff with excitement . . . One heard Frenchmen going about saying this was probably the last friendly visit the Germans would make in Paris. . . . . But Paris has been for long full of Germans, not only Jews but all sorts of refugees. The Luxembourg sounds like the Tiergarten . . . Germans sit there talking more happily than I ever heard them in Berlin, though. They look as if they had arrived in Paradise. . . . It is not my imagination, just because sometimes I have the feeling that I too have arrived there. But of all foreigners in this place, the Germans always seem the most pleased. There is something shining in their eyes . . .

Your description of the Christmas festivities wrung my heart. I hope you wished just once that I was there.

And now, Caroline, we are coming to America. Here is the plan. This is final. Nothing short of death can stop us now. We know where the money is coming from, and that is all that has been stopping us. Gene got full pay restored and then a raise, and so its settled. August first, we go to Salzburg for five days, (just the time it will take to hear Figaros Hochzeit, Rosenkavalier, and Falstaff conducted by Toscanini, two concerts and the Alpenabend). One day at St. Wolfgang at the White Horse Inn, to swim and sun. Back to Paris and down to Cherbourg or wherever the City of Baltimore sails. We land in Baltimore and go down through Virginia, Tennessee, Carolina, Kentucky, etc, to New Orleans. From there I go to Texas and Gene to Colorado, (to see our families) and we shall meet some where on our way to New York where we aim to look in for about ten days, and so back to Paris. . . . We have three months leave, on condition that we go to our native land. Otherwise, only a month. So the trip is going to happen, and we should certainly be near you by the last of August or the first of September. Will you have gone back to University by then? I hope you'll still be at Benfolly. To see Benfolly has become an obsession with me, its now six years or more overdue, isn't it? Or five, anyhow . .

Of course, I know its pretty hot weather for travelling in the south, and what about this bus thing? Is that a good way? Of course we have not and shall probably never have, a Ford of our own. So its train or bus . . . What do you advise? We mean to take it calmly and travel light . . . We shall have no mission, we shall not collect a single impression or statistic on purpose, we are just coming home for a visit. Gene is trying to work up a little southern blood on account of his great grandfather having founded a little Presbyterian seminary in South Carolina, I think it was; I've forgotten the name of it, but I'll ask him again. Anyhow, he's never seen the south, but is in love with the idea, and doesn't want to go anywhere else . . . So I return the courtesy of being Pennsylvanian on account of General Andrew Porter of Morristown . .

You're right about Josie's second book,[85] It was such a disappointment I haven't had the heart to write to her about it. I liked the first sincerely, I still think it is a good book, and I wrote her a long enthusiastic, and judging by the quoted fragment, ungrammatical letter about it. I was a little taken aback at the sight of my name on the slip cover to this one, which I don't like at all, and the quotation edited to appear as if I had written the praise for a review. . . . However, I suppose it doesn't really matter, and I certainly told her long ago she was at liberty to use anything I said or wrote to her for publicity. . . . Hacienda will be out soon . . . Harcourt Brace is going to reprint Flowering Judas, using all the other stories too . . . I'm trying to get the manuscript together now. Brace will be here in a few days. I mean to give him tea in the garden and try to wangle a more generous contract out of him.

That's probably just tall talk, you know I shall never unless I am born again be able to wangle any real money out of publishers. The book is going to be brought out in England too, and there will be an advance, which Ford says is almost invariably fifty pounds, of which I would only get half. And that is what I shall get if I get anything at all.

—On the fourth page I decided to wind up this letter, but must say one more thing. About the reviewer who complained there was no problem in Aleck Maury's life. . . . Yes, its a symptom of something when a man's life-long battle to preserve his personality, independence, and to pursue a certain way of life precious to him, is no longer considered a problem. I had thought it was about all the problem there was. There is one point I thought about: that it would have been more dramatically defined, so that even a newspaper reviewer could have seen it, if you had brought out again, as you did in Old Red,[86] the real conflict between him and his wife in this matter: their silent struggle, hers for moral and spiritual supremacy over him, his to preserve himself intact against what is, I think, the most terrible calamity that can happen to anybody, man or woman: the invasion of one's own inner life—(and that is an inner life, no matter what the hard boiled realists say—) even by the best beloved being. By God, that paragraph almost got away. Did, in fact. But it makes sense enough, I hope. But you were right not to do it, because Aleck Maury would not be the sort of man even to hint at such a state of affairs between himself and his wife. It comes out fairly subtly in incidents; and this is not just the history of a man, but a whole order, a kind of man, and if you had him speak out of character in order to point up the dramatic conflict, it would be wrong. And I think the plan of your next book is magnificent, too! You are surely building on a pretty hefty scale, more power to you!—

Josie's people; yes, they are dreary. I didn't find them so in Pity Is Not Enough. I thought some of them had human feelings. She is best at depicting that period which touches her most; the youth and later life and old age of her mother. But you must remember what kind of people she writes about, and oh, what hundreds of thousands of them there are in America; the second and third generation of European peasants, hungry, anxious, struggling, gaining a little and getting rapacious and dishonest. Envious and really lacking feeling except of the most ungenerous kind. When I consider that this will be the ruling class in America if it is not already. . . . . It is from that class that all the foul politicians, the newly rich who are really brutal to the poor, who really respect money and power and nothing else, and use them without any scruples at all, are rising. . . . . . I'm going to stop writing. I have just discovered the serpent in our little Eden. My windows are open over my deceptively quiet looking little garden, and from the court beyond, four different radios are going at once on four quite oh quite different tunes, and all full blast. I give up. Its no use trying to say anything clearly, with both ears shrinking—Lord, what a din. . . . Well, now I know the worst. We kept wondering what we would finally discover not perfect in our house, we are so pleased with it. This is it.

Love to the three of you, I long to see you . . . Katherine Anne

To: Ford Madox Ford TLS 2pp. Cornell

70 bis rue Notre-Dame-des-Champs, Paris VI
3 December 1935

Dear Ford:

We-all were happy to have your letter, but would have been happier if the news had been better . . . We were looking forward to having a Christmas hullabaloo in the Atleay, which is good for just that, and nothing else. I have just got another piano—rented—and I mean to practise there at least an hour a day, so the gaunt painter in the red felt liberty bonnet next door will probably dynamite the place very soon, and you may never even see it—

When we see that Provence[87] was positively a best seller, we settled back with great wreathes of satisfaction hanging all over us, and thought, NOW things are all right. But we might have known. One thing in your letter struck me—can one, even in New York, ring up, bedevil publishers about checks, and really GET them? I had never dreamed of such a thing . . . My contract says royalties such as they may be are paid twice a year, the first time six months from publication, so I have until next April to soothe myself with hopes of a pretty check. . . . But of course, you do have so many books, and they must be bringing in something at irregular moments . . . . I didn't get an advance either. . . .

I'all do take interest in politics and public affairs. I always did, I cannot help it, it isn't that I expect to find the Sacred Emperor in this particularly low tea-house, it is that I am outraged at their not being anywhere a high tea-house with a human being in it ... There should be one, after all the talk.

Speaking of talk ... I spoke for forty-five minutes at the top of my voice at the Club the other day, on Legend and Memory[88] as the Sources of literature, and the papers reported me as a "rugged individualist" giving advice to young writers.... I can only say that I know better than to go around speaking, and I'll never do it again. It was all very serious and well managed and not half the ordeal I thought it would be, and afterward a dozen women came up with copies of Flowering Judas which they had bought for me to sign. Which I did. And then they fed me very nicely on young venison, chestnuts and apple tart. And then I rushed off just a little late for my music lesson ... And that is that for ever and ever.

The reviews have been very friendly, but not many of them very clear. Ford, you know that one's best friends do not listen to what one says, or if they do listen they never get it straight, so why should one be unreasonable and expect multitudes of strangers to do better? I don't trouble at all about my place. Writing seems to me to be my private occupation, my way of living. I want to write and shall keep on with it, and the reputation may fall where it shall fall. I have nothing to do with it.

Your weather sounds enticing. We have been having variety, that is the best can be said for it: Floods, lightning, thunder, fog, hail, winds high and low ... And steady vicious cold. The furnace works. I experimented with making a goose paté in crust and it was such a success, I mean to make it all over again for you and Janice.

Maybe we can go again to the Midnight Mass, fasting this time properly, and have dinner on Christmas Day, where it belongs. I don't mean altogether fasting. We could have Noche Buena salad, or something of the kind ...

I had some very damned odd reviews.[89] Friendly, all of them, meaning well but misguided. You know the distressing kind I mean ... One fellow said I have learned much from Somerset Maugham. This is the cruellest blow I ever received. I never read a line of Somerset Maugham except OF HUMAN BONDAGE, it must be fifteen years ago, and once I saw a play called RAIN, made from a story of his....[90] I almost broke my rule of not answering back. I had a violent temptation to sit down and tell that fellow that he is a gourd headed imbecile, but I have managed to hold myself. There'll be worse coming, no doubt. Some one else said my work had had a powerful influence on the young writers who contribute to STORY . .[91] They'll be pleased with that, they will. And without having seen STORY since it left Europe, I am quite willing to say its not so. . . . . This is a dull subject. Let's drop it.

Paris is cold, rainy, dark grey; I seem continually to be catching busses to go to music lessons in a melancholy drizzle, having forgot my umbrella. The weather, confound it, is all over the place. One can't escape it for a minute ... Our cat, Skipper, is a good Parisian. Pays no attention to the weather. Sits in the rain with his feet in a puddle and watches the sights, never misses anything. Runs to the top of the gate when the bell rings, runs back to tell me some one is there, anxiously leads me down and goes back to the gate with me.... He's the very nicest cat I ever knew. I enclose a snapshot I made last August. I have a whole collection of them. He loves to pose for the camera, lets me maul him around to get the best light. Stands quite still when I weigh him on the bathroom scales. He weighs eleven pounds, and is about fifteen months old. His fur is so long and thick and fine there may have been generations ago a scandal with an Angora in his family. Otherwise he has the beige and black-grey markings of the Paris cat quelconque.

Don't forget about Christmas, let me know as soon as you can. I remember that you usually came up later, but this time I heard, as I say, that you might change your plans....

Same old love and affectionate remembrance from both of us, to both of you. Let me know your latest alarums and excursions and what good luck and cheer you are having, I should prefer good news, if possible, but the real news in any case....

Katherine Anne

To Eugene Pressly TLS 4pp. WSU

April 20, 1936
In Houston, Texas

My darling, I began twice a letter to you, once just as I was leaving Boston, and again here. The first page I cannot find, but I send the second pair, for the record. You remember that I never disputed your findings in the bus travel business, but I wished to know for myself, too. Now I know. It seems to me I was not so badly done in as you were, for I recovered my spirits after a day and night in bed. Meantime, I saw kinds of people and scenes I cannot not see in any other way. Sailors and soldiers, moneyless, melancholy, one of them drunk, going home after many years' absence, on leave. A horrible crew of drunken missourians boasting of their southern blood. A nosey Indiana female who lectured against cigarettes all through Indiana. That

midsection of this country is more appalling than any other to me. Genuinely spiteful, nasty manners, petty tight faces; and the only place where
women write quite incredible filth on the station toilet walls. But really brutal, I was astonished. It would have been astonishing in a low-white section
gang's toilet, really, I think. And no where else but in these mid-states did I
see this.

Texas is pretty appalling too, in some ways. I should like to write it now,
but I wonder if you can believe me when I say I have quite literally fought,
ever since I came, for this one afternoon in which to write to you: and this
minute, just as I had everything cleared up, my niece Dorothy Ray, class poet
of her graduation class, rang up to ask me if I had finished her graduating
poem yet. . So I know well she will never be a writer, or any other kind of artist, even if I had not known it already by the specimens she showed me. Even
at seventeen a real writer would want to do the job for himself . .

The speed is unbelievable, the whole family is on wheels, three motors
in Baby's family, one in Gay's, three in Paul's; and they all simply go day and
night. I stopped with Baby first, then with sister, where I am now. Sister's house
is larger and has fewer people in it, she is a little quieter, but Daddy came up
from Mission, her son and daughter-in-law joined us, so with Anna Gay we
are six in family, and we have all talked ourselves quite hoarse . . .

Don't worry, my darling, I'm coming back by train. And by now you know
about the ticket business, so we needn't go into that. Aside from being worn to
death, I am having a good time. You are right in your notion that I can really
fall back into family life.

I have been interrupted three times since I started this, but now the
young ones are gone, Pop is down for a nap, so is sister, Niece Dorothy cannot
arrive for another hour, (I hope) so let's make hay.

As I was saying: We play the races by day, play poker by night, as we drive
the radio plays jazz or Texascowboy songs; the Centennial is in full tilt, and
the folk arts are rampant, food is good and abundant, nobody drinks, almost
no one smokes—my sisters don't, and neither of them can finish even a bottle
of beer—the young are all reactionary to an indescribable degree, full of local
patriotism and all of them leaders in their school organisation, most of which
have a military manner, at least at a parade. . . We stood modestly on the
sidewalk, we elders, and watched our young going by with their battalions,
musical comedy uniforms, trumpet corps, drum and fife corps, all snapping
along like tin soldiers, little ninety pound school girls rending the air with a
trumpet corps that out-trumpeted the marines, who were also present. Little
skinny boys stomping along with their bands playing oompah-oompah. Two
girls, two boys, from our family among them. It was disheartening, but to me

only. The others were pleased that the young were doing so nicely in their school work, getting an education ..

Cowboys from a famous rodeo went yip-yip-yeoooow and whirled riatas, while their paint ponies danced. Wobbly old Confederate Veterans went by on a float, with the Stars and Bars flying, giving their famous Rebel yell in shrill cracked voices. Gold star Mothers and Navy Mothers rode in beflowered motors. Marines and soldiers tramped. Everywhere flags and confetti. And all military. I got along very well until I heard a faint reed flute music with strange voiced drums; and about two hundred Indians, in full costume, men ahead, women following, marched by .. Darling, I do not need to tell you that my heart almost cracked. They are the last of an almost extinguished race, and their walking in this celebration was a cruel spectacle. The conquered dragged at the chariot wheel. The mob yelled joyously and waved greetings to them, and for one instant I too lost my head and forgot what this march really meant, and waved and called out to them as if I expected to be taken for a friend. They marched straight by, their heads up, a running fire of scarlet, in majesty, their faces fixed, not one gave a sign they heard, except two or three men who frowned from the corners of their eyes.

The women walked like the Tehuanas, each wrapped in the strange burning red. I did then as Genevieve Taggard did when she read my story: I wept for all of us, I could not stop myself; it was an abominable sight.

I said to Baby: "Haven't they found any Mexicans to help them celebrate the victory of San Jacinto?" And yes, they had. A whole float of them in the Charro and China Poblana, strumming guitars and singing.... I tried to imagine a Confederate soldier marching in a Grand Army of the Republic holiday, and wondered what these Mexicans were thinking about. It is no good trying to imagine.

+++++++++++

Gay has had the influenza, and is very pale and very tired. She took a few days leave, and one morning about five o'clock, she, Mary Alice and I set out for Mission Valley, 365 miles away, to visit Dad. Mary Alice drove. This is one of the most beautiful countries you could hope to see. Warm green spring, the whole land covered with gay flowers, blue bonnets and Indian paint brush and buttercups, plains crossed with rivers. Roads run twenty miles straight and smooth without a turn. We bowled along, radio going of course, stopping to look now and then at the fine world we were in, talking and singing, stopping again for coffee, Baby driving at a steady sixty five miles for hours at a time, seemed to me ... We took seven hours for the journey, being leisurely with pauses. The orange country is heavenly, the air is so fine and so sweet smelling. When we drove up, Dad was sitting, in white clothes, white hat, field boots, talking with the man who brought in his fine inexhaustible well. It had just come in that morning, after many trials. He was so engrossed he just looked up and said, "Well, what are you doing here?" The man moved away and I sat down beside him and said, "Why, I came to see you." And we hugged each other and just sat. I was very happy to see him, and he looks marvelously well. A really hale, handsome, old man, energetic as a man of sixty, more than most of that age, and his place is one of the best in the Valley. He's just unable to be an optimist, as you know. I expected to see a few withered stumps, after all his calamities. Not at all. The place looks as if three landscape gardeners had been at it . . .

I took a picture of him, which I send. There is too much light, so I over-exposed the film, but it is a perfect likeness. You see how strong he looks. We had three days there, warm bright days, cool nights; we visited a famous cactus garden, and drove in all about two hundred miles a day here and there, seeing everything. It is just across the river from Mexico, and is half Mexican, or more . . .

The well was much too good for the dams and channels that had been built for irrigating, so everything broke with a whoosh and the place was flooded; we had meant to bring Dad back with us, but he could not leave. So we drove back, and Dad and Breck followed two days later . . .

In a few days Baby, Dad and I leave for San Antonio; we are going to visit all the ancestral shacks, birth places, graves; Dad has not been back to Indian Creek since that time he took me there when I was two years old. This will be the last visit for both of us, for, as you advise me, I am going to finish up here, now, once for all. . . . It was time, and I want to do it, and certainly I do not expect to see Dad again. So we are doing everything now. . . . Baby is monstrously fat, not well, not strong, there is something very wrong with her. But she is the same forthright creature she was, and her eyes and skin are as beautiful as ever, but otherwise I look twice at her sometimes, trying to see her as she was. Gay, on the other hand, is thin as a lath, with the same mulish temperament as ever . . .

Anna Gay is a graceful, beautiful girl, but darling, she is not a dancer, and will never be. I saw this clearly the very instant she stood at the bar. She knows it, too, without being told. I cannot tell how disappointed she is, she is so shy and so reserved; a lovely young thing, I wish her talent had been equal to her work and hopes. . . .

Paul's children are all goodlooking and full of a variety of talents and bursting with energy and ambition and will no doubt get on nicely. I choose Patsy, now about ten. Paul himself is worn to death, lives in his car looking after a dozen fields, got in from Louisiana this morning at six, slept for two hours, came over to see me for half an hour, and was to be off to Arkansas this afternoon. I do not quite see how he can keep it up, but he has now, for fifteen years....

It is odd what people need. They all have pianos, radios, victrolas, motors, their own houses, farms, summer camps; they fish and hunt and take trips. There is not a really good musician among them, there is not a single book of any interest nor a page of music worth playing, in all three households—four, even. I don't know what became of Dad's collection of books. Scattered and gone.... Not a decent picture.... Not a single piece of really good furniture.... But they are all having a good time, they really do enjoy their lives and like what they are doing. There are the usual family intrigues, cross currents, sniping, jealousies, gossip; but they form a whole little society, and wouldn't know what to do without each other.... I couldn't live here, but I'm glad I came. And in many ways that I could not describe without thinking it out, I am one of them and awfully like them, in character and in temperament.... A mass of contradictions swirling around a central force of will.

I am so tired all the time my head buzzes. We leave about Wednesday for the San Antonio trip, to be gone about three days, maybe four. It is only 120 miles. Then Dad goes back to Mission, and I shall go on to Tennessee to the Tates for a Day, and back through Richmond and Washington and so to New York and there about ten days and so home. This is the best I can do for a shedule, darling. But its pretty plain I shan't catch the President Harding on the 29.....

It will be so beautiful to be home again, but I know that I am always tired in the middle of any project, and I shall not let my fatigue keep me from finishing my trip as I planned, for I shall have time to rest and think it all over afterward, and there must be nothing left undone this time. I am even having family photographs copied. One of my mother, one of myself a sulky little baby, another of Mary Alice, Grandmother and me, when I had become a sulky little infant of three ...

The weather is so hot here, I have no clothes for it. I wear borrowed things from Gay and Mary Alice. But I mean to get a cotton dress or two—they are cheap—soon. About a dollar each ... I carry the camera and take pictures, but I expect really to spread out on the San Antonio trip.

Isn't it odd, my sweet, you were a merry baby and I was a gloomy one, apparently, and now you are gloomier than I am, mostly ... Dear love, I know you got troubles, and you may be sure I know they are worth telling, and I am the one to hear them; for then we can find a way out. Your skeleton plan was good. We'll settle everything when I get home ...

There are thousands of things to say. I have to get this letter off, the first since Boston. . . . So hoping to begin another tomorrow, my only love in this world, I send you oh how many kisses, how much love, and Lord, how much plain old fashioned home sickness. This is my body's native land, but not my heart's. . . . . . . We'll find a place of our own.

I love you truly my darling, I wish I could go on writing until I could <u>say</u> it, really, but its no good. I must see you and kiss you and lie down with you in love and joy and sleep with you and get up with you and wait to see you again in the evening as I have so long, and then everything will be quite all right again. . . . . But I can't regret this long curious journey . . . It has meaning, it is clearing up something, you will see . . .

Blessed dear love, this is no answer to your last letters . .

Tuyo, tuyo
Katherine Anne

Dad is waking from his nap. I must go in now. He wants to spend every minute with me. He is very sweet. Has come to that strange benevolence of old age, tenderness, and the special beauty of eighty years. His skin and hair are finer, his eyes bluer, he has a little pet dog he takes every where with him and spoils as if it were a little human being . . . Darling, I am <u>very</u> glad I came back. It would have been terrible not to have come. I felt it would have been and I was right this once.

To: Eugene Dove Pressly TLS 2pp. WWSU

I have a small furnished apartment in a big private house, not bad—
218 West 15th Street, Houston, Texas
January 11, 1937

Dear Gene:

Today I took a step that may surprise you; I filed suit for a divorce. The grounds in this state are much more civilised than in most: simple incompatibility, or if one must, mental cruelty, which seems to me one of those useful little phrases. . . . I will send you a waiver to sign, my lawyer says you are to go before the American Consul in Moscow to sign it. I hope you will do this for me; I cannot imagine you contesting it, really, since you must know that our marriage is ended, and has been ended for a good while. I do not like the dubious status I now have, and I have plans to settle here or near here—I prefer south Texas, - I wish to plan my life definitely with no more threats of change and uncertainty, and waste and frustrated hopes.

I am here for an odd reason: I came home for Christmas, meaning to stay for a few days. I have had a violent and terrible cough, such as I had in Paris all that winter before I went to Davos. So I went to a doctor here, a specialist, who X-rayed my chest and found a well developed ulcer on my right lung extending into the bronchial tubes. He is giving me intravenous injections twice a week, and is making tests to find out just what kind of ulcer it is. So I must be here for several months, perhaps, and after that I mean to go to a dry climate to live. . . . On getting this diagnosis I went back to New Orleans, packed and was back here in four days. It is nothing to tamper with. My lungs last January were clear, and this new thing is real; I saw it the minute I came into the room where the picture was set up, put my finger on it and said, "This wasn't here last year." The Doctor said, "That's good news, we'll catch it before it really gets a start."

I have been very tired and troubled in my mind, and though I have worked pretty well, it has been against fatigue and sadness of heart. I want the rest of my life for myself, I have something to finish. . . . My dear, I hope you will agree with me that this is best. All the things you have sent me of yours, and the things in storage, I will keep for you, and I hope you can send me a little money as you planned and as I refused. Not much, and when you have it, but I am going to need it for a little while. I hope to get the Guggenheim, and I am almost finished on the story that will pay me well, but I have none of this yet. . . . .

Dear Gene, I received your Christmas present, and was so touched by it. And the lovely Breughel monograph, and all the little things you remembered that I like. Bless you for your goodness, my dear, and please think of me as well as I think of you. But you know we shall never live together again, and I think you will find it better to be free, really, to make a life of your own. This way, it is nothing for either of us.

There is just now nothing more to say. I feel somewhat better with the treatments, but I am very uneasy. Not that it matters much what happens one way or another, but I do want a little more time, and I want to know exactly where I stand, and what I can expect. The Doctor has promised to tell me as soon as he has finished the tests. . . . . I will let you know. I am sending a copy of the Winter number of Southern Review with Pale Horse, Pale Rider in it. . . . Not long ago I received a copy of a collection of American short stories translated into German, and my Maria Concepción was in it, with a very praising sort of note about me.

Goodbye for the moment......
Katherine Anne

Please don't think I believe that this illness is going to be fatal, but I do know that I shall need to be careful for some time, and of course, any talk about illness always seems more serious when ... I don't remember what I started to write, but no matter.... Please sign the waiver when it comes, and send it back as quickly as you can.

K. A.

To: Caroline Gordon TLS 1p. Princeton

[spring 1937]

Caroline, I am sending this because you probably won't be able to get a copy......
    Darling, if this review[92] is not about your book and your ideas, then I should stop writing because I no longer know what I am doing. It's a tribute to the Confederacy, all right, but so is your book. And though the emotion in the writing is mine, still I am explaining to the best of my ability what you were doing ... I meant it as a tribute all around, and I hope it will be understood as such; Book, writer, cause, and all.
    Caroline, I am a pacifist.....
    Snarl, snarl, ... I know just how that dear old general feels. I've been kicked around by militarists.
    ......I am a pacifist in this our day and time, because I do not approve of the trumped-up causes, and the munition-manufacturers' wars, and the sacrifice of millions of human lives—the best, the kind we need to keep, if the race is not utterly to degenerate—to help big countries to over run the little ones; I am not in favor of sending our men to die so that Italy can keep Ethiopia, or Hitler can get more territory. I am for a defensive war only. I am against Fascism, and against Hitlerism, and Stalinism, and I don't care much for England's Imperialist policies, either ... This country, such as it is at present, is all we have......If our luck had been better on a certain celebrated occasion, I

believe firmly we would have had a much better country to fight for. But this is the one we have. I should like it not to get any worse, if we can prevent it, and I should like it to remain intact and to develop in its own way. . . . For this I would say, yes, I suppose we must fight. It certainly looks that way. Very well, up and at 'em. . . . But I still think its a waste and a horror and I shall regret the necessity that people must die who are much better fitted to live than their murderers. . . . . . . (Item . . I am a born agrarian, and I have a good argument which I need not trouble you with, as you know it already.)

The French have a very good law. The man who strikes first is in the wrong, and automatically becomes the defendant who must explain and justify his act, or go to jail . . .

Its a very good beginning to teach people to keep their hands to themselves and to respect the human rights of others, even if they don't agree with their notions. . . . . . .

I realize that this is all very eighteenth century and Encyclopedist but here it is. . . . I am a disciple of Erasmus and Montaigne, when it comes right down to it.

K.A.

Show this to Andrew[93] if he's there.

To: Caroline Gordon TLS 2pp. Princeton

543 St Ann Street, New Orleans
October 2, 1937

Caroline darling It occurs to me I didn't answer your last letter which had your plan for the Texas student . . . It would have been quite all right, I would have undertaken the job for a smallish fee, not feeling justified in more; but she has not written me, and it seems reasonable enough that when one chooses a certain critic, just any other one won't do. . . . So I imagine that is settled out of court.

I slip this note in with my heavy business letter to Allen . . . There has not been a whisper from Baton Rouge since the first week end, you'll be glad to hear. Or I am glad to tell you. I am leaving for Texas for that wedding, later than I expected, but my domestic trials have been such, SUCH, as would be hard to describe. Gene suddenly decided to take action, went to Washington, went back in the service, tore the Perry Street apartment up by the roots and loaded it on a train—or boat, I can't make out which, and has set it down upon my neck at vast expense without even asking whether I had the money to pay for it . . . I have, thank God, but quite by accident. . . . . He has kept the wires and the air mails hot with conflicting statements, confusions; really, it has been as reasonless and mysterious as a cyclone, and I cannot put my finger on the causes or actually tell what has happened or why. . . . . But this will be the last. In the midst of it all, dire threats—of nervous breakdown, of suicide, of an immediate trip to New Orleans; strange love-letters and wishes for reconciliation, if not now, two years hence . . . The strangest kind of a break-up; and <u>it came of him not believing that I was going to stay away, just as I had said.</u> It has all been very tedious and shocking at once, and I have been too upset to think about or do anything else . . . His refusal to listen to, or believe, one single thing I ever said to him, until this very last minute, accounts for so much that I have not been able to understand until now. . . . Its really very strange, but now it is done, and I can begin to pull myself together . . . It has been quite horrible, in fact.

+++++++++++++++++++

I never have had those pictures of Nancy on the pony developed, because I am discouraged in advance, believing them all to be light struck. But when this rain lets up—it has an air of permanence you would have to see to believe—I shall see about them . . . My mind is made up to stay here, maybe for good. . . . I have all my plans made for the next year, at least; it had been my hope to have until January to think about it, but my household being dumped on me makes a sudden anchor. One can't go hauling things back and forth, no one wants to. I bought a season ticket for the Civic Symphony, first concert on the 11th of October, last one in March sometime. Now that makes me a citizen, doesn't it? And I changed my bank, or am just now changing it, after the little muddle of accounts is straightened out. I am a femësole for fair, now, forever, I hope, though there is no woman who needs a husband worse than I do. But I mean a husband, not a household pest. . . . .not a spoiled child, not an irresponsible—well, let's not go on. Its not my husband I miss, it is the mythical male being that women were brought up to believe in—the Man Who Knows What To Do Next. The Head of the Family. The Good Judge and Benevolent Autocrat. The One You Can Depend Upon. That's the fellow I haven't been able to locate. . . . . Like all myths, he must have had a foundation in fact once, but when, and where? And—this is the real question—how on earth was I, of all people, ever taken in by this teaching? For certainly I was taught it, seriously.

"Promised Land"[94] has not progressed, but I think now it may. Things seem to be settling down . . There's one pleasant prospect—now I will have all my music here when you come up for the winter months. I still mean to stay in this attic until I have finished my book, and one story besides at least, then I shall get a cheap apartment: I can get one unfurnished in this quarter, pretty decent and liveable for $25.00 a month, which I have set as the limit. A coat of paint is what all of them need; and knowing myself, it will take me a month to get settled. So I shall leave most of my things in storage and wait until my job is done before beginning that sort of thing. .

Well, my dear, I hope you are working powerfully, and that your work pleases you. . . . .

With my love to you, and to Nancy
Katherine Anne

Jackson Park is knee-deep in a grey pool—I can tell from here. I shall put on raincoat and goloshes shortly, and venture forth. I love the rain, but not umbrellas. That makes it difficult.

To: Albert Russel Erskine Jr. TLS 1p. Maryland

Saturday November 13, 1937

My darling
Having come out of my swound at least, I can begin another letter. The writing is not going well; I lose confidence in what I am doing and the thing has become monstrous to me and so it must end. If we make it, its going to be by the narrowest squeak we ever saw. I still, in spite of your telegram, momently expect to see you at the door, and the fact that nothing exists upon which to base such an expectation does not make it any the less real. It is four o'clock and your telegram just came, <u>what</u> a telegram, bless you forever.

Miss Katzelbow the poet has not made it back yet, but I wait with fear and trembling for Monday to end, hope for once you lose a bet.

Today Gertrude Stein's book[95] arrived but I don't have to do anything about it until around the first of December. I looked at it a little, and I think it is going to be very funny reading. You remember my story about Meraude Guinness?[96] Almost the first name I saw was hers with Miss Stein's own view of her painter-sailor (from Aix, it seems, not Provence as I thought.) Her travels in America ought to be something to hear about. I was at Gertrude Stein's only once in Paris with the Tates. I sat in a corner with Alice B. Toklas (who has as fine a set of mustaches as I ever saw) and we swapped cooking recipes and mange-cures for dogs; she gave me her formula for making blackberry or raspberry cordial, and I told her what to use to make her hair shine. Across the room full of horsehair covered sofas and little tables was Gertrude, surrounded by young men. Her manly voice went round and round and I never heard but one word, "perception" which flew past at intervals like the brass rings you reach for on the carrousel. One line struck me: "It takes a lot of time to be a genius, you have to sit around so much doing nothing." This was in the book, I mean, not in the rue Fleurus.

+++++++++++

Next day, Sunday Noon.
My dear love, I have read your letter so much it is quite limp. One thing to remember: I want to see the very bas-reliefs you worked on when I come to Baton Rouge. . . . . Darling, time hurries, even when we are not seeing each other. Not counting today, which is half gone, there are five days only instead of your eight, which sounded so hopeless. That is not time enough I am afraid for me to do what I must do before I see you. I wish I had twice my energy, I am tired and everything is an effort. But that has nothing to do with anything much, it is to be expected and I must use what I have. I learned this from the French who are so admirable about limitations, and so sensible in most matters, so I adapt as well as I can their state of mind.

I am going out to mail this now and then back to my typewriter. Darling it would be very nice and very consoling to me if I could tell you how much I love you, and maybe you would like it too, but I think it takes more words than I have, and maybe you will not really know until next year or the year after, and maybe never. So I am not going to worry about that, and you mustn't either. You know well that I do love you, and as you said, it would be a pity to sound like Mrs. Browning. . . . . .[97]

With all my heart your very own
Katherine Anne

To: Caroline Gordon TLS 3pp. Princeton

Kean's Apartments, Chimes Street, Baton Rouge
May 7 1938

Dearest Caroline:
This apartment we "located" was, is, just the little two room bath kitchen affair which harbored Albert during his bachelorhood, in those intervals

when he had not given up in despair and sublet it to the first-comer. Lease runs out first of September, thank God, and meanseason we go about stepping on each other and saying "sorry," and stuffing things in closets where they get lost; but at least we have a southeast exposure, and our hopes.

The actual wedding ceremony was one of those highly secular affairs beginning at eleven o'clock a.m. with drinks—Planters Punches, three all around, in the St. Charles Bar, now a wreck of its former self with Surrealist decorations—a bar quelconque, en effet[98]—Red was best man, of course, and so by logical sequence, C.[99] was best woman or whatever that rôle is called; Wedding party, decorated with lilies of the valley to which was added three pink roses to the shoulder knot of the bride, erupted out of dusty cars before the Court house (Palace of Justice to New Orleans) on Royal Street, where we interrupted the judge who was trying an all-negro case. We walked through a dark cloud of witnesses to a small room beyond. Red noted that we had an unusually large number of faithful family retainers on hand. The judge came in, a little busy Jew with—I don't know where he got it—a pure East-side accent, informed Albert that the license had been issued in Baton Rouge and the ceremony committed in New Orleans, that would cost him a dollar extra. To which Albert consented cheerfully. He then asked me the date of my divorce. I replied it had been granted ten days before. There was a sinister silence. After which the ceremony proceeded without incident except that Albert answered I do and I will indiscriminately three times out of turn, so that when my time came I barely mustered up one feeble I do, also no doubt out of turn. But the judge seemed to consider the matter as legally binding, we signed papers, got out of there and took our lilies of the valley to another bar for another drink. I have a broad gold ring and Albert has a long document to prove that the event actually took place, befogged as we all undoubtedly were . . .

We stayed in new Orleans two days, then decided we should be burning leaves and chopping weeds at the Cares,[100] and came back; and Life, or anyway, living, goes on with a pretty steady cheerfulness, to put it mildly. I expect gradually to dwindle into a wife (remember The Way of the World?)[101] and being a husband sits very gracefully upon Albert who remains quite as he was, which was quite good enough.

Red is in the throes of finishing his novel too.[102] I am also in the throes, but have been so long it is no more a matter for comment, I just try, faithfully, every day, to work a little. This place is too small for hired help, I do everything myself and it takes time; but little by little I expect to know what to leave undone, an art of itself in my situation. We go to the Cares in our Willys coupe (26 miles to the gallon, hosanna) and dig and sweat and labor mightily, but make very little impression on that wilderness. That there can ever be a house there seems improbable, it makes my head ache a little, too, but a house we must have and it is to be there. Its that or rent forever, and here, houses are scarce, small, expensive.

Your New York trips sound exciting just the same, I shall be glad to see that place again, and some friends there, but the chances are slim for the moment. I am going back to Olivet[103] in July, Albert may come for me and we shall drive back around, and that will be vacation, no doubt. By then I hope to have a book off my mind, and some Guggenheim cash in hand. Wasn't that a pretty little surprise? I had no hopes at all, just half heartedly applied some time last fall. It is going to be a help.

The last three moves I have made have been the occasion of desperate threats and more than rash vows about what I would do to myself and my environment if ever I must move again. I have moved and nothing has been damaged except my belongings, nobody hurt but myself . . . Now there was at first vague talk of taking a house, sending for the furniture, setting up a half-household while we waited to build. But no, I won't, and there's an end on't. One final grand slam of a move, and I hope to be carried feet first out of that place in a very distant future . . . Now Caroline, you know well how much weight my hopes have in the matter. Still I record it.

+++++++++

I saw a photograph of Edmund and Mary Wilson somewhere or other; reading a book together, as was fitting. Books in the background. This is frivolous of me, but when I think of Edmund Wilson I think of I Thought of Daisy, and wonder how any woman could read that and not be frightened off afar . . . Or maybe Miss MacCarthy is a mean enough little girl to enjoy his befufflement. (That was a typographical error, but it seems to be the right word.)[104]

++++++++++

As to Flaubert, his influence, I read Bouvard and Pecuchet, and Madame Bovary,[105] at about fifteen, went on reading them at intervals until I was past twenty, never read them again. But during that time I read Wuthering Heights at least a dozen times. As I remember, at that period the cleanly coldness of Flaubert's style, his famous detachment, repelled rather than attracted me; Emily Brontë was my notion of a novelist.[106] Do you know who influenced you, really? I don't. My whole life from the time I learned to read until my twenty fifth year was one long orgy of reading, and one of the most difficult questions ever asked me was: "Who are your ten favorite authors?" It was so difficult I simply didn't try to answer it. I know this—I never read any work of any author earnestly in the sense of hoping to get something for my own writing from him. Hopelessly frivolous in that: I just read for pleasure . . Somewhere, somehow, no doubt something soaked in, or I hope so.

Bibi Fellow sounds enchanting, you know what I thought of Vili in spite of what Vili too apparently thought of me....[107] I could not but respect such constancy and depth of devotion in his nature, but it did make things difficult for the bye-stander at times. Never will I forget the time you left him in my care for—was it three days?—and he refused all aid, comfort and assistance except now and then a snack when I was not looking, and for the rest, howled like a ghost at midnight..... Such intensity makes most human beings look fairly washed-out emotionally.

This letter has been going on in fits all day. First one thing and another—lunch—visit to doctor, callers—Tinkum Brooks, her mother, sister, and Jean Albrizio,[108] surely the nicest person I've met in a long time—and then Albert comes in, and there is dinner, and for hours we have pored over house plans, and now it is eleven and bedtime, and not one stroke of work have I done.... Nor have I finished this letter, of which more tomorrow ... Good night ...

Tomorrow is here, and it has been as busy and disjointed as yesterday. I manage to read a little, too—things as dissociated as Ransom's The World's Body and Gide's Voyage to the Congo.... I had read the last in French, now in English, stands up fine in either language.

This afternoon we are going to the Cares. A good rain here for two days, so we may transplant Bermuda grass from the corn field where it is a nuisance to the place we hope to have for a side lawn, where it will be a delight....

Still, it remains that I share Andrew's wish to "get away from everybody," or "it all" not because I think that is a desirable way to live always, but because it is the only way I ever get any work done. I have been trying for ten days to catch a few solid hours, but it is hopeless, I'll just have to look about and discover a hidey-hole when I really make up my mind to finish something, quite as I always have done.... I shall ruin my story if I work on it in patches after it is finally ready to march.... How many good stories I have spoiled and thrown away on that account. After all, the supply is not unlimited, I think I'll try to save the rest....

+++++++++++++

Your old ladies—what luck they have, with their privacy they don't need at all perhaps......

++++++++++

Must stop, get into overalls and rubber boots, gather up hoes and machetes and get to the country....

Your news seems good and cheerful, I hope you are all in good health and spirits. It would be charming to see you anywhere, in Greensboro, here, at Benfolly, in Connecticut—you seem to be working eastward little by little, and I do think the change of scene is good if only for confirming again your own choice in such questions as <u>what</u> scene you will have. . . . . In general, I think it can be said that, where ever I am, I can think of fifteen or twenty other places that I should like to be, so a change of air really does me no good. In many ways this is a pleasant place, and if I can live anywhere it should be here. When I remember how I used to sit in Switzerland and yearn for Louisiana, I hardly dare be anything but damned pleased I am here. . . . At any rate, I never in my life yearned for Switzerland . . .

Good bye for the moment. Love to Allen and Nancy and love to you. Let me hear from you. Albert sends love (actually, what he said was, "Tell 'em hello" but I feel my translation is quite exact.)

Katherine Anne

To: Josephine Herbst TLS 3pp. Yale

901 America Street, Baton Rouge, Louisiana, March 21, 1939

YOO HOO, Josie, First day of spring, darling; and here the day is half gone before I had time to think of it. . . . And having thought of it, I remembered that your last letter had said you were going on to Florida where you would drop me a line in a few days . . . Like a noodle, I am—or was—still waiting for that line to send your letter direct instead of all the way to Pennsylvania first, or to your publishers as I do with this one. I wish you were here, or I were there . . . In fact a wild notion was in my mind that I might rush down to Florida for a week with you. Wild, indeed. I rush nowhere, as usual. At any rate, we are in the same publisher's catalogue at the same time for once,[109] and are you surprised that I finally pulled myself together and realized I had a book all this time if I would just break down and admit it? I'll swap you one if you like. . . . . .

I am half way through a full length—or nearly—novel, that short novel Promised Land kept growing and spreading; I have just let nature take its course, which I should have done from the first.

Where will you be from the latter part of April until the latter part of May? I expect to be in the East, having at last been given a pretext for getting there. To be visiting conferee, or whatever, to writing classes in half a dozen colleges, Vassar, Olivet, Bennington, Shipley etc., the scheme being that I am to stay two or three days at each and give a little advice to the classes. No idea of mine, Josie; it was all worked out at Vassar, but I am pleased, because it will bring me east for a little while, and I'm not nervous about the work because I have trained in for two summers at Olivet at Joe Brewer's College. . . . I hope you will be at the Grist Mill, or in New York. Do let me know.

As to other things, I have grown a little benumbed by events in Europe. I don't trust any country but Russia to stop Hitler; I don't trust England at all under any circumstances, and as for France, already half-fascist to put it mildly, Daladier[110] has at last succeeded in getting the powers of dictator which he wanted. I notice—a mere detail no doubt—that his first act was to get the new forty hour week changed back to the old sixty hour, for high patriotic reasons, of course. I fancy that after the workers have been put back about where they were, Daladier will go on taking slaps from Hitler, and France will descend to a third rate power where Germany has always wanted her to be. My hope is that the workers won't be so easy to set back as they once were. But I cannot say I have a great deal of hope about anything. I think Hitler will go on up to the border of Russia and stop there for a while. When he moves again, it will not be towards Russian territory.

I wish I could see you and have a long talk. This is all too much too complicated even to try to mention it in a letter. Do let me have a word saying where you are; if you cannot come through here on your way back, and I wish you could, tell me where you will be later, so we may see each other. We have a tiny apartment, but could put you up a night or two, if you could stand it, on the front room divan, quite in the old New York style of long ago, among struggling literati. . . . We have a good cook named Bertha, a good woman who is really a saint. I mean literally a pietist who puts her beliefs into daily practise, but she isn't smug. She is big and warm hearted and the joy of my life and likes being around here. So we wouldn't have to worry about keeping house, Bertha turns that out with a twist of the wrist, murmuring hymns in a fine contralto, and laying her plans to educate her children. The other day something happened to upset her at home, she was telling me about it, and said, "Honestly it almost made me mad—but I know I should even say that word in a whisper to myself". . Think of a soul like Bertha's in this methodically brutalized world we live in. I think of her a great deal, with immense respect.

She isn't simple minded, either. She has all the natural wit and common sense and understanding anybody needs, self taught and well taught, and both feet on the ground even if her spirit does enjoy the upper air. And a lovely sense of fun; and says, when we play Mozart on the radio: "My, what sweet music that is." On her account I can work regularly every day, and I do. Her son wants to be a doctor and her daughter a trained nurse and I'll bet they make it.

It seems odd to have your book reviewed with Dorothy Canfield's,[111] I have seen it done twice and its strange company for both, with all the advantages on her side. . . . I don't hope for much this round, though H-B and Company have promised to give me a little advertising. The local scene has been buzzing with reporters and camera men, and <u>Time</u> sent reporters and a camera man, then wired to a newspaper man in New Orleans for more stuff. He called me by long distance and interviewed for an expensive forty five minutes, saying he was going to wire the interview to Time. All of which merely makes me nervous. I still think authors have a right to a private life and I hate their damned personality sketches. I also know that if reporters get a down on you they can be very nasty. So I tip-toe along on this thin ice, trying to avoid a show-down, which would make it all seem much more important to them than it should be. If people would only buy books and read them and let the writers of them alone. But I suppose that would be eating your cake and having it too. I wish I <u>could</u>, I'd love it. In this particular, it may even turn out that I <u>can</u>.

Tell me how your book goes, how you feel about it now. I'm awfully anxious to see it. But yes, even more anxious to see you, for the book will always be there, but you are very hard to get hold of nowadays.

With my same old unchanging love, Josie and tremendous hopes for your good luck and good health. I suppose by now you're hard at work again, and I hope so.

Albert is in his quarterly flurry getting out the spring number. A really fine feller, you'll like him, I do believe.

Good bye for the moment,
Katherine Anne

To: Caroline Gordon TLS 4pp. Princeton

1050 Government Street, Baton Rouge, Louisiana
June 9, 1939

Caroline darling:

Your big fine letter came when I was in the uproar of getting away for the spring barnstorming tour, I re-read it on the train and again. Since then, I went east to Vassar, Bennington, and Shipley—the Bryn Mawr annex—on to New York for visiting, back here after five weeks; and within less than a week of arrival, found myself moving, lock, stock and barrel into a house. I had my stuff sent on from New York where it had mildewed in storage for two years. We found this nice spacious rather shabby old raised cottage, five big rooms, kitchen, bath, halls, porches, a sizeable yard planted in a random sort of way with camellias, magnolias, arum lilies, camphor trees, flags, a rose bush or two, a bamboo thatch, a vitex, a wild cherry, and so on and on, all completely out of hand and each trying to push the other off the lot. They will have to carry on the war without interference until I can get this house straight. Oh God, how trash accumulates.... I hadn't time to weed out in New York, couldn't decide what I might need, so all of it was dumped down upon us here, to an outmoded gas heater and bath tub from Paris, complete with plumbing fixtures, and big taps saying <u>chaud</u> and <u>froid</u>. But my little spinet is intact and beautiful, I had forgotten how solidly comfortable my beds are, I was delighted to see the big mirrors and the 1850 English armchairs on rollers,—oh well, all the bits and pieces. The pine furniture looked like something fit for packing cases. But it is scrubbed and waxed now and cheers me up again. I hope to God we stay here indefinitely. No question of building, simply out of the question. For what we could afford to pay, we could get only a dreary little shoebox of a house. I like this pleasant old place with high ceilings and plenty of outsize windows and tall green shutters. We'll just go on paying rent for awhile.

+++++++++++++++

Albert proceeded Master of Arts at Vanderbilt and is now getting ready to proceed Doctor somewhere else. I said, NOT at this place. He did a fine piece of work. He is tired. The other day he played his first game of badminton in two years, with Duncan Ferguson.[112] I watched and they were a good team. It was amusing to see them work back into form in about three quarters of an hour.

+++++++++++++++

The tour was a success, it seems, because it is to be done again next year, but for two months at least; about a dozen colleges have engaged me—two days work with students at each—and I expect to hear from more. I am charging one hundred dollars flat at each place, and they don't seem to mind. It is the most gruelling work I ever undertook in my life, more concentrated than at Olivet, even, and the constant lunches, teas and meeting strangers is enough to scare the life out of me, in memory and in anticipation. But the money is handy, and the colleges seem to take to the idea. The idea, by the way, was not mine, but the inspiration of the head of the English Department at Vassar. She started it and the whole thing grew out of that first engagement. Next year I will go in February and March.

If we don't get to see you this summer, we will meet again next spring in the East. The Princeton thing seems pretty good the way you have it arranged, with still a toe hold in North Carolina. I heard you were at Princeton for a little while this spring, but it was mere rumor.....

7:30 A.M. June 10

I started this letter yesterday, it is morning again and I am trying once more to live through a day; the end will find me blunted, numbed and speechless with fatigue; since the fifteenth of April I have been an ox on a treadmill, one ox on a treadmill with three or four levels all to be kept going at once. It has been such a mixture of catching trains, talking to crowds, meeting strangers, trying to wedge in a little work, running to appointments with editors, publishers, photographers—and then here, a simple matter of lifting and pushing furniture, housework of all sorts, and so on and on; I feel damaged for life, yet I know a week of, not rest, but diminished activity, would restore me—or nearly. The uphill road does grow steeper steadily, doesn't it? I shall be scaling a cliff with finger and toe nails before I am through, at this rate.

+++++++++++

I must do four promised articles, get some work on Promised Land, and then dive off to Olivet. Promised Land is going to be done by late fall, though—hot or cold, it leaves this house in November . . . For the present, I am feeling very well about the way it comes on.

My cousin Lily Cahill was in New York, in a beautiful apartment over the river in East 72nd Street, elegant as ever, looking like a little sketch in Harper's Bazaar; Gertrude the Beautiful was visiting with her, and I visited too. They gave me a cocktail party; twenty five or thirty persons dropped in, such a mixture as Carl van Doren, Jean Charlot, Rose and Manson, Glenway, George Lynes and Monroe Wheeler; Paul Rosenfeld. . . . I can't remember whether there was any one else you'd remember. Jared French and Paul Cadmus, two awfully good young painters. . . .[113] The book signing party at the Gotham brought out a real mob, bigger than Atlanta, even. I still think the author has enough to do to write the book, I object deeply to going on the road selling it afterward. Mr. Brace said, "How do you like being famous?" I said, "I shan't value being famous until I am so famous no one would dare insult me by asking me to sit in a book shop autographing my books so they will sell." I mean it, too.

++++++++++++++

Edward Donahoe came to a party Glenway gave for me; he was awfully gentle and pleasant, invited me up for a week end in Connecticut, but I couldn't make it. At that party he was a kind of link between those friends of mine, and Albert. The only one who knew us both.

++++++++++++

Let me tell you about my birthday, because it was so nice I think it should be the last official celebration. George Platt Lynes took a fresh set of photographs of me. He gave me the works, lights and backgrounds such as he uses for his five hundred dollar sittings, and turned me out in such a style as you will not believe even when you see the prints. Birthday present. Then Monroe came for me and took me for cocktails in the back room of the Plaza, a real masterpiece of 90ish interior decoration, all fluted pillars and wrought iron. We then took a carriage through Central Park and drove up to 89th Street slowly through the declining day. It was that kind of tone. We had dinner there, the four of us, (Glenway added and dear old Henry McBride,[114] for the reason that he is a love in his ancient years.) Then Beulah Wescott, Glenway's sister, came in and a few other friends. Glenway played her accompaniment, she sang a whole group of my favorite Schubert songs, and ended with another set from my French song book. . . . . If I ever had a pleasanter birthday I don't remember it.

==============

I went to the opening of the Museum of Modern Art; was a guest at one of the fifty odd dinners arranged before, all over New York, with international hostesses, and guests drawn from positively every land and level under the sun. This was Monroe's idea (he is head of the membership committee for the museum) and it worked wonderfully. Six thousand people came to the opening, and complained bitterly about the crowd. I saw and spoke to Peggy Bacon, William Gropper, Brancusi,[115] Ezra Pound, etc .. saw in fact about two hundred old familiar faces. The show was really good, too, as I discovered on going back in the morning a few days later . . . The building is fine for its purpose, all glass brick and indirect lighting. .

And so on. . . . . At Shipley I followed Auden,[116] and it was rather hard going because Auden wears mismatched shoes and lets his hair go wild, and was altogether the ideal figger of a literary man to the girls; they wouldn't believe I wrote the book because I looked and behaved, so far as they could see, like anybody else . . . Mildred Lynes,[117] head mistress, told me they wanted fearfully to work up some sort of lurid past for me, and had I belonged to that Lost Generation in Paris? At the Gotham Book Mart I followed the party for "Finnegan's Wake," and had echoes of that. Good God, I almost forgot. Mary Rose Bradford of New Orleans cornered me there, the most appalling female I ever encountered, barring not even C. . . . .; and I had to fly to the cubby they set aside for me, and ask to be rescued. This was done.

++++++++++

I missed Erika and Klaus Mann,[118] they were out war-mongering, as usual. It annoys me the way our distinguished refugees fly from the wars and woes of Europe and at once begin agitating here to make a shambles of this country, too. Damned short-sighted behavior. Here is a rather anti-Semitic joke going the rounds of New York: The Jews naturally would like to see the ears beaten off of Germany by some country, they don't care which; and their theme song is "Onward, Christian Soldiers."

++++++++++

Red is off on the first lap of his Guggenheim race. To Nashville. C. . . . . . saying she is ashamed of him getting such a low appointment, and that Nashville is going to be a terrible bore. And announcing to the papers here that most of their vacation will be spent in Italy. On another page of the same paper, interview with Red, announcing that most of their time will be spent in Nashville or at least America. He must do research at Nashville. C. . . . has lost her job in the University, says thank Gód now she can get some writing done. Low gossip, but low facts.

++++++++

It is almost impossible to think of your grandmother as dead. She had such a deep vitality it must have been a great wrench that snatched her out of life. I couldn't imagine her letting go easily.

++++++++

Good heavens, I haven't begun bringing the gossip up to date, but it can't be helped. This must stop. Meantime this morning I have had breakfast, read the morning mail, seen Albert off to office, talked to Bertha about dinner, and now must go to work. I now have 72 unanswered letters, but they must wait.— Just this minute something occurred to me about the summer. I must be two weeks at Olivet. Joe wants Albert to come too, a manifestly impossible thing.

Why couldn't we drive to Monteagle[119] a day or so before, let Albert visit there, I go on to Olivet and come back for another day? I haven't said a word to him, I just this second thought of it, so it may not be at all feasible, either for you or for him. What do you think? He has no plans for vacation or visiting or anything at all . . . May have to go to Memphis. Hasn't been for a year and a half.

+++++++++++

How is Nancy? Odd thing; that remark she made—what a serpent child—about your reason for using the time shift is exactly what Glenway Wescott said to me years ago in Paris about Ford. . . . "He <u>has</u> to use that oblique method simply because he is a man incapable of telling a straight story." That is something that no one could ever say of you, no matter if you chose to write in the shape of a chessboard overlaid with interlocking circles. . . . You <u>can</u> tell a straight story and, time shift or no time shift, do tell one. But Nancy has undoubtedly many times witnessed incidents with you, and has been mystified by your account of them afterward, not having seen at all the same thing, not understanding symbolic truth or the art of presentation. Oh, the young. . . . . I have been so tangled up with the young in the past few weeks, it is a heavenly relief to get back to the adult mind again; no matter if the adult mind is probably as muddled as the young mind, still it is a muddle I can see my way through. But Nancy always seemed to me far beyond her years as to mind.

+++++++++

Well, goodbye for the moment. Please don't owe me a letter but write when you get to it. Paul Rosenfeld sent you his devotion. His very word.

With love
Katherine Anne

My book went into its third printing six weeks after publication, and they tell me it is selling steadily, and may reach two or three more. . . . . I hardly believe it, even though I did see the figures. And HBC[120] seems to be advertising it quite a lot, nearly all in the New York publications, though.

=====

Gret God, one final word . . . About the hindsight of my young people in Pale Horse etc . . . We really did feel and talk that way; and I have had many letters from persons who knew me then, saying never had they read anything that gave a straighter account of the way the young people were talking and feeling and behaving towards the end of that war. Remember, we were all reading Siegfried Sassoon[121] and the other war poets and listening to the dissenting voices from the Left Wing and from the Irish revolutionists, Some of us were cheering our heads off for the Russians; that is the way it was, my dear, in my company and situation. I was threatened direly twice by the Lusk Committee[122] for not having the right attitude towards the war. And as for Alexander (Adam)[123] when I was ill I said to him: "Isn't it strange. Here we were so certain you would die first, and after all, I am the one to die." We were completely fatalistic, by accepting death in advance I think we hoped to cheat it, somehow . . . And some of us did.

Part Three

1940–1949

The 1940s was a decade of shifting foundations for Katherine Anne Porter. Bolting from Louisiana and Albert Erskine (and a marriage that was over before it began) to the security of the artists' colony Yaddo, she faced a string of losses that began with the upheavals brought on by the Second World War. When her beloved Paris fell to the Nazis in 1940, she lamented to Erskine, "[I]t is the end in my time of a world I knew and loved and from which I drew strength." She had a terrible feeling about the war even before the United States was shoved into it in 1941. "We are in for a period of unmitigated evil," she wrote Erskine, "in some ways the worst in the history of the human race, and it may well last our time."

Between 1940 and 1949—while grieving over the death of her father and her divorce from Erskine, buying and selling a farm near Yaddo and a plot of land in the high California desert, ricocheting among Yaddo, Washington, D.C., and California, criss-crossing the country in a string of appearances on college campuses, indulging in one brief but serious love affair and one fantasy affair, and trying to find purchase in her chaotic life—she continuously refined her political positions. She leaned more left than right and was more Democrat than Republican, but in the 1940 presidential election she considered "throwing away a vote" on the Socialist candidate Norman Thomas. When her story "The Leaning Tower" was published in 1941, she said that rather than having applied hindsight to the setting of her story, she had acquired her basic knowledge of European politics in Mexico in 1920–1921 and had felt the "infection" of Hitler in the Berlin air in 1931. When the war ended in 1945, she saw other threats emerging in the cold war. In 1947 she remarked to Josie Herbst, "You know I don't like Communists, the American brand. But I hate to my bootsoles the Fascists who are doing so successfully what Hitler did: using the popular fear of Communism to cover the trail of his intentions, giving the people an enemy to distract their minds from the worse and real enemy in their own country."

One result of her intense contemplation of the world war and its aftermath was the crystallization of the theme of her long novel-in-progress, the first pages of which she had written at Yaddo in 1940. "My book is about the constant endless collusion between good and evil," she wrote to Herbst. "I don't offer any solution," she said, "I just want to show this principle at work, and why none of us has any real alibi in this world."

At the same time, she clarified her view of art, coming down on the side of Eliot and Pound: "The experimentalists," she told Monroe Cockrell, "seem rather embittered with those of us who believe in the great unbroken line of development in all the arts, in all life." She had embraced Henry James's definition of art, "a game of skill," which means "courage," which means "honour," which means "passion," which means "life."

She also was becoming more outspoken in her views. "Isn't it odd," she wrote Herbst, "how after years and years of saying nothing, under a certain pressure you find yourself blowing the cap and saying what you really think about somebody or his work or both, because they are most certainly related, if not one thing." Part of her candor encompassed her support of younger writers she considered promising, whether poets such as Theodore Roethke and Harvey Breit or fiction writers such as Eudora Welty. That generosity had become part of her modernist code of morals.

To: Albert Russel Erskine Jr. TLS 2pp. Maryland

Yaddo, Saratoga Springs, New York June 18, 1940

Dear Love:

What do you mean by "Your other letter"? Have you had only two?

The mail seems so slow, and your air letters don't seem to travel much faster than the ordinary, and I have a vague feeling that I never get any kind of answer to my questions; it occurs to me that probably I didn't ask them, but only thought them; or that you have never received the letters, etcetera. It is one sign of the general emptiness and acedia that sits upon my spirits . . . ah, yes, I did feel badly, and worse than that, about Paris, and nothing could exceed the way I felt yesterday. But I have written you and by now you have my letters perhaps, so now, today, I am really trying to overcome the pain and out-live the blow. This is not the end of the world, I tell myself; but I do know it is the end in my time of a world I knew and loved and from which I drew strength. This is not the end of the world, it is only the end of my world. The furies really have arrived, and the terrible thing about it is that they did not come uninvited.

I have been trying also to examine my state of mind about war, and it has been a fearful strain, for after every argument has been disposed of, I know that very deep in my mind is a perfect knowledge that if France had crushed Germany I would have felt the whole war well justified. Yes, that is true, that is the way I really feel. I am at that point now where I would be quite willing to die myself in the next effort to beat them. I hope this government will act at once against every Fascist and Nazi organization in this country, stamp them out here and now without any hesitation: and they should be rooted out of South America, now, and suddenly, and by force. It would save us a great war, but it will not be done. We will have the war instead, and it could be prevented now. . . . . . I would shoot without even thinking about it any one who tried to break into my house at night, and I would root up and throw out any individual in my personal life that I knew was insinuating himself (or herself) into my affairs and my interests to undermine and ruin me. And I feel now the same way in the larger question. This is a badly managed country, and we are a badly governed people, but I have believed always in the autonomy of nations; it was not Nazism in Germany or Fascism in Italy or Communism in Russia that I objected to: it was their efforts to undermine our system of government, it is the presence of their agents in this country living off of this country and working to destroy it. I have never believed that democracy should go so far as to tolerate that, and I believe so less than ever. . . . We should stay here strictly on our own grounds, but send the Fascists and Nazis away. But as I say, nothing will be done for any good reason. Power politics will decide this country's fate as it has the fate of the others...... Russia and Germany between them now control Europe and the Balkans. Japan is their ally, and we are arming Japan against ourselves. As you said about France, England and United States combining to re-arm Germany because it was such a good market they couldn't pass it up, so our war-merchants can't resist the fine Japanese trade, either.......... Some fellow here the other day told a funny story about the taking down of the Sixth Avenue EL. The scrap metal was of course to be sold to Japan. He remarked that it was all very well to be sentimental about the disappearance of the dear old El, but we'll feel differently when it shoots us.

Your letter was written on the night of the fourteenth, day of the fall of Paris,[1] and you say: "It is after twelve, after two in Yaddo. If you aren't asleep you should be. . . ." curious co-incidence. You must have had a hunch. You know by now that I was anything but asleep, for later on some one told me it was nearly three when we got in from that evening in the bars. I wish I had been with you instead, <u>both</u> of us sitting in that blue chair.

Give Nell and Jane[2] my love when you go to Memphis, tell me about the young nephew, and meantime, tell me about yourself. It seems you are having another rainy summer like the first one we spent there together— remember that long season of rain and terrible heat, and terrible suffocating unhappiness? I simply don't remember it except as something long past..... I would never have dared hope then that we might come to the feeling we have now for each other; I truly do love you, and you are my dear faithful friend besides.

Good bye my darling for the present. I love you.
Katherine Anne

To: Albert Russel Erskine Jr. TLS 3pp. Maryland

Yaddo, Saratoga Springs
New York, August 26, 1940

Dear darling:
    That there is no news here at all may be good news for you. I have gone back into my own life and closed the door; there are still sounds from without, and it takes a little time too for my mind to arrange itself properly to its own state once more, but still I am quite safe for the moment, I think nothing

shall happen soon to drag me forth again. Its wearing, this constant effort to keep a balance, but still I do reach it now and then, and something gets done.

The weather was warmer today, and at midday I flattened out in the hay-field for about two hours; the light here is beautiful now, the colors all changing very softly and gradually. I thought about the book, and then came in and wrote down what I had been thinking about.

I would like to have about two months of the year full of action; going about, seeing all sorts of people and things, doing readings, and all managed so well it could be done and finished in that time: and so back to quiet and inwardness for another ten months. I should like a place finally and once for all my own. But it may not happen. In my journals I ran across several allusions to Rainer Maria Rilke, when I was reading his poetry in German with my teacher: and lately I am reading his <u>Letters in War Time</u>.[3] Do you know, <u>all</u> his life he wanted a quiet place of his own, but he never had it. He lived as he could, in borrowed houses, in rented rooms, in several countries, and died in a friend's house in Switzerland; but he did get his work done, really finished. His example gives me great courage. The measure of all deprivation is <u>need</u>; and what might have been a fairly adequate life for another sort was for him a terrible form of struggle. Still, he won, and it was a fine victory. And millions have died for nothing since and we don't know their names, but we have him forever.

+++++++++

Perhaps we might say, it is a lucky being who has a friend's house to die in now; Ah, yes, of course.

Your account of August weather in Louisiana makes me think the world is coming to an end. Some one here last summer, a playwright, a Communist one, I can't remember his name, was saying that weather-students—what is the scientific name for them?—seem to be discovering that modern wars change the weather, actually the constant heavy explosives change the air currents, the seasons run at odds; this is the kind of theory that sounds fantastic enough to be pure old-wives' tales or cold scientific truth: to one so uninformed as I in such matters, the scientific mysteries have a lingering air of miracle about them.

+++++++++

Please do send me a copy of Burke's book,[4] I am so anxious to see what you have made of it. Write something in it for me. Don't forget.

I have hardly seen the newspapers, this afternoon David Diamond[5] passed by and stopped long enough to remark that it was wonderful the way the British were holding off the Germans; so apparently yesterday was an important day for them. And what you tell me about the "wealth-conscription" bill is

most remarkable. The only thing that I cannot understand is this: the "100&
(if they can get it) patriots" have so utterly exposed their hand, so cynically
and shamelessly declared the true purpose and motive of this war, you would
think that every man liable for conscription would simply revolt; you would
think there would be millions of them going toward Washington to protest
together. But no, not at all, now or ever. (I happened to notice my 100& above.
This keyboard is known as Author's Keyboard, and the designer was quite
right: the average author has no need for a per cent sign.) What I wait to hear
next (again) is that labor must cease its selfish demands for shorter hours and
more pay, and must tighten its belt and get ready to make patriotic sacrifices.
That comes next in this dreary, all-too-familiar routine. And also, that the
income tax exemption has been lowered to $500 a year, and taxes must go up
at once. . . . Well, business has this country really by the throat, and won't let
go until it hears the death rattle.

+++++++++

A man got on the bus the other day, on the way to Bread Loaf,[6] with a
tabloid newspaper; I saw huge headlines, Trotsky is Dead,[7] and a photograph
of his mangled, bloated face and bandaged head in death. It is strange, a man
was willing to risk his life to kill Trotsky, but not one has appeared to destroy
Hitler, or Stalin, or Mussolini, compared to whom, Trotsky was quite harmless. I know you will add to my list a British Prime Minister or two, but assassination would be quite pointless in a country where after all, they had only
to put him out quietly, and send him down to the country.

++++++++

The German White Paper[8] came today. I shall read it shortly. I wish we
could have all the Color-papers from each country. Just for comparison. Of
course the full records can't be published now, may be never. . . .

++++++++

Truth is, darling, I have no hopes at all. We are in for a period of unmitigated evil, in some ways the worst in the history of the human race, and it may
well last our time. The little good there is will go on, but there is not enough
for the present; but we must still plan and live and feel as if things were otherwise, or at least, that they might be, may be yet, much better. I shall try to do
some good work. And you will too.

Good night, my dear darling. I love you.

Katherine Anne

P.S. Diego Rivera is the same unscrupulous opportunist he always was![9]

To: Albert Russel Erskine, Jr. TLS 2pp. Maryland

Yaddo, Saratoga Springs, New York, October 18, 1940

Dearest Albert: How you must have changed since I saw you. And for the worse darling. You must have turned red-headed over the draft? But the last time I saw your eyes, they were a light tawny tan with quite definite green spokes around the pupil, and little occasional flecks, mustard color, the whole effect being of a very pleasant and of course I thought perfectly beautiful, hazel. And your hair at times (in the house, or at night,) was a kind of polished tan leather color, edging towards straw at the temples and neck, and in the light it was just a mixed, bright straw-blonde. Very handsome. And your complexion was a fine sunburnt olive the last time I saw you, no matter what they seem to think has happened to it since. They should have let me fill in that part of the document.[10] However, it is not so bad as my passports used to be. I would describe myself meticulously, even to the little scar in my left eyebrow, and the passport would come back; Description: Eyes, medium, Hair medium, complexion medium, distinguishing marks, none. And in this disguise I used to land safely at foreign ports.

One of the notables of the draft of course was Mr. Oscar Levant,[11] who got into an argument with the registrar about his complexion. He said, "swarthy." She said (it was a she) it was sallow. They compromised finally on "ruddy," a word they like perhaps because it connotes health and spirits and fitness for service.... I have seen the full questionnaire published in several newspapers, and thought of sending it to you, but it seemed likely it would be published there, too. Well, my darling, you are a character in a novel by Kafka now,[12] and so are we all. I saw the little note from our President, also. It did seem rather the last straw.

About voting: it seems I can't vote after all, anyway, you'll be glad to hear. I lack not quite two weeks of the proper time of residence. I hope you will believe me when I say, I was wavering when the moment seemed to be approaching, and was thinking of throwing away a vote on principle for Mr. Thomas.[13] I too am sick of the main candidates, it is no choice at all, except, yes, I'd rather see Roosevelt win than Willkie,[14] but I'd like best to see Norman Thomas in. What do you want to bet that when and if we go to war, Mr. Thomas is going to jail? Mr. Debs,[15] Socialist candidate, did the last time, and maybe that is one tradition that won't be broken. I do wish now I had a chance to prove my good faith by voting for Thomas, but maybe you'll feel easier to know I'm staying in the farm house that day, the nearest substitute I can find for woman's proper place, The Home. Elizabeth[16] is keeping open house on Election Night, and I'll go there for a little sprightly listening in on the returns and watch the Willkieites faces as the news comes in. <u>Maybe</u>. Yaddo is pro-Roosevelt to a man or woman, now that the last Pro-Thomas crowd has gone home. But all up-state New York is just moss-back Republican come weal, come woe, and no back-chat. What I am doesn't count because I am not a good citizen: I have no vote. My own fault, too. And yours for not registering properly long ago. One more vote for Thomas, two more, would help …

It is lovely to know the records sounded well, and as for the radio—well, you never seem to get anything else for yourself, it seems to me little enough to have a new radio. Its a progressive affair, though—do you remember the modest little cash-on-the-barrel-head one we got first, in America street? To say nothing of your pint size portable in Chimes? And now way up to a One.[17] I too wish I could hear it.

About the Bach concerto: I loved best when I heard it the slow movement for just the two pianos, so perfectly blended it sounded like one, though I suppose a pianist would need four hands to play it alone. Today, Elizabeth sent me an old fashioned hand winding Victrola, and David brought me an arm load of records from the Skidmore library—some Mozart quartets and Monteverdi and some Schubert songs, so I've been having music too, today, and it does make a great difference. I know I am writing badly and dully, but my tooth has begun to make trouble again: I put off the dentist until after the Skidmore thing thinking I could make it, with the treatment, and I can, but in fact it is a miserable business. Don't worry about it, though, for by next Wednesday I shall have relief of some sort; permanently, I hope. Mean time again I am not able to work, I simply can't. I had meant to read the stories here, but I shan't be able. Instead, I am going to read the whole manuscript of The Old Order, and one other thing if there is time. I have been lying down mostly, reading, or maybe just lying down, and "missing you more than I can say," too, but still occasionally (what are words for? or must I decide that writing is a useless trade?) trying now and again to say how much, and making a very poor thing of it . . In missing you, I miss just about everything: maybe that will do for the moment. I feel sometimes that in writing you, I should try not to say much about all such things; for it may trouble you, and you cannot answer, because you "do not like to talk about it." I do understand this in you very well. Our temperaments are fairly different. And in this situation, quite different things have happened to each of us. Oh, darling, I'm quite worn out with this too—but I think it is not useless to say, I love you, nor to love having you say it to me.

Now I must stop because I am tired and don't see the keys very well. To bed and to sleep. I'm delighted to know the S.R. is on its way, I <u>like</u> that magazine … If you'll give me a latish deadline, I'll get a story in the December number, cross my heart. It is rotten luck about this dentist thing, but there would be something—maybe there always will be, I'll do what I can in spite of. My story is very horribly melancholy, a real Season in Hell,[18] but if it is good enough, let's not mind. The Berlin story is melancholy too—and the third one scares even me.[19] But I don't suppose that any one of them are really any worse than Noon Wine. And you told me once that was the most "painful" story you knew. By the way, some one wants that for another textbook of literature. Published by Ginn and Company, but the textbook writer's name not given. It would appear that in my life time I am to become one of those authors students hate because they had to study the works in school. I hope not.

Good night, my dear darling. I'm going to my nice warm bed and sleep, sleep, sleep until tomorrow. It is only eight o'clock, so I think a huge bath first. Absurd how delicious such comforts seem at this moment. When I am ill I feel so unbelievably lonely; I don't want to complain to any one, but just to have company. I am going to stay with Josie Herbst this time, she is always so good to talk with: I go on liking her with firm friendship, year after year, and she is always the same with me. She is having the devil's own time with a book just now and I don't feel any too good about not getting my stories done, so you may well imagine we shall have a fine cheerful time thrashing out the mystery . . .

Darling, my dull letter is no return for your dear good one, and that I wanted so badly to write to you is no excuse. Don't mind it, I am really quite all right, and shall do much better very soon.

With my same love, your very faithful
Katherine Anne

To: Theodore Roethke TLS University of Washington

Yaddo, Saratoga Springs, New York
March 10, 1941

Dear Ted:

Your book[20] came a day or so ago, I have only just looked at it to see what they had done for you in the way of type, margins, paper, and what you had done by way of arrangement. It all strikes me as a fine job of work all around, I am going to read in it for a great while from time to time as I do read poetry. . . . . At this very moment I find myself in a real sweat of anxiety about finishing my novel, time is simply exploding around me, it no longer runs orderly and smooth at a fair pace. But I do know I am capable of sustained effort, and I depend upon that second wind I get at a certain point of exhaustion. So I'll make it, and do pray for me, too. Blasphemy? I think not. I can pray for you sincerely in what I would consider perhaps the only legitimate pretext for prayer: If God will not help a man to be a good artist, then where does He use His powers? As to your fate at the hands of critics, perhaps that comes under the head of worldly <u>biens</u>, maybe praying for that doesn't help, but still I am willing to try. . . .

I agree with you and with our friend the poet in placing John Peale Bishop first or in first rank of American critics, either of poetry or of prose. But never would I be so rash as to say, in this country which has and has had for some time the best critical writing in English, that there are only two. There are a number of firstraters . . . Tate, Blackmur,[21] Warren, Wilson, Bishop, to name my first choices among perhaps a dozen, and any one of these five can give our poet his come-uppance if he starts scattering his personal likes and dislikes under the guise of critical or poetic principle. Believe me, I know that by habit writing people do not behave very well to each other—the critical wars are another version of the perpetual dog-eat-dog of the human race. . . . . Therefore all the more important for the individual able to think a little to have an extreme sense of responsibility for his words and acts. . . . . . and oh, how distressingly tactless and blundering so many of our new citizens-to-be are. They dash in, opinionated, full of snap-judgment, and begin stepping on the nearest toes right heartily. . . . . There used to be very bitter criticism of certain kinds of Americans in Europe, just criticism, too; the badly behaved ones were taken as the type, the others were ignored. . . . . I am afraid we are going to get all this right back in our laps. . . . . Here, the second-rate, pushing, brazen opportunist European is going to make a nuisance of himself and harm all the others with us, just as the same kind of American used to do in Europe. . . . Take a look at the list of writers merely from France alone: the Bernsteins, the Maeterlincks, (well, Belgian) the Chadournes, the Dekobras,[22] and a host of nonentities hardly less pretentious, <u>all</u> are here, adding to the muddle. Valéry, Gide, Aragon, Larbaud, Duhamel,[23] where are they? In France, where they know they belong, and where, if anything can save the spirit of that country, these spirits can. . . . .

There is this about us, dear Ted: no matter what happens, <u>we have no place to run to,</u> here, and now, we must make our stand and see things through. I for one am most grateful for this. Here we must live and die; and we none of us can escape the responsibility for what life in this place shall become. Believe me, I lived in Europe for years, I loved living there, and may I say in my own defense that I lived there working in silence and with a sense of modesty as a stranger who wishes only to accomodate myself to life there, and to disturb nothing. But this I know: Europe has its own vulgarities, confusions, its own kind of baseness, also. And I think we do not need those things added to our own. . . . . . . Surely we still have the right to choose what we shall accept, and what we shall develope as our own . . . And indeed I have a very definite point of view about this sudden stampede of noisy and vulgar strangers who were no good to their own countries and will bring no good to this one. . . . . And it is going to work such hardship on the good and valuable people whom we should make welcome, and do not—often cannot, for they cannot be seen or heard in the uproar created by the others.

Well, this train of thought has gone rather far away from its starting point; but to tell you the truth, I would like to repeat the compliment to John Peale Bishop, and shall if I am permitted to change it a little to a simple word of praise as a first rate critic: but J. P. B. would resent the notion that there are only two good critics of poetry in this country: he would name you quite a list of his own. . . . . After all, our dear poet, who, I believe with many others, is a good poet, doesn't absolutely <u>know</u>, so he shouldn't be so rash. . . . . . But more power to him as poet, and to you and the whole brave company. . . . . . . I hope everybody gets on with his business without trying to be Messiah.

++++++++++

"Saving America" of course is now for a great while going to be a free-for-all scramble. I hope it will not sound too severe if I say that all these people who could do nothing to save Europe, should be appropriately discreet in their efforts to help save this country. . . . .

++++++++++++++

I have just made an act of faith equal really to having twins. I have bought 105 acres of land with a good sized house and a small house on them. It is a good solid house, no architectural jewel but honestly made in its time, which was 1780. I am going to move there in late spring, as soon as the novel is finished, make renovations and necessary changes, and live there I hope for the rest of my life. The soil is good, well watered, there are woods and fields, and I am very happy planning it and thinking about it. . . . This is a good part of the country, not too picturesque but very pleasing to look at, a fine climate of four well defined seasons. I mean to dig out one of my trout brooks into a good sized pond suitable for, and tempting I hope, to wild ducks. The government will send me the eggs if I will get them hatched out and be responsible for the fledgelings . . . I can't eat them, though. Its part of a scheme to re-stock this country where everything has been so shamefully wasted and mis-used. I shall have sheep, too, and turkeys and pigeons, but not this year. I shall plant flowering trees all over the place. . . . . . anything that thrives here. . . . I have plenty of room for a tame deer, but I must first get a good fence so he will be safe. . . . same for the sheep, who are so timid they never thrive if they are once frightened by anything . . .

+++++++++

Well, as my good friend Glenway Wescott says of himself, "I am a loose fool" for daydreaming here when I have still nine sections of the novel to go in six weeks. . . . . So here is an abrupt stop. . . . . . Best of luck to your book, to you; give my remembrance to Bravig and Valeska, and to their dear Jane who is a real little person on her own already.[24] Bravig exaggerates, bless him the kind of exaggeration no one could mind: but it is true I fancy myself as a cook and Bravig can afford to be generous, for (this is true) I think he is a better chef than I am. But then, we are both pretty good. (Amateur cooks are not expected to be modest. They are a braggart kind.) You are good too. Perhaps you forget how I ate? that was a beautifully planned, most successful dinner . .

Thank you for the name of the wine: I shall get some at once . . . A friend is leaving, I mean to have a farewell dinner: sweet breads with mushrooms, sour cream and white wine sauce, with quenelles and a dash of estragon . . . So I'll get that wine for it. . . . .

All good wishes to you
Katherine Anne

To: Morton Zabel TLS 1p. Chicago

Yaddo
Saratoga Springs, New York
December 27, 1941

Dear Mr. Zabel:

Your lovely card and note made me very cheerful indeed, for the festive season found me in general a frustrated and contentious woman. I meant to have a little picture of South Hill on a postcard for my Christmas card, and the difficulties I ran into in that simple matter damned near got me down. After two failures, I just took what I could get in the business, and sent it on. You can see what the place looks like, at any rate, or did, on December 10. It has gone on a little from there . . .

The arched space will be closed with small paned glass like the windows, there will be green shutters, the arched room with fire place is paved in lovely soft colored flagstones from Vermont, and the court outside is paved also, with space between the stones for grass and little rock plants. . . . . I hope you see it some day, and will visit me there and sit before the fireplace in a high backed chair and have eggnog or whatever the season calls for.

Marjory[25] told me some time ago you would like a copy of that photograph in the HBCO catalogue, and I have taken steps to get it and it will be on soon. . . . It is lovely to know you like it. I chose it from a great number of poses because it resembles the grandmother I am named for. Her very look and posture. . . . I should love to be like her, and when I saw that photograph, I had hopes . . .

By now you must have the evil news about the Southern Review.[26] Suppressed, finally, once for all. On grounds of reducing expenses. When I think of all the hundreds of thousands of dollars that University has poured down the sink in its filthy activities, I wish to protest, to tell the bitter truth, somehow to get their skins for what they have done . . . You know how many enemies it had there, and they have never given up hope of destroying it. . . . They have used the emergency of the war as an argument, and their victory is a most sinister beginning of what we must expect from every side I imagine. . . . . It chills my blood a little, it was so prompt and accurately timed, and they had been waiting a long time for some such chance . . .

I loved the Review dearly, it was such an act of faith, such a work of love and disinterestedness. . . . So it must be the first thing to go in these evil times . . . I have cried over it as at a death and it is a death. . . . .

The announcement of the contents of the Yeats number came: it is going to be wonderful, a real blaze of glory for the finish. I mean to do something I don't know what, to be in the last number as I was in the first . . . . How well I remember my eagerness to make the first number and resolved that was a deadline I'd keep if it was my last act. I made it, too. . . .

Yes, I prefer my first title, but there were so many arguments against it, I gave way. . . . .a mistake, maybe. . . .[27]

May you have a good New Year; health and good fortune to you with all my heart

Katherine Anne Porter

To: Cleanth Brooks TLS 2pp. Yale

Yaddo, January 9 1942

Dear Cleanth,

The issue (re VWB et all)²⁸ stet! is precisely what you say it is, and what has been done to the Southern Review is precisely the sort of thing that school of thought would like to do to all such as we . . . Will indeed use the war as pretext, excuse and shield. . . . Oh, boy, have I got sumpin to say? Tell me more or less how many words. I imagine Two thousand would be enough, maybe fifteen hundred, maybe what? Let me know. I can't give the title yet, because actually I haven't focussed on the point of attack, but I will get there on time, don't worry. . If you have any idea of what some of the others are going to bear down on, you might suggest to me some point to emphasize, to avoid repetition.

The Yeats number is magnificent, the real word for it. Nothing better could be imagined, and everybody seemed at his high level best. As usual, I admired Zabel, heavens, what a civilized mind it is, T. S. Eliot was intelligent and cagey, Blackmur, Ransom, Burke, Tate, oh well, ALL of them, simply hauled off and made a first rate job of it. This sun does set in glory.

One thing strange: that refrain 'I am of Ireland And the Holy Land of Ireland'²⁹ which runs like the basic theme through the whole collection of essays, haunted me from the first, it makes my hair rise. It was the point of that poem, the reason for its beauty and meaning, and I thought it was the greatest refrain Yeats ever wrote. . . . . . and at this late day my ignorance is rebuked; I don't mind, ignorance should be rebuked—but for some reason it made me happy to learn that that song was old and known and part of the common memory of Ireland; I'm glad Yeats didn't write it, for this way, it belongs to everybody. . . .

I could love Yeats if only because he loved Dean Swift. I am apt to be fond of persons who are fond of (1) St. Augustine. (2) St. Francis. (3) Joan of Arc. (4) Sir Thomas More. (5) Dr. Johnson. (6) Dean Swift.³⁰ Why are those my particular loves and heroes? Some of them would gladly have burned some of the others at the stake. But I feel some mystical quality, or element, common to all of them, maybe I could name it, but it is enough to know it is there. . . .

Hello to Tinkum, with my love. I must get to work, time's a wasting. . . . Let me know as things happen. I should like to sign something that was going to the General. . . . . . Or give me his name and address and I'll write to him. I feel that simply General Hodges³¹ isn't quite enough.

Love to you both
Katherine Anne

To: Gay Porter Holloway and Harrison Paul Porter Sr. 1p. Maryland

Yaddo, Saratoga Springs New York January 24 1942

Dear Sister: Dear Brother Paul:

After all the rage and hatred and anger, and the last weakness and fear, it is ended; and tonight I looked at the cold stars and the half-moon in the deep sky, and could think only of our little, old sad father lying alone for the first night in his grave; and he seems to me like my own child, as if I had grown very old and he was newly born again ... And this morning I saw the first sun he would not see, and though we had waited for this day, still all day my mind has been suspended, blank, and my heart full, as if I were still waiting, as if something else could happen. But it will not, and now I hope we can go our ways in peace and forget some of the evils we have known, and that the old grudges will die; remember how grandmother's children turned away from her grave and hardly saw or thought of each other again, and no doubt were better for it. . . . They did not love each other; there is something loveless in us; and it is a terrible pity.

The telegram came at half past two this morning.

I sent Talisman roses because those were the roses Dad chose to take to Mother's grave when we visited it together that spring when I first came home, and he said, "We used to have these in the yard," and he said, "Its a pity they must fade so soon." So it seemed to me his rose.

Tell me something about the last days if you know about them. Death is not an unhappy ending, it is simply the end. It is only unhappy for the living who remember what went before. . . .

I can think of nothing but the little tired man folded away to sleep and to go to dust forever. . . . . . it makes me very lonely and tired too.

With my love, I hope you are well.

Katherine Anne

To: George Platt Lynes TLS 3pp. Maryland

South Hill R.D. 3
Ballston Spa, N.Y.
July 8, 1943

George darling:

If I were there, I'd hope the gayerty might go on as it does, if it is not to your ruination, which you seem to think it may be. It would be heavenly no less to see you, but I am up to my ears in deadlines, and you know my kittenwits can't take much distraction. If I get out and start pleasuring myself, literature gets derailed for God knows how long.

I miss the little virginal,[32] but then I missed it for more than a year now, and it is very consoling to think it is in order, being cherished and played again. It demands, in its offish little way, to be tuned and played upon every day, really: Marion is very nice to share attentions with a foster-child, considering how absorbed she is in her own. Meanwhile, now and then I spread the music before me and totter through Lord Zouche's Masque or Wolsey's Wilde[33] on the edge of the table, a dull thumping noise being all for pay, but I at least do the fingering and the rhythm . . .

I am driving better now, in a slaphappy way; and my Cousin Lily is sitting out under the maples this minute reading Proust, which makes the place seem less a hermitage with briars growing before the doors. I am up here making the last copy of my James essay which should have been out of the house a week ago. In another day it will be gone, blessed be. I love James dearly, he is my great admiration, but he makes me feel like an amateur, and at this stage of my career perhaps that is not a good thing for me. Besides being the most complete artist of his century—unless Yeats can edge up for place—oh <u>how</u> he was a <u>writer</u>, in the sense that apparently he wrote all the time . . . So I crawl through my little piece about him feeling very crestfallen and insufficient, which of course may be good for my soul. But I'm fed up with having things good for my soul. Darling, I do deliberately plan, when I am through with this round of things, to come to New York and see everything and everybody (you know who) with not a deadline hanging over my head . . . That will be something new.

It is full summer now, with tiger lilies blooming wild all over the place, and little green grapes with wild cherries and tiny apples beginning to show up. The whip poor wills still yell in at the window. Traffic on the road is very congested now: about four cars a day; the nests are full of squalling naked birds, and the landscape is simply a horrible warning about letting nature run wild: all blousy and out of shape like an old fashioned trollop.

Our Victorian Gothic radio died on us, and as we do not take in a newspaper, and haven't been to town for a week, we really couldn't say what goes on outside: nothing whatever goes on here, though, and do wish for me that this little state of things doesn't change until I am over my deadlines ... After that, the more change the better ...

With my devoted love; do save a few fragments of your being for when I get there: an early grave is not your style really, it isn't becoming to you and you won't like it.

Love again,
Katherine Anne

We have got a bottle of good Bourbon in the house—that's news. I almost forgot: Who is Peaceful Allen? Any kin to Preserved Smith?

To: Margaret Bishop ALS 4 pp. Princeton

Good Friday [April 7], 1944

Dear Margaret,

John so young in death has been in my thoughts all day, for I believe he looked upon me as a friend, even though not a close one. And I was reading in my favorite collection of poetry and copied out for you Prudentius' Burial of the Dead—

I wish I had written to John but I did not realize the seriousness of his illness until I saw your letter to Allen a few days ago. All my sympathy to you

Katherine Anne

The Burial of the Dead
[Humnus circa Exsequias Defuncti]

Take him, earth, for cherishing,
    To thy tender breast receive him.
Body of a man I bring thee
    Noble even in its ruin.

Once was this a spirit's dwelling,
    By the breath of God created.
High the heart that here was breaking,
    Christ the prince of all its living.

Guard him well, the dead I give thee
    Not unmindful of His Creature
Shall He ask it: He who made it.
    Symbol of His mystery.

Comes the hour God hath appointed
    To fulfil the hope of men
Then must thou, in very fashion
    What I give, return again.

Not though ancient time decaying
    Wear away these bones to sand
Ashes that a man might measure
    In the hollow of his hand.

Not through wandering winds and idle,
    Drifting through the empty sky
Scatter dust was nerve and sinew
    Is it given man to die

Once again the shining road
    Leads to ample Paradise:
Open are the words again
    That the Serpent lost for men

Take, O take him, mighty leader
    Take again thy servant's soul
To the house from which he wandered,
    Exiled, erring, long ago.

But for us, heap earth about him
    Earth with leaves and violets strewn,
Grave his name, and from the fragrant
    Balm upon the icy stone.

Aurelius Prudentius Clemens
348–c.405 A.D.
Translated by Helen Waddell

Copied by Katherine Anne for Margaret
on Good Friday, April 7 1944 in
memory of John Peale Bishop.

To: Orville Prescott ALS 3 pp. Columbia

[Letterhead: Hotel New Weston
Madison Avenue at 50th Street
New York 22, N.Y.]
September 19 1944

Dear Mr. Prescott: Ordinarily I think it the most unprofitable thing in the world to question any critic's view of my work: but in the case of your review of The Leaning Tower,[34] I hope it will do no harm to say, it might have been better if you had known something of the history of that story—First, I have not been "politically unconscious" as the saying is, since I was twenty at least. In Mexico, in 1920–21 and surprised, I got a good view of European politics, for the Mexicans are much more informed as to what goes on in Europe than are Americans, usually. I learned to hate Mussolini long before I ever saw Europe, or heard of Hitler. I recognized on sight what Hitler was driving at, in 1931, when I was in Berlin. At that time I wrote to the editors of several magazines here, offering them articles about the Nazi movement. Nobody believed, nobody was interested. The notes for this story The Leaning Tower, were made, and most of the conversation in the café written in Berlin in 1931-2—and in Paris 1933. I wrote the story from these notes in 1940, It was first published in 1941, spring. You seem to think I am writing from hindsight. Dr. Canby[35] tells me an Austrian friend says I must have brought it up to 1931. The state of mind I could have found light years earlier in Berlin. Alas, he is wrong too—The story was based on what I found in Berlin in 1931, and oddly, there was then very little talk of Hitler. There was only the infection of his ideas in the air, and the most familiar remark was "what this country needs is a Mussolini, and Hitler looks like the man."

Yours sincerely
Katherine Anne Porter

To: Charles Shannon TLS 1p. Maryland

[Yaddo
Saratoga Springs, New York]
21 December, nearly midnight 1944

Charles my dear: This note is for you and so tear it in little bits and drop it in the wastebasket.

Today being the shortest day of the year and the winter solstice, it happened also to be the first day I had time to burn my letters to you. I burned your letters at two o'clock A.M. in my own room in a horrible fog of drunkenness and nightmare, threatening everything here with being burned to the ground. But mine to you I burned in the little stove in my cabin, in a beautiful clear winter light, along with a lot of other rubbish, poking them up to make them burn better, without any regrets at all.

I have been just packing up again—things seem to consist of taking things out of suitcases and putting them back, nowadays—and tonight I have been reading poetry and a very nice piece about Henry James, whom I love, and there was this quotation from his own writings: He says, "Literature" (we may say, any art) "is a game of skill," since "skill meant courage, and courage meant honour, and honour meant passion, meant life."[36]

It is so reassuring I send it on.
With my same love,
Katherine Anne

To: Herbert Schaumann TLS 2pp. Maryland

House Address: 333 25th Street, Santa Monica, California
12 April 1945

Dear Herbert:

After finishing the first volume of Chin P'ing Mei, I am pulling myself together to begin the second.[37] Being only a real westerner, and a woman at that, I am a little exhausted with the crescendo of erotic sadism, whippings, tricks about money, thefts, murders, amorous cheats, deceits, and suicides. If this were all I knew about China, I would prefer, if by hideous fate we really are to be born again and again, to settle for a peaceful civilized life as a woman among the head-hunters of Borneo. I can see, (dimly, dimly) how you might like to be reborn Chinese, but as a woman I must decline the privilege. And after all, you would have to be Hsi Men; you wouldn't want to be any other man in that book, would you? And yet, even Hsi Men. . . . . . Is that an enviable fate? He is pure scoundrel, and yet look what fools his women make of him at every turn . . . One of the most interesting things about the book is its wonderful slow cumulative tempo. Step by step, or rather, woman by woman, you see Hsi Men, and the women, coarsening, grossening, the affairs one by one grow more sordid and dirty, the petty crimes grow into great ones, the human feelings (such as they were, for they are pretty poor in the first place) are gradually blunted and finally brutalized altogether . . . Its really a terrifyingly moral book, isn't it? Ever now and then I would have to turn back to Monkey for a little refreshment and reassurance.[38] But then, I always turn with relief from the Satyricon to Horace, let's say. In fact, I haven't seen the Satyricon for years and probably never shall again.[39]

This is the literature of decline and death, and I realize something about China that I had not before: that its period of decay set in several hundred years ago, about the time when England was producing William Byrd and Shakespeare, and that they have produced very few things or men of any importance since. Still, believe me, I prefer them to the Japanese. But in general I have no leaning at all to the Orient; and if I had to be born again I would want to be a woman—of high station in life, of course, otherwise one would be a slave—in almost any period of Greece from—well I'll settle for Heraclites or Pericles.[40] But I do not want to be born again at all. Once is quite enough. And when this is done, I hope for eternal oblivion. I think when the anima escapes from the body, it might very cheerfully join its native air again and forget its identity. What I should like is that the human identity, here and now, should be acknowledged, recognized, and treated well.

My thirteen weeks option will be up in just nine days, and I have been hoping they would not, as the saying is, exercise it. So afraid did I become that I went privately to my producer[41] and told him that I was certain this work was not good for me, that I did not in the least belong here, and I hadn't got the time to spare doing the wrong thing, even for another month. And I asked him to let me go. He was fairly thunderstruck, said he was sure I would feel differently if I would stay on. I said, that was the point. I couldn't stay on . . We talked it over a little, and of course, he agreed to let me go. A little while back when I said something of the sort, he hit the ceiling. So I am afraid we just agreed between ourselves, and then I broke the news to my agent when he came in next morning. He was also agitated, and immediately began talk about placing me somewhere else. I explained, and it took an immense amount of explaining, that I was not going to do any more work for the moving pictures, anywhere at all, any time. I think they've got it all straight now. I have been very thrifty and have saved quite thousands, and shall be quite all right. I shall stay on here for the climate and the doctor until I am altogether well. He has told me I will never get well if I go on with this work. . . . So, I hope you feel much better. I do . . .

Paul's[42] last letter was rather depressed: the 9th had got stymied in a spot and had to stay there to look out for counter-attacks, and they were all completely bored, wanting to go on forward. He said the only bearable thing is action: the minute they have to stop, everybody goes into nervous tension. Truth is, they think now they can see the end: and it cannot be made to come too quickly for them. By the news today and yesterday, he must be feeling much better now, for they seem to be going forward without much opposition. He said that the ruin of the cities is complete, there simply seems to be nothing left worth trying to build up again. There is this to be said for it: I hope everybody, above all the Germans, will have to stay at home and forget about war and preying on other countries for a while, and build up their cities again, and make a government that human beings can live with . . .

I think your part of this war has been in a way more difficult than that of the men who are now going towards Berlin and Tokyo. You cannot now imagine what it would have been like, but you would have been better off in the midst of it. I never heard any solider before going over but said he loathed the whole notion of what was going to be required of him. But you see they are doing very nicely indeed. And so would have you . . . and your whole feeling would have been different, and better. . . . . news and pictures keep coming in showing the treatment our captured men have had in Germany, worse if possible than in Japan, and it has had the effect on me it should have, was meant to have, and I believe on a great many others: the last soft spot in my heart for the Germans has hardened and for good. I do not in the least care what becomes of them, the people or the country.

Oh but think, this war might end soon . . . even our war in the Pacific. It turns out, doesn't it, that we are fighting two wars: one with Japan alone, and one in Europe with the Allies. The Allies never seem to notice this, I must say. Even most Americans do not seem to realize what we are doing. I must say, as a military performance, it is not bad. And by figures I read from somewhere—War department, I believe, at least two-thirds of our armed forces are in Europe. Yet we have enough for Japan, too. But it would be nice, wouldn't it, if our Pacific war goes on longer, if the Allies would help us a little? I am afraid they will find plenty of good reasons not to, but still I can hope.

I look forward to the next few months here, settled in this house, free to finish the novel and also a short novel I have on hand. Then for a handful of short

stories. Wish me luck. It could happen. I think you do miracles ever to get a line
of poetry written, and I do wait to see what you are doing. I wish you were out
of the army, but ah, so do I wish for about 9 million others, for this is a weariness
of the soul to all of us, and none of us can flourish until all of us are out of this. I
sit here safely making my plans because somebody else is giving his life to make
it possible, and believe me, my sense of obligation and guilt will end only with
my life … My dear, I know what things are wrong with this country. But at least,
we have another chance now. Think what it would have been if Hitler and Mussolini could have done to this country what they have done to their own and so
many others. We are not as free as we should be, but if we aren't, its our own fault.
We can be as free as we will. I am sick of the suicidal, maggoty-minded Europe,
and I can see working here busily all the same elements: all these fraudulent
refugees—I can see especially great numbers of them here—who have brought
their sickness with them, and they infect the air.....

Tonight I am going to see Katherine Dunham and her dancers:[43] a very
lively performance, if it is anything like what she used to give. I am not a
palpitating savage, and have no intention of trying to be, and the excitement
about negro art bores me a little, but just the same, its very interesting dancing, and worth seeing.

Yours,
Katherine Anne

To: Herbert Schaumann TLS 2pp. Maryland

333 25th Street, Santa Monica, California
11 May 1945

Dear Herbert:
Among all the many thousands of quick thoughts that flashed in and out of
my mind, no doubt a little dazed by the inordinate fire-works of recent events,
one came back, as if it meant something more than just itself—How Herbert
will get out of the Army. You won't be the only one, thank God, (I have some
hope, but less, for Paul) but it does seem reasonable (as if reason had ever had
anything to do with ANYTHING in these past years) to suppose you can't be
really needed if you ever were, any longer .. Do tell me what your prospect is,
I shall be keeping you in mind.

We have all been put through so many and such various kinds of feelings
lately, I shan't make any attempt to say anything about them. But at any rate,

half of the bloody mess is finished, and the Russians really did get to Berlin first on foot, though by arrangement after our Air Forces and the British air force had reduced it to a pulp. You cannot know how pleasantly pure the air feels in this world to me to know that at least Hitler and Mussolini and a few minor infections are out of it, and Berlin is destroyed.... It frightens that they didn't shoot Goering on sight, but then, you know the truth is, we have some native Nazis, and they are some of them enormously rich and powerful, and they have been dealing with Germany all along, and Goering, though he is a horrible clown, and comic even now in some perverted way, is also dangerous because he can practice some very pretty blackmail ... I am just hoping now that some one man or a small group will, after a decent interval to give the authorities a chance to show good faith, just dispose of him quickly as was done with Mussolini. We can lose this peace again, but I think not so easily and completely as we did the last time. But at least the shooting has stopped, nobody else need die in Europe for this criminal enterprise; (except I hope about five-hundred Nazi and Fascist leaders) at least we gained the first point, without which nothing else could be done, a real undisputed military victory. So we can all breathe easier for a while. We aren't any of us going to be put in local Dachaus after all.

+++++++

My birthday is coming soon, do you remember the funny party I had in Washington?[44] This has been the longest year of my life, and in many ways the most difficult. Even those situations you might think would contrive to ease life a little, bring along with them some complex means of making it harder. That other birthday was pleasant enough for personal reasons, but this one seems to have nothing personal in it to speak of: yet it is a better day than that other, and I shall be happier to see it ...

++++++++

A good while ago I finished our Chinese novel, and the second part is so much finer than the first, it is astonishing. There is a kind of tragic weight and progression in it. ... of course, the first half was all preparation for the second, which is good enough strategy in more things than literature: in fact, it is almost natural law, isn't it? The most impressive thing is that terrible procession of spirits announcing their return to life again, and the scene where Moon Lady's son is taken ... It is quite wonderful. Now I shall wait a while, and read it again, and it will be more absorbing in the light of what I know....

You never did write me about Apartment in Athens.[45] I reviewed it in the Herald Tribune, rather hastily but as clearly as I could. Glenway is some-way not a novelist, but I approved that book with all my heart and mind even though it is flawed somewhat. He called it his "war work" and so let it be that if he likes, but it is a good deal more, and I hope a great many people may read it.

I have been reading a great deal, too much, and practicing—I can never say playing—on the piano, and working but fitfully, not in the right rhythm at all, on a story. Still uneasy and unsettled, as if there is too much unfinished business in the world which concerns me for me to attend to my very own . . . I know, I still do know, the proportion of things, but I am not strong enough, or is it self-centered enough, to do my own work just now. I hope my mind will turn that way again for good, and soon. But I am pulled too many ways at present. I have been here 17 weeks and two days today, much too long, really, since far from settling, I just now begin to feel it is time to be going somewhere else. But uncertain where to go, what to do when I got there, I cannot imagine. So I shall stay on here until something happens to take me out of the place.

This letter must end. May it find you looking outward very hopefully towards some life of your own again: really you have earned your citizenship in this place if ever a man did, and perhaps you don't even want it now. But look around you at countries available. This is not the best of all possible places, it is only for the present the most possible of all places, so be reconciled so far as you can. You have had a trying time of it, but you might have been smoked in an oven years ago, and I for one am glad you were not, and I am going to believe that you are too until I hear to the contrary from you.

Do write me, my dear. When everything is fairly shuddering on the edge of enormous change, again, again, let me know how you are, and what happens to you.

With my love
Katherine Anne

To: George Platt Lynes TLS 2pp. Maryland

201 South Bentley Avenue, Los Angeles 24
California
2 September 1945

Dear George:
    At last and on the very right eve, I broke down and celebrated a little, not believing at all this war was over until I heard the proclamation. A nice funny sort of young man who interior-decorates night clubs here[46]—or did before

the Army snagged him—took me to dinner at La Rue's, where there was a fearful mob. Then we went on to a party at one of the fabulous Hollywood "estates"—all Neo-Spanish with grill-windows, and wandering all over a huge amount of territory with a wonderful view from the top of a high hill. I knew their names last night and they are very pleasant youngish people. I cannot tell the age of people here—the mother never looks more than five years older than her grown-up daughter. There were about a hundred people scattered all over the lawns and the long, open cool rooms, and every single one had trade-mark names—you know, like Atwater Kent.[47] For some reason that is the only one I remember at the moment; no matter. But it was dull. My young man doesn't drink and neither do I, and really nothing was going on but that. So we straggled out discreetly as hell about half past 11 and went to a little night club called the Gala, run by one Baroness Erlanger for her boy-friend Johnny who sings . . .[48] I remember her name because she was in some way muddled up in a murder case in New York last spring.

It turned out to be as amusing a night club as I ever was in, with a really gay air in it. Johnny is a well weathered Irishman who does things like The Duchess is learning the rumba, and Bury the Hatchet. A woman named Edie Griffiths who looks like a Toulouse-Lautrec woman from the Lapin Agile sings too and plays the piano. That's all. But you'd have to see and hear them. It was like the easiest little clubs you ever saw in Paris; only I thought nicer, somehow. Better humored . . But there must be a lot of New Englanders out here, for they have the oddest little blue-nosed regulations in the midst of all the gayerty. Curfew law says firmly and means it: No drinks sold after midnight. Well, everybody just got to buying six drinks and standing them in a row and lapping them at leisure between twelve and three a.m.—So now, the rule has been made fool proof until somebody thinks up a way to get around it. At half past twelve the waitresses come and take away your glass or glasses. We had a little tot of Bourbon and ice that wouldn't have staggered a flea, but were so late we had to swallow it whole. Nothing like that goes on in New York now, does it?

Well, I am back in circulation officially and it was a very nice little get-away. . . . My young man informed me that I had better come out of my shell for people were beginning to talk. Mostly hints of a subterfugeous (I just made that up; Pretty, isn't it?) love affair, and other little improbabilities. That I was really living alone and liking it is what They—whoever They are—could not believe for a split second. I told him I couldn't be blackmailed into doing a single damn thing that I didn't want to do, and the next time any one inquired, tell him or her I was out here counting my toes trying to make them come out even.

My real situation is now this: Robert Lewis is coming back next Saturday, so I must give up the house.[49] The packers will be here Friday—I brought all the things I had had sent to Washington here, alas—to take the truckload of gear away, but where? Nobody knows. I have not even the shadow of a house yet, and only one hotel will even toy with the notion of letting me have a room, and that one, the Bel-Air, not until the 11th of Sept, when I must have one by the 8th … It does not seem possible that I shall really have to live under a bush, but if it happens I'll let you know what its like. Meantime, write to this address, it will always be sent on.

Russell and Mildred invited me to put up with them for a month, if I came back to New York. But now it seems my agent—I have a new one, Harcourt Brace's agent here—is out peddling me up one side of the street and down the other, and he talks in such astronomic figures about money, it sounds more like the war debt than my wages. And I am wondering now if I should ever have invented that story about the woman who wanted only to live a chaste life, but couldn't afford it—if I never told it to you, I will sometime if you like. And in the meantime, brute curiosity keeps me here, I do want to see exactly what I really can fetch in the open market. And the climate is good and travel is horrible, so it may be spring again before I get back to New York. O dear, let's not think about it. Why did I bring it up?

I had dinner the other night with Dorothy Parker,[50] and she is coming this evening with me. I was amazed, though I don't know just what I did expect. She is so little and so pale and ill and melancholy and simply soggy with fears and self-pity. Still in love with that really nasty cad of a husband,[51] which seems to me such rotten taste to say nothing of judgement to say nothing of feeling. Apparently he has played about every crooked little trick there is on her, and she comes back groggily for more … She doesn't drink though, which helps a little.

… I just remember in time something I have meant to ask you to do for a great while, but never thought of it when writing to you .. Harriet de Onis[52] is going to write something or other about me for a South American review, and asked me to let her have a print of your photograph of Paul's drawing of me.[53] I have only the one you gave me, and am not able to persuade myself to part with it. Would you let me have another one? I have sometimes wanted to ask you to let me pay for a lot of them, because I have had literally hundreds of requests for that picture, and there are a few persons—fifteen or twenty, that I should really like to send it to. . Would you do that? I would be so pleased if you would … Oh yes, its time for photographs again, isn't it? I do my hair up now, very slick and plain, and am thinner but looking quite healthy, and it would be nice to have that on the record …

Your house in the country is lovely, and I wish—I wish—and what's the good of that? I miss you very much.

With my love   Katherine Anne

Stay out of debt this time, darling. Its fun.

To: Harvey Breit TLS 4pp. Northwestern

843 6th Street, Santa Monica
California 4 January 1946

The new date comes so easily, dear Harvey, I haven't missed it once yet, because I was really glad to see this year come in, thinking that at its worst it would still be better than any the world has seen lately; and at its best—hope, hope, it's my besetting infirmity—it could be really new.

I had the impulse to reach out and gather in again everybody I ever knew that I remembered having known once, from merely pleasantly to memorably, a kind of roll-call, a mustering-in of human forces. And with you I feel a very gentle sort of bond, so many many things: I don't know whether first because you are a good poet or because you are a good human being, and I shan't inquire. Let it go for just what it is . . . it is quite good enough, and should last well.

Tomorrow will be one year since I left New York, and it has not been the worst year I ever knew. I have really got well, for one thing, and have had time to think a little about all that has happened, and some leisure just to be quiet and by myself, and it was all preparation for something further on. I had come to the end really of physical resources, apparently I had been going on a narrow margin of nerves for a good while . . . I had virus pneumonia three days after I landed here—a cynical friend says it was caused by seeing three of Sydney Franklin's pictures in a row, and indeed, after I got up and went back to MGM, life, capital L, went to a level of despair such as I never knew, and possibly one can only afford it on a salary of two thousand a week. But I got out of that at the end of the first fourteen weeks, and then floated along for a good while . . . Last October, my agent, who thinks he owns me, got me another assignment with Charles Brackett and Billy Wilder[54] at Paramount, to work on Madame Sans Gêne—you remember that old Sardou war-horse . . .[55] Well, they are wonderful to watch as a team, and it has been interesting, but what am I doing there? In fact I am not there at all. I have sat out ten weeks again without doing anything much, just as I did at MGM. . . . I know there is something here I could do, but where is it? and what? and why do they employ me? But it will be over soon, and out I go again, and this time really for good. One thing, I have been sensible and am saving money, and that little question will be settled for me for quite a while. I live in a little $65 a month flat—furnished partly, in my favorite among all these warring little suburbs, Santa Monica, six blocks from the sea, and at night sometimes I can hear the surf smashing on shore and the stars look as well here on clear nights as they do in Texas, which specialises on big glittery stars. Never let them tell you you have to buy or rent an estate with a gold plated swimming pool just because you are in the pictures. . . . You don't have to do a damned thing you don't want to do, here; Hollywood may be a state of mind for some people, but for me its just another place, and there are some very nice things here, but you never read about them. . . . People are magically friendly and pleasant to me, I get an illusion of perfect peace only dispelled by reading the newspaper occasionally. Girls murder their mothers with butcher knives, men cut off women's heads and throw the trunk down a gulley, an average of three persons a day are killed by automobiles, six masked men held up a private rich-off gambling hell the other night and got away with 40,000 dollars. And this morning at the doctor's I talked with a gambler who was there, and he said it was the slickest job he ever saw: no shouting, no shooting, just zip and away. They didn't take the customers' money, only the proprietors' . . . Betty Grable[56] screamed and one of them said, "Shut up," just like in the movies. But as I say, where e'er I walk is perpetual June, and even when I go to a party where Charlie Chaplin[57] and his entourage are—and quelle entourage, my God—what happens? His fifteenth child-wife[58] sits and knits blue booties for two babies, one outside and one still inside her, and dear Paul Green[59] talks about God . . .

I must finish that novel—did you see the bits published in the Kenyon Review and the Partisan Review? Surely you remember that novel?—and do a little job of editing before I leave here, so it will probably be full summer before I get away. I mean to go back to South Hill, but I know I can't live there. I was there a whole winter, spring, summer, part of fall, it is very dear to me but it isn't a one-woman job, that place . . . It takes two, a man and a woman, to run a house, alas. I never had a man who would really undertake life with me, something seems to scare 'em off—could you, as an ardent student of the human predicament advance even a small reason why, and what? I mean so well and have such workable ideas, it seems to me. But work they do not, after all. Anyway, I shall probably sell dear South Hill, it was just as lovely as I thought it would be, and I hope somebody who likes it will buy it.

There is something deeply and—unless something overturns from the very bottom—incurably wrong with the pictures, the way they are made, the reasons, everything. No good at all thinking about them any more. Somebody may do great things with them, but not I: this is not my place, I have a previous engagement. The climate is as beautiful as everybody said it was, and I do enjoy just being easy in good weather. Being a semi-tropical plant, no one can persuade me there is any special moral beauty in fighting the elements. I can put up with a rotten climate if I have to and to hell with it—further than this I do not commit myself.

Do you see anybody we know? I am not lonely either, one finds a little good company anywhere, but still one's friends are one by one, no two alike, none can take the place of any other; and I do miss and want to see some nice, old familiar faces—yours, for example, and soon.... Tell me something about yourself, your life. The boy must be a big one by now, does he flourish? I hope so; this place is simply carpeted with babies, and even Judy Garland[60] was half again as big as a house when I saw her last.

I "meet" absolutely everybody sooner or later, and yet I go very little, there isn't time and it isn't interesting. Everything to make a world capital is here but the spirit: I still feel one comes here to live in the country, and somehow I almost manage it. . . . . Yet,—typical Christmas present—I got a basket of champagne from my agent, and a corsage of white orchids, among other things . . . Twice in my life I have worn orchids, and both times right here. I dislike them extremely, and so think this is no place for me; just another symptom, that is . . .

Let me hear from you. Are you writing, have you had anything published? I mean poems, of course. Let me know where.... Or copy out and send me a new thing or two . . .

With my love
Katherine Anne

To: Josephine Herbst TLS 3pp. Yale

843 6th Street, Santa Monica,
California 23 January 1946

Josie darling I can't wait to tell you how gay it made me to know the warm winter sun is shining on you, too. Leave us brag back and forth a little: I am in the bay window and my neck is burning and these keys are hot, and it seems just right . . . I hope you can stay there until the novel is finished, as I mean to do here, and then we will both have a free foot—one apiece, and ditto consciences.

That part of the novel you saw has been written since 1940, late summer, and I have done a lot since, but it was always torn up again by forced changes, and now for the first time in my life there is nothing pulling me this way and that: I have really got things in control and can keep them that way until the job is done. . . . That seems to me a change for the better, and what a lot of doing it has taken, what a lot of just sitting firmly saying "I shan't be moved" like the old Negro spiritual . . It has been the devil's own job to do, you're right, but it can be done, I find; that is, things do come out, people are accounted for, I <u>think</u> the point will be made. . . . It is made in my own mind, so maybe it will be bound to come out if only between the lines . . . Your undertaking sounds like a real one too, and even the way you write about it hastily has your own kind of truth and poetry in it—I insist that truth and poetry are one and indivisible, and you know this hasn't always been a popular notion. My book is about the constant endless collusion between good and evil; I believe that human beings are capable of total evil, but no one has ever been totally good: and this gives the edge to evil. I don't offer any solution, I just want to show this principle at work, and why none of us has any real alibi in this world. Just the same, there are degrees of guilt, and it seems to me most important to keep this in mind, especially now. But then, I had my plan and my conclusion all worked out ten years ago, and nothing has happened to change my mind—indeed, everything has confirmed my old opinion . . . My original title for this book was <u>Ship of Fools</u> and I am now busy working on my publishers to change it back. . . . . The original manuscript has that title. . . . It is a one-draft book. I just write ahead by the grace of God for a good stretch, then something happens and I must stop and later comes another stretch. I have 240 pages finished, and the total working time has been 2 months, 1940; 2 and one half months, 1942:—1 month and a half 1943 at South Hill; and not a lick since. Total: Six months and not a page re-written . . . But I doubt if I could have done the same thing if I had gone steadily ahead for 6 months. . . . I have stopped fretting, in any case . . . I will do what I can, which is all I ever did.

Now I am coming back to it with a good stretch ahead and it should finish in the next blow. At least I know exactly what I want to say, which is something . .

As to my good news from Europe, it mostly comes from France and from friends there, and is personal. That is, they did survive, they are going ahead with their lives again. They have no coffee, tea, chocolate, soap, stockings, underwear, wool, paper or coal or wood, very little electricity, and so on. But it doesn't seem to slow them down as much as one might think. They do seem to have their minds on something else, fulfilling previous interrupted engagements and plans. . . . Their courage and hopefulness are simply magnificent, and they are doing some work . . . How would I dare to despair, Josie, in face of this? The little I can do is absurd. I send boxes regularly, half a dozen persons I know do now and then have a little soap to wash with or a cup of hot coffee to drink during their long cold days . . . I send books, and newsletters, you might call them, and am trying a little to call attention to writers here unknown there, and have a connection with a publishing house, which will listen at least now and again to my suggestions.

Were you ever translated into French? I know you have been in Russian, and other languages? If you have not been introduced in France, would you like to be, and what books or book would you choose? Tell me. Then get your publisher to send a copy to

Mlle. Marcelle Sibon
5 Quai Voltaire, Paris, VII France . .

She is my good friend and translator, does beautiful work . . . The advance on royalties will not perhaps be much, $300 or so, but that is only an advance . . . She tells me the French are really wanting to read American writing, and has already sent me wonderful reviews of Flowering Judas . . . The other two will come on shortly . . . Let me know about this, I think it is important . . . As one of my reviewers said, it was strange that France had known no American writers except Sinclair Lewis, Steinbeck and Hemingway. Not until 1933 was Dos Passos translated, Faulkner even later . . . And where, he asked, had they been hiding me? So, I think it is time for the ladies to step forward, Josie . . .

When I know your book is chosen and sent I will write to Marcelle, who knows English as well as she knows French, she will read it, and the thing will be started. . . . One of my reviewers mentioned that the one thing against me would be—guess what? the same thing that has been against me here. I write short stories, and they, like Americans (not so much now) want novels . . . So you are one up there . .

++++

Josie I must interrupt here to say that another Christmas Overseas box I sent my nephew last October has just come creeping back . . . I sent four in all besides two later not meant for Christmas and so I suppose I will be taking back the mangled things that started out so brave and hearty so long ago. This one contained a can of tuna fish, a smoked cheese, a pound of jordan almonds, a pound of chocolate-nut-nougat candy, and a box of rye wafers. The only thing not practically pulverized was the can of tuna . . . The other one contained toothbrushes, razors, shaving soap, bath soap, wash cloths, face lotion, Arrid, foot-powder, and a fruit cake wrapped in the wash cloths . . . It came back with the soap and fruit cake so crumbled together you would never know which was which . . . Yet I had packed them so carefully following all the instructions, everything carefully padded with kleenex tissues, and so on. Mashed flat, Only the strings held . .

I carried on correspondence with more than 600 men in service in every army on every front, they wrote to me after my overseas edition was sent out.[61] I sent three of them boxes—including my nephew—and so this was what the good, gallant spirits wrote so fulsomely thanking me for. Dear God. . .

+++++++

Next war, I'll know. Send everything in tin cans . . . Above all fruit cake.

::::::::

Well, I just had a kind of final check-up with my doctor, who is getting ready to wean me and high time. I am a year-old patient by now. I just decided that since I had at last found a real doctor, I would stay on and do as I was told and get well. He says I am well and sound, to go ahead and try not to be foolish or wasteful of my health. It is wonderful to feel easy all over, all through, all the time. . . . It was worth the year and the money—though he is very reasonable, a good ethical man—and I wish I had the chance to do it ten years ago. But now is all right, too.

+++++

I have Dostoyevsky's short novels with Mann's preface,[62] and I must say I was repelled by the preface too . . . Art comes out of health and not disease, from the strength of the artist and not his weaknesses, and his work is weakened by his diseases just as his body is. And that rotten nonsense about the young and strong eating his sicknesses and turning them into health . . . If you eat sickness you may be strong enough to resist infection, but that is as far as I would venture on that road. . . . I have said of late, we have all the sicknesses of Europe coming in on us to add to our own (and Mann is one such, I do believe) and it is true that we can always catch each other's diseases, but no one can give his health to another. . . . A man like Dostoyevsky had a gift great enough to carry his sickness, and it is true that he was strong enough to use it, to turn it into art. And none of us are sound altogether, we must work with what we have and are and make what we can of it. . . . . Mann's pseudo-mysticism has always seemed to me false and even invented, I do not trust him in anything. I do not even trust his motives for leaving Germany. If you want really to have a glimpse of him that will raise your hair read a little story called <u>A Man and His Dog</u>[63]. . . . It is one of the foulest little records of pure sadism I know about.

Your account of what you see at different times of day in just light and air was lovely. I watch this world, or live in it and soak it up, in the same way from hour to hour. I see the sun rise and set, I watch the moon's phases, it is exciting to know whether the tide is going out or coming in, sometimes at night I wake and hear the sea pounding on the shore. Life is an end in itself, more and more I wonder what it is in people that makes them pant after "meanings"—the meaning is already there, if they would stop their invention and their lying long enough to see it. . . . I am sick of mean little souls in a highfalutin search for God . . . Kierkegaardism, etc., or worshipping sex in a kind of impotent orgasm—Lawrencism, etc. . . .[64] I wish they could really just once <u>see</u> another human being, even just once would help.

Well, darling let me hear from you again as soon as you are in the mood. With my love

Katherine Anne

To: Herbert Schaumann TLS 4pp. Maryland

843 6th Street, Santa Monica,
California 5 April 1946

Dear Herbert:

You with your returned soldier, and I with mine—at least you seem to be stubbornly staying in your own house, which was more than I had force for. . . . My blessed Paul finally arrived, and the whole situation promptly stood on its ear . . . I had tried but in vain, but <u>vain</u>, to find him a room. Then I had to buy a bed and put it in my living room, which is also my working place . . . He came in (I was and am heavenly glad to see him) and did just exactly what every other human being on earth does near me: sat down in perfect serenity and folded his hands . . absolutely confident, as everybody always is, that I can and will arrange and do everything . . .

Well, my producer at Paramount thinks that, too, and so does my publisher. And I was up to my neck scattering bits of mss. to them to maintain their belief . . . Also, as a long second thought, to get my work done, which is after all the only thing that gives me any real happiness. . . . after <u>all</u>, I mean that literally. That is my only source of nourishment and renewal—everything else gnaws me away at the roots . . . unless I can see some relation to my work with what is happening.

In two weeks I was a mere wreck, a ghost talking in its sleep . . So I left the apartment: we had advertisements in all the papers, and friends looking for a place for Paul—and bolted to the desert, there to wrestle with the devils—multiple, a single one would be a great change for the better—where naturally, on the second day, an enormous blizzard blew up, blew a window sash in front of my worktable out and bashed me over the head. I never had a bash over the head before, and it is quite something, isn't it? I am now full of curiosity as to its effect on my future mental processes. .

I stayed there three weeks and damned near finished the Paramount play . . . I should think I'll be out of there in another week or so . . . I hope, anyway . . . And Paul finally got himself settled permanently for two months in a little beach apartment. And I came back and went to bed for three days, and cried quite a lot, which with me is no sign of weakening, but nature's own announcement that I am getting my sleeves rolled up really to go into action. Now I have the house to myself again, Paul just comes in now and then and we listen to music and talk about everything on earth—he is really good company for me, and loves being around—and I have been sleeping ten hours a night for some several nights now, and all at once Life, the sabre-toothed tiger, is back in his cage. . . . .

But oh, never think that I don't know what is happening to you. I like to feel I wouldn't need to experience it to realize: but having the same thing happen to me at the same time does make a bond, somehow. . . . I do hope by now you are out of it. By tradition, upbringing, two thousand years of history, I am Christian in essence and believe firmly that we should bear each other's burdens . . . But the hell of it is, nobody will help me bear mine—or more justly, nobody can. And apparently I can just take on anybody's,—for a time, at least. But something incorrigibly human in me saves the pieces by causing me to rebel finally. And then I find that the other person can go on very well from there without me, which is always a terrible relief to everybody . . .

All this is not about Paul: Paul was just the last straw . . and bless him, nothing was his fault. . . . He's all right now; I'm having him done over completely, façade and all, by my wonderful doctor. And he is pulling himself together beautifully after all these years of abominable, abnormal army life and war . . . He is probably wallowing in the sun on the beach this minute: I hope so.

About Europe: I agree with you, it has been the bad lands and is. But not France. It was odd. In the old days, Americans loved France and Germany:

quite often the same American could love them both equally for their different qualities. And Germans loved Italy . . . Sometimes I have theories about
this which sound reasonable. But let's not go into them now . .

I don't like Italy at all because I loathe their whole 19th century. I am sure
it is the most lovely country in the world, but the people have shown themselves so weak and so frivolous and so gullible and so damned dishonest and
fuzz-minded I have no patience with them at all . . . And I hate the way they
simply escape all the consequences of their idiocies—I used to remark about
this in Germany when I was there . . . The Germans seemed to hate everybody else on earth, but they were as indulgent to Italy (who is not and was
never their friend, nor anybody else's) as an infatuated man would be with
a seductive, kitten-witted unfaithful woman; and even though Italy had not
supported them in War 1, and had run out on us, and had shown itself utterly
irresponsible in every way, they still never lost hope of winning that enchanting country to them . . . Well and so they did, and what came of it? But as the
French say, the heart has reasons the mind knows nothing about, and I don't
suppose the Germans can learn anything by history any more than any other
people can . . .

The ancient Italy—what is left of it—is valid, there it is, or rather, there
it was. I am for saving every remnant of it, loving it, studying it. But modern
Italy has very little to do with it: Like all of us, it has made little use of its
great past. I wouldn't go to the country because Mussolini was there; it had
been enough to have to be in Germany when Hitler was there. Now maybe
I shall see Venice and Firenze too . . But I'm in no hurry. I want first again
just to see the stones and hear the good speech of Paris—But the prospect
is a little further off now. . . . It recedes somewhat as I approach . . . I don't
know when I shall go. But some day surely . . . not to live there. I live here,
in this country. But for a lovely look at the beloved place and the faces of
friends. . .

This immediate moment, tomorrow, next day, next week, next month,
must be got through first, and they are not the worst hours I shall spend in
the world either . . Things seem very pleasant and possible. First, I shall take
a plane out of here towards the end of this month—date depending on the
American Air lines—(or I may get a place on the Constellation[65]) to New
York, to Saratoga Springs and—this depends on the date of the Library of
Congress Annual meeting of Fellows[66]—even to Washington . . . You know
I never go anywhere unless I have an absolute errand to perform; this is not
a rule I made, but the way things happen: and I hope the meeting will be in
early May, for I could attend. . . . For some reason or none I remember Wash-
ington pleasantly. And my real wish to be there now is that we could see each

other. . . . I'll know in a few days and in any case will send you a telegram before I arrive, if I do . . .

Almost I forgot to tell you something which may turn out to be important. I bought a mountain . . There was a nice honest Swiss kind of man in the desert who also owns a gold mine. He says it is full of gold and he needed some cash to work it. He wanted to sell his mountain, which apparently is without gold, but it had a good many things I prize more: Two springs of water, government tested; they produce thirty thousand gallons of pure cold water—oh such lovely water, every day. . . . He has got it piped all over the place for irrigation, I can run an electric light plant by water power . . There are 160 acres in a fertile little valley on top of a mountain, a little orchard already planted and in bloom when I saw it, a little house and some odds and ends of barns and so on; Best of all, he has loved the place and has really seen it—its true shape and what it needed to be more beautiful, and even his little domestic buildings are disposed in a harmonious design. He has terraced a place against a hill where he meant to build his house, and the whole thing is so bright and gay and heavenly up there just under the clouds, I took one look and said, "I'll have this." It is my extravagant belief that you can see two thousand miles every which-way on a clear morning, and the air—well, I was so accustomed to its purity and lightness in two hours the desert was almost unbearable when I got back to it . . . And I wanted next day to go again to my mountain, and the day following. And I am homesick for it now . . . I hadn't really expected to buy it, and didn't have any money or checkbook or anything with me. I borrowed fifty cents from somebody near and made up ten dollars in loose change, gave it him, he wrote a receipt on the inside of a packet of matches, and next day we went to the bank and put the thing through all the necessary formalities, and I handed over the thousand dollars in cash—money I never saw, actually, but I knew where it was . . .

I plan to build a long adobe ranch house there, with the pointed beamed ceilings, thick walls, enormous windows, patios and terraces and a bath for each bedroom which is rapidly becoming a typical American domestic architecture . . . It pleases me to the bone, I live at ease in such houses. It is a deep melange of Spanish, French, and early American country house thing: something peasant, something aristocratic in it, and the most comfortable house I ever knew. The walls will be at least three feet thick, tile roof, rambling, plenty of places to go, privacy and space for everybody . . Do you find this a pleasant notion? I go to sleep every night planning my house. . . . . .

It can be a self-sustaining place, and I am going to look very carefully for a good farmer who will run it . . . There will be, besides horses, goats, burros, guinea hens, pigeons, and peacocks. You find this last bird out of place? It is hard to explain, but in the San Bernardino valley (where my mountain is) people have peacocks . . . Even the most shattered looking little estate you can imagine, with sagging barns and sunken little shacks, have peacocks roaming around them. . . . God forbid I should fail to fall into the regional customs, whatever they are . . .

This is the reason Europe recedes. . . . this is for me the most compelling kind of reason—of the heart—to stay where I am, and make something beautiful around me. It is only a three hour drive to Los Angeles, seven miles from Lucerne Valley Center, in the very edge of the Mojave Desert—such a blooming, fertile desert, with water just under the surface. . . . full address: El Pedregal (name of my place) Lucerne Valley, San Bernardino County etc . .

I happened to pick up a book of Thomas Wolfe's—you can imagine how thunderstruck I was for something to read—and he wrote, over and over, about the "desolation" of this country . .[67] There is no such thing as a desolate country. The desolation was in him, in his own soul. Believe me, he could have taken this desert and made it bloom, and he would have done better to do it than to let his own fears eat out his substance. . . . . I was shocked at his book, what a coward the man was. . . . How deeply unimaginative . . . how negative. Self-love, self-absorption, self delusion—with the airs of neglected genius. . . . On a huge scale, a portentous sign . . .

What do you mean when you say "love"? I think I know what I mean when I say it to you, but do you know? The word has its own meaning for each one, and maybe the secret of happy love (does it exist? is it possible?) lies in two people understanding each other's meaning; for maybe it is not possible they can mean the same thing. I read the scratched out phrases too: they make a different meaning from those you left clear, yet they do not really contradict each other . . . or maybe I only hope they do not. . . . . You know I am afraid of love and do not trust it; yet this is something that comes out of mere experience, my instincts were precisely opposite. I have not found in any man any faith or stamina of heart for human feeling: I cannot know what flaw you find in women, (in principle) but that it is there I feel certain. But don't you think it was strange there was no man who had the courage to make a life with me? Or who had enough force to make a life of his own that I could share and live with? Or better still, to have been able to share a life in which both of us could grow without damaging each other? Isn't love something a little beyond sensual captivation, hasn't it some real bond with the life we live every day humanly, doesn't it relate somehow to our death, too? . . . well, these are only the dullest most superficial of my questions. . . . but you see the word sets up endless echoes in me. . . . And still I do have feelings about you that I can recognize as love, and when I sign my letters "with my love" I mean it,

even if I no longer can say just what it is I mean, because it is an airy kind of thing, nothing has touched it – it has had no test of any kind, no obstacle, no proof. Just the same, I am now going to bring this enormous letter to an end, and really I can say in all faith, With my love
Yours
Katherine Anne

I suppose you know by now, have known for a good while, that your poor student who reads the criticism and not the poet is just one of several million.

To: Albert Russel Erskine, Jr. TLS 5pp. Maryland

SEND BACK?
843 6th Street, Santa Monica, California
15 January, 1947

Bless you, my dear, by now you should know no asperity can trouble me if it comes of solid, but slightly harried, statement of belief. You speak of three letters that shocked you. All too obviously two of them were mine—or am I reading in a hurry again? God knows I have not time for anything else—but the third? Never mind, it probably does not concern me. P.S. I just found my first letter, which I had forgotten.

I don't want to write to you at all unless this time I can really take time and choose words to make clear what I mean. Yet the misunderstanding goes on compounding itself because invariably you take any attempt of mine to explain why I cannot accept certain books as an attack upon yourself: and that is rather benumbing to any true exchange of ideas.

But anyway, to take your letter from the beginning: You have never understood at all my attitude towards the Germans. I know too well they are a part of the human race, and any part of the human race is "worth saving." I simply do not think that the way to save them—if we could, which is a question—is by criminal collusion with them in freeing them from all moral responsibility for their acts, and building them up again, at the expense of the rest of the world which they have damaged so much, so they may repeat their attempt again. I am appalled by this talk about how Europe needs a strong unified Germany in order to be prosperous and at peace. We have had a strong unified Germany for four generations, and they have invaded first France, and about forty years later, have fought with France and England, (and us, incidentally) and a generation later have involved the whole world in disaster. . . . It is no good to say we are all to blame. We are, but there are degrees of guilt, and no one, not even the Germans, can deny that they are the ones who always deliberately planned war, prepared for it, provoked it and marched first. A favorite argument is that America, France, Great Britain, sold them the material to prepare for war. And so they did. But what they sold them was not necessarily material only for war. It could very well have been used for prosperous peace time purposes. The guilt of the other countries lies in the fact that they knew Germany was preparing for war again, and did not prevent it. You know that will lead us into the whole question of the international cartels, armament industries, power politics, and the men who make wars as Big Business. We know that both Mussolini and Hitler were financed from this country as well as from England and France: we know the role the Catholic church has played, and why the three Fascist countries, Franco Spain, Italy, and Argentina are more tenderly treated by our state department than any of our Allies . . . We know that Great Britain (which might be understandable,) and America have opposed fiercely in Italy, in Greece, in France, in Poland, all attempts of the people to form any kind of decent governments. And what I cannot make clear to you about my feelings as to Germany and the Germans is this: that Hitler was a popular idol, there was nothing in his ideas in the least strange or repellant to the Germans, even those who fell into trouble and had to run away, even those who were sent to concentration camps, did not quarrel with his principles of government. Their opposition was Party opposition, they wanted the same kind of thing but administered by another set of people. We used to hear a lot about the good Germans and the bad Germans. My idea is that the difference between them is that the good German lets the bad German do his dirty work and then goes out into the world to explain and apologize for him. Witness Niemoller,[68] who was allowed to come here (and typically the first thing he asked for the Germans was food and clothes, as if they had not robbed all the food and clothes in Europe for six years) and he had not one word to say against Nazism—only that we must all be good Christians and love one another and send at once a lot of help to the Germans. . . . Well, my horror is this: not against the Germans, they are what they are, and what they have been from the beginning, only of late they were more dangerous because they were stronger—but against the rest of the world who, instantly the war is over, transfer all their interest and pity and charity and concern to them, and will go on helping them rob and cheat and plunder, by withdrawing help from their victims and giving it all to them. And the Germans go on saying smugly, "If you make us pay anything for our glorious binge, you are just as bad as we are," and alas, we feel just guilty enough to let them get away with it. . . . .

Have you read any of their books? You should read <u>The German Talks</u> <u>Back</u>.[69] You might read <u>The German Record</u>. Or you might just listen to a few "refugees" such as infest this coast. . . . . Well, Spender[70] has done a painfully honest job of trying to see all sides of the bitter question, and of course, he does lean backward now and then to be more than fair to the vanquished enemy—who has already announced once more, as he did the other time, that he was not really beaten, it was just time to call time out for the present—and he quotes a great many German speeches and comments without seeming to understand the double talk and the meaning between the lines, but just the same, he has done so much better than so many others, and does speak so plainly now and again for a kind of human common sense as against the morbid sentimentality of so much thinking about the Germans—really, how people do love them, deep down. Is it because they really have the guts to be as evil as the others would be if. . . ? I have thought about this a good deal. Is it because they are the people who can find no middle ground, but must either wallow in brutality like swine or go star chasing? What could be more ethereal and spiritual than a German when he is not kicking somebody in the face? What <u>is</u> the beastly attraction they seem to have for the rest of the human race, so that no vileness is too great to forgive them? The Germans go over Europe—and they marched first, remember, I think that is all-important—and over Russia with the most awful slaughter and rapine the world has ever seen, and the loveliest places in Europe are bombed out and the villages and farms destroyed beyond rebuilding, and it is surprising how calmly a great many Americans took it until the Allies got to Hamburg or Frankfurt, or Rome. One little church knocked down in Rome seemed to be more important than all the other glories destroyed in Europe by the Germans. And when the Allied Armies got into Germany and behaved pretty much as Armies do, only not so badly as the Germans had, the bawls and yells of protest filled our press. You would have thought we were our own Enemy and the Germans our dear abused friends. . . . really, Albert, it is a perversity I cannot fathom. Truth is, long before there were any wars, I thought them the most naturally unattractive people in the world. I admit there is something in the German mind that is unsympathetic to my own. And I have not really liked their ways since 1914. But that would still be no reason for mistreating them. I don't want them mistreated. I simply do not want them treated better than we treat our friends. . . .

The question is so deep and so complicated, there are so many elements involved, and I am full of scruples, and trying to find my way through a very dark night to some glimmer of daylight truth and some final balance of justice. . . . . Back to that line which so distressed you: "Fascists are born . . ." I have had a little trouble getting through your paragraph beginning with that quotation, but you seem to say that no one except the "irreparably flawed" is born to incurable evil, and I say I believe you are mistaken. I know that people are born into this world with a natural bent towards evil that no amount of teaching, of persuasion, of examples of goodness, will in any way touch or change and they are not mad, they know what they do. They are perhaps not so many, but they do exist. Most of us are a mixture of weaknesses and strengths, and are teachable and will go more or less according to our early influences. And there are some great ample souls capable of enormous evil or enormous good, and who knows why one will be a great criminal and another a great saint? And you must know that among the Nazis there were many strange idealists, who were poetically and mystically devoted to their religion of blood and power and murder, they did not think themselves evil. They were doing great deeds, living and dying cruelly and heroically—the words seemed to mean the same thing to them—so, in the end, if you are going to ask, how can we know, who is to tell us, what _we_ are, my dear, that thought which you say you find terrifying, does not terrify me at all. But then, do you remember once when we were out somewhere in a summer night in Louisiana, and I said that I could not understand Pascal's feeling, though I sympathized with him: the silence in the spaces between the stars does not affright me, as it did him.[71] So I am not frightened at the possibility of being judged, as to my acts and motives, by others ... But I agree with you utterly—is it because I was taught this when I was young, do you remember a passage in Old Mortality? that life was something to be taken hold of and formed to our beliefs, that the wish to be good is first necessary, the first step to virtue, and we must work it out ourselves, with the help of those who have attained it to whatever degree—for I think it is true there is such a thing as pure evil, but goodness alas is always qualified and imperfect—and though we cannot expect to ever reach anywhere near perfection, still if we really love goodness we cannot be discouraged or give up.

Well, we are arriving by slow stages to Lowry's book, but we must first go through Red's again.[72] Its no good, in the first place, saying Huey Long[73] is not the main character. Jack Burden—protagonist then, you big purist—is, I think, in spite of him being the narrator, the eyes that see the thing, is only what Henry James called a _ficelle_. He is a hero-worshipper, always a poor thing at best—that kind make Mussolini or Hitler followers, it is sinister that they never pick a _real_ hero—and Red does a strange thing; for he shows the demagogue to be just that, and though he tries to make a case for him, a great soul gone wrong, he never gives any satisfactory motive for him having gone wrong. There was really no reason at all, except for the little rotten spot in his soul that simply grew by what it fed upon—power. And Burden himself is a weakling, man without a center, I've seen dozens of newspaper men like him; and if the demagogue was not intended to be Huey Long, it was another man very much like him, I see no point in making distinctions there. The point is that Red never once makes clear his own position in the question: and I say that the reader must know where the author stands, no matter what his characters say or do. <u>The attitude of the author towards his theme and his characters is the important thing in any book, and the great ones never leave you in any doubt.</u> I seem to remember it was Huey Long who said that when Fascism comes to this country—it is already here, you may have noticed, has been here for a good while, and is growing stronger—it would call itself anti-Fascism. This is a good typical Fascist saying, creating mistrust, scumbling up the boundary lines, confusing the issue, throwing the monkey wrench—a damned smart crack, I admit. And Göring once, when asked why the Nazis didn't keep a larger number of paid agents in this country, said: "Oh, America will be an insider job." And so it is, too.

+++++

I noticed at once the beautiful mottoes for Lowry's book, some of the most beautiful in the world, and not just for sound either, and they set the tone, and I began to read with great pleasure, and it seemed to me a good book, and I was happy, until about half-way through. And chilling doubts began to set in, and when I closed it I was disappointed and let down. If I had had time to read it four times I might have been able to give a better judgement. But in God's name and I hope all modesty I ask, did you ever have to read anything of mine four times to understand what I was saying? I know that one can get from good books something new and deeper, and little slant-ing rays on surfaces with every reading, but it does seem to me the great, the major, theme and point of view should come through almost at first sight. And I simply could not see it. I closed the book thinking, But just what did he mean to tell me? Even with all your citations, I still feel they are not strong enough, not well placed enough: put it down to my own failure of imagina-tion, I could not see the point. I have re-read the passages you marked; except I did not really have to go òn from page 241 to page 252, for that scene to me is the most memorable, the peak and the crucial point of the book. And later, the man with the two hats displaying what he had stolen, and no one doing anything at all. After all, whose business was it actually? I don't suppose you remember, but this is the theme of my novel, the whole point of it, and believe me, after this it is up to me to make it clear. . . . not the point, but my point of view in it. I did not read into the scene of the dying Indian a parable of Loyal-ist Spain, that would be too local, it was something that belongs to all human history. That passage, I thought, should have led the whole thing out into the open. It is after that, you remember, that the consul breaks out and makes his scene, and it was there that for me the spine of the book was broken. You say, "Why should the author even imagine. . . . . that the reader would attribute these speeches to <u>him</u>?" Of course I imagine no such thing.

What I cannot understand is why the author gives us no real clue to the helpless, spineless, shameless descent into hell of a man who, after all, is only a medium sort of man, with no real destiny, with no real capacity either for great good or evil, with no true passion about anything except negation of life which in the end is just self-indulgence . . Let me try to tell you: I have known so many people like that, who could not bear their own mediocrity, and I have seen them, drunken, drugged, deliberately making a drama of destroying themselves and others, creating melodrama in which they may play a leading role: they abound in life and in books, and I think for such a man there was no call to prepare us with Sophocles and Goethe, though Bunyan is apropos: he "did not desire deliverance." The stupidly faithful love of an abused woman is common in life and in fiction, and the devotion of friends to a worthless being: but in art at least, this kind of character should be deeply understood by his creator; and I think Lowry had a first rate idea which he was not strong enough as artist to carry out, and I say the weakness is in him in the sense that he is divided in his own feelings about the man. That is not the same as to say that the speeches of the character are his own . . . Please don't think me too stupid if I say I lost the thread, not of the author's story, but of his intention. Even all those strange characters, the man in dark glasses, and the shadowy beings the Consul seems to take for spies who mean him harm, all the extraordinarily sensitive and exciting clues and threads—well in the end, one of his friends talking to another says, it was not true. . . . Is this to stand as a symbol of all his illusions, for really, he never, so far as I can see, saw anything straight . . . And the sign about the garden, which he mistranslated, and Hugh later translated correctly—was that another point of the same kind?

This letter is getting too long also, but I suppose it will go on for a while, because I so truly would like to make myself clear, and you know my favorite line—I think from Voltaire—about not having time to make it shorter . . .[74] About Yvonne's death. Your conclusion "that no man can do violence to himself alone" seems to me the truth of truths. But it is only that most authors can never think of anything to do with the main woman character but kill her off; unless some dismal end like streetwalking or drugs or getting bogged down in baby diapers and unfaithful husbands. But mostly they just kill her off, until I am inclined to think they do on the printed page what they would like to do in life. I wonder sometimes if it is not the expression of some deep male resentment of the fact that women have destinies of their own, they cannot be absorbed, dominated, nullified; they have an awful vitality and recuperative power, in life they are damned hard to kill except by violence with weapons, a practise which is increasing to a scandalous degree in this country. Well, the incidence of mortality among book heroines resembles the traffic death statistics in greater Los Angeles. And Yvonne's death seems to me just rather fortuitous besides horribly symbolic and melodramatic: but her soul wings towards the stars, you remember, while her husband's body is rolling into the ravine with a dead dog thrown after him . . . No I do not accept that as good in any way, no matter what the author was trying to tell.

Albert, I am working on four things at once, and here I have sat for hours off and on writing this, and wondering all the time what it can come to, will I have said anything that will really convey to you what I think and feel, and will you take it as I mean it, or just as a personal attack on you? For I am not attacking you, or your right to your own choice of books to publish; but dear me, you should know me well enough by now to know that when you ask me a question you really will get an answer, and it will be what I mean, for I take it that is what you meant—or why ask, and why answer? Time is too short to waste in any such way . . . I suppose because I was interested in what you had to say, but anyway I cannot see on your pages quite as much asperity as you seemed to feel when you wrote them. Besides I never minded a little heat in discussion, if the thing discussed is real and important to the debaters . . .

Our society is very sick, and it has been badly for a hundred years at least. There were sick souls from the beginning of our western civilization, for there were always two parallel lines of thought in Christianity, one of hope and one of despair . . . The despair has won slowly, we could begin roughly with Kierkegaard, for our century-span, and all over Europe and Russia the hopelessness spread—almost the whole literature is sick, and I think the crisis has about been reached. We must either find a cure or die . . . I don't know whether the literature, religious and philosophical ideas, and art and even music, laid the groundwork for our political disasters, or whether the artist simply reflects the tendencies of his times . . . But believe me, we are sick. The evil are very active and devoted and methodical and sleepless, and the good are amiable and slack and divided and half-hearted, because they feel defeated. . . . How can we say they are good when they have such weakness? I speak of their feelings, their hopes, their intentions. . . . but by their weakness they connive with evil, and assist it.

++++++

More than enough of all this, my dear. I too, have about you some personal notion that has not changed for the worse in all this time. And when I say I give you up—well, that was the kind of thing one needs to <u>hear</u>, I can see how it looks, chilled on the page. Yet it was meant for a kind of facetiousness, I not wanting to be after all too damned solemn, which perhaps I was anyway. . Never mind, I have no intention of giving you up in the sense of our present relation, imagine being so dramatic.

So, yours relatively, as before, and hoping firmly that all this typewriting is going to be useful in shedding some light on what seem to you, I'm afraid, very dark corners in my mind . . . Dear Albert, I always found that the great trouble with marriage, or even just love, was that one couldn't say what one really thought any more, and I found it most hideously wearing. It is the charm of friendship that no truth should offend, and no expression of honest opinion should be followed by any such condign punishment as if inflicted in marriage, just as a matter of course. Please keep in mind that no matter what we were, we are now good friends, or so I hope . . .

Yours again
Katherine Anne

Never think either that I mean by spoken or written word to attack the book. Oh dear, why wouldn't you know? This has all been exactly for you. Please let me add: The almond trees are beginning to bloom, and the mourning doves have come back!

To: Josephine Herbst TLS 2pp. Yale

843 6th Street, Santa Monica
28 January, 1947

Josie darling:

I do hope you are still in the pleasant warm place with the good friend and the good food and not out battling the inclement winter scene somewhere else by now. After having had spring the year round, we now have winter for a week—chillish fogs, high winds, floods of rain, and I being the <u>frileuse</u> sort, am sleeping under three down comforters with the little electric heater going. Its fun for a change, but not cold, really—if it ever hit freezing point here I think everybody would curl up and die not from cold but from injured illusions . . .

There seems to be a great deal to say, and I notice almost everybody's letters begin of late "I have been meaning to write to you for months" or something of that kind, and all my letters begin the same way . . . The best I am able to say for 1946 is that it got us safely out of 1945 and into 1947, no small feat. I'll begin with today though, and let the past come in where it may. The thing that really got me to this typewriter was a letter in the morning post from The Worker's Defense League, asking me to write to Prime Minister Mackenzie King[75] requesting him to lift the ban on James Farrell's <u>Bernard Clare</u>.[76] I send a copy of my letter. It is most surely to God the principle of the thing with me, for I find it very hard to go to bat for James, not because I think he is dangerous, but because he is oh so dull and incoherent I can hardly get through a paragraph, much less a whole book. So, without having read it, or knowing why it was banned, I hit the line as I always do in these cases . . . I don't know if James is a Communist or not now—he was, I know—and I think rather sourly sometimes that if he is, he is working for my extinction and the extinction of all like me, and he must think me a real sap for defending his liberties when I shudder to think what his crowd would do to me if they could—but damn it, one is either a democrat or not, and I am one, and I don't believe in censorships. We are plagued with them from every side, and no matter what they call themselves their aim is a totalitarian repressiveness; The one difference I can see between Communism—I don't really mean true Communism, I mean as the government in Russia which calls itself that—and Fascism, is that Communism does guaranty at least a measure of economic security in return for serfdom, and Fascism does not even do that. As for our own country, well, the battle between Capital and Labor is now getting into its second century and a high crisis. Capital is really making the big push now, but Labor is a giant too: between them they may very possibly destroy this nation. The terms are getting so mixed. Was it Luce who invented that bastard Siamese twin, Capitalist-Democracy, and laid it on the doorstep of the founding fathers? Lately, I notice, several people have come forward to state that a Republic is not necessarily a democracy: and Hearst has coined Red Fascism further to confuse the issue . . .

Next day: Spring is here again, all bright with sun, and my gardenias and Azaleas and Camellias are pushing out, budding, blooming. I solved the need for something of my own growing near me by simply buying young trees and shrubs growing in big half whiskey-barrels painted green, from a nursery near by. Now I can spray and pick off dead leaves and water and give them fertilizer and vitamins and give myself as much trouble and enjoyment as if they were in the ground . . . Every plant has a name and its own face, and they are divinely beautiful. My little dining room is now full of bookcases with ferns and ivy sitting on top, the azaleas, the whole dozen are on a big stand in the front room window, the Gardenias are on the front balcony in full sun, and the Camellias are in the back yard under a trellis, where they belong.

Josie darling, On the other side is a letter I began to you so long ago it seems like B.C. You know the old routine, for me at least. I begin a letter, get interrupted, take it from the machine, do something else, it slides quietly under the nearest stack of paper and hides there face downward, and weeks months or years later it comes up to the surface . . . But I send it anyhow, because it was something I wanted to say to you, and also it is funny, for I have never had a word about whether the protest had effect or not. . . .

Anyway, so far nothing has had any effect, but at least there is no longer any doubt which way things are moving, it is not possible any longer to say <u>Maybe</u> something even yet can happen, can be made to happen to halt this progress to ruin. It could be made to happen but it will not; we are going towards Fascism, the western form of the totalitarian state, and the coalitions are forming very clearly. . . . Europeans have been saying for more than a hundred years that Russia was the great threatening power that would engulf Europe, and it may be so. But there will be a war of annihilation first. I believe in the principles of Democracy, in the republic as a state form which may even yet be tried fairly, though not in my time: and in the possibility of improvement though not the perfectibility of man. So you see I shall soon be as the dodo if I am not already, and if I stay around to see the next uproar, my rôle is not really enviable, for I hate both sides equally and just quietly know—with the same kind of mystical obstinacy of an early Christian, that they are both wrong and in the same way. You are right it is only a struggle for world power, but what has statecraft ever been but that? And I envy those people who can be so simple as to believe in the rightness of one or the other of the contenders. . . . . I don't really envy them. It is just that sometimes I am tired of being morally responsible. It is a great weight. But actually I feel about corrupt beliefs of all kinds as I used to say about Christian Science, I'd rather die honestly of what ails me than to be cured by any such fraudulent means. . . .

xxxxxx

Those X's mean the telephone rang and a woman pianist I knew in 1918 in Denver, ran into again in 1935 in front of the Café de la Paix in Paris, and have never seen or heard of since, just called me to say she had seen my picture and interview in a local newspaper, and wants me to come for dinner at her new house; her husband is frightfully rich now and they bought the McCormick estate. . . . well that will be something to see. But the point is, he is Rex Miller of the Christian Science Monitor and she is Christian Scientist also, and I haven't thought of them or of Christian Science for years, and had barely written the above line when she called. This is just one of those little no-things that I find interesting.[77]

Well, darling here I am writing another letter. Stop me, somebody. I've got to get to work this gay bright morning.

Love again
Katherine Anne

To: Josephine Herbst TLS 3pp. Yale

843 6th Street, Santa Monica
California 20 July 1947

Josie darling:

It is now seven in the morning, closed in fog with the foghorns howling among the fishing boats and pleasure boats and life rafts in this funny no-harbor. It is a beautiful sound; and the mourning doves always complain more than ever in such weather, and sometimes in the night I wake and it is so still I can hear the Pacific beating its head off on the sands and rocks, with an actual splash that sounds as if it were just over there, in the next block. I wish I could have a house on a little cliff where I could look down into the sea, but they all seem to be occupied, nobody seems ever to move away if he can help it, and neither would I. One only drawback: the fog shuts off my breathing a little, I find myself sitting around drawing in air very carefully, which can't in the long run be a good thing, so I suppose I ought to try to be sensible and move back a little out of the fog belt, as Santa Monica is called by the outlanders.

I woke at five feeling very fresh having been asleep since nine, had a lot of coffee, went down and cut the morning crop of roses—few, but roses, and they never do what is expected of them. I selected very carefully four shades of pink, from shell to pale rose red, two deep velvet reds, and white, hoping to have them all mixed in bouquets. Well, Caledonia, the pure white, blooms madly all by herself; when she gives out, on comes Rose Marie and Otto Thilow, two pinks almost the same. They stop, and the Doctor puts forth, and so on, with Hadley, Ami Quinard, and Etoile d' Hollande, all deep crimson, holding out until they can all bloom together . . . But every little face is dear to me at no matter what time it chooses to poke itself out . . . I must have told you I am looking for old roses, and there is a big garden in the state which has them: Moss Rose, Damask Rose, Cabbage Rose, and the mixed red and white which is called—falsely, I am told—York and Lancaster. But at any rate, it is several hundred years old and a beauty. They are going to send me their famous catalogue, and if you like I'll get you one. Nursery catalogues are often my favorite reading matter.

+++++++++

Also I am going to have a new camellia, Lady Hume's Blush, the oldest named Camellia known, and named I believe for Alexander Hume's mother. This need not be right, it is only what I was told .. But it is the most delicious shell pink extremely formal flower; I have already selected my tree at the nursery, but left it there until it blooms because I want to be sure it blooms true to type. They sometimes don't and you'll find yourself stuck with a sprout, or even the wrong one for they do sometimes get mislabelled ...

++++++

Today I am finishing up Gertrude[78] and it will be published in the November Harper's. That is because Russell Lynes is editor there now and finally got round to asking me what I was doing that they could print. They never asked me for anything before, and of course I never thought of sending them anything, looking upon it as a dull little magazine, which it still is and will be I don't doubt. But Russell did get a fine piece from E. M. Forster, who talks a kind of civilised good sense that I love; and in this series, Pritchett takes a real fall out of that wormy fake Koestler,[79] Glenway Wescott does one of his two-way de-appreciations of Somerset Maugham, and I do Gertrude. Gl. is one of the most divided minds I ever knew and you can hardly tell whether he loves what he hates or hates what he loves, best. (That sentence got away, but you can make it out.) I neither love nor hate Stein, but I do find in the end that she was a kind of huge comedy-figure, tho, as I mention, "practised with increasing facility and advocated as virtues five or six of the seven deadly sins, of which avarice became her final favorite."

It is a fact that after you read and think her over for awhile, you realize that she was a total monster of just plain, pure selfishness, laziness, greed, acedia, avarice, and God knows what. She just ate her way through life like a big slug, and digested it all in wads and called it genius.... But that is not all, and the thing is taking about fifteen typewritten pages to give her portrait as she portrayed herself....

++++++

Isn't it odd how, after years and years of saying nothing, under a certain pressure you find yourself blowing the cap and saying what you really think about somebody or his work or both, because they are most certainly related, if not one thing. . . .I don't think I ever mentioned Farrell to anybody before, the occasion simply never came up ... What you add of course is fascinating, for after all you knew him long and well; I used to be indignant at the way he slandered what I am sure he called the proletariat. I never knew any proletariat but I have known a lot of people who worked with their hands for a living and they none of them were so dull and mean and malignant and stupid as he makes them out. In fact, some of the most interesting, complicated, generous, warm hearted people with basic mother-wit no matter how uneducated they were, that I ever knew, were among such people. . . . So I am unable to imagine where he got his stuff, and I think it must be out of himself . . . I think he just can't see or feel: as when he intends to make a brilliant mind of Bernard Clare and turns out a dull boor . . . Its just true that no one can write without giving himself away.

+++++++

· · · · · · ·

When I read about the Communist-hunt in Washington, I remember that you were one of the early victims. You know I don't like Communists, the American brand. But I hate to my bootsoles the Fascists who are doing so successfully what Hitler did: using the popular fear of Communism to cover the trail of his intentions, giving the people an enemy to distract their minds from the worse and real enemy in their own country . . . Well, let's face it: no country will get any help from this one unless it is Fascist Argentina, Franco-Spain, the reactionary elements in Greece and Italy, and so on. Every foul reactionary in the country is back in the driver's seat, and this war did what wars are supposed to do: throw everything into confusion so the reactionaries can get the power. The passing of the Taft-Hartley bill. The removal of price controls. And now the open plan to build up Germany's industry, especially steel production, this time to use Germany in the war with Russia. This to the destruction of France, of course. And Tscheko-Slovakia, a country which really made an experiment in decent government, is first run over by Germany and then grabbed by Russia. But you know, things are really smoked out, and it is almost a relief to have them just finally come out and say with total cynicism what they mean . . . "Whoever controls Tscheko-Slovakia controls Europe." Not even the shred of pretense that perhaps that country should be allowed to control itself. I wonder about the use of the atomic bomb. I remember how no country used poison gas this time, because it was simply too dangerous, too destructive and unmanageable, and their aim is not to destroy the world, but to keep it continually in a state of war and confusion. The atomic bomb would be the end of everybody including those whose business it is to keep war going. Which makes me think they may come to some agreement about its use, and of course for the same evil reason that they have finally decided to give aid to Greece. Greece is not of course going to be aided in any sense that makes human sense. And if we don't get dissolved by atomic bombs soon, it is only because the people who cause them to be used stand a chance of being destroyed too. Its a thin hope, of course. I think Russia has the bomb too—it is certainly behaving like a country which knows it can hit back, or even attack if necessary. Josie just in the most unexpected way I ran into books lately that reminded me that Britain has looked upon Russia as its great potential enemy for more than a hundred years, Communism is just their pretext now, they hated and feared the Czars, just as much. And Germany also has had the same fear and hatred. It is simply nothing new, it has been working up for generations. . . . . . It is just that the grand show-down is about due. And Russia has certainly done its part to bring it on.

++++++++

I feel very detached about my personal fate. After all, we have had nice long lives, relatively speaking, we weren't wiped out just when we were starting, that is a piece of personal luck which we can just take for what it is worth. There has hardly been a time in the history of western civilization when I, for example, wouldn't have been a candidate for the dungeon, rack, and stake, given always my same kind of mind and temperament. I am a heretic and dissenter born, and even now, my luck has been largely geographical. Suppose I had been in Europe. . . . . born there. . . . And with the Fascist-Catholic combine on the one hand, and the Communists on the other, golly, they may get me yet. But they can't change the fact that I had my chance to live and say my say just the same. . . . So I can't complain about myself. But I wish the people who have a future could realize what is being done and fight harder—still, I wish we had, too. . . . And that regret I imagine is what all of us die with, if we are capable at all of any thought or feeling.

++++++

Angel, I've got to get to work. . . . I'll make myself another round of coffee, smell the roses, look over the mss and finish the copying. Get it off tomorrow and start something else . . .

A funny thing. I wonder what's cooking. Or is it just the summer season is coming on and the editors are looking for light reading. Time sent a reporter and photographer and took a long interview. Now why? And here is a little squib by a local paper who wanted out of a clear sky a story about me. Its just sweetly silly but not malicious. I send it for fun, and for the picture. You can see that your old friend now really is beginning to look like the Dean of Women, leave us face it . . .

Write again when you can, darling. You must be very happy to have got your book off; Lord, what a job, so just breathe easily for a while, and wish me power to get mine done too . . .

With my love
Katherine Anne

I forgot to say: I was shocked by Warren's book, a sentimental apology for the worst sort of Fascist demagogue, the most awful slack kind of fatalism. There is a lot more to say, but this must do. One key is this: once in a discussion when I mentioned universal franchise, he said flatly, "I don't believe in universal franchise. The right to vote should be very severely restricted."

To: Monroe F. Cockrell TLS 1p. Maryland

8706 Sunset Plaza Place
Hollywood 46, California
5 January 1948
Monroe F. Cockrell, Esquire
Continental Illinois National Bank
and Trust Company of Chicago
Chicago 90, Illinois

Dear Mr. Cockrell:

Your letter (Dec. 22, 1947) reached me today, with the clipping from the Chicago Tribune;[80] the delay making me feel again how very far away from center, my center, I am. Let me thank you for your generous re-assurance, and assure you in turn that I shall not, indeed, cannot change, for this contest between my "conservative traditionalism" and the vanguard of experiment in writing has been going on all my life as a writer. I have always known just what I was doing, and sometimes even I knew why, and I looked upon my experimental stage as part of the apprenticeship any one must serve in any art or profession. Painters have a homely name for their trial sketches and marginalia: they call them studio sweepings, and rightly. Mine went to the wastebasket where I was sure they belonged, and what I have published was only what I believed to be finished so far as I was able.

The experimentalists seem rather embittered with those of us who believe in the great unbroken line of development in all the arts, in all life; but they never troubled me deeply, because I think they are useful. They keep the forms from hardening, provide a stimulus, even if only that of annoyance, their excitement is catching, make discussion. All this is to the good. None of us can mortgage the future, we cannot tell what even next year's reader will choose. So I write as well as I can, always in the charming hope that the next piece of work will be better; and, next to the work itself, which is a happy occupation, the pleasantest thing in life is to be reminded now and again that I have readers who re-read and still can praise and write me such a letter as yours.

You may be pleased to know, by my publisher's last account, that the students of eighty-five colleges and universities of this country are being dipped in the dye-vat of my traditionalism, so we'll see what comes of that.

Sincerely yours,
Katherine Anne Porter

P. S. I do know the banks of the Trinity where you grew up but San Antonio is my stamping ground.[81]

To: Monroe F. Cockrell TLS 3pp. Maryland

8706 Sunset Plaza Place
Hollywood 46 California
14 March 1948

Dear Mr. Cockrell:

Though I fondly make plans which always seem simple, natural to my state of life, calling, and temperament: and though they are always based on what appears logically to be the next step, the fact remains that there are times when I feel that Life, capital L, has simply taken me by one foot and is whirling me round and round and round, myself an unwilling partner in an acrobatic dance. I have just been set down on firm ground once more after one of these spins, and discover as always to my surprise, it was no interlude, it was not really confusion, things were really getting on, and what seemed like pure tangent was a long advance on the right road.

I distrust very thoroughly these perky little psychologists that insist you always get, and do, what you truly want in this world. Every little want and wish, every smallest plan, is provisional and contingent upon the wants, wishes and plans of everybody nearest you and by radiation extended to include God knows who all—hundreds, tens of thousands of other people no doubt; and if each one of us is the center of his own little universe, there is another universe of which none of us is the center, and its that one we have to look out for.

For three years I have not been well, an "incurable" bronchial trouble, and I know now that all the doctors who pronounced it so meant only that they could not cure it. And then one doctor did cure it, simply and within a fairly short time, and I found myself well, able to do what I liked so far as it can ever be managed. At once a moving picture company offered me a writing job. The State Department offered to send me to South America to lecture about American writing. A magazine offered to send me to Europe for a series of articles. My publisher was delighted that now, now at last I would finish that novel. I found myself in the situation of that legendary animal who starved to death surrounded by food because he was unable to choose where to start eating. (Oh dear, that was a donkey, wasn't it? Must have been.) Then to cap all, seven Universities invited me to come and talk to students, beginning the latter part of April and ending the latter part of July. Where to begin? What to do?

So I haven't been writing letters as much as I should like. Friends and family have begun to write hopefully inquiring if I am dead? Out of the confusion I chose in the following order—the motion picture play which I am working on now. The University engagements because I shall just take a few suitcases and troupe all summer, combining travel with the society of students, a species that interests me deeply, for they are the future. The novel troupes along too, and will get written in hotel bedrooms, trains, sorority houses, university guest rooms. There are only about sixty pages to go. Then Europe in early fall, and next year, if the State Department (a mere Pixy, as we all know) doesn't change its mind, or just forget all about me—South America. It sounds wonderful, doesn't it? Let's see how much of it comes out.

Ah yes, Robert Penn Warren's dedication to me of The Circus in the Attic[82] was very touching, that is my third dedication and no one could offer a more charming present, that is, if it is a good book by some one you like. We are old friends, he is much younger than I, and I read his first poetry long before any of it was published. I think him a superb poet and critic, I think less of his novels and stories, but he is a good artist and cannot do anything inferior in grain, so it is easy to trust him.

The other day I was re-reading some essays of Hazlitt, whom I used to love, and find I still do, (in spite of his worship of Napoleon, poor misguided man. But then he had not seen the type run to poisonous seed in Mussolini and Hitler and Stalin) and fairly opened the book at his essay On the Want of Money.[83] Of course, when you are making a little anthology, you must choose from bales and bales of related things, and you probably know this piece. But if you don't: He begins—

"It is hard to be without money. To get on without it is like travelling in a foreign country without a passport—The want of money I here allude to is not altogether that which arises from absolute poverty—but that uncertain, casual, precarious mode of existence, in which the temptation to spend remains after the means are exhausted, the want of money joined with the hope and possibility of getting it, the intermediate state of difficulty and suspense between the last guinea or shilling and the next—This gap, this unwelcome interval constantly recurring, however shabbily got over, is really full of many anxieties, misgivings, mortifications, meannesses, and deplorable embarrassments of every description."

He then goes on with a brilliant account of that condition, with special reference to authors, actors, and all those who live, usually from hand to mouth, by their wits. God help us. He makes it funny but grim.

Doctor Johnson was grim on the subject, not funny. Oliver Goldsmith had something to say—which you quote—and as for Balzac, to whittle him down to two sentences is a masterwork of selection, since you feel sometimes that he wrote and thought of nothing else.[84] But his was not real poverty, but love of money for its own sake, which is another thing than dear Hazlitt's point of view.

For myself, as artist, I have been a little amazed now and again by the attitude of the general public towards the artist and money. If he is honest and refuses to sell out to popularity, they take him bitterly at his word and begrudge paying him for any of his work. If he shows a natural anxiety as to how he shall survive on air, they say triumphantly, "Aha, so you're not so high minded after all." And if you refuse to write to order, they say, "Very well, go your own way and starve if you like." I should know, I've been the whole long road from the beginning until now, and I know exactly what it has cost me in cash on the barrel head to insist on doing my own work in my own way in my own time and then to have it published just as I wrote it and not clawed to death with an editor's blue pencil. I won, and it was worth it. And far from feeling injured, I saw no reason why I should be paid for doing exactly what I pleased and having my own way—On the contrary, I have taken jobs and worked at all sorts of things to support my writing, as a matter of course, and quite agree with whoever it was who said, for the good life he gets out of it, and the pleasure of being a free man, the artist should perhaps be made to pay for his privileges, instead of expecting pay for them. Well, I have paid for mine and joyfully. I shall never be rich, but I do not need to be, nothing depends upon it; from the beginning, I loved luxury, ease, beautiful houses, noble and beautiful objects, expensive clothes, ample surroundings—there could be quite simply no question at all of making money enough for all the things I could buy, for there is no end to the money that I could spend.

I faced this out with myself early, and made my choice, for I had a choice in a sense that I could say when the time came, "I will take this road instead of that." Yet it is possible that I had no choice at all in the sense that I could not, given my deepest beliefs and preferences, choose any way but the way I did take. Only this morning I was talking with a friend about the plans for this next year, and he said, "Why don't you go to Europe for N—Magazine instead of X? X pays a lot more." And I said, "Yes, but N—prints my stuff as I write it, and X wants to edit everything. So I pay that difference for my favorite luxury of writing as I please."

Do you know, if it is a question of power, I choose Gandhi's kind instead of Stalin's for example? Moral force is taking an awful beating at this time, but it has taken a good deal before, and will again, and it does not die. I don't deny—could this be spiritual pride?—that so long as they will have me, I mean to stay on the side of the angels simply because I prefer the company.

As for money, it is most remarkably useful stuff. I never despised it as such, and I know just what it is worth to me. The only interesting thing about a rich man is not that he is rich, but how he made his money. Second, what use he makes of the great power it gives him. And these two points, it seems to me, are the ones most completely ignored by people, for the truth is, most of them would make money by any means they were able, and so the whole evil is in human nature and not in money. How seldom do you hear the phrase correctly quoted: "The love of money is the root of all evil." And the lack of it is the root of too much human suffering, if we went into that, we should have to pull the whole material system of this world apart and put it together again, wouldn't we? And I don't feel up to it, do you? Not this afternoon anyway.

Well, thank you for your little book, which as you see set off a rather erratic train of sparks in my mind; I hope sometime you will add to it, for the only fault is, there could be a lot more of it.

Indeed yes, if ever I am near Chicago, I should be delighted to let you know, and to see you. Unless I have a map, I only know where I am, but not where I am in relation to outlying territory. So, I shall be at the University of Kansas and the University of Missouri in June. Where they are as to Illinois I wouldn't know. I used to go through Chicago on my way to a little college in Olivet, Michigan where I talked to summer students about writing, but that course of study ended now, due to the trustees' apprehensions that too much study of literature was dangerous to religion. In that department they were teaching that the world was created just about six thousand years ago, and that original sin with its attendant dangers of hell fire came about because a serpent gave Eve an apple which she shared with Adam, a real apple off a tree, probably a Delicious. I tried to argue with one of their theologians that the fruit was really a pomegranate, as apples did not grow in that place at that time. But I was roundly snubbed for this heresy, and was looked upon afterward as a bad influence. So much for the education at Olivet.

You can see that letter writing is with me a vice, and now I must stop this pleasant pastime of speaking my mind, but really hoping to entertain you at least a little, and get to work, which in my calling, knows no Sundays or Holidays.

Sincerely yours
Katherine Anne Porter

To: Wallace Stegner TLS 1p. Stanford

Stearns Hotel, Ludington, Michigan
14 August 1948

Dear Wallace:

Well, it took some doing, and like the philosopher's Porridge, "There's lumps in it,"[85] but I do know well what goes on with Administration, and all; and think, everything considered, you have worked no less than wonders ..

I received the big official blanks to fill out and never did I realize so well my total lack of official or academic standing; there is a whole world—another—in which I fit into no category whatever. So I covered some of the open spaces with irrelevant information about my past activities, which seem to have nothing whatever to do with education. At last at one point I simply had to break down and confess that I was just merely a professional writer and nothing else much ... I hope they knew this all along and weren't expecting a long row of Ph.D.'s, M.A.'s, D.D.'s, and so on. Hell, I'm not even a D.Litt: though I will be if ever I can get to Olivet at the right time for them to hang it on me, as they so elegantly phrased it.

The one point which troubles me is the withholding of credits from the students who work with me. You know what tigers they <u>have</u> to be for credits, and also it makes me feel rather marginal; and frankly, I didn't answer your first letter at once because I had real doubts, deep uncomfortable ones, about this clause, and have been all this time making up my mind to accept it ... It puts literature and the artist in their place, all right, something not to be taken too seriously in academic life, an imponderable "good influence" or some such, and certainly we should be used to this official attitude by now. But I admit it does still chill me to the bone, for it is not only in education we find it. In Washington during the war when sometimes I spoke of morality in politics, my hearers looked at me as if I were something out of a zoo. . . . Something not "real" in their peculiar use of that word.

Well, so it is ... I will do the very best I can with my assignment, and you know I appreciate your generosity and kindness in thinking of the plan in the first place, and I shan't forget how much trouble you have gone to about it ... Actually, just personally, I am pleased to have the chance to look for promising talent and maybe be of some use to a few but I was and am afraid that many will be hampered or prevented by the weight of their other work and the lack of credits for work with me. ... It cannot be helped, we will have to work within our limitations. .

Well, I want to finish my novel before I come, and since I have a choice, I take January first to August 25th ... The problem of where to stay and how to live will have to be settled, also, and this will take some time. Also I engaged to lecture at Chicago U. on October 21, and may as well hang round in this vicinity until then. It is wonderfully pleasant here, the midwestern landscape has its own rather grand charm, and above all I am <u>here</u>, which is always a prime argument with me for staying anywhere.

I hope the Indian runner overtakes you with this; and that all of you are having a splendid summer. All my thanks again; consider everything as settled, and don't give it another thought.

Yours
Katherine Anne

To: Janet Lewis Winters TLS 4pp. Stanford

Stearns Hotel Ludington, Michigan
18 August 1948

Dear Janet:
It seems only yesterday we said goodbye on that rainy day, but this could be because I was a good part of the time since unconscious. That gay little tour of Universities turned out to be in some ways a species of traveling gridiron on which I seemed to be stretched. Even when I <u>stood</u> on it, it was still spiky. But I would not have missed it for anything, I would do it all over even knowing what I know now, and I did survive, which is a main point, though that was not what I started out to prove ... The going got tougher and tougher as I advanced into the old-fashioned honest-to-God writers' conferences in the middle west, complete with the standard gimlet-eyed old lady in the front row who is deaf and full of curiosity, the temperamental young women who have fits of hysteria; always one person, male or female, who should have been

certified long ago, a few amateurs who thought this would be as good a way to spend their vacations as any; and then never failing, the one or two or three for whom the whole show was got up and who make it worth doing and who leave a good memory.

But just the same, I was out on my feet when the session at Lawrence ended, and had to cancel Seattle. Being a small woman with a long history of fatigue, naturally I feel a heavy sense of guilt when I get tired; but it did console me a little, made me feel a little less inadequate, when great tough towers like Walter van Tilburgh Clark[86] got circles under the eyes and a caved-in look around the middle. I landed here in a daze and by happy accident. George Davis, an editor,[87] advised me. He said it was his home town and a pretty little resort mostly frequented by the unrich, and he knew a friend who had a little hotel, and indeed he arranged everything and we traveled together as far as Chicago, and he saw me off on the second lap, which included an eight hour trip across Lake Michigan . . . I slept for 17 hours on arrival and then slowly started to pull myself together. It has taken about a month though. I have done a little work, but not much. I suppose this had better be my farewell tour . .

Did I tell you, or had it happened then, that Stanford made me a kind of offer to come back for a while, which I accepted. It began as a truly brilliant generous plan in the imagination of Wallace Stegner, much too beautiful to be true, and was finally put through the administration machine, from whence it emerged whittled down to scale—their scale, never mine or yours, or Stegner's . . . Just the same, after going into a brown study for three weeks, I decided to do it. So, there remains only to try to finish the novel here, stop in Chicago to lecture at the University on 21 October, and so trail West again to be ready for work by the 21 January . . . This means trying to find a house by long distance, get my stuff, poor little stuff but my own, my darling little household stuff, in pieces by now and who cares? Moved once more, for though my appointment is only for a year, I see no reason to move away again if I can get decently settled. Of course I have my romantic dreams of something inhabitable not too far away from the University, but not too close, either. . . . You know too well what I mean. I should like to be able to provide properly for a cat and to raise a few flowers, being, as Yvor noted, feminine. Or did he say that raising flowers was effeminate? I believe that was it . . . Well, it's a fact I have the damnedest most effeminate tastes and habits you could ever hope to see. I wish some of them weren't such hard work, like cooking, or mulching and spraying and weeding. But so it is. . . Anyway, it will be pretty nice to have a place where my papers can accumulate on tables for months if I like, instead of having to take them off the bed every night and every time the woman comes in to clean.

Do you know anybody with a house to rent reasonably, or know anybody who knows anybody? Don't work at it, though. This is formula question One, I am asking others at University, and also should, I suppose, have the name of a real estate agent. Only, they are always determined to sell you something. I should love to buy something but there is no sense in being <u>too</u> romantic.

Here it has been a cool cool summer after coming through the furnaces of Purdue, Columbia, Missouri and Lawrence, Kansas; this is the Epworth League and Chatauqua part of the country, Republican party-lines, and the people who bought all those copies of <u>The Robe</u>.[88] They look to Dewey[89] as the second saviour, he is going to get this country out of the grip of labor and all those gangsters and Communists of Roosevelt days, and put the government back where it belongs—in the hands of business and free enterprise . . . I'll bet he does it, too—he's really got the backing.

Why should the contractors build houses? They are not allowed to make any money out of it. Why shouldn't there be peace time conscription? We're going to war with Russia any day now. Besides it will get a lot of these idle boys in the army where they'll learn to respect authority. And if food prices are high, it's the fault of the farmers. (I don't quite follow this last, but that's what they say.) I don't remember all the rest, but you can read it in any republican newspaper.

****

On the other hand, members of the English Faculties in several Universities explained to me that they let their students study second and third-rate writers because they weren't prepared for the good ones. They had to be led up to it gradually, through Steinbeck, et al., and they seemed very serious about it. At Lawrence, Extension, studying the list of writers engaged—Caroline Gordon, Allen Tate, Frederick Nims,[90] myself, and so on, said there wasn't anybody there they'd ever heard of, and they stood to lose two thousand dollars on that deal. We must have a drawing card, said Extension in chorus, so they brought in Erskine Caldwell. . . .[91]

When you see him close, he looks like a goat in the eye—I almost expected to see the slit pupil. He was not happy, but it was nobody's fault. We were all on our nicest behavior . . . Caldwell, too. .

Well darling, this must end. Its really to let you know I'll be back and glad to see you again. Love to all

Katherine Anne

Dear Janet, for the first time in my life I have been making copies of my letters on this trip, because it was my only chance of keeping a kind of record.[92] And now comes up a really good reason, for I am certain I mis-addressed the letter I sent you yesterday or the day before. So here is the copy, having found the address book and realizing I did not remember the address correctly.

Well, I'm off to New York in about 10 days, plans changed, mail reaches me there care

Harcourt Brace and Company

383 Madison Ave

New York 17

N.Y.

But I'll be seeing you sooner than I thought when I wrote the foregoing.

I expect to cancel Chicago but can't know for a few days

To: Herbert Steiner TLS 2pp. University of Washington

768 Santa Ynez Street, Stanford

30 January 1949

Dear Mr. Steiner:

My failure to reach Seattle for the Writers' Conference was a most terrible disappointment to me also, and the finishing touch to a season that came very near being total calamity for me. I am not yet recovered altogether—that is to say everything is still in arrears, even letter writing has been completely impossible. Now I am settled more or less at Stanford, giving two lectures a week to a large class of student writers, and shall begin to get my affairs into some kind of shape. I shall be here until the first of September next. There have been several invitations meantime to attend conferences in various parts of the country, and single lecture dates, but I am refusing them all, in favor of staying at home and doing my own writing, which has suffered deeply from my inattention.

So I am sorry, for I can't think where you might hear me except in this place, and this year only, for I have very firmly resolved never to do any pub-lic work again. I thought and do think it was part of my professional duty to work with students for a part of my time, and for twelve years I have done a good deal of this ... So now, it is really farewell to all that, and back to my own desk until I have got my own work done, so nearly as that can ever be made to happen ..

I do thank you for your letter, and for your interest, and above all it touches me to know you found one of those little war-time books. 150,000 of them, a little more or less, were distributed, and I had many—more than 600—letters from all parts of the war front, every branch of the service, about that book, and it was rather more than wonderful for me to know that something I had written was bringing a little however momentary comfort to people in such situations...

Happy New Year to you, in turn, and if you should happen to write again, tell me what special branch of athletic sports and recreations you practice?

Sincerely yours,
Katherine Anne Porter

To: Herbert Steiner TLS 1p. University of Washington

13 May 1949

Dear Mr. Steiner:
You might think all your pleasant beliefs about me were a little mistaken if I could be so rude as to fail to answer your letter, or to tell you how I liked the flowers: they arrived in perfect freshness, and were beautiful for days, and they came just at the right moment, for I was having pneumonia, a dull illness at best, and very wearing to the spirits ... Flowers help bravely in such a situation.

It is just now, in the past few days, that I feel a tide turning back to shore; not only shall I live, but I am going to like it again presently, it seems certain. I consider that Life, capital L, is a cross between a saber-toothed tiger and a protracted game of gin rummy, but I am used to it, I could never consent to get along without it. So rather slowly things are pulling together again, and I find myself reaching out into distances with letters once more, always a hopeful union.

May I tell you in turn that I was charmed with your visit to me, and that your letter would quite touch the heart of any woman at no matter what time of life; for I do not believe that the love of praise and appreciation comes of vanity, but it is just true that we all love reassurance that we are cared for, liked—what could be more simple and human? Some one, I cannot remember who he was, and yet he was some one famous and memorable, spoke once of "the noble pleasure of praising."[93] And it is noble, and a pleasure. And so I thank you, for it is pleasant to receive, also.

I hope you had a good summer, and are doing well now. Let me hear from you when things happen and changes occur. I am going back to New York in the early fall, and shall give a series of three lectures at Williams College in Massachusetts, and (a man's college) and one at Wellesley, a hardy old pioneer in female education. This seems to me very nice—I look forward to it. And this is <u>very</u> confidential: I am finally to be stuffed and put in a glass case at the University of North Carolina on May 30 next—they are going to make me a Litt. D. (I like Doctor of Letters better) with a walloping black and violet hood to hang around my neck on all future academic occasions . . . I am not supposed to tell this, and so let's consider it untold. It's a merely formal secrecy: it wouldn't cause a riot in the streets anywhere, but you are charged not to mention what I couldn't help mentioning myself. This is not fair, of course, but there you are!

We did have coffee and cigarettes together, yes, I remember. And your list of activities remind me of the times when, without being an athlete at all, I used to sail a cat boat, and swim four miles, and take three months horseback trips in Mexico, and dance all night, and get up at six o'clock in the morning to bowl, and it was all heavenly fun and I'm glad I did it and it would be nice to do again, but more tiring now, I imagine. . . . . .

With my best wishes,
yours
Katherine Anne Porter

Part Four

1950–1959

Katherine Anne Porter settled into the 1950s with the full intention of quickly finishing her long novel, excerpts from which she continued to publish. Sustained work on the novel, however, was difficult because she seldom had the privacy or peace of mind required for serious creative work. She described to Ignatius McGuire how "being alone" was the price she paid "in order to have the repose of mind and use of my time to work." It was a steep price, she said, because "I long for human society." She also faced again a string of distracting losses of persons she loved—her brother, Paul, her editor Donald Brace, her friend George Platt Lynes, and her cousin Lily Cahill. A frenetic schedule kept the grief at bay. Almost continuously accepting speaking engagements and social invitations and finding time for an occasional romance, she worked on the novel whenever she could, visualizing the final stage of it only in the last year of the decade.

If the completion of "Ship of Fools" was eluding her while she was on the college and university circuit, joining the American delegation at the Congress for Cultural Freedom in Paris, and wrapping up *The Days Before*, her first collection of essays, she was further refining her position on literature and especially on the novel genre. She had her favorites among younger writers, such as William Goyen, Walter Clemons, Daniel Curley, William Humphrey, James Purdy, Flannery O'Connor, and George Garrett, all of whom received her endorsements and patronage, often in the forms of nominations for grants and fellowships and encouraging letters. When she became vice president of the National Institute of Arts and Letters, she took her position seriously and used it to bring into the organization the best of the younger generation. "[Y]oung ones are coming up," she wrote Faulkner, "and I mean to try to persuade them in, one at a time." But she was equally firm on what and whom she didn't support. In fact, in 1955 when she was invited to speak on the state of the modern novel, she rhetorically asked Ludwig Lewisohn, "What makes them nearly all so bad, so shapeless and confused and grubby and gritty, or soft and supperating at the center?" Aside from the work of her protégés and a few others, she found little to admire in what she regarded as a widespread "mediocrity" in American letters in the 1950s that was in part simply the dissipation of the modernist aesthetic.

In the 1950s book-length studies of Porter's work began to appear (all of which appalled her), and she was having to stave off would-be biographers. She referred to the authority of Henry James and others who argued that the public had no right to an author's private life, and she declined the offers as they reached her. Although Edward Schwartz reminded her that she would have biographers and biographies whether she wanted them or not, she turned down his request to write her biography, partly because she sensed he might inject Freudian psychology into his account. She simply told him, however, "I think the blood pressure of your interest is not really high enough for a biography."

As she closed in on the final stage of "Ship of Fools" she was organizing her life, or so she thought. Misunderstanding an offer from the University of Texas, she promised her papers to Harry Ransom for the new library being built that she presumed was to bear her name, a prospect that delighted her. And she was more than content with Seymour Lawrence, her young editor at Atlantic–Little, Brown, where she had moved after the death of Donald Brace.

To: William Faulkner TLS 2pp. Maryland

108 East 65th Street, New York 21 N.Y.
17th April 1951

William Faulkner, Esquire
Oxford, Mississippi

Dear Mr. Faulkner:

For the next election of members to the National Institute of Arts and Letters, I have proposed as my candidate Miss Eudora Welty, and I am required to have two members of the Institute to second this nomination.

Would you be so good as to allow me to name you as one of the seconders?

I cannot suppose you take much interest in the goings-on of this society, and neither did I for years after I was elected. It seemed to me a morgue and I said so. I also sent them a list of nearly twenty names representing the various arts which I missed from their membership—just nearly everybody in this country whose work I respected. Well, all but two of that list are members now, and the place is anything but a morgue. Of course, young ones are coming up, and I mean to try to persuade them in, one at a time: I think we should have some kind of center in this country, and as the Institute is already a going concern, why not let's see that it really does have as members those who genuinely practise arts and letters? It has always irked me even to be asked to belong to things, I manage to evade or ignore the whole question. But after having consented to be elected one of the Vice-Presidents of the Institute last year, I decided to take on two jobs: first to get members worth having, and second to try to snag a few of those thousand dollar grants for the right people. I failed to get the grant for my this year's candidate, but am putting him up again for the next. And I do intend to get my candidate elected. I think and have for a long time that Eudora Welty is a beautiful writer and as a friend I am devoted to her. So please help me if you can. You have only to let me know that I may give your name to the committee. I shall be very grateful.

++++++

One gets too many letters from strangers, asking for things; it is one of our occupational hazards. But I hope I am not altogether a stranger to you; as for myself, I have known you well and for many years, in the happiest possible way: reading all you publish and re-reading many times my favorites, finding always another kind of newness in them, another refreshment, an endless excitement to the imagination, some increase of courage in my own mind. I wish to thank you for this now.

Yours
Katherine Anne Porter

To: William Goyen TLS 2pp. HRHRC

108 East 65th Street New York 21 N.Y.
19 July 1951

Bill my darling:
    Your letter with the passage about Mr Gruesome Caputt[1] came almost at the moment when I was going through my books, this time looking for Hogarth's Text Book on Painting,[2] which I realize now Paul must have absconded with way back in Santa Monica, and there fell out instead a rare item I forgot I had: blue-bound uncorrected proof of Other Voices, Other Rooms,[3] with an inscription from the author himself, dated December 1947, which runs "For K . . . A . . . P . . . from T. . . . . .who admires her more than he could ever say."
    I had not been so embarrassed since Henry Miller inscribed Tropic of Cancer[4] to me in Paris. But at least I was able to read that, and with the best of intentions I was not able to get past the first twenty pages of this opus. I have never been able to finish anything by that singular genius, until now. He has shrewdness, and inventiveness, and effrontery, I gather from what I have seen; But it all seemed so heavy and contrived and made up and what-of-it? But I did read the Grass Harp[5] because almost in the beginning I caught the echo, on a shallow, easy level, of some of your rhythms and even words; so I read on through to see if the impression would hold. It did . . I hope you appreciate the grisly humor of the Lady Patroness of the Arts warning you that you must imitate your imitator, as you now have him to measure up to; it is such an example of the crabshell temperament as I mentioned to you yesterday.
    Now you may remember my experience of a certain young woman novelist who spent a good deal of time re-writing several of my stories. I hadn't read them, but I could see it after it was shown to me. That all passes, it has nothing to do with you or your work. From what you said I had thought it was an unholy combination of Cerf AND Lindscott[6] who had wangled you into the best-selling Sodomite division, (if indeed they really did. I always thought you maybe exaggerated this a little, but then,) what a horrible sort of category

even to be threatened with; you are right to take it seriously and simply see that it doesn't go on.

++++++

It is nice to know that even when he tries to imitate you he is just as dull as ever; a brightish brat making up stories about paper-dolls. His characters were never anywhere but in his book, and not alive even there. Look, if I have to put up with being mentioned in the same paragraph with C.McC[7].... why then, my darling, try to be patient under your present affliction. Both will pass. I used to be mentioned with Kay Boyle![8]

++++++

No doubt I shall be mentioned in time with Jean Stafford.[9] I hope it does them good. It most certainly can do me no harm.

++++++

Well, by all means send on something to that superb international catch-all, the Dark Warehouse.[10] I hear it pays well, sooner or later everybody lands there, it seems, so wade right in. You will meet with some of the most interesting jellyfish, beside a few really good writers. Darling, there are never more than a very few at a time, so maybe we shouldn't be too severe with editors who HAVE to get out a magazine of a certain size, and must appeal to all kinds of tastes. But I could wish that the editors knew the difference between the work they print. I simply don't believe they do.

It is half past twelve noon and we are having a very noisy thunderstorm. It is dark as seven o'clock evening and the thunder roars so the house shakes and one expects the bolt to crash through the roof. The lightning cracks and little metal objects about the room go "ping!" Guinelda[11] who is here today turned her fine jamaica-rum colored face upward and said, "The sun is fighting with the rain, but he will win!"

We know that your devoted Cyrilly[12] will take a story if she can possibly fit it in to her strange publication. Yes I know what it is like to try to live on a Guggenheim anywhere, anytime. My hope is that you will be able to sell many parts of the book in several places, and also get a renewal of the grant, so that it will be a kind of foothold and not your entire income. And our words are always crossing—yesterday I tell you to save yourself a little for other work to come, and today you say you are trying to do that .... Please do take a little vacation somewhere quiet and cool, near water, before you plunge in again to a heavy piece of work .. I love you tenderly, I will live in the nest of your mind a little blue egg, happily. But when I am very tired, and very lonely for you, I wish I could rest my head in your lap; and when you need food and rest, I wish I could give them to you ... Darling, I'm afraid I think of love as a daily thing to live by and with; lovers should not leave each other to their fates, this is what everybody does; but should do for each other only those things that real lovers in their love can do for each other.

I wait for the things you want me to see, the things you have gone farthest down to bring up; they will be very precious, for they have cost us both dearly, dearly. Try not to trouble about what any one will say about you, or the work itself. Cut it away from you, float it out on the tide, let it go, it is not yours any more. Time will take care of it. Go on to the next thing.

Well, let me go on to my own work, and take my own good advice. I shan't write to you so much, for my mind does leave this place and go out looking for you, and it is no time for me to be making such journeys. Let me know what happens to you, and I will tell you what happens to me. This has been for me such a dark night of the soul that nothing worse I do believe could follow. Everything in my life that could go wrong has gone wrong with the steady implacability of Nemesis: simply, the Furies had been on their way for a very long time, and they finally arrived. We do know that they arrive punctually— I have said that somewhere before—but when they have done their worst, I expect to be still alive and able to finish at least a part of my work . . . it is not possible to believe otherwise. So keep faith in me, and with me: I need the faith of those I love and believe in as much as they need mine. Remember.

And remember that I love you, and take care of me in your words and your thought and your acts, as I do you.

Your
Katherine Anne

To: Robert McAlmon TLS 3pp. Yale

108 East 65th Street, New York 21 NY
25 January 1952

Bob darling:

When I speak of you, which is quite often, my most persistent pleasant memory always pops up: about how, after any irregular, unmeasured lapse of time, out of silence and distance, my door bell would ring; I would open the door all unsuspecting, and there you would be, fresh from God knows where, but always somewhere I hadn't been, or not lately; and after a very short accounting, we would go out on the town. . . . This happened after all, only in Berlin, Paris: where else was I when we knew each other (as if we didn't still!) except for that first meeting in New York, with Helen Black and Agea,[13] quite years ago. (Had you heard that Helen Black died about three months ago? It is hard to believe—that great strapping fine girl. But this is my early memory—I had not seen her since before I went to Mexico, and afterward to Paris.)

Well—the other day I was going over papers, scratting happily among the hills and dales of the past, when I came across one of those complimentary New Year Calendar and account books such as were put out by the Gas Company in Paris. I had started a diary in one of them. It says: "1 January, 1935; at nine this evening I went to answer the door bell, and there stood Bob McAlmon and Roland Hays,[14] fresh from Spain. They spent the evening and told the most incredible story about......." and that is the sole entry for the entire year. I must have got interrupted, and you know how it is—once interrupted, I can stay that way for years and years. I know there are, or were, two Roland Hays—one a Negro singer and who was the other? And WHAT oh what was that incredible story? I have been thinking about writing a little in an autobiographical way, but it is such items as this that stops me in my tracks ...What really happened, and when, and why? What was the truth of the matter, as distinguished from the mere facts? And if I can't get the facts straight, then how in hell can I hope to tell the truth?

Your book[15] makes it all look so easy. You just go along putting events down in their proper order, and making your marginal notes and opinions as you go, expressing your ideas as they occur, or so it appears. It was that misled me. So I tried it ... The entire past on its five hundred levels of consciousness piled up on my head, and in no time at all I was swamped, drowning, and barely scrambled out. I just don't think I'll ever be able to write about what happened to me, above all, what I happened to; for you know we have both acted upon our lives quite as much as our lives have acted upon us. So much for autobiography.

****

Got a Christmas note from Jimmie and Tania,[16] with photograph of the so-typical English farm house they found for the winter. Jimmie gave me your address in El Paso a good while ago, I wrote you a letter—got one from you, too, have it yet—but this particular letter of mine was returned to me. I still have that, too. I don't know why it came back, but it discouraged me. I was talking about you to Norman Pearson[17] when I was up at Yale visiting my old friends Tinkum and Cleanth Brooks. They have got one of those classic old middle-seventeenth (or late) Connecticut farm houses, all giant rough hewn beams and eight foot wide fireplaces, with ceilings so low only miniature shapes like me can get around without bumping my head, and I must say the Grooves of Academe (as we used to call them in the convent, to the annoyance of the sisters) are less stuffy there than in most Universities. One surmised that a little honest misbehavior might just possibly be going on behind them bushes, and that nobody would be much shocked. I read Flowering Judas to the Elizabethan Club there, and they gave me a clay pipe which is the sign of new membership. (It's all male, of course, and ladies are only let in on leashes, unless as in my case, they were getting two hundred and fifty dollars worth of work out of me for nothing—Cleanth got me into THAT) and so I understand that a clay pipe with my all-too-feminine name on it is hanging on that sacrosanct rack . . . Its a funny finish, somehow. .

****

No, Bob, I am not a recluse, only that my same old botheration, chronic bronchitis, recluses me from time to time, and it doesn't get any better, and will not, and will get worse; I know this now, and have just set myself to handle it as well as I can, staying in when I must, and getting out into circulation again as soon as possible. I miss some entertainment this way, and yet when I make up my year's account, there was always quite a lot of fun, too. Just now I am barely up from a siege that has lasted with intermissions, since last October, and I don't feel too certain that this is the end of it, but I do try: I don't like being ill, or even thinking about it. But long ago I faced a simple day light fact that we live in our human frames and they are of mortal substance. So I do as fairly as I can by mine, giving it the chance for survival I suppose I should have given it earlier. . . . as if any one could waste time on <u>that</u>, with so much to do!

****

Bless you, the only streak of common sense I ever showed in my life was just exactly where it would do the most good to my work, if that doesn't sound like bragging, which it is . . . I am the first author, dead or alive, who demanded, and got, a clause inserted in a publisher's contract that, so long as I live, no book of mine is to go out of print. So, every little book, all three of them, and a fourth to be added soon, are still circulating like mad, and can be got for the asking. Thousands of bookshops may not carry them regularly, but they can order them. Flowering Judas was in the Modern Library for ten years, then Harcourt took it back and put it in a cheap edition of their own, and sold Pale Horse, Pale Rider to the Modern Library instead. But you just be patient until I get on my feet really, and I will send you signed copies again, because I do want you to have them. You were always so good and friendly to my writing, and you know it wasn't at all liked or known when it first came out. God, look at the field we ran with, and what kind of writing! Joyce, Stein, Hemingway, and then Faulkner . . . the wonder is that I wasn't lost in the shuffle entirely. But no, after all these years, I have been translated in French, German, Swedish, Norwegian, Italian. A lot of authors now—well, I can think only of Robert Penn Warren at the moment, but I have heard of others—get this clause about not going out of print, and I wonder why they did not demand it from the first. It is absolutely horrible to see the way books worth keeping just float up for a minute on the dirty tide of the Sunday Reviews, and then go down forever. What do we live and work for? I told my publisher I would as soon let him expose a baby of mine in the ashcan as to have my books treated so. As you remarked of a girl in one of your stories whom you called stupid, or a bitch, I forget which, "she (he) understood."

****

Your desert sounds pretty nice, in spite of the special grey weather in which you were writing. I was at Stanford for a year, talking to writing students; it was a dull time, except for the students. They were all right. But the littery faculty was the worst I ever found anywhere—fifth-raters and barely that. So the company and the tone were poor. There are fine people on other faculties there, but I was so bogged down with work and so benumbed by the situation I had tripped into, I hadn't got time or spirit to look for them, or encourage them to look for me. (Let me here except Yvor Winters and his grand wife Janet Lewis. But then I never got them identified with the faculty, somehow, or even with Stanford. They are just Yvor and Janet, where ever they might be.)

****

I haven't heard from Bob Wetterau[18] for years. Do give him and his wife my remembrances . . . I was to be godmother to their first baby, and of course, fell on my face at the last minute with—guess what? Bronchitis.

****

I wouldn't know just where to place the apex or zenith of living in the world at this moment, either. Nor the nadir. The younger set of writers, painters and all here don't seem to be having much fun, though an awful lot is going on, in a helter-skelter sort of way. But the writers seem to be just fraying out the last loose-ends of something that was getting to be old-hat fifteen years ago, and they don't seem to be reading anything except each other's books, trying to find the same thing as they can. (Looking back at this sentence, I do not believe it is English—but I do hope you can guess at what I am trying to say . .) There is a young woman, Eleanor Clark, who will have out a book this spring, not fiction, called Rome and a Villa. And William Goyen will bring out his second, Ghost and Flesh. They are the only two I can think of just now that seem to be stayers, and getting better as they go. There are entirely too many infant prodigies, which is quite correct in music, but doesn't go so well in writing and painting, which requires one to grow up in order to be effective. And the plague of writing schools has taught everybody "how to write" before they have anything to say. I have also a theory that most of the advertisements for fashions, deodorants, perfumes and life insurance are written by the writing school students who didn't quite make the grade in third-rate fiction. So they write fifth-rate fiction and sell it to advertising agencies. Lord, Bob, when I was on the West Coast all tangled up successively with MGM, Paramount, and Columbia, the saddest thing in the world—mind you, I don't mean to make you cry—was the long row of movie writers, on contract at salaries from three thousand to five thousand a week—them was the days!—who sat in my office telling me how they were still hoping to save enough money to live so they could at last "do their own work." They were, they said, just simple, honest artists at heart, and were capable of great things, but somehow they had just never been able to free themselves and make a start. I used to tell them my story about the girl who loved virtue above everything, but couldn't afford it; so she went in a whore house and worked like mad for years saving up so she could live a pure life. They simply hated that story.

****

I think perhaps now that Life, capital L, is where we are, each one of us, I never found it dull anywhere, but certainly it has been better at different times and different places. Mexico was wonderful for me, and so was Paris: but then, here would be quite all right if only I could have a little more steady health. My life in California was all muddled up with the moving picture studios, and was not right for me. Imagine that my happy memories there are of growing camellias and roses and carnations and azaleas and irises, but there are worse occupations! Now, I must not start another page—this gossip could just go on forever . . . I would so like to see you, we would quite talk our heads off by now. Tell me really about your life, what you are working on, how you live; of course no matter where you are you will find the possible human beings for company; that's a lovely thing about you. . . .

Now then, this will learn you to write me a letter—see what you get back! Let's not lose touch again, even if we can't write steadily—who does? we can surely keep each other up on news, and above all, let's tell each other where we are! Its always nice to know that.

With my same old love,
Katherine Anne

To: William Goyen TLS 4pp. HRHRC

Hotel Chambiges, 8 rue Chambiges, Paris V111
2nd June 1952

Hello you darling yourself—

The Festival really closed, last night, with a big farewell concert. I didn't go, but rested in bed the day-long, having done motion pictures the morning before (with Glenway and two members of the Hindu team, in a new little Café called <u>Les Enfants Terribles</u>, a perfect Fairyland of putrid little near-Cocteau decorations, with large plaster-casts of the hands of the Master-baiter showering blessing on the inmates.) Well believe it or not, we four sat at little tables near the bar under the murderous lights, and with the camera grinding away at our faces, talked as seriously as possible in the circumstances, about—well, about how writers, artists of all sorts, should make their separate peace among themselves, and from there on we talked a little about ways and means of doing this. It was strange, the place crowded with camera men and reporters and the windows crowded with onlookers from the street: and oh very tiring. Then I went to lunch at Pauline Potter's;[19] she lives in a princely old house at the very point of the Quai Bourbon, in such lovely austerity of bare floors and windows, baby-blue satin upholstery, stiff taffeta hangings, enormous garden of white lilies blooming against a bare wall: a delicious house. There were Janet Flanner, Glenway, Virgil Thompson, Cyril Connolly, Philip Rothschild, a most attractive man, friend of Pauline's, and his beautiful young daughter: beside her discreetly a beautiful young man whose name I did know but now cannot remember, Pauline and myself.[20] Heavenly champagne, lovely food, and you would have been pleased to see how four of the most opinionated people in the world, (Flanner, Wescott, Connolly, and Thompson) minded their manners and got along prettily. I have a feeling it would not have lasted long, but it lasted the luncheon, anyway. Well, then, home and Calvin[21] called. He had just got in from Amiens. In the evening I went at last to 4 Saints etc,[22] with Marcelle, after having dinner with the Lowells, and there was Calvin who had managed to get a ticket. You are right I believe about the piece: It is rather touching and awfully well done, pure amusement so far as I know or any one seems able to find out or to care: I kept thinking I should have brought the children, it had so the air of a Christmas pantomime; though there is, as in almost everything done for the theatre now, that corpse-like fetor of sodomy. But I think children might just get the absurdity and the really witty music. A little girl said to me the next day, 'I think I liked it, but I didn't understand it.' I said, 'No one does; no one is supposed to.' I must say she really looked mystified then. I had a diabolical impulse to add: 'No one really understands anything, nor really wants to. . . . .' but held my tongue, believing as I do that children must not be deliberately confused, nor be subjected to premature experience.

- - - - - - -

It has been a tremendous round, and I have lunched, aperitiffed (<u>could</u> that be a word?) dined, gone to cocktail parties, attended conferences, been interviewed, every day at such a rate that of course, I collapsed, at Ciro's, of all dull places where I had blundered in with a party of very rich Americans seeing Paris, with a General or so from Eisenhower's staff, and altogether, I evanesced and was carried limp into the green room where the floor show troupe rested between shows, and after an hour was brought home, spent three days in bed, French doctor gave exactly the same diagnosis as Dr. Coppersmith, but a slightly different treatment. He is right not to trust me to be able to ward these things off, and now every morning I take two impressive looking ampoules full of a strange tasting liquid, and haven't had a symptom since. Still Allen Tate and Glenway crossed their hands and together carried me up the stairs when we were invited to lunch at the restaurant Laurent by the publisher of Le Figaro.[23] I must say the literary gentlemen (the French ones, I mean: I was the only woman present) looked a little astonished, and far from explaining anything, Allen said gaily, 'O, this is a customary way in America for ladies to go upstairs'. Wasn't that charming?

I suppose I should tell you who I have seen. Curtius[24] didn't come, a rumor that he got his feelings hurt—I didn't hear how. I found Allen, Glenway, Stephen Spender and Natacha,[25] The Lowells, (Elizabeth Hardwick) all runningtogether more or less, and I saw a great deal of Stephen, first and last. Marcelle laughed: she knows my stance on this topic. And she said, that the first half dozen times she saw me, I was either getting in or getting out of a taxi with Spender: which was true. He is so goddamnably amiably <u>impervious</u>, in some sort of mysterious way, I just gave up any notion of making any sort of stand about anything: He finally went to England. His wife seemed to me so incredibly superior to him; and she carries her dubious, humiliating, insulted life with such dignity and seems so strangely vowed to it, actually the daily, visible sordidness of his behavior (such as bringing the French journalist mentioned in his autobiography, to lunch with all of us, sitting huddled up with him, Natacha present) seem somehow reconcilable with human decency, which of course it is not. I said to Glenway, that he seemed not in the least to realize the nature of his acts. Glenway said, it was simply almost total insensibility: he did not know he was treating her badly, after all he never treated her any worse than he had treated everybody else. I said, that homosexuality in either sex had this peculiarly brutalizing effect: and I wondered if the dirty habit itself was not the sign of an original <u>thickness</u> of some sort, either a blunted or an exasperated nervous system which could only respond to violations of one sort or another. They simply violate everything they touch. But I don't mind if they would only stay on their side of the street. And I am shocked at women like Natacha who consent to such a parody of marriage, which for creatures like Spender is only one more theatre for exhibiting himself. I can only suppose she has in her some deep sickness also.

xxxxxxxxxxxxxxx

Calvin and I went out last evening, pooled our finances, and sat on the terrace at the Marignon, on the Champs-Elysées, under a cloudy sky which finally burst into rain. I <u>think</u> I invented a new aperitif for Calvin, who hates sweet drinks. I just take Cinzano or something of the sort. He took gin, but didn't want a cocktail. My favorite tipple is Perrier—do you remember that delicious sparkling water?—so I ordered a little cold bottle of it, a slice of lemon, ice, and Calvin simply mixed his gin in that, and of course, you or any one is free to say that combination is old as gin itself, but just the same, I never saw it. He said it was wonderful. Then we moved inside, and had red-hot buttery-burgundy-garlic snails, a plateful each, a tremendous Chateaubriand steak, rare, and wound up with Crêpes Suzette, the first I have had here: coffee made at the table in a little glass machine, and Calvin took a <u>fine champagne</u>. We drank a bottle of <u>vin rosé</u>,—which is more popular now than when I was here before) and we just had all along the most euphoric, dreamlike, almost spiritual feelings such as only wonderful food and wine in a gay beautiful place can give: at least to such earthly beings as we agreed we are.

It cost us just four thousand francs, including a very good tip, which comes out to something a little over ten dollars: it was the kind of food you get only in the Brussels or the Chambord in New York, and would cost twenty five dollars at least. Everybody screams about the cost of things here, and things are dear, but nothing to compare with New York. Fact is, the screamers are tourists, visitors, birds of passage, and they must have the best of everything and buy all sorts of stuff, and they do indeed scatter their money, and it disappears at a dismaying rate. At home they know the value of the money, and don't toss it around so freely. But then, no matter what it costs, I still feel Paris is worth everything.

- - - - - -

I was going to talk some more about people, but every name has a long history attached to it, we have simply met up everywhere in slightly changing, dissolving groups; I saw Auden only at big parties or at the conferences; Faulkner didn't show up at least not near any one I knew, until the last day, when he appeared and made an unbelievably inept little speech. By that time we were all tired of his rudeness and so Lowell, Glenway and I, who sat together on the platform just back of him, decided that our great man could go to hell in his own way, and didn't shake hands. Childish of us, I suppose. But natural. I found here people I don't suppose you know, which I knew years ago, friends then and now of Jimmie Stern. Jimmie and Tanya were here the day I came, but left almost at the same time. Asked for me, and Glenway told them I was too tired to see anybody, which was true but would not have been for them. I am so sorry not to have seen them. Louis McNiece married Hedli Anderson[26] the young singer who was first engaged to Darsie Gillie, (London Post correspondent)[27] then to Jimmie, while Darsie was engaged to Tanya, and then she married Jimmie, and here seventeen years later, all passions spent or presumably, they are all amiable friends, and I was delighted to see them. Of course there may be every sort of banked fires and private dramas, but as you know, I have learned to stick to appearances, the surface of things is quite enough for me in my general personal relations. I want my friends for comfort and conversation when my own inner hell is too much for me: and sometimes I think they most of them want that from me, too: at any rate, it seems to be what I have to give.

XXXXX

France was never so beautiful, from Cherbourg to Paris, all Normandy was one green glory. Paris was never so beautiful, I never loved it so well. This is my city; I belong here, I am at home here in a way that I never was anywhere else, and somehow, I can't quite see how, I shall manage to live here, or at least have this instead of New York as my point of departure and return. I have already set the date for coming back up to September 5th next. Meantime next Thursday the fifth (just one month since leaving New York) I am going to Brittany for a month, to a little inn, and sit down and work, and get something really finished. Then I plan to go to the Basque country for a little visit with Marcelle on her vacation, THEN back to New York to close up that house and dispose, one way or another, of my household stuff. And come back here for good. Nice young John Ransom (JCR's nephew) came bringing roses and Bourbon, and when I said, 'If I must live in misery, I had rather it in Paris than New York.' He said very sweetly, 'But you know it is very hard to live in misery here—you are always too happy!'

Glenway is off to Italy and then home, Allen to England and then home, the Lowells got off to Austria this morning, Cyril Connolly left Pauline's lunch table before dessert to catch a plane for London, the Spenders are gone. I think Allen is visiting them: I haven't seen or heard of anybody today except Calvin, who rang up to inquire how I had survived the evening: we sat up here on my balcony until 2 this morning talking about Life capital L, over John Ransom's Old Granddad, which somehow makes a pretty picture in my mind of an old gentleman extended like a table between us. Pentecôte as you know is a full bank holiday here, and everybody who can, leaves town. Marcelle[28] is in the country with friends. And so on. I just sit here in my tacky little fifth floor room, with its great double windows wide open, and just there, every time I glance up, is Paris, great tall eighteenth century greystone façades, iron balconies with green flowering plants all over them, the chimney pots, the arched dormer windows, and above the lively moving illuminated clouds, and the sweet clean air of this place, purified by its long vistas of trees and the spring rains. I am perfectly happy, if I know at all the true meaning of that word. I want nothing at all just now but what I have: I miss nothing that I ever had, I want nothing back; tomorrow may come when it pleases . . . I know where I am and what I need to do, and every step I take is in that direction. Oh blessed good time that I had almost lost hope of coming to. . . . .

XXXXXXX

Well, I feel that this is a dull letter, for it seems I have told really nothing, and yet, here are all these pages . . I have been trying to keep notes, a journal, but it is dull work, I haven't had time for anything but dates, names of places, reminders of things to tell fully later . . . I must stop, my darling, I can hardly expect you to read this! One's little adventures after all can't possibly be so absorbing to any one else: perhaps I really have nothing at all to tell: for what is really happening is very quiet and deep and it does not have a great deal to do with people or events . . . So take it as what I am able to do now, I did not want to wait too long to write, because then who knows when I should ever? I will send my address from Brittany, but meantime if you write in care of Marcelle, it will certainly reach me.

Take good care of yourself, love me in whatever way you <u>can</u> love me, as I do you: what is there we can ask of each other? Maybe we will get in the habit of remembering each other tenderly, forgetting all but that face we now and then showed each other that no one else ever saw, nor can ever see, because we created each other's faces in that moment. And then, our horrible year will maybe just break off our lives and sink away and not be remembered any more. It is all still such a nightmare to me that now as I write I begin to feel again that deathly sickness of the soul of this time last year . . and must really stop now.

Good-bye, good-bye: I don't in the least know what you mean when you say you love me, nor even what I mean now when I say it to you. Yet there is something, and we'll call it by that name until we find a better. So, I love you. Let me hear from you, and especially when you expect to come to Europe. I should be in Paris in August, certainly towards the end. If we can manage, let us see each other then. With my love,

Katherine Anne

To: Gertrude Beitel TLS 5pp. Maryland

Hotel d'Isly, 29 rue Jacob, Paris VI, France, August 14th 1952

Gertrude darling: Brittany is now a green memory, surely one of the most serene and lovely of my life; and did you ever during last June, sleeping or waking, intercept even a little wandering thought from me? For you were constantly in my mind, and I missed you as if we had been used to each other's company, and now were separated at exactly the wrong time. I simply wished every day that you were in Pont-Aven too, so that we might see everything together, and talk about it. Maybe it was your letter that came there so sweetly and familiarly as if you had walked into the Inn that caused me this longing for your society. Whatever it was, you <u>were</u> there in somewhat baffling fashion.

As you know, I went there to work and to recover a little from the enormous strain of the past few years. I was too tired to work very hard or steadily, but I did get far along with the corrections and revisions of the proof of my new book, "The Days Before." I must have told you this, it was about all the news I had at the time. Well, I finished it here, got if off three weeks ago, it is announced and will certainly appear in October. You and Lily will have your copies the minute I get home and can sign them. It is a collection: in case I didn't tell you, of my occasional writings, essays, criticisms, and "personal and particular" as the publishers have entitled one section. We think probably everything worth saving has been gleaned out of Sunday Book Supplements and weekly magazines and literature reviews. It was astonishing how much there was of it, all buried and forgotten for years. But I did have friends who remembered certain things, and even friendly strangers wrote and asked me why I didn't have such a book published. After all, it is an important part of the work of almost any serious writer. So we did. And my publishers seem most happy about it, and tell me the advance sale is good. I hope so. I long for many readers, first, and I should be happy about a little money, too. The work was not done just for money, it was the best I could do at the time, and always something I wanted to do, but now it is done I don't pretend that I shouldn't be pleased with a fine sale. But I am not anxious about anything; it is always this way with me after finishing a book: it is cut away from its mooring and launched for itself, it no longer is mine altogether: it belongs to whoever reads it, and my feelings become serene and impersonal: I am not nervous about the reviews, and have never had a clipping service, even. I thought once or twice of taking a service of the kind, if I stayed in Europe, but nothing has been done about it. My publishers usually send me a parcel of reviews sometime or other, after a while. There is one thing though about this book that I noticed as I was correcting proofs: it really is for my friends and family, I believe they will like it whether anybody else does or not. I look forward with pleasure to your reading it for you will recognize the family voice and tone in it.

XXXX

Alas, I did not get to Mont St. Michel nor even to St. Malo: but then, I am coming back, and what I have seen of Brittany will prepare me for that. I joined religious processions, went to Pardons, (how easy it would be to be Catholic in that country!) and street markets: did have a few wonderful sunny days in Quimper, Audierne, Lochronon, gazing and dreaming: believe me, the ancient Druids breathed their magic on that place once for all, but you know and have seen everything that I did, and more too: and yes, the smells and colors, and above all, the flowers, were something I had known before, long ago: I felt at home there. Oh the smell of camphor and cedar—and did your grandmother, sister to mine, strew dried lavendar petals in her linen? We called it lavendar, and it looked and smelt like lavendar, but some erudite told me that our Texas shrub was not true lavendar, but vitex, a horrid name that reminds me of toothpaste or patent medicine. . . . . . It is strange how we let everything go and just for the reason you say: because we did not in the least realize what we had. It was just the natural thing and would go on forever. In our poor little farm-house on grandmother's land between Austin and San Marcos, we had fine old walnut secretaries full of wonderful old books, and walnut bedsteads, and all sorts of odds and ends which we did not even consider worthless: we simply never thought of them at all. I have seen the same things in shops in Lexington and Madison Avenue at unbelievable prices . . . . things that should never have been for sale at all once they were set in their proper houses.

XXXXX

Do let me know more about the novel about the Skaggs family. I do not know the writer, but Seward, (if he is a Seward) is surely a connection.[29] I am very anxious to read it. I have many times been tempted to go to Kentucky and dig out the annals of that family. I found priceless bits of history in the Library of Congress. Probably could find everything there in time.

Speaking of family, I believe this will amuse you. I was invited to dinner by a very charming French family, and among the guests were a young journalist who proposes to write an article about my work for Les Nouvelles Littéraires here, and another young publisher. During the evening, the young publisher said, "I know a great deal about you, your personal history!" I asked him where he learned it. Our hostess at once produced a huge tome, (that is the very word for it,) called Webster's Biographical Dictionary. A book I did not know existed. He turned to the right page and showed me the little outline about me. I said, that I did not know I was in that book, and how pleased I was to be right in with my family! So I pointed to six times great grandfather Colonel Andrew, and Cousin Horace, (ambassador to France for eight years). And David Rittenhouse Porter, brother to Andrew and Father to Horace: and sure enough, Katherine Anne is there too, the first woman in the family to be seated on the platform with her menfolk! Now, I want to see that book closer, and look for the Skaggs. Would you mind looking for them? This edition is a late one, of course. I can't have been in it very long. But don't you think its fun? I've a good mind to drop a note to the Webster publishing people and establish my relationship with the others of the name, for their next edition. They mention the relationships between Andrew, David, and Horace, and I belong there too. I just don't want to be taken for a stray in that company.

XXXXX

Here is an ironic note: my nice new French friends, who know very little about Americans, were plainly impressed by that Ambassador cousin, and could not conceal their surprise that I knew who my Pre-Revolutionary grandfather was. They had not known that Americans had any ancestors to speak of. Their frankness in the matter was delightful: they thought a great deal more of me when they discovered I had relatives of some public distinction: I do not believe that any people in the world have more respect than the French for success: just almost any old kind of success will do. They can be, in respect to Americans at least, comically mis-led by it.

XXXXX

Alas, no, I have not seen Colette.[30] She is crippled with arthritis, lives in bed or a wheel chair, yet lives a very public life and writes constantly. I am sure I could see her if I asked, but I hesitate, because she is so surrounded and so occupied: I speak French so little and so badly—it is strange because I did well enough before, but I have forgotten the speech: I should need an interpreter, and that would make much too "set" an affair of it. It is of no interest merely to meet some one in such conditions. Maybe something, an occasion of some kind, will take me near her: it would be delightful. Her vitality of feeling and speech are wonderful. She is called upon for her opinion about almost anything, and gives it; wittily and charmingly and acutely. Her photographs snapped at random show her wonderful old face beautiful and alive and sparkling. I hope something happens that I shall have an excuse to talk to her, or just see her. Proust's niece[31] is another matter. I am waiting for a French friend to come back from vacation to take me to her. I'll tell you all when it happens. Ah, and Montaigne's house! But never mind, I'm coming home to straighten up my little affairs and get ready for an absence, and then I'll make your pilgrimages for us both!

Just today, just an hour ago, I had a letter from—well, I suppose Director, I don't know his exact title—of the American Academy in Rome, asking me if, just in case, I were invited to come to Rome for a year as a Writer-in-Residence to the Academy, would I accept.[32] Oh, would I? So I wrote him a carefully dignified but pleased letter, trying not to convey the notion that the wild horses couldn't keep me back if they <u>did</u> invite me. I suppose it would be some time this fall or winter, the beginning. Now, as you know, in diplomacy, it is custom before inviting any one to anything of a public or official nature, first to write and ascertain privately if the invitation can be accepted. If not, it is not given. If accepted, it means that you are, for all practical purposes, already invited. Well, this is not exactly diplomatic business, but I imagine it is run on the same principle. So I have accepted, and if they don't invite me now, officially, I shall be surprised, very unpleasantly, because they won't be playing the game according to the rules I know and it will be confusing.

If I go, I will be the first in that chair. It is a new thing. It is not exactly a surprise, because friends have been talking around and about it for a year, and I have been recommended over and over again, and I met Mr. Laurance Roberts last February in New York at a dinner got up specially for us to meet by a friend of us both. So his letter surely means only one thing: that I have been chosen for the place. I am told one is given a beautiful apartment in a palace, travel expense and a modest but sufficient stipend. It sounds almost too good to be true, and I'll be sure to keep you posted on all the changes, variations, and mischances if any, as events unroll. No doubt though, it is an honor, meant as such, and I take it as that .. Though such public honor as I have had until now does very often turn out, practically, to be hardly that. We'll see. It would be so pleasant to receive a real one that I could respect. I must modify this a little: I was pleased to be a Fellow of the Library of Congress, and I was re-elected Vice-president of the National Institute of Arts and Letters for my second two-year term last spring. Two terms are customary, there are usually five of us at a time, and it is a very rotating kind of office. They haven't required anything at all of me, and God knows this membership is a mere catch-all: still, if we do have a perfect zoo of hacks and climbers and third-raters, we still do have almost every writer, composer, and painter of stature in the country. If we haven't, it is because they refused membership.

So I am glad to have been chosen as an officer. But generally speaking public life is not for me . . . . not that phase of it. However, one thinks of the family: and every year another line is added to my biography in Who's Who, so all of it must serve some good purpose. I remember how annoyed I was to learn that Great- etc., Granpap Andrew had refused the post of Secretary of War I think from President Monroe on the trivial grounds that he was getting old and was tired. He should have done it for his descendants. So I take everything as it comes along so the family can be proud of me. I notice I am proud of those who made a little mark on their world in their time. I believe this is quite natural and somehow associated with our other and greater longing for immortality of the soul. All the known energy of our ancestors seems to give us energy, of a spiritual sort, which is the best sort. I love Lily's honorable life and the way she respected her gift and developed it and never misused it; as a friend of mine who saw her once remarked: "When she comes on the stage the whole tone of the play rises by many degrees." We saw her together in Life With Father,[33] a play certainly not good enough for her, but she <u>made</u> it good enough. Bless her.

Well, my dear, you see I have come to a breathing place, and here is a long rambling letter—one-half of the conversation I wish we were having, and I hope to hear from you soon. I shall be here in this funny little hotel on the noisiest corner in Paris, Bonaparte and Jacob, until September 4th. At least I am supposed to sail with <u>La Liberté</u> on the 5th. If you write before then, give yourself time, even by airmail: not later than September 1st.

With my devoted love, and tell Lily a mss. will fall on her, next.

Katherine Anne

Speaking of mss.

Its no good to try to tell you how anxiously I look forward to seeing your Hamlet;[34] still I do know its no good trying to hurry you, it must come in its time. Your trouble is over-richness of material: it must be almost impossible to know <u>what to leave out</u>. That is the great problem of any writer who really has something to say. But do try to finish, and be sure not to destroy one note as you go. Keep everything. The sources are always fascinating for others to study.

Love again, KA

To: Cora Posey TLS 2pp. Maryland

117 East 17th Street, New York N.Y. 21 October 1952

Dearest Miss Cora:

All my gratitude to you for sending me the copies of my father's letter to you written after my mother's death. They are most painful to read, and haunted my mind for days with the same kind of bitter melancholy I used to have as a child when the gloom and darkness of his nature darkened the very air around us. I noticed that in these letters he did not once mention the children: we early learned not to speak of our mother, his grief and regret belonged to him, we could neither share nor lighten it. I know that he loved us, and did what he could for us, but I always felt we were an immense and bitter burden to him, on his heart and in just the daily life of trying to care for us.

All life of feeling seems to be so tragic. And as you were very near to those lives when they were young and hopeful, and when they were ruined and desolate, I say to you what I would not say to any one else, unless to my older sister, Gay. Did you receive your copy of my book, The Days Before? I dedicated it to Gay for a birthday present, the little foreword was written on her birthday, 25th July, in my noisy little hotel room on rue Jacob, near the corner of Bonaparte, Paris . . All these years my sister never forgot to tell me that she believed in what I was doing, in my work and my life, which are, after all, the same thing. This book, with work in it reaching back through thirty years, seemed to be hers, naturally.

Let me tell you before I forget again: I have a package of my father's and mother's letters before they were married, which you sent, I think, to Gay a good while ago, and she sent on to me. But of course if there are all these others I want to see them if possible. There is some talk now of being invited to Houston to speak or read, perhaps in November: if so, I do so want to come to Indian Creek to see you. Nothing is certain yet, and I will let you know as soon as the question is settled. I can never afford to travel unless I go on what I call "a paying errand." It is odd, but I make much more money talking around the country than I make writing. But maybe I would do more writing if I stayed at home more and didn't go off lecturing and reading in colleges and Universities. But it is interesting and I enjoy it.

Miss Cora I shan't start another page, because if I do I'll just run on and on, and my book is coming out tomorrow (no, day after, and things are piling up as they always do: and it would be easy to feel a little harried at this moment. Yet it doesn't happen often that I bring out a book, so I do rather enjoy the hubbub, and even look forward now to seeing the reviews! A health-ier state of mind than <u>that</u> I can't imagine.

Bless you, and thank you for everything: hoping to see you this fall or winter, with my love Katherine Anne

Niece Ann's six months old baby has got both his parents licked to a standstill: he is spoiled beyond words, but <u>so</u> sweet and smart he is charming anyhow.

To: Thomas H. Carter TLS 1p. W&L

117 East 17th Street, New York 3 N.Y.
9 March 1953
Dear Mr. Carter:

Maybe you will be surprised at this: safely shut up in the bottom of the Spanish cupboard, (safely for the present, that is) stands a 1-quart bottle of Virginia Gentleman. You remember there was none to be had in Lexington. I tried again in Washington, meaning to give it to the friends I stopped with— no luck. I settled for Jack Daniels. By now it was a crusade. So I called my little liquor dealer just around the corner and down a ways, and he sent it right over! So now you know where it goes and why Virginians must go on a wait-ing list. Its not right.

++++++

I saw Ezra, and his wife, and a young man whose name I don't remember; my friend Marcella Winslow went with me. She has painted two portraits of him, both excellent, and visits him. My feeling is that everything went very well; he was in fine spirits, and lost not an instant in the business of setting me right on all points where I erred and do err, and I sat down under it like a lamb; he did not want to quarrel with me, only to <u>tell</u> me. I am going back to Washington April 1 to read at the Corcoran Gallery, and mean to stay several days, and take notes of his talk, and copy them out for him, and for myself. It is just a good moment to listen to him, he really has something he wants to talk about. Where he was, the air was not hospital air, or the air of madness; he is profoundly eccentric, he is really a Fascist by a kind of emotional <u>bent</u>, and I cannot, cannot understand one word of his economic theories: so I tried without I hope being too obvious to keep the talk on poetry and personal his-tory. . . . He <u>is</u> in prison, you know; and it seems strange to me now how free he was—all the walls disappeared.

+++++++

I must have been temporarily deranged if I promised you a chunk of fiction, for the only finished things I have are chunks to be excised at will from
the novel; and there is such a passage lying around here somewhere, I thought
it right here on this table, but I can't find it anywhere . . . I meant to send it to
you, and will when I see it, which could be any minute, it is absolutely in this
room; and though of course you must be the judge, I wonder about its suit-
ability. It consists entirely of a low-comedy love scene on the ship's deck, from
thence to childish improprieties in the bottom of a life boat, and an autumnal
seduction scene, consisting entirely of conversation between a fifty year old
Countess who takes ether and the sixty year old ship's doctor, who has heart
trouble. The Countess of course is the seducer. Doesn't sound like me? Well,
its part of the novel, remember; the whole book is not like that. If this interests
you I'll be pleased to send it, when I find it.

O everything was lovely at Washington and Lee, and now I really understand a friend of mine when I told her I was going there: "Its my favorite place
of the world." And she has really seen the world. You were all so charming to
me, I felt wonderfully at home. Please will you send me Shenandoah regularly? I told the girls at Sweet Briar they should all be reading it. I want to
write to you in particulars about the magazine, but it must be later. I am off to
Chicago University now. What a change!

With my happy remembrances
Yours
Katherine Anne Porter

To: George Platt Lynes TLS 2pp. Maryland

Hopwood Room, Angell Hall, University of Michigan, Ann Arbor Michigan,
24 November 1953

George Angel Love
I hurry to grab the few minutes before my next student appointment to
answer your letter, for it is fascinating to me that you still after all these years
look upon me as a femme mysterieuse, if not, oh never, fatale; the legend that
I disappear, taking my secret life with me—that, even and perhaps, I work a
machinery of mystification on purpose—well, what could be more interesting, and alas, further from the facts.

About this last business: simply, the New Weston had no room for me,
my fault for delaying too long in asking for it. In Baltimore I was put up at the

Sheraton Belvadere by my committee, and the management kindly offered as a matter of pure business to reserve me a room in the New York Sheraton, which turned out to be way to hell and gone on the West side in what Charles Henri Ford's mother in her Mississippi accent would call the theatrical dist-ict.[35] I arrived so exhausted I fell into bed and slept until time to go to the Poetry Center.

But the <u>news</u> you give me! Lightning has been striking all around me for weeks. On the train as I left for Baltimore I read about the death of Dylan Thomas, who had given a performance of the Milk Wood just the Thursday before me at the Center. Ten minutes before I started my read-ing, the news came that my sister Gay had had a coronary thrombosis and was not expected to live. She did live, but must live carefully from now on. Then Glenway's father died, and you are in a motor accident. . . . Now when-ever I get a telegram or a long distance call, I have a real shudder of fright. Everybody at the Center was crushed by Dylan's death, and John Malcolm Brinnin, who had sat up with him for four days and nights, looked really like a shadow. Nobody I knew came to hear me this time, but there was an immense friendly audience of strangers—a packed house, and it went off very well. You know, I have been doing this sort of thing for years upon years, all over the country, and not until last year—no, it was at the Museum of Modern Art, before, did everybody I knew ever have the faintest notion of how I had been spending these strange jaunts I took about the country . . Alas, for mystery. I never thought to explain because I never dreamed any-body was interested!

This last trip about did me in . . . I could do nothing between times but go to bed, have food sent up, sleep, and try not to collapse . . . You don't realize darling, that I live in this place and any school where I am, out in the open totally exposed to ravening cannibals who nibble and gnaw on me all the time . . . I am supposed to have a buffer, an assistant who finds out whether the person has any real business with me, as half of them have not, and fend them off for me. But she just turns them in in droves. . . . I am so tired all the times it is physically painful. . . . . . .

Ah well, there it is, and I have no right to tell you such a dull story . . . it is <u>not</u> that life is dull, but unbelievably wearing and incessant. . . . I like what I am <u>really</u> doing, the thing I am here for, its just all the huzza and hullabaloo on the periphery that grinds me down . .

Now, I begin vaguely to think of Christmas vacation—we have two full weeks—but it wouldn't surprise me if I spent them in bed with a good book and a bottle of Bourbon. But one day, one fine day, or rather night, I expect to curl down under that bearskin cover, your happy guest.

Do let me know what happens; I am just going through my paces as well as I know how, trying to be a little saving so that my next time of freedom won't find me also broke, for I do so want to work a little on all that unfinished business of mine that you know so well. Everybody I see here is pleasant; this is a fine faculty, those I have met, and though this University no doubt suffers all the debilitating effects of that Giantism which does afflict this world now, the Biggest being per se the Best, it is a good University in many of its separate departments. So I don't intend to do anything but live here as amiably as I can, and leave without incident. . . .

Bless you, I wish you were happier, please tell me you are following your "diet"—remember? and that it works. Here is my sabre-toothed student prowling outside . . . always a different one. . . .

My same old love. And give my love to Glenway . .
Katherine Anne

I suppose Monroe is well away to South America now. He sent word he was going. They invited me here to stay on for the 8 weeks of summer school too, so I shan't be out until late in August.

To: Harrison Paul Porter Jr. TLS 3pp. Maryland

25, Avenue des Platanes, Cointe, Liége, Belgique: 11 December 1954

Paul darling:

The little girls are most certainly lovely,[36] and its a real test to come through that kind of occasion and that kind of camera. Katherine Anne resembles you, me, and your sister Dorothy—we all have a strong family look, and your father used to look like you—But Connie simply has the wittiest, most humorous, most acute look I ever saw in a child's face; if she has not a superior temperament and mind then she shouldn't have that kind of face! Its misleading. Katherine Anne seems to look out towards her world as if she wondered what it thought of <u>her</u>; Connie is regarding it very objectively, and what is important to her is what <u>she</u> thinks about it. But they are both delightful looking, each with a most strongly marked character; not so beautiful as their mother, but that could hardly be expected; very few girls are as beautiful as she was. . still is, no doubt. But it has been years since I saw her . .

Oh dear, wouldn't it be wonderful to think that they were getting a real education and had something to look forward to? But I cannot take on that worry . . . I cannot understand the fear and even the suspicion and hatred that that family have for superiority in any form—even Ann who had such a quick, though certainly not deep mind, seems hardly to be able to wait to be as dull and stupid as Walter . . . Its a pity, but it is simply not my affair.

++++++

I am leaving here—do tell dear John[37] that I am going to get that ride in a helicopter at last—they fly between here and Brussels to make connections with international airlines—on the 21st, will record on the 22nd, fly to Rome on the 23rd; by train to Paris on the 30th—with Marcelle Sibon, who will meet me at the Albergo d'Inghilterra in Rome—a little hotel where English and Americans go—Via Bocca di Leone 14, put that in your address book in case you ever need a little hotel in Rome—and from Paris to Liége on the 3rd of January . . .

So the two main Sitwells are in New York again.[38] I wish I had time to see Sachie and Georgia,[39] but they are in Northamptonshire and I can't, this time. But I'll tell you all about everything when I get back . . People do give awfully good parties for the Sitwells in New York. Well, I gave one myself for the other two!

Copy out the Roethke poem for me, with date of magazine where it appeared? I might use it for my anthology . . . He is growing fast, I cared nothing for his early poetry, but I have seen some wonderful things in the past two or three years. Ah. love, etc., and don't think it hasn't a great deal to do with a poet's poetry . .

+++++++

I started this last night, but was too tired after a long day of just letter-writing about every kind of detail—lectures, of anything, the trip—God it takes fifteen letters to get the smallest thing arranged, and so gave up; Day before yesterday there was sunshine all day, for the first time in fifteen or sixteen days; but yesterday and today are back in the groove—wild, windy, bitter-cold, dark, rainy—oh, well, I'm going to stop writing about the weather. It is simply damnable and thats all. Darling, I remember the New York winters, too—yet there are a few days in it worth living!

But first, for your ear-ache I want you to do something very pawky and sensible and effective. Get a little box of lamb's wool: the same thing ballet-dancers put in their box-toes, I think you can get it at drugstores—and simply wear little boluses in your ears when you go out. Cotton won't do, it takes wool. This warms the inside of the ear and keeps the wind out, and you'll see what a good thing it is if you try it. Carry the stuff in your pocket and you can always remove it in the house . . . You have apparently some deep allergy to cold—that itching, and so on. Does it break out, or is it just that terrible nervous surface itch which comes of skin allergy? Well, anyway, I had a post-card from Monroe Wheeler the other day, from Puerto Rico, with a wonder-ful beach scene, and he said, the University there would be glad to have me if I cared to come; and it never got colder there than 80 degrees... I'm really thinking it over! Maybe you had better, too. Is there not some well-paying chore that a promising young man could snag for himself with some Ameri-can company, equivalent to your rock-salt enterprise, in Puerto Rico, or some interesting tropical Island? I hate to think of you sitting there in New York itching yourself to death every winter...something should be done about that.

+++++++

Your notes on the aspect of the school children of your time, and the way you managed to register on film the smell of "restrooms" of elementary schools, is merely wonderful ... I noticed when I was even a little girl that little boys smelled like goats, and I have often wondered how little girls smelled to little boys? But the fact is, for some silly reason people think little boys like being dirty, which I have never been able to believe. I think they are told they like being dirty, and so they act out the part assigned to them ... Little girls are simply washed and combed more, and they are sprinkled with talcum powder, too: it all helps. These little nieces of yours have the most beautiful hair so beautifully cared for, and I bet their little boy cousins are let go shaggy and unwashed. It is not fair ... I remember Thomas Jefferson's letter to his daughter Maria, warning her that she could not be too careful in her personal cleanliness: "Nothing," says he, stuffily, "offends my sex like a want of delicacy in yours."[40] I was about fifteen when I read that; I didn't need the advice, I was clean as a cat all my life; but I was not too young to look around me at the other sex who would be offended if I lacked delicacy, and to think: "Why doesn't it occur to them that we might like a little delicacy from them, too?" But apparently it never has occurred to them.

+++++++++

Oh, that's not fair either ... I have known some very sweet-smelling men.

+++++++

I think little boys are taught, perhaps, at least by implication that dirtiness and roughness are proof of manliness; something of the kind. Whatever it is, we may be sure it is all nonsense.

++++++

I am very pleased with that review in Time: it is so sly, and friendly and witty, and obviously the man really respects that collection: I wish I knew who wrote it. I love especially the way he takes Melville for the standard—his natural grandeur and nobility, his fearless high style; even in English, The Overcoat[41] manages to be one of the very greatest stories ever written. I wish I could remember who said that the short story—short novel?—as we know it, the whole thing, was hatched from under Gogol's overcoat. Its just true.

Darling, this must end—it is pure self-indulgence, in a way, for I do suppose that you like to read my letters as much as I like yours. So thats my excuse....

Now then, Merry Christmas and happy New Year, and don't send any present!

About that 150.00 if you want you can do it easily, simply send a check to
    Norman A. Ottmar, Vice President
    Ann Arbor Bank, State Street Branch
    Ann Arbor, Michigan
made out to me, signed by you, and on the back, "for deposit to checking account only." It will be safe. I should be happier if you put it in your own savings account, to my credit, you might say, so that if ever I got in a real jam I could ask you for it. But just do as you feel about it ... it makes me so happy to think you are so confident you can do this! Darling, I do not like poverty and misery. It is just too great a burden and drain on the energies. Try to take care of yourself and get a little back log, so that when you are ready to take the next step you will be able to do it!

With my same old love
Aunt Katherine Anne

To: Ludwig Lewisohn TLS 1p. Maryland

117 East 17th Street, New York 3 N.Y. 5 May 1955

Ludwig Lewisohn, Esquire
Brandeis University
Waltham, Massachusetts

Dear Mr. Lewisohn:

Thank you for your kind invitation to take part in the symposium on the present status of the novel, and I am happy to accept for Thursday, June 9 at 2:30 on the campus of Brandeis University.

My own view of Mann, the old death-bringer, is that he had a compulsion to elevate his own weaknesses and lacks into a canon of art, and I think he did more damage to the whole idea of art, the place and meaning of the artist in society, than any writer of his time or after, and that his novels are like malignant growths on literature. Just the same, some one who must be dealt with seriously and taken into account: his short novels are miracles of form, at least four of them, and it is not just accidental—that corpse-like fetor that breathes from every line of his: child of his time, echo of its voice.

I have been reading a good many new novels lately—not exactly on purpose, publishers send them to me, and curiosity does the rest; so now, in light of this symposium, I shall begin to look at them a little more closely, and try to find out what it is that makes them nearly all so very bad, so shapeless and confused and grubby and gritty, or soft and suppurating at the center; yes, and often a combination of these two sicknesses. Yet now and then comes a little honey out of the horn: enough to keep us encouraged, and to remind us that the average of any human endeavor is never very high. There is the average—and then there is the rare and not to be classified superlative, given us for nothing, for certainly we do nothing to deserve it! Please don't think that because very little pleases me I am disillusioned about literature—no, alas, I have as great faith and expectations in it as ever, but I do know its no good to make excuses for mediocrity, and mediocrity is what we are getting mostly now, as ever.

Yours sincerely
Katherine Anne Porter

To: Edward Schwartz TLS 4pp. Maryland

Roxbury Road, Southbury, Connecticut, 5 November 1955

Dear Mr. Schwartz:

Its very long since I had your pleasant letter, but I have had enough change and upset since then to account for any failure in letter writing. I suppose if I told you, it could make half a chapter in that biography.

On my Fulbright Grant I broke down completely, not a nervous collapse but just exhaustion, had to be sent home, (honorably, with a lovely send-off and a beautiful voyage from Cannes to New York, and all, as if I had covered myself with laurels!) and then followed a long expensive idle kind of cure, but it was a cure, and I can still hardly believe this health is really mine—no cough, no fevers, no dolors of any kind except the minimum to remind me I am mortal. But I learned something. Friends helped me find this house, I have taken a lease for three years, and plan to finish up my four next books, and I have stopped trouping around the country and Europe reading and talking about literature. I intend to produce a little of my own, such as it is or may be. I moved entirely from New York on July 28, last.

Now then, about a biography. . . . I feel that all such things are just ways of stuffing me and putting me under glass while I am still walking around: how can we write a story until we know the end? In a special and almost literal way, <u>In my end is my beginning</u>;[42] nobody will be able to see what my life meant until it is ended; how can you sum up my work until it is finished, or at least, all I am going to be able to do? But I suppose these are my questions, not yours: I should like to have your reasons and ideas on the subject.

This house is nearly ideal in all sorts of ways and then fails in the strangest particulars. It was built as a kind of summer pavilion, though it is very sound and easily heated and ample—but there is nowhere enough unbroken wall space to build bookcases, and my books nearly all of them are still in cartons in the garage, and so are my hampers and hampers of letters and notes, and steel cabinets of mss . . . How would you go about getting to them? You on the west coast, and me in the lost deeps of Connecticut seven or eight miles from a trainstop, with slow busses running about four miles away, if I wish to take a taxi to go catch one! I love it, I feel settled here, this is the best place I know of for me, and I seriously expect to stay and get my work in hand again. I think you have no notion of what you would be up against in the way of documentation—I have no time at all to help in it, or to send things—No, I think it is impossible. . . . Another thing, my life has been exciting enough, I think it may have been interesting enough to tell about, but also a great many sufferings, hardships, troubles, and if the truth were to be told, it would cause great trouble with other people, and pain which I have no intention of inflicting on anybody. And what is the use of telling anything but the truth, so far as we are able to find it out or recognize it in the clutter of events?

I do not know if you still have any interest in the bibliography, or are keeping up with "items" for a later new edition: but, July Mademoiselle Magazine has a piece of mine <u>Adventure in Living</u>. . . . I wish you would read it anyhow . . . Some Sunday this month of November I imagine, my notice—it can hardly be called a review, they limit one so—will appear in the New York Sunday Times BOOKS, of John Malcolm Brinnin's memoir of Dylan Thomas, which appears on November 15. My review should be printed sometime about there. And in Harper's Magazine for now, November, a little poem is on Page 44, with a note on page 25 about when and where it was written. . . .

I'd like just the same to hear about your adventure in Mexico . . . My adventure in Mademoiselle is in Mexico, too—bullfight and St. Augustine all in a row!—and it is strange how we all feel that whatever happened to us there was possibly the most exciting things that ever happened, and so many people get fiercely possessive and jealous of the place, almost at once, and indeed, it is a place that will grapple your soul to it if you don't look out and get out in time—I think I did, but I wasn't the same girl at all when I left that I was when I went in. Oh not at all!

So on this semi-autobiographic note I had better end. Please give my best wishes to the wife and child I have never seen, indeed you hadn't either when I saw you, did you? and I hope you all last each other a good long life-time and bring each other joy. . . . There's not much point to anything without this . . . Within two months I have lost in death three persons each one in his degree dear to me,—a favorite cousin about my own age, who had been a sweet friend and a charming artist; an actress, that I could admire and respect for her temperament and gifts; and my only brother, and it has been very like a part of myself going down into the earth with him: and then, a long way after, but painful, my friend and publisher of twenty-five-years, Donald Brace; and all this happened between July 20, Lily Cahill's death, and September 21, Donald's death; my brother had died on the 19, two days before. It was like a deluge of stones on the heart. I am still dazed and full of tears. . .

++++++++

Thank you for your letter, and maybe some day you will write a book about my life, and I shall try if I can later, to put you in the way of some papers. But I have promised my papers to a University, and I have an executor if nothing fails <u>there</u>, but you know, the Universities put everything in order and photograph everything, and then it will all be at your disposal . . . I am going to do a series of papers, not fiction, I might say selective autobiography, and I will let you know when and where they appear.

Sincerely yours—
Katherine Anne Porter

To: Gay Porter Holloway TLS 4pp. Maryland

5 December, 1955 Roxbury Road, Southbury Connecticut

Sister darling   I found your letter and my first Christmas card in the post-box down the steep hill beside the road, the box with my name on it in red paint, lettered by Paul. I haven't sent any cards and yet I do mean to; and I am sorry if my letters to you have been sad, but I have been grieved over Brother and Lily, and have had besides the hardest year I remember for a long time, making a desperate sort of last stand to get settled somewhere, and get free of all the things pulling me in every direction, and of late I have had a long contest trying to get free of my old publisher, who has simply let me lie on the shelf for a good while, and of course everybody there put as many delays and obstructions as they could: so yes, maybe I did sound a little melancholy now and then. But darling, don't look upon yourself as a Rescue Party—I'd just as soon write to you, and get letters from you, when one or the other or both are merry and well ..

It looks like a lonely Christmas for me too, though I am on the very point of getting off my ms. for the Atlantic Monthly Serial, which will appear in the March AND April numbers. It is just that my photograph will be on the March cover. I will send you and Miss Cora a copy of each; please give me her address. I'd like to write to her anyhow.

But angel it is as you say: I too much prefer to be alone than to make do with almost any sort of company. I long sometimes for company, but just any old face won't do—I want the special ones I love, and lacking them, I'll choose nobody. I have beautiful music to listen to, many delicious books to read—or re-read, which is fun—and at last, after all the time, and work, and terrible expense, I have got my life organized so that my time is really my own. I get up very early, about six or a little before, and light my little "Coffee-fire" in the big beautiful room downstairs, and make my breakfast; and by half past seven I am all shipshape and at this typewriter. I have worked four hours, and am tired and shall stop and do something else—wash my hair, maybe, or do a little very light dusting and cleaning—I don't believe in wasting energy on that stuff! but no matter what I do, it will be what I want or need to do, and these two things are very often the same.

Well, in the last two days I did finally wring my release out of Harcourt Brace publishers, and am off with the Atlantic Monthly raggle-taggle gypsies O! and they have bought me out, paid my debts and are going to make me a nice new advance which will pay my other debts, and give me an adequate income for a year, so that I need to do nothing in this world but write my books—can you imagine anything more wonderful after all these bloody years of exhaustion teaching and trouping the country reading, trying to make a living so I could afford to write? Well, I just had an offer from an agency to make a 9-week transcontinental tour reading my stories, and he could guarantee I would clear at least six thousand dollars in that time; and I was happy to say, No thanks, I've GOT a quarter—remember my favorite old joke about the little negro boy who was offered a quarter for an errand?

Next morning, fifteen minutes to 8, 6th December, Tuesday—I put it all down because sometimes, somewhere, I lose a day, or add one, but this I know I have got straight. The other day I was sending a telegram, and first

I asked the operator—"This is Friday, the 2nd, isn't it?" She said it was. "Will you give me the exact Western Union time?" I then asked, and discovered that my three time pieces, wrist watch, desk clock, and electric oven clock were all varying in time within fifteen minutes, early or late! So little by little I hope to be able to give up this preoccupation with the day of the week and the time of day, and live as I like, that is by the tides of the moon, as I did once in Bermuda, the best five months of my whole life . . I did eleven chapters of my Cotton Mather book there, (still not finished, because my little bit of money ran out and I had to leave) in the most concentrated and sustained period of work I ever had, and it was divine then, and wonderful to remember. Now, I feel something of the same state of mind settling down in me, not quite the same for I am so much older, and just by that more tired, and I also know that such balance as I have managed to get can be destroyed very easily, and I am walking carefully, trying to save what is left of my life to do the work I was meant to do. But it has been wonderful to have an abiding interest, to have loved something better than I am that can not fail me, to have had a guiding force in my life which without it would have been so pointless; even as it was, so difficult.

(Sister, I am going to put something in here that will seem like a fable invented for illustration of what I am talking about—really, the destructive, the murderous impulses of people who can't resist trying to devour and kill whatever they cannot be, or understand. I have always had people around me who sponged not only on my material, no matter what it was, but my spirit and mind. And so—just this minute I looked up at the sky—I work in a glassed-in porch which combines all the beauties of indoors and outdoors at once—and saw the three hawks flying over once more. They fly straight and hover surely, for they are hunting. And they are hunting the little sweet birds I have brought to this place with setting up a feeding station for them. It is only a large round disk of wood near the wall on the front porch, protected yet open, and they have been coming by hundreds for food there for weeks now. I saw them the first time yesterday afternoon. I had been wondering why the little birds had not been appearing—they have almost regular hours, all flying in at once in a great flutter, and all taking off within a few seconds. When I saw the hawks, I understood. And you know it is not that this episode is fitted to my situation, but that my situation was what made me think particularly of the hawks. I do not think of myself as a bird pursued by hawks . . . not at all. I am just once more a little baffled by the problem of Good and Evil, which is strictly human, and the birds know nothing of it. The little innocents come here by the hundred for the food set out, but they try to chase each other away from it, after all they eat live worms, and so on. But my astonishment is this: that knowing so well as I do the nature of this world, and the creatures of this earth of which I am one, how could I be so horrified at what, in my eagerness to help the birds live through the winter, I have done: attracted them to one place in such numbers that they in turn have attracted the hawks who will destroy many of them! Look, it is a very obvious irony, I shan't try in the least to make anything of it. But my big table of grated suet and mixed bird seed is untouched this morning, the little birds are all hiding I hope in the evergreens, and the three hawks are flying, flying with the purposefulness of all predatory things . . . . Yet, I know they are trying to live too, and no one is going to help them; but why should we, anymore than we should warm vipers? Note: the charming grey squirrels are swarming down from the woods to the south to pick up the peanuts I scatter for them every few days. They too come in a scattered body and depart in a huddle several times a day. I expect any day to look out and see a fox with a squirrel in his teeth.

About typewriters, this is an Olivetti (Lettera 22) of Italian make with an international keyboard, meaning it has such keys as é £ $ ç + ¿ ¡ % ! " ^ ` ´ ~ _-º ? ,/ and so on; if you know how, (which I don't always), to get the right accents, you can write German, Spanish, French and even English (£) on it. It has a small type as you see, but it is tiny, weighs only 8 and three-quarters pound in its little cover, and is a jewel and costs around $70.00. Don't judge its virtues by my performance—I simply have never learned to operate any mechanical object however simple, and after typing for now going on, indeed fully, forty years, I still am hit or miss, Hunt and Peck system. I use two fingers on my right hand, two fingers and a thumb on my left. Its a bore but that's the way it is. Just the same, the best typewriter I ever had was a Remington Portable which I bought when I went first to Mexico, end of 1920, and which I replaced with another R. Portable in Paris fourteen years later; and I believe that if I had kept it until now, it would still be better than any I have had since. I paid an enormous price for a Remington Portable about six years ago, and it was such a tin rattle-trap, perfectly worthless, that I finally gave it up and got this last spring. Its an improvement all right, but after years and years I simply don't like typewriters.

XXX

Your story of the visit to Miss Cora makes me feel that, if I can get my affairs settled, I should around the first of the year just ask her if I may fly down there to see her. I shan't have to stay in the house, but just go out and see her for a couple of afternoons if she pleases. Her story of going into our old empty house to weep for her friend, our mother, and hearing the sound of weeping, and looking through the window from within the house to see our Grandmother Jones[43] peering through, shading her eyes, is quite simply the most tragically, frighteningly moving thing of the kind I have ever heard; and it is not altogether because I am so near to it, to the women in it, but the whole desolation of all human loss and loneliness is in it. And I have seen that house, the place where we were born, which must have been desolate at best; built as it was facing the north, the front door opening directly into I suppose the living room, heated only by that little fireplace—no wonder our mother died of pneumonia after the exposure of childbirth in January in that house! And the house was just such a house as was built in that time by men who had lost the art of building houses, and women had nothing to say at all about what they needed in a house; it can even now, yes you are right my dear, break the heart to think about it . . . . . I thought I would cry myself to death this long year, there were so many and such various griefs I was confused; yet I wept again for my mother, and for the gentle beautiful little grandmother I never knew: and yet it was positively endearing and I could laugh over the vital spark of human rage and remembrance in Miss Cora and Miss Mary McAden[44] when the subject of that snake in the grass, Aunt Sally,[45] came up! Now do you know, I wish you would tell me what kin Aunt Sally was to us, and how she got into the affair. I remember always vaguely in my childhood that Aunt Sally was somehow the villain of the piece, I never knew just why: but I made her into a great-aunt in Kentucky and put her, fanged and clawed, into <u>Old Mortality</u>—remember? And I knew that our mother's mother was supposed to have spent the last years of her life in a home for the insane—melancholia her trouble was then called: and very well named no doubt and she probably had good cause for it. Yes, God help the old; but we need not be victims, I mean you, or I, not at this point. But it is true I have gone about freeing myself from anybody, kin or not, who would simply leech on me until I was exhausted if I would let them—even now! I still have a future, and it looks very bright— rather brighter than for a good many years. I am not desolate, I am not lonely, I have done some good work in my time and I am going to do more. I have a little picture of my mother in a silver frame on my little old French fruitwood desk downstairs - she would have loved my beautiful old furniture—and now and then I look at her and say, "Don't worry about your child—she's coming through!" Angel, I must stop. Got to get on with my Atlantic job! Same old love—Katherine Anne

To: Edward Schwartz TLS 2pp. Maryland

Roxbury Road, Southbury, Connecticut 1 July 1956

Dear Mr. Schwartz: It has been in my mind for a long time to try to answer your extremely interesting letter of last February, giving the history of your interest in my work, the strange reasons for reading it at all, and what came of it; but when I had the time, I had not the mood. When I felt I could write to you, I had too many other things to do...... I have been trying to get my life in some sort of order and to work regularly, and have pretty resolutely put everything else aside for the time being.

But maybe the real reason I have not written is just this: your letter confirmed my belief that you should not do a biography of me, for neither your interest or your feelings are really in it; and you show almost no understanding of my character or temperament; and there is plainly to be seen though under the surface, your own determination to fit my life into your own idea of what it should be or you think it should be, instead of making an attempt to discover what it really was.

I have always been of the opinion of Henry James in this, though I felt that way long before I knew that he did—that it would be better for writers to burn every scrap of private papers, letters, and force the biographer to face the published work in order to get at the real nature of his subject. And I have always felt that publishing books should not deprive the writer of a life of his own: it is my book that is public property, not I! You say, that while I am walking around, I might as well keep the clutter of events accurate! There are a great many things happening all around me, among other people, things being said and done, that I don't even know about, that no doubt are influencing my life profoundly in ways I shall never know. This is the kind of thing the biographer has to find out. For myself, I do my best to keep my own accounts straight, but there are many situations in my life of which it is nearly impossible for me to know more than my own side, or at best partial views and feelings of others involved...... I am writing and hope to get in shape for publication, quite a lot of autobiography, but it is not the regular chronology—it takes the form of my notes on the origins of Noon Wine, to be published next fall in the Yale Review, and also in Red Warren's new edition of Understanding Fiction. Or the Adventure piece in Mademoiselle .. I hope you saw it finally. In these fragments I was trying to set down <u>what happened</u>, what I saw and felt, what the event seemed to me to be and to mean to me, at those turning points in my life—for me, this is the only kind of autobiography worth writing, certainly the only kind I can read; and I refer you to three tremendous, beautiful, essentially true, works of this kind, so different they might have been produced on three planets, with one great likeness: the work of men trying to get at essentials: Autobiography of W. B. Yeats, (Reveries etc. Trembling of the Veil etc) Henry James, <u>A Small Boy and Others</u>; <u>Notes of a Son and Brother</u>; and even the unfinished third vol, though it was much less <u>innerly</u> than the others. You will see what I mean, and the third, Sir Osbert Sitwell's five volumes, Scarlet Tree, Right and Left Hand etc..... again, the fifth volume is a little like an amiable courteous bread-and-butter note to Life, but why not?[46] A man may be a gentleman even if he is an artist—we have enough examples to be able to make a rule, almost! Even if it seems to be pretty much out of style just now ... Is it my longing eye that sees signs from afar, or is it a fact that thuggism and hoodlumism and whorism are going a little out of fashion now, the endemic typhus on the bowels of our writers from Ben Hecht to Norman Mailer to Saul Bellow to Jones, to Nelson Algren:[47] all second-rate, it is true, but noisy. I throw in also Steinbeck and Caldwell, but they aren't so forward as they were. In all of them I have the feeling of something weak dirty, crumbling, shaking, and contagious, all at once—they really do breathe out disease.....

If I say this to you, you will better understand why I turn to my three great, really first-rate artists above....

Well, I simply can't stick to the subject of my own future biographer and biography...You remind me that I shall have them whether I like or not, with I think a shade of vengefulness in your tone ... Know please that I sincerely do not care; I shall not be here, I shall not know; and I trust time to take care of the truth, as I have seen reassuringly often in the case of others. I believe, I hope, I shall have my place in the story of American literature; even at this point, how could they write it and leave me out?—and, far from taking Henry James's advice (to himself) and burning all the records, I am leaving them all to a University to be arranged and put in order and left open for all to see and examine for whatever they are looking for! And in the meantime, I must be working at the things I want to do; I do not like being made self-conscious about what is going to be written about me after I am dead—or even while I am alive, for that matter. It is just that, for me, the interest of my life lies in other directions. I think your bibliography is a fine piece of work, and I am happy that it has been done. But I think the blood pressure of your interest is not really high enough for a biography. First place you haven't got a notion what you are asking for. Bushels of papers and letters, filing cabinets of note books and unfinished mss. The marginal notes on my books alone was undertaken, and given up in despair, by a young friend. And think of the chronology! and the places I have lived or visited, and the <u>reasons</u> for my being there.

Friendships, love affairs, marriages. . . . ideas of a life time, varying and changing and coming round again. And the genesis of stories, and how related to
my experience. . . . . this and a lot more is what you undertake in an honest
biography, and I advise you just to be my friend, as I am yours, and not think
about this any more. I <u>have</u> to stop; its a heavenly day for work!

Yours with affection and remembrance
Katherine Anne Porter

To: Edward Schwartz TLS 2pp. Maryland

Roxbury Road, Southbury, Connecticut
22 January, 1957

Dear Mr. Schwartz: Your delicious gift of dates was all the more welcome
because it was just the size and shape of the average manuscript as it comes
through the mails, and when I discovered it was nothing I was expected to
read and then write a letter about, Oh, God, I could have wept with surprise
and joy! So I ate three dates one after the other just to prove to myself that it
was no mirage, and I hurry this morning to write you my thanks—they came
yesterday afternoon, probably delayed because I have been snowed in here on
my hill, (temperature between 4 and 10 degrees below zero for at least the last
two weeks) and the postman couldn't get up to deliver packages. He will leave
letters in the box down at the road, where I can do a little xxxxxxxxxx mountain climbing in the snow, but not packages. All this stricken out passage is
not indecision as to words, but an incurable inability to hit the right keys for
even the simplest words . . .

I shouldn't be writing letters at all, I am trying to get some work done, real
work, a novel and several occasional pieces I want to do, and I am more and
more convinced that words are quite useless as a means of conveying thought
from one person to another; yet I must try now and then, again, because words
are, after all, about the only means of communication I have. So here goes
again about that project you had of writing my biography. I have your letter
somewhere but not at hand: I believe I remember the crucial paragraph. You
said something about it being better for me to do what I could to getting the
truth told while I was still alive, adding that it would come out after my death
anyway. You had told me the story of why you undertook the bibliography in
the first place—awfully interesting as a personal experience, and it most certainly led to a fine piece of work. But there is still a great difference between

a bibliography of an author's works and a biography of the author; and my doubts were not at all as to your methods or point of view, but simply as to your final fitness to undertake such a work. To begin with, you have no right to a point of view until you have seen the whole record and made a long study of your subject. To illustrate what I mean, compare Leon Edel's biography of Henry James with F. W. Dupee's ..[48] Edel, beginning with that most debased of pseudo-sciences, Freudianism, sticks firmly to all the stale old clichés of the school, and goes on until he reproduces Henry James, with his unique genius and his special unmatchable history, to the same dull stinking mud that the Freudian method can reduce anything human to at last—and this is false as hell, and the work of a mean mind incapable of admitting superiority or even excellence in another. Freud himself lived to learn his limitations and even almost to admit them, in spots. He had a great idea, but his awful obsession with being right and exercising messianic authority made him incapable of passing on a workable method—it was most corruptible and it has been corrupted until it can no longer be touched without contaminating the one who touches. It has even brought a kind of low jargon into the language which completely distorts any psychological insight. Read Dupee's book. You will see what I mean. It is almost certainly perfect—the best thing of its kind I have seen for years. So, I surmised—and I may have misunderstood, that is always possible—that you have an idea of a biography as an exposé, a searching out of "secrets" and a method which begins on the assumption that the subject did not know what he was talking about, did not understand his own motives or acts, and was in fact, to be "smoked out" and given the works—your works.

This is not a good way, and if I am mistaken in what I took to be your point of view, I am sorry.

But as you say with such admirable frankness, about your work: "Even though it was to have been about you, I felt no obligation to explain my methods or point of view." You are quite right, and it was never my intention to dictate an official biography. The main objection to any kind of biography while I live is that it is bound to be fragmentary, incomplete, and even now biographers (except perhaps Richard Aldington[49]) still have some respect for the feelings of the living, if not of the living subject himself (in this case, herself) still for the surviving family and friends. It would take you five years steady work to get through my papers and records and really find out what is in them in the way of personal history: I want the use of my papers while I live; and as I said, I shall leave them to a University Library where they may be available to any one, AFTER my literary executor is through with them and releases them. (This decision is new, and follows my revised will made recently. I mean about the executor.) Then too, I have had literary friends who have died within the past few years, and all my letters to some of them have been impounded in various libraries for twenty five to fifty years: this is the right of literary executors if requested. If seems an odd sort of right over what should be the property of the writer, but it is legal. Well, let's wait and see whether any one cares any thing about this topic in fifty years!

This is now the 26th of January, and I have been writing this in snatched time, and I do think I have nothing more to say. Did you see the Fall number of the Yale Review? They published my piece about the sources of Noon Wine. Christmas number—next to last—Woman's home Companion, a Christmas piece . . .

With my thanks again for the delicate Californian sweets, and my best wishes to you as always,

yours sincerely
Katherine Anne Porter

To: Daniel Curley TLS 2pp. Illinois

Roxbury Road, Southbury Connecticut
3rd February 1957

Dear Mr. Curley: I hardly dare wish you anything after what you say about the effect of my Christmas wish, but still, I am an incorrigible good wisher, or at least hoper, so I <u>hope</u> your time at Yaddo was good for you. I know—we cannot always know at once whether anything was good, or not—it sometimes takes years to find out. I have not been there for six years just about now.

I am delighted to know the arrangements for publishing the stories and a novel are complete. I can't write anything for the jacket, because—it sounds like no reason, but it is a good one—I never have. And the reason I never have was because I never liked the custom. And—you will find this out for yourself after your books come out, you will have so many requests you cannot possibly keep up with them. What I always used to like to do was to review the books I liked, and then the publisher could use extracts if he liked. But of late I am so overwhelmed with just trying to get a little work of my own done, I cannot even do this any more, or not until I have finished my own novel. You will understand this I know. I am sorry.

Do you know, I began reading Freud when I was about eighteen, and read everything more than once, and then Jung. and then Adler,[50] and so back to Freud, and the upshot is, I am at variance with the whole psychoanalytic thing, and think it nearly worthless as any sort of key to human nature and motives. Your friend's gospel that "Happiness can only result from the fulfillment of childhood wishes. That is why money, not being a thing desired in early childhood, cannot by itself bring happiness." My earliest memory was wishing for money, and I said often, "When I grow up and am rich—" and it was not until I was past adolescence that I lost entirely my wish for money, that is, for the power and freedom of riches. By that time I had begun to try to write, and the wish to be a good artist took the place of many other things that had interested me from time to time. I have in fact managed to make quite a considerable sum of money over the long years, that is, considerable for a person who never tried to make it, and never took it seriously; and what happiness I had was in the partial fulfillment of my later wish—to be as good an artist as I was able. The trouble with the Freudians is that they try to make a few generalities explain millions of particularities and they succeed only in covering them up, like a tent! I am at the point where I consider them about on the level of astrologers, only more expensive and not so entertaining, and I don't patronize either for one very simple reason: they don't know enough.

Do you know, I left school at sixteen, and have not cracked a book by way of formal instruction since, and the first time I ever set foot in a University was to lecture on English literature and teach a writing course. And I have in the past twenty one years since I came back from Europe visited more than a hundred fifty colleges, universities and writing conferences for this purpose, and have just cancelled five more for the next few weeks, besides a Television program called The Last Word.[51] But I had never been flunked out anywhere, I never expected anything except to graduate from my girls' school in time, I didn't feel I was really getting an education anyway, I was reading and studying years beyond my class, so I just skipped out and got married and Life, capital L, took me on from there at top speed. So I missed the dizzying sense of triumph when the higher education called on me for help. I had never even thought of it, but when it came, it seemed only natural. Most of my disappointments have been in <u>myself</u>, not in the world or the people around me.

++++++

Now I must stop, and go to work. I have been very tired ever since my tour escapade last fall, and am going very slowly; and I am afraid now I shall never finish even a tenth part of what I had planned, and have in so many cases half written or more. But this novel IS going to be finished, if I live another month! And may you work well and in good spirits.

Yours sincerely
Katherine Anne Porter

To: David Locher TLS 2pp. Maryland

Roxbury Road, Southbury Connecticut
30th December 1957

Dear David: The exquisite Rosary came safely, and will always be a treasure to me. I am going to get a special little jewel case to keep it in the next time I go to New York, and there will be a little inside sort of flap, I know—there always is—where I can keep your letter with the passage about the multiple blessings it carries for me. Bless you for thinking of all these, I need all of them! Just as an object in itself, aside from its meaning, it is the most beautiful Rosary I ever saw, and I have seen some very wonderful ones; but this one has crystal and silver, two of my favorite materials, and the filigree on the Pater Noster beads gives such light and shimmer to all the rest. Well, I suppose this is vanity—I was always told by the nuns that the plain wooden beads carried more merit, and it may be so—but I could never understand why this was so, when nothing is too rich or magnificent for the altar, the statues of the saints, or the robes of ceremony—why then may not we also say our prayers on a beautiful Rosary? I think the answer must be, we may, or you would not have made me this one; and so, the first thing I did was to say Five Decades and meditate on the Joyful Mysteries, for you.[52] And I shall go on being grateful for the rest of my life for such a lovely gift which no one else ever thought of giving me.

After reading your report on what happened to some of the other rosaries you have made, I took a careful look at the one you gave me in Ann Arbor, and I can see no signs of deterioration—the metals parts are perhaps a trifle darkened, but so little I would not have noticed it by myself; and it has lived a varied life, crumpled in my hand bag, tossed at the last minute into the pocket of a suit case, hanging at the bed head in all seasons year in year out, it has not been idle or cared for tenderly—just a hardworking set of beads, and it looks as if it, too, were good for my life time!

Tell you the truth, I wouldn't have dared to be seen reading "Sanctuary"[53] in public anywhere. I think it is a truly scandalous book, scandalous in a way that the cheap sensationalists who don't pretend to offer anything else, cannot really be! Yet, it is a masterpiece in the way it presents the criminal world and its female camp followers: and surely one of the most utterly gruesomely comic scenes in literature—anywhere!—is the passage where Miss Reba and her lady-friend are drinking beer and talking over the funeral and having a maudlin jag, and Uncle Bud keeps stealing their beer right from under their elbows. It took a real artist to write that book, and yet it is a terrible book, and

YET I can't be sorry he wrote it because he does hit a bedrock of the evil in human nature, with a kind of offhand authority and dead-certain swing that reminded me of Bing Crosby playing golf![54]

He didn't have to wind up—he didn't have to say to himself, "I know how to do this," he just did it, spectacularly well, and moved on to the next play.

I think that little reminiscence of Susanne Peplinski[55] was, is delightful, and it is so much the kind of thing that people DO remember: I had a Christmas letter from some one else who was there then, saying he best remembered me one cold winter morning coming into the Hopwood room wearing my Brittany fisherman's jacket! And last year on my tour (reading) I met a former student in Chicago, a beautiful and talented young woman, who told me she remembered best something I had said in class one morning about love—but it was after a reading and there were people about, and she never got to tell me what it was I said, and so I'll never know, probably, yet she said she would remember it all her life! That sort of thing is a little frightening. I don't remember the episode of the 2 p.m. breakfast either, but I do very well know it sounds perfectly characteristic and true.

Let me know if you are not able to get a copy of Mademoiselle, I am sure there are still copies in the New York office and I will have them send you one. It is very good of you, and better than that, to see that my works as well as Faulkner's make their way into your library. And it is good news too to find you settled in work you are really prepared for and like and can be active in— there isn't anything better in life than to find out what you want to do and can do and then get on with it.

Well, talk about verbosity! But I am an incorrigible long-letter writer, and quite often do that when I should be writing a review—such as the Dylan Thomas letters to Vernon Watkins, deadline tomorrow. Not finished yet, won't get there until the first or second of January. So now I must get back to it, but I couldn't have been easy in my mind until I let you know about the Rosary, and my news such as it is. Did I tell you that my story Pale Horse, Pale Rider, has been made into an experimental play and is now running off-Broadway, and has had now altogether counting pre-views, twenty-nine performances as of tonight. The critics didn't like it, but somebody does, because the people keep coming in, and my friends seem to love it, and I saw it twice and thought it most impressively done, and such old pros as the critic on Variety, and Tennessee Williams, and William Saroyan[56] and my dear friend Robert Penn Warren rushed to the rescue and are being quoted in the advertisements. So it goes on, but I think it will not last very much longer, the audience for that sort of thing is limited, and nobody expected it to go as far as it has! Anyway if I haven't told you this piece of news, I shouldn't want to leave it out.

I wish you a wonderful happy New Year, just the kind you will like, and please don't worry to answer this, either, as it is really an answer to your letter, but tell me your news as it comes up, any changes or good or bad luck .. We mustn't lose sight, after all.

Yours
Katherine Anne

To: Glenway Wescott TLS 1p. Maryland

Roxbury Road, Southbury Connecticut
6th April 1958

Dear Glenway: Got the notice here of the Grant-in-Aid list of candidates being made up. We have a good crop of more or less new ones this season.
My choices:

William Humphrey,	Home from the Hill.
J.M. Purdy	The Color of Darkness
George Garrett	King of the Mountain
Daniel Curley	The Marriage Bed of Procrustes

Its true Humphrey—a long time admiration of mine—has a best seller, could have been helped by a grant before, after his first book. Purdy, who sent me a pre-view of his stories a year and a half ago, is I believe tangled up with Lilian Hellman writing a play—maybe HE doesn't need help either. I don't know about George Garrett, that phenomenon snuck up on me—a real surprise, but simply wonderful! Publisher Scribner's.[57] They sent me an advance copy months ago, and I meant to do something or other about it, but didn't .. I hear it is out now but haven't seen any reviews. Daniel Curley (care ACCENT,) could I know do with a little aid right now, and I think his stories are splendid. My all-time favorite is The Night of the Two Wakes ..
Flannery O'Connor[58] hasn't had a grant, has she? Well, why not? She's a special talent, all right, but that is what I am looking for special talents .. I went to Macon last week to read at Wesleyan, and she and her mother invited me to lunch with them in the country, and it was also pretty wonderfully special and I will tell you when I see you. Now frantically trying to catch up with my mail so I can get back to the nobble. Please let me know what steps I should take beyond this to get one or the other of my choices on the list ..

I have to decide on one, I don't believe in scattering one's forces, such as they may be!

I'd love to see you! Got a post card from Monroe in Jamaica saying we should all spend our winter vacations there. I'd love it except I don't seem to have vacations, either winter or summer!

Love as always
Katherine Anne

To: Ignatius McGuire TLS 3pp. Maryland

Roxbury Road, Southbury, Connecticut
21 May 1958

Dear Ignatius:

It <u>was</u> a little unnerving to be snatched so suddenly thirty four years backward in time, and set down in the midst of a summer in another part of Connecticut which I feel free to tell you now, was for me as near Purgatory as I expect to be in this world![59] But that, no one could know but me, and it isn't in the least the point. All of it has been somehow absorbed, lived over, lived down, you might say; and alas, I have no such electrifying memories as you; the crucial, important experiences of my life were not there, nor with any one there. It is charming, (and that is not a trivial word to me—it is charm as magic) and enviable of you to be capable of such love and remembrance, of such deep faithful feeling in that decade especially when it was fashionable to be "sophisticated" in those matters, to have "love affairs" instead of love. It was a peculiarly detestable decade to me, and I have very few recollections of it that I can enjoy.... yet no doubt at all it was making the future in its own way, and "Lo!" as Cotton Mather would say, "It came on, and see what was in it!"[60]

It is strange, that not one soul I knew, and took then for friend, remains of that period. They have disappeared into death, or into the void of this world. I have not seen or heard of Katharane since I saw Covarrubias[61] (now dead) for the last time, certainly twenty five years ago. He told me about her being in Bali at the time he was there, or this is my impression, that they were there at the same time. Do you remember the Dalletts, John and Liza? I won't go on, the very look of the names on the page give me a deathly sense of dreariness. It is not their fault—it is only that I was in the wrong place with the wrong people, and I was in a wasteful and suicidal state of mind, and I had to find my way out of a personal predicament—it was all necessary, I suppose. And I think I remember you with a kind of pity for your bedazzlement and anguish and rapture and innocence and foreseeable disaster. Yet look! how it lives in you and how you wish to remember everything, and not only that, but to know what I remember, too. Well, I remember that about you! But—David wrote that you spoke one day of your wife—imagine, I never knew that you had married Katharane! Well, at least you did see things through to an end no matter what, and that is all to the good of everybody concerned.

Your photograph is very nice indeed, and perfectly recognizable. I am sending you one of me, to show what thirty odd years have done . . . I live in the country on a twenty acre place with a pleasant house, very airy and spacious for me, with all my European loot gathered around me; and here I have really been alone by choice and by will, because things have not changed for me in this regard—any one who lives near me wants to absorb all my time and attention, will not admit my vocation, and becomes such a burden and curse and liability I feel as if I were being bled to death! So the price of being alone in order to have the repose of mind and use of my time to work is, that I must be alone when I long for human society! I have dear friends and people I love and want to see, but they are all so scattered, and all so occupied with their own lives and work, I see very little of them; but we hold together by letters and messages and occasional happy meetings. You must not think I am cynical or misanthrope (can't even spell it!) oh, on the contrary! I am sure that my own nature is what I have to fight, and not other people.

Interrupted here by some frightfully dull little people trying to convert me to some particularly dull sounding little form of Christianity—they have been here before, I know, because I would return home and find leaflets tucked in the screen door, inquiring: "Are you Saved?" or "Is your Soul Right With Jesus?" or some unimaginably ignorant interpretation of Bible passages. This time I was out in the heavenly spring day looking at the new Iris blooms, the first are always a marvelous deep pure blue-purple—I'm almost sure it is a Black Douglas—and they came whizzing up the hill and caught me as the saying is flat-footed. I am quite capable at sight of a strange car of dashing back into the house, locking the door and pretending I am not at home, even if they have seen me clearly in broad daylight. I thanked them for their interest in my spiritual welfare and explained that I was already baptized in a religion which seemed to do very well for me; They stood staring in my living room (for of course, they got in) at my sixteenth century polychrome Spanish statue of St. Francis, my early nineteenth century primitive Mexican Indian painting on copper of the Flight into Egypt, and my Three hundred year old great silver Trinitarian Rosary hanging on the wall near them, and apparently none of it conveyed the least light to them. So I finally said, "I'm sorry, but I haven't time to talk; and I am a Catholic." And <u>They</u> said "Oh—well then of course you're not interested in the Bible!"

So I said, "Goodbye, and thank you for calling!" and came back up to finish this letter. And such a divinely beautiful day, too, as I said, and those weaseling little minds out spreading their ignorance on it!

Now and then all through the day, I go down and go out into the light and air, how I do love the visible world, how I do love being here, and how grateful I am for having been born—think of all the chances against it! and so, I go out in joy and run into that sort of thing!

Well, so it is. I am going to the University of Virginia to be writer-in-residence for a semester, and then to Washington and Lee for the next semester and meantime, I am getting another D. Litt—my fifth, though I have been able to accept only three—this will be the third. Its very expensive rushing across the country to be present, and I can't always afford it! but this is nearby.

I shan't start another page .. David[62] can't tell you very much about me, because there is really almost nothing to tell, thank heaven. I have a kind of public life of course, but I am not a public figure. I have a private life which is really private, and of course it could be stuffed with all sorts of fascinating mysteries and even scandals, if you like, but it isn't. . . . If I tried to tell you about it, it would sound duller than my missionaries, even. But it isn't dull to me, my dear, and I hope you have a good private life of your own as simple and incommunicable as mine!

Still, please try to communicate from time to time. Now that this thread of memory has proved to be unbroken, let me hear about you, from time to time, tell me what happens or what does not happen to you; it is very pleasant to know you are going on so well; I like an occasional Bourbon, so maybe we will drink one—unless you prefer Scotch—everybody to his own choice!—together sometime but <u>after</u> this book is finished!

Yours
Katherine Anne

To: Walter Clemons TLS 3pp. Maryland

Outpost Inn, Ridgefield, Connecticut
18 August 1958

Dear Mr. Clemons:

Maybe we'll be able to swap books by then, for I am towards the end of the triple-copy stage with my <u>Ship of Fools</u>, which began as a diary on board ship August 22, 1931, from Vera Cruz Mexico to Bremerhaven Germany. What those passengers have become since would startle them. It even startles me sometimes. It is like everything I do, based on actual events and real persons and just how and where it becomes absolute fiction I simply am unable to say; but it <u>is</u> fiction and nothing else by now, I even based one of the characters very lightly on myself, but she got away long ago—was indeed one of the first to escape. In fact I have now become all of the people in the book, the fat man in the cherry colored shirt, the captain on the bridge, the drowned man, the hunchback, the Jew, poor obstinate David, all of the women I'm sure, as well as the ship's cat and the sea-sick bulldog, and sometimes I have the oddest illusion that I am the ship, too. Well, here it is getting towards the end of August again, twenty seven years and three books later, and a second career of reading and talking in Colleges and Universities to support the first,—you may know by now that writing so far as money goes, is as chancy as the Irish Sweepstakes—and the minute I get to the last page of this job, at which I am now so utterly exhausted and in such rebellion at my self-enslavement I can hardly hit the right keys any more; sincerely I don't give a damn what becomes of it or what anybody thinks of it, just so I never have to read it again! I am on my 322nd page, written from top to bottom and to both margins—about four hundred twenty five words to the page every one of them hand-picked, you might say; yet plenty of them I stop to think about, and reject, and find another that nearly pleases me for the moment, and I dare not keep the mss. near me. As I finish a batch, I mail it to my editor, otherwise I'll never finish. Yet it is strange, for I really want to write, I can't imagine life without it, and when I do write it is always at top speed, and as my husband once remarked, with my hair on fire. Its the long pauses between these outbursts that take up the time, and I need a lot of time to do all sorts of other things while I brood; but my present editor is rapidly losing his mind, so I took drastic steps also to find utter freedom to do nothing but this one single thing until its finished. I gave up my house—lease expired—on Roxbury Road at the end of July, and I don't go to the University of Virginia until the first of September—one full divine month I am stopping here at this country Inn. Breakfast in bed, the only place I enjoy it, up and to work by 9, solid work until three, a good lunch, and back to work about five, and stop for supper between 8 and 9. Well, my notion of the Earthly Paradise! I used to work that way at Yaddo, I wrote the first fifty pages and the last three of this book there in two months, the summer of 1941; then I was interrupted by unhappy personal concerns and didn't do anything until the next year, and it has been stopped and broken into and left for five years at a time with an unfinished line; taken up again in the middle of a sentence and carried on; and now I am copying into the same paragraph lines written from notes made twenty five years ago, and passages written ten years ago, and things written last month and something else I just thought of a minute before; I have some good writing friends who have read quite a lot of this manuscript and they will not believe that it was done that way. Two of them are extremely good writers as well as critics, and they declare on honor they cannot find any seams. . . . . . Well, I had never meant to write a novel, I was and am a short story writer and that is simply another metier, a different thing altogether. Yet I am glad I wrote this novel; the material ran away with me, and I have never been able to shorten it or hurry it or do anything but go on with it when it was ready to go, and I could make time for it. . . It is nearly impossible to explain this to a man who has to explain to the business department why he can't seem to wring a book out of me. But he really has got one now, though he still doesn't quite believe it because he hasn't seen the last page yet. He is a very nice man—Seymour Lawrence[63] at Atlantic Press—a naturally impulsive, eager, perhaps even impatient man, who has been so entirely friendly and patient and encouraging and hopeful, I feel it is just not fair to draw out his ordeal a minute longer than I have to, a body can get a real psychic damage from being forced to be too good and too virtuous for too long a time. I am afraid he will just explode, so I am hurrying like mad now. The thing is finished, and it is the only novel I shall ever write, so I may as well let it go; I do know how the old fashioned authors felt when they wrote Finis Laus Deo[64] and laid down their worn-out quills.

Your own feelings at this point are very right and normal, I hope you'll be glad to hear. And it happens one time or another with every book as it comes. I expect to revive later and view my own work with horror and dismay and plan to go live somewhere else under an assumed name. That will pass, I assure you. You will wonder at yourself, and go through it all again with the next one. You know, I have been trouping the college and University circuit for twenty-years, reading my own stories or talking about literature and allied subjects—which is everything under the sun—and I still tremble with stage fright the last five minutes before going on! No hidin' place down here, is what I'm trying to tell you! As if you didn't know.

Thank you for reading my stories and the odd fragments of the novel, and for your good and very welcome praise. I think so well of your gift and the way you are going, and have such faith in your future,—saw your first published stories and "found" them for myself,—it makes me very happy to know that you read my work and believe in it. Naturally we all of us want as many readers as we can get, but it still does make a great difference to know we have the confidence of the <u>kind</u> of reader we long for..... If you really did spot me at the <u>Theatre de Lys</u> that afternoon, (I was wearing a conspicuously large grey draped felt hat, of which I was very proud, and I hope you did see it and liked it.) I wish you had spoken to me; people do, utter strangers in the street who never wrote a line in their lives (as we use the term) and I should have been glad to see you. Well, the play did move up town to that ill-fated Jan Hus—never without a play, and never without a failure, I believe the saying now is about that house. The young producers who took it over also made it over to a wonderful degree, and it got better and better, and clearer and more touching all the time; the young ones got stronger and more confident and they gave the minor characters more to do, and so, by hook and crook and fine words from such assorted persons as Red Warren and Tennessee Williams and Saroyan, they kept it alive for fifty performances in all, and went down with all hands on deck, flags flying and the band playing. What I am really saying is, that the understudies had never had a chance to show what they could do. So they played the very last performance one Sunday evening—January 12th I see by my calendar—no ticket sale, but contributions for the Actors' Fund, and I was told they had the best house and took in more money than any other performance. I found this spirit and freshness of feeling and just good conduct under fire so appealing it makes me merry to remember it even now. The original cast sat in the audience and applauded—don't you like this story? I do, and its all true. The young producers drove from New York to my Roxbury Road hermitage to tell me all the last things, and bring me a beautiful album filled with all available souvenirs of our venture—even programs and tickets as well as all the reviews and wonderful photographs of scenes . . It didn't feel like a failure to me, there was too much good work in it. . . .

I haven't seen Jarrell's collection,[65] but shall when I go through New York. I do remember "Rothschild's Fiddle"[66] and God knows it is heart-breaking. But then, wringing your heart when not engaged in breaking it was Chekhov's speciality. I am still amazed at the widely spread critical opinion that Chekhov was a "light writer." But then, so was Colette all those decades. Have you read <u>Sido</u>, or <u>My Mother's House</u>, or <u>L'Etoile Vesper</u>?[67] I don't think this last has been translated yet. So much for critics, most of them. Don't let them trouble you.

I'll be in New York sometime during the day of the 28th August, but I must shop that afternoon. 29th, but I have to spend it at the hairdresser and the photographer—Editor wants new photographs for his publicity. (And oh, yes, my original title was Ship of Fools, but they persuaded me to change it at Harcourt's .. when I went to the Atlantic Monthly Press I took back my first title, the only one I wanted.) 30th, so far, I am free. I leave at five, first of September for Virginia, Yes, if you are in New York, I'd like to have at least a little cocktail hour. I'll be at the Winslow, 55th and Madison. Please call me there, and leave a message if I am out. And now, I must get back in my imaginary world which seems quite as real to me as the one I am manifestly in!

Sincerely yours
Katherine Anne Porter

Part Five

1960–1969

At the end of the summer of 1961 Katherine Anne Porter completed "Ship of Fools" and sent the final pages to her editor, Seymour Lawrence, at Atlantic–Little, Brown. It was published in 1962 on April Fool's Day to highly laudatory reviews followed by immediate appearance on the *New York Times* best-seller list and before long a contract for a film adaptation. "I give most of the credit to my publishers for simply blasting me off as if I were a rocket," she wrote to Red and Eleanor Warren, "and this time," she said, "they hit the moon."

But there were disadvantages to the success. First, the great amount of money Porter earned was largely out of her reach owing to rigid tax laws in 1962 that allowed "the revenooers," as she called the Internal Revenue Service, to demand more than ninety percent of her income for tax. To protect her, Atlantic–Little, Brown withheld and invested the novel's profits and provided Porter with monthly stipends at a lower tax rate. While she had more money to live on than she had ever had before, she didn't have the enormous wealth she might have had. Separate contracts for additional books would partially bypass the problem, and she halfheartedly resumed compiling anthologies of her favorite poems and stories. She also approached screenwriter Abby Mann about a consulting "chore" on his film adaptation of *Ship of Fools*. Nothing came of those efforts, and she had to contend with other distractions that followed in the wake of the initial response to the novel.

Porter was dismayed at the reviewers, including those that praised the novel. Not one, she said, "got at the vitals of my theme." But the negative reviews, which were far fewer in number than the praising ones and began to appear in the summer after publication, disturbed her even more, despite her declaring to Red and Eleanor, "I don't pay any attention to the reviewers" and assuring Raymond Roseliep, "I don't mind." She described unfriendly reviewers as simply boiling her "in oil" and passing her around "sliced with vinegar." It was, she said, "as if they hated the book so much they hated me too."

Since 1930 Porter had enjoyed nearly total praise from reviewers of her collections of short novels and short stories. It had been "a nice little snug world of few but friendly readers and critics," she recalled Caroline Gordon's telling her. Now, she was in what Gordon had called "the hot dusty arena of Literature" where writing a long novel—and a best seller at that—had plopped her. She feared that some persons, "astonished bystanders," even thought she had abandoned her artistic principles for the sake of writing a "popular" novel "on purpose." "Honey," she said, "I didn't do a thaing but write a book."

The joking didn't eliminate what she admitted was her "melancholy." Swept up in a whirlwind of attention in Europe during her year-long sojourn there in 1962–1963, she relished much of it. But even that wore thin. "I expected to enjoy my life a little," she sadly wrote Abby Mann, "and I don't really enjoy the strange gritty world of publicity and 'celebrity.'"

In 1966 Porter's *Collected Stories*, brought out in 1965 by Harcourt, Brace, won both the National Book Award and the Pulitzer Prize for Literature. She settled in for the remainder of the decade dealing with what she called "the seamy side of being an artist."

To: Robert Lowell TLS 1p. Harvard

3112 Q Street, N.W.
Washington, 7, D.C.
10th May 1960

Dear Robert: It wouldn't be human for us both not to be always a little dazed when we meet, for it is always, and was from the beginning, in the middle of huzza and hullabaloo of a more or less Litr'y nature. Remember Olivet? Paris in 1952? I forget where else until Washington, 1960: only the scene changes, not the situation. Well, if those are the terms, we'll make the best of it, and yet maybe some day we <u>shall</u> sit down together in a quiet corner together and talk a little. I have your books, I love your poetry, and I think your latest is your best, which is the way things should be, so I want to say so now, in flight, as it were, while I can. It was delightful to see you, and I didn't notice anything strange about your manner at all—you have a very reposeful silence, not indifference or weariness, but a very live and shining look, as if you might burst into speech at any moment. . . .[1]

I wish I might have seen your little daughter, and Elizabeth again before you went—but, touch and go! that is the way it is. Well, when the book is really out, I'll be in Boston I hope for a few days anyway and hope to see you again, happily.

Yours
Katherine Anne

To: David Locher TLS 2pp. Maryland

3112 Q Street, N.W.
Washington 7 D.C.
18 January 1961

Dear David: No use asking me not to worry or to be horribly embarrassed by the request to do a line for Father Roseliep's book of poems,[2] Oh dear, how little we know about our friends, how little my friends seem to know about me. Yet it never seemed anything worth talking about . . It has been simply a rule with me for all the time that I have been a writer, not to write anything at all for the jacket of any book, even of my best friends or the people whose work I admire most. . . . This because I really detest the whole system, and have been embarrassed by eulogies on dust jackets of my books, and without exception I have refused to write even one, though I have an average of I daresay fifty requests a year! What I have always done is this: when I review a book the publisher is then free to use any part of that published review he finds useful, and in that way several lines of mine have appeared on dust-jackets—very few. Also I have just had trouble about Jay Laughlin[3] using a paragraph from a letter of mine to him about James Purdy.[4] Two or three years ago, about, Laughlin brought out a book of Purdy's short stories[5] and asked me to write something, that the man was in great straits and could not get published, and I gave permission to use part of my letter—against my life long belief and habit—that <u>one time</u>. Purdy, three books and two publishers later, is still using that paragraph on the jackets of books I never saw, because Laughlin, who is tricky always and about everything, told him it would be all right. This is just being thrashed out, and I have been much agitated and worried over it. But David I have no way to explain to you what a siege I am under all the time, I feel as if I were being pulled to pieces with fishhooks, too many persons want too many things of me, I am distracted and wasted every day of my life; because I cannot be indifferent, I <u>must</u> listen when people ask me for something, but oh, what a disturbed, uneasy life they give me! You know I have not seen many of Father Roseliep's poems, but I know he is a real poet, and I would be happy to praise him if I knew how. But I am not a poet, nor really a critic of poetry, and I am not competent to write about it—I have some wonderful poets as my good friends, and I have never written a line about them because I do not feel able to do so; it is simply not my territory, and I do know my limitations. But I am sorry because I should like to be able, and I am always distressed when I cannot do something that seems perfectly reasonable and right, like this, but it isn't, and I am the one who knows it.

At this moment of course I am in a dreadful crisis of work, with my publishers going mad and threatening to come down and sit on my desk, my University of California engagement coming on, trying to finish another story, and then—the Inauguration! Of course I was invited to everything, but I must go and pick up my tickets and sign my name in a souvenir book for the dear and beautiful Kennedys—gladly, but still it is a chore. Then on top of that they asked me to take in another visiting literary person—you remember my guest room—and who should it be but Tennessee Williams? I was dismayed and looked for ways out, but this morning a telegram came from Mr. Williams to headquarters saying he is not well, on tour in Florida, so I am saved once more by the eyelashes . . .

I have a notice from the Post Office that a piece of mail is being held there, I suppose insured or registered, because the postman tried to deliver it

and I was gone—so I am going there this morning after I get my letters written, and I imagine it is Father Roseliep's book, or ms. because I do not expect
any other special mail. David I can't say how I regret this, but it cannot be
helped.

I would say to you what everybody says to me, Now don't worry, don't
give it a thought. Allright, my dear, you try it! You know perfectly well that
these apparently small things—I don't think this is small, really—are what
wear away our lives and nearly spoil our days, because—as for me, and I know
I am not so singular in this—I wish to do what I can for all the arts and
whatever I am able for those who practice them, but I <u>cannot</u> do more than
a limited amount and so I find myself refusing where I do not wish to refuse,
that makes me unhappy. But so it is, and now bless you and good bye for the
moment. I can't write any more, so read not only the lines but between them
to know what I feel and mean.

I wonder about Hemingway, too. I don't know if he is still a Catholic.
So many of them fell away, those converts. Tate and Hemingway the most
famous ones... You do not see my name in the papers much because I am not
"news" in the newspaper sense. I don't want to be, and hope I shall never be.
But yes, I am one of the 156 chosen ones,[6] and I have seen the list, and a fine
kettle of fish they turn out to be. I would be ashamed to be seen or heard in
the company of all but a dozen, more or less, mostly less. Who did the choosing I don't know: they are referred to as an "anonymous jury" and they'd better
stay that way for the sake of their reputation as pickers.

Life was always difficult, but it gets heavier and harder and more complex
as it goes on. <u>Up hill all the way</u>, I believe good Christina Rossetti discovered.[7]
And so do I.

Yours
Katherine Anne

To: David Locher TLU 2pp. Maryland

3112 Q Street, N W
Washington 7, D.C
3 February, 1961

Dear David: Your little busy bumble bee of a nun is a charmer, I'm not surprised it was accepted.[8] Your letter turned out indeed to be a mine of trea-
sures, they kept coming up and up at me. To have my membership care of

the Jesuit Seminary Association, what a truly divine Christmas present from you! and a copy of Hemingway's letter about your rosary, and your poem to him,[9] and last but beautifully in its right place and importance, your poem to me....[10]

AND the letter itself. Well, I thought for a moment it was my birthday. Bless you for everything. I think your poems are firmly shaped and they have a kind of confident movement as if you really knew what you wanted to say, and you do say it well and with a happy sense of words. One of the fine passages: "His are granite mountains, overhung/ crags where winds blow around the upper/ earth," etc., it reads aloud splendidly, you really should hear it to get the swing of it.[11] And as for my poem, I am shy of touching it (What, ME shy? Yes, I am about a good many things, and so are you!) but just the same, like you I can sometimes venture. . . . . "poetry in the curve of the line/ falling into song with a Latin/ beat . . ." I love it. I wouldn't take anything for it. Thank you altogether, entirely! And the little note at the end is all too generous. What was I ever able to teach you? Yet I did try, but I think you just went on your own way! Maybe I was able to tell you a few little things, or remind you of something, or stir up a new thought in you. I hope so, you have turned out so well I would be proud of taking a little credit for it, but I do know better than that, David!

I was reading this morning in the New York Times how a Catholic columnist says the Catholic laity have not contributed much to the cultural and intellectual life of the nation but from the names he mentions, like E. McCarthy and Sharper, the editor for Sheed and Ward, and Father Weigel and Msgr Ellis, and others, I think he hasn't much interest in the Catholic writers in this country—novelists, short story writers, poets, critics.[12] Allen Tate, Ernest Hemingway, Flannery O'Connor, Caroline Gordon, J. F. Powers,[13] KAP, just to name the first who come to mind; their work seems to be of no interest to Catholic critics. I went for the first time to a Catholic University to speak last year, at Georgetown, and then La Salle, and I am invited back to Georgetown this next summer, and you know I have been barnstorming around this country for twenty five years, and publishing, if not copiously, for thirty years. Every University and College of standing has had me to read or speak, except the Catholic ones. I feel that when Mr. McDonald (the columnist) says culture he really does mean intellectual activity, philosophy, theology, political theory, etc., and not the arts, not the life of the imagination as we mean that word in the arts. This is a pity, for all the great art of Western world was Catholic for sixteen hundred years, I almost said in spite of hell . . . but that is a little too rash . . . I think in general the Catholic layman is not exactly anti-art, but just merely indifferent or ignorant of it, and this could be the fault of the Catholic system of education. In my time, they read St. Thomas to us at the table, and discouraged our reading any secular poetry because it would put romantic notions in our heads, We read it anyhow, bootlegged it, and they were right, it did not exactly put romantic notions in our heads, they were already there, but it did make us feel that poets sometimes knew more about people than the theologians and philosophers did. Well, in the long run, I believe it did us no particular harm; as one grows, things fall into line, take their proper place and proportion. I love poetry, life would be very sad without it, I still read good love poetry and the lyric short singing poems that just speak of the human heart, and of course with quite a different mind than when I was young and everything was new and happening for the first time....

If the Church loses her artists and intellectuals and leaders, need it be all their fault? Well, David, I must stop this. I am packing to go, and up to my eyebrows in little jobs to do. I will write my California address on the other side.

Your news about Tennessee really IS something!

Feb 5 to March 1 1961
KAP   Care Department of English
        University of California
        Riverside, California   That's all,

To: Glenway Wescott TLS 2pp. Maryland

3112 Q Street, N.W.
Washington, 7 D.C.
20 March 1961

Glenway darling: Here is the postcard one receives from the Secretary or somebody of the Institute on such occasions and my answer has been for too long, "Sorry!" which I was, but it couldn't be helped. I nearly see my way to getting there this time, and after my wonderful California trip, and a few days rest in bed, I was so exuberant at the idea I wrote to you instead of to Felicia.[14] So here it is, on second thoughts, and I sent her another, more sedate reply.

Of course I got back exhausted, got a sore throat, and had to rest in bed a few days. This always restores me, and I am in good energy again, with too many things to do of course, but at least with the hardihood to try, which is sometimes beyond me.

I am so very touched by your fine speech to the grantees, in the Institute report. The whole ceremony, at least of the speakers, seemed on a much higher level than many such events before. The one thing that shocked me was the grant to Norman Mailer.[15] I do not think we should encourage a middle-aged juvenile delinquent even if he has had the courage to write one of the foulest books ever printed in English, and has also had the courage (when blind drunk) "to explore areas of human experience" usually left to adolescent moral imbeciles. Still, I suppose this criminal collusion on the part of the Institute with a particularly cowardly sort of would-be killer, a born thug, is balanced by sending Walter Clemons to Rome, and by a grant to Philip Roth.[16]

Auden's long meditation on an unwritten poem is, I think, the best poem he ever wrote except "Lay your sleeping head, my love . . ." which I believe to be the best love poem of my time, at any rate. I had seen this meditation in his Homage to Clio.[17]

Red Warren will be here and we shall lunch together on the 27th. Meantime I am to speak or read at a dinner of the contemporary Arts club this coming Thursday, my only March engagement. April and May are crowded. Note on the persistence of creatures: For 26-or-7 years—since the year O'Brien died,[18] for I wrote the letter to him—I have been steadfastly refusing to allow the Foley's Best or O. Henry or any other such thing to reprint any short story of mine. They seemed to me then a fringe of small parasites on the ears of literature, and it was no honor to be selected by any of them. Yet every time I publish a short story here comes another letter from them asking for it for their collection. Fact is, they have improved in their tastes as time goes on, but I still don't like them or their racket. This morning comes from the Foley outfit a request (with contract enclosed) asking for The Fig Tree. Wouldn't they just, with Holiday in print? They aren't going to get either.

Oh I want so badly to know about Monroe, and how he really is, I want to see him and hear him talk. I am going to write him and ask him to come and visit with me for a week end. I hope you are well and happy—

Love—Katherine Anne

To: Thomas S. Knight TLS 2pp. Yale

3112 Q Street, N.W.
Washington 7 D.C.
21 June 1961

Professor Thomas S. Knight,
Division of Behavioral Studies,
Utica College of Syracuse University
Utica, New York

Dear Professor Knight:

Your letter inviting me to contribute to the Racine Press series of scholarly monographs entitled "Great American Thinkers," was received yesterday. It is true I have in hand a full length biography of Cotton Mather with eleven chapters complete of a 20-chapter plan, which I still hope to find the time to complete. But it would be impossible for me to undertake such a work as you propose, for several good reasons. First, the impossibly short deadline: even a properly annotated bibliography would require longer than that, especially as I do all my research and slave-work myself, I have no assistant. Second, I would not think of calling Cotton Mather a "Great thinker." If my thirty-odd years of study and intermittent contemplation of that mind has led me to any just conclusion, I should say he was no thinker at all. I think he was a species of genius, and certainly one of the most brilliant, copious, and maggoty-headed men who ever set pen to paper in this country. His brains worked and seethed, boiled and bubbled, day and night in his obsessions, and his unresting, overwhelming unscrupulous ambition to lead and rule and get a supernatural hold on his congregation, on New England, and—by his own word—all the world, simply did for a while carry everything in its flood. He most certainly did his best to fix on American religion, social customs and political practise, some of the most vicious and immoral doctrines of not Europe only, but from the most ancient evils practised in the name of religion and government. He provides material for a remarkable study of self-deluding mania, (of grandeur, of power, of saintliness!) with a childish personal vanity, and an emotional instability that led to sexual disorders finding outlets in many forms of cruelty. The Salem scandal was only one, but important because it was after a certain point almost entirely his own doing. He left an evil heritage and we still suffer from it. But does this sort of thing come under the head of "great thinking"?

I am writing this at top speed, early in the morning when I meant to get to my own work at once, but I am so shocked at the entire project you are undertaking, I cannot refrain from a few marginal comments on it. It frightens me absolutely when I think what is being done in the name of Education in this country.

First, why the word "great" in a list of "thinkers" that includes Bronson Alcott,[19] as cheerfully typical a mushhead theorist as ever lived anywhere, I do believe. Not that he hadn't got an array of touchingly harmless virtues, he was a good kind man if nothing was demanded of him, but he lacked two strengths that would qualify him for a place on a list of just thinkers, much less great ones. He could not really think, and he lacked the force to act on his moral beliefs.

Samuel Johnson? Is that our Great Whale, or some American I haven't heard of? If it is The Doctor himself, how does he get on a list of Americans? Then why not include Voltaire, or Diderot or Rousseau? Reinhold Niebuhr?[20] Is it not a little early to sum up his influence on American theological disputations? However, he IS a thinker; of the sixteen men whose names and works I know fairly well on this list or so, he is one I should put unhesitatingly in that category. But I wish to know on what grounds you include such as Brand Blanchard, Orestes Brownson, Rudolph Carnap, Morris Cohen, Herbert Feigl, James McCosh, George Mead, Samuel Miller, Charles Peirce, George Ripley, Paul Tillich, John Witherspoon, John Woolman, Chauncey Wright?[21] I have nothing to say against any one of these perfectly worthy men who achieved some distinction in their various fields: but in what possible way do they merit the title Great? That is a serious tag to pin on any name—it should be used with discretion or it loses its meaning. We have a plague of Best thises, and Greatest thats, and Most whatevers, and they turn out to be again some passable anthology or collection or series compiled by quite earnest-minded honest people doing their best, but under the cloud of not knowing just what such words mean.

Why did you leave out Thoreau?[22] Not much of a thinker, but surely as clear as Bronson Alcott. A delightful cranky sweet-styled writer, an artist really, but still he had and has his pervasive lingering influence on the native atmosphere.

Why leave out Thomas Jefferson let's say on Ethics, or if you prefer, the Humane Arts. Or education, unless you might allot that subject to Horace Mann. What became of William James in this mad scramble to collect Greatness in a two-foot shelf of paper covered volumes to be distributed widely at a reasonable price in the hope of raising the intellectual standards of the American public? Or do you feel they have been over-sold?[23]

There is still a great deal to be said about them, and it will be well to keep them before growing minds, which sometimes easily confuse the second— and even third—rate, for the First, Especially if their teachers do not know the difference themselves.

With my Thanks for your letter, and all personal regards and good wishes, yours with perhaps a reader's sincerity—Katherine Anne Porter

To: Robert Penn Warren and Eleanor Clark Warren TLS 2pp. Yale

3112 Q Street, N.W.
Washington 7 D.C.
17 July 1962

Dear Red and Eleanor: Your welcome lovely letters came a good while apart, but still from the same slightly mystifying address, and I hasten to answer this very morning, though by now it has got to be July 28, and I had started this page—date above—then went out, caught my toe on the edge of the stair tread, twisted my left instep, called the doctor, went to bed xxxxx—can't hit the right keys, never could, never will, I suppose—bed for two days, got up on the third, took off by airplane for a previous engagement to spend the week-end with my editor publisher Seymour Lawrence and his most lovely wife and their two angelic children, the family a ringer for your own as to beauty, intelligence, pure deliciousness, but in their own style, not to be confused above all with Rosanna and Gabriel,[24] but just younger, two and five, Macy the daughter and elder, the little boy looking like one of those cherubs in the Italian art hovering around the throne of the Virgin and Child, just as Gabriel did and no doubt does, though the age of divine infancy that can do no wrong is probably passing into a more interesting but difficult time. Macy at five is a sweet obstinate hellion on wheels which is perfectly normal, I believe. It does not lessen her charm. Oh I wish I could see my Rosanna, my most loved child in the world! When are you coming home?

Ann Gay kissed her roaring boys goodbye at Idlewild and got off with me by jet first to Paris, then to Rome and at last to Taormina, for a twenty-one days escape to the very nearest thing to an earthly Paradise I ever expect to see. You know what value I give to a tranquil garden with the ease of heart and mind, no matter how brief a let-up from the hell on earth I have lived since I can remember; I don't know why, no longer have any theories, but so it has been—and I got good and sick of it long ever ago. Well, my darling Ann is the best of company, a beautiful creature formed by fire, a genuinely grown-up person that doesn't need anything explained to her.

At this point the telephone or the doorbell rang, or something of the sort, and here it is the 31 of July, same year though, and as you see I had put the line spacer back on Writing, capital W as distinguished from just writing, like this. Events have proved one superstition I have as well based: I make a rule never to take a page of Writing out of the machine until it is filled, because if I do take it out, it could easily be a year before I got it back again. And this works for letters, too, only not so drastically.

Red, you and Eleanor have been wonderful about that book. I have had good reviews, that is, praising ones, but none that seem to have got at the vitals of my theme: and a good many reviewers have simply boiled me in oil and vinegar as if they hated the book so much they hated me too, or maybe the other way about. But the wonderful thing is, I have so many, many letters from readers, and they are so warm and sincere and good I don't pay any attention to the reviewers. And the great joke here seems to be that I should be thanked for staving off Herman Wouk for seventeen weeks, or maybe 18 by now.[25] Whenever this is mentioned to me—and never think it isn't, often—I remind them there are something like 170 million people in this country, and Mr. W. and I simply haven't got the same set of readers. I am not running a race with anybody. I never have. Caroline Gordon years ago reproached me for living in my nice little snug world of few but friendly readers and critics, and admonished me for my soul's good to get down in the hot dusty arena of Literature and see how I liked it. Well, I seem to be there, not knowing in the least how I did it, nor how I have been no.1 best seller since the week the ship was launched.

The odd thing about all this is, to me, the utter tomblike silence of my old friends and reviewers: I could put down here twenty names of fellow-writers and editors that I have known and been on good terms with for twenty five years, and not one of them has sent me a line: I was told that John Palmer printed a very nasty review, but I haven't been able to get a copy of the Yale Review: I wrote to him asking for a copy some time ago but he has not answered . .[26] Well, this is funny, but I suspect not unusual, and I suppose all those people who said they just <u>knew</u> I would write a best seller if I could, are now saying, I told you so! even if, so help me, I don't in the least know how I did it. I give most of the credit to my publishers for simply blasting me off as if I were a rocket, and this time they hit the moon! As I keep pointing out to astonished by-standers who think I did it all on purpose, "Honey, I didn't do a thaing but write a book."

My favorite light reading matter at the moment, Barbara Tuchman's <u>The Guns of August</u>, and Emlyn Williams' <u>George</u>—simply a delightful beautiful book: I bet you'll like it![27]

hours later, same day, though. do you-all remember Carley Dawson, the beautiful daughter of that Mrs. Robinson of Kentucky who called herself Mary Chess and got up some delicious perfumes and made millions and Carley inherited the business and sold it, and she lives just round the corner and down the street aways, as who doesn't in Georgetown? Just in case you do remember her; she has a wonderful little house in West Virginia—an old mill with waterfalls on each side and a fine big lawn, with some woods attached. She has loaned it to me for the month of August and I am going to try to get out my poetry anthology in that time. No good trying to do anything here. She wants to sell it, preferably to me, because everybody knows I have made nearly 3 quarters of a million this spring and naturally must be rolling in gold dust. It aint so, but try telling anybody that. The Revenooers would take 91 percent of it away from me on sight; so I am on a nice solid little income for life, but every month it will go just so far and not a nickel further, and everybody has turned into saber-toothed bandits and can't wait a minute for all that cash on the barrel head. Its rather embarassing. The Princes[28] are driving me to the house this afternoon and we will stay over night to get acquainted with the place, and I'll come back to get whatever I need there, mostly mss ... and settle down to my notion of heaven—no telephone, no doorbell, no mail, no chance strolling visitors, just freedom to breathe and live round the clock and work in my own time and way ... When I have been able to manage that, I have always brought out a piece of work. So wish me luck.

I am horrified at Rosanna's broken arm; kiss her for me, tell her I am sorry and hope it has stopped hurting; and I am very glad she is a brave person, because it is a lovely grace to have ...

Well, this is my last or next to last month in this house where I have put in three of the most baffling frustrating devilish years I ever knew and it wasn't the book that troubled me: it was the everything else, everything that took my time and attention and wearied and worried me, I shan't go into particulars, you know well what happens, that kept me from my own work. But after the poetry mss is in, I'll go back and finish Cotton Mather. Where, I haven't a single notion. I refuse to plan even one day ahead in that business. I keep thinking of Rome—Einaudi[29] gave me a cocktail party and everybody came, and they all remembered meeting me at Denis's party in Rome all those years ago, and again, Moravia and Milano the critic, of coming to dinner with you and Red and me, and Milano says I saved his life by giving him sleeping pills. Silone and his wife promised to help me find the right apartment, then everybody said he would help![30] It was fun, but I shall not make them sorry they saw me, but look around for myself first! IF I GO!

I now have a second string of pearls with a fine emerald and diamond clasp, and a twenty-one carat emerald ring surrounded by twenty-four small but nice diamonds, so I am very cheerful and that is the end of jewellery for me!

Love again, then and now and on—
Katherine Anne

To: Raymond Roseliep TLS 3pp. Maryland

Hotel Eden, 49 Via Ludovisi, Rome Italy 12 January 1963

Dear Father Roseliep:

The title of your new book of poems is entirely taken from one of the very loveliest and tenderest and most humanly heartbreaking poems in the English language and I daresay in any other.[31] Did any four lines of poetry ever carry such a shock of feeling? I have another favorite, quite different, but an in-love-with-life poem too, that I found once years ago in a little anthology in Sylvia Beach's bookshop in Paris—then it disappeared and I could not find it again, but years later it appeared in Norman Ault's anthology of 17th century poems. I had memorized it just by standing there in the shop reading it a few times,—why I didn't buy it I don't know, but I suspect the same old reason, temporary financial insolvency. But I have recited it over and over as an encore all these years I have been speaking and reading—twenty five years, and more than enough—if my audience is specially friendly and it has been a pleasant evening; and now you'll never hear me say it, because I made my last appearance and said my goodbyes on the 4th of last November at the Poetry Center in New York, being the only engagement I had been able to keep after my accident and that only because I was in a hotel not far away and could get there easily and away early. So here is my poem: (Anonymous)

As life what is so sweet, what creature would not choose thee?
The wounded hart doth weep when he is forced to lose thee.
The worm doth strive 'gainst fear of death,
And all choose life with pain, ere loss of breath.

The dove which knows no guilt, weeps for her mate a-dying,
And never any blood was spilt but left the loser crying;
If swans do sing, it is to beg of death
He would not rieve them of their happy breath.

Isn't it lovely? After all these years I am uncertain about the old fine word rieve—reive? Remember the old Scotch ballad beginning "O the reivers (?) have stolen fair Annie, and taken her ovver the sea?" And in my part of the country the really old fashioned backwoods folk were still reiving shingles, that is splitting them with a sharp, shorthandled axe, or anyway the biggest broadest hatchet I ever saw. I was really pleased when Faulkner called his comic last book by that name.[32] I miss him—he had the most gorgeous broad comedy sense of anybody in all American literature, maybe not more than Mark Twain, but Faulkner was bolder, he didn't have William Dean Howells and Livvie holding him down.[33] I think the chapter in a novel that I can't remember, but this part I love is quite often published separately and called The Raid, is one of the most deliciously comic things I ever read. And Spotted Horses![34] Bloodcurdling, but horribly funny, just the same! And that chapter in Sanctuary, where Miss Ruby and her battered ladies and Uncle Bud, the little boy, have got back from the gangster's funeral, and are having a little refreshment of beer. And conversation. Do read it again.

History of Calamities with a Happy Ending.

On the 28th of October 1962, the movers came in and started to pack up my 13 tons of household gear, including books and papers, all except a small truckload the Library of Congress had taken away to "curate" as they say, and as usual they started by dismantling all the beds, and packing up the kitchen and dining room things first, so the unfortunate pilgrim has no where to lay his head or make a cup of coffee; so I took the hint and packed for Europe and got out and went to my favorite nice theatrical hotel the Jefferson, and just went back to Georgetown in the mornings and spent the day overlooking things. This went on for two days, and then the first gang moved out and a second came and began loading the vans. I then went to my hotel and rested for three days and off to New York, a reading at the Poetry Center, the YMWHA; and rested some more, saw friends and relatives, and on the 8th of November my niece and her husband and two little boys came in their big white station wagon—five rooms and a bath, as I describe it—and took me and my half dozen suitcases to the Leonardo da Vinci where a lovely crowd of friends had gathered, and we had champagne—I was sent one magnum and two ordinary bottles, all in iced buckets, and at eleven o'clock in the morning, we lapped it all up. Flowers came until the cabin was full, and then overflowed in set pieces along the passage way outside, looking very like a festive, second class Mexican funeral. And after goodbyes, the ship got away with all those majestic signallings and bellowing and orders bawled through loud speakers, and the passengers lined up on the rail and the friends and family lined up on the water's edge, crying and waving and throwing paper streamers back and forth, and so, blessed be, it was over and I went straight to my little cabin which I had all to myself, and went to bed, and there I stayed in a blissful trance for three days. It was a happy easy voyage and I drove around Naples while waiting for my train, and came to Rome at half past six of a dark, rainy evening; my driver from my agency remembered me and my niece from last June, and the people in my little old hotel remembered me from the time before last, and welcomed me very nicely; and I slept and woke, and here I was in Rome, just where I most wanted to be, and I had only to be quiet and rest. . . . It has been a strangely rainy winter, but the warmest place in Europe and it would seem, in America too. It has been like a fine late spring, and when the rain clears, the sun is wonderful and the skies are blue as sapphires, as always, and full of little wandering 13th century Florentine School white clouds. I love it. I moved to this big fine Eden so I could have two rooms and work a little, and start answering letters, and of course I still have all sorts of things to do, to look after, but I am easy in my mind and happy. I wander about, go to the Vatican in good weather, to the Borghese Gardens, to the Via Appia, to the Spanish Steps, I went to see Keats' room once and he was like a nearly visible presence in that place. I go to the places I knew, and find new ones and oh this is a place like no other. I shall stay for a long time, a year if I can. I will visit shrines for your beloved mother, and for you and for me, too: it is <u>easy</u> to be a Catholic here, it is just as natural as breathing, doubt seems so foreign to everything. And I love the way the nuns and brothers and priests of all orders stroll about here each in his own habit and going about his own affairs perfectly at home. They are everywhere and I love to see them.

I mustn't start another page. But I do want to say, the summer was rather peril for older people. Your mother's accident in July, late, wasn't it? Well, on the 22nd of August, in the afternoon, I fell down my own stairs and fractured six ribs, and was in the hospital two weeks, and six weeks getting over it. BUT, that same morning, Eudora Welty's mother had fallen out of her bed and fractured her hip. And—this is the grand climax, at 9 that evening, U.S. time, General de Gaulle was shot at twice on the road by the bandits who have been trying to get rid of him, and I wrote to Eudora that at least we, her mother and I, had been in very good company! It was the first time in my life I ever had a broken bone, and it was very surprising how painful it is. But here is something wonderful. I was brought up very severely about confession and holy communion and I did not know the rules had been changed. So a young Jesuit priest heard my confession in hospital and then told me to go to Holy Communion every day if I could, and I did not need to go to confession until I knew that I was in mortal sin. "And you do know when you are, don't you?" he asked me very severely. "I think I do," I told him, and we both cheered up. And it has been such a new wonder, such confidence, and then, such a guardian kind of thing, but I need not tell you, or try to explain. But I do believe you will like to know.

I must give up this suite on the 31st of January. it is reserved for the season, but I have a place in the Boston, just around the corner, for the month of February, But it looks as if I shall be driven to taking a flat.

We'll see. If you have time to write, address the American Express, 38 Piazza di Spanga, Rome Italy, until I am settled, I'll let you know.

Thank you for your prayers and your friendship

Your devoted friend
Katherine Anne Porter

Except for 3 or 4 good friendly reviews I have been boiled in oil and passed around sliced with vinegar in England. I never dreamed of such malice and hatred. But I <u>don't mind</u>. I know my friends, and they are enough for me!

To: Erna Schlemmer Johns TLS 2pp. Maryland

Hotel Eden, 49 Via Ludovisi, Rome Italy
5 February 1963

Erna darling: It is marvelous to see your well-remembered handwriting, so very much yours, so clear and steady, like your mind—a positive treat to my eye and heart and a rebuke to my wandering erratic script—my French translator calls it <u>Pattes de Mouche</u>, which I suppose means more or less fly-tracks, or as she says, fly-<u>feet</u> tracks, a little better perhaps but not much. So I write on this machine and even so don't always hit the letters I want, but still you can read it, and that is something.

Your letter was not too long, I should have liked it twice the length, but I'm glad you didn't tire yourself writing it all at once; writing is hard work, even if it is fun too—like canoeing or horse back riding or even just playing poker, it takes a lot of energy and concentration.

I am glad you are still in Berlin, its hardly any distance away by air; I know how homesick one can get, even if, as in my case, one really has no home to mention: yet I still have a native land, and like you, am grateful for it. But I like very much to have now and then a change of sky, as the French say. But it seems so possible maybe to see you before you go. If I knew in time to make a little plan, why—I just take a morning plane, spend a few hours with you, and return by dinner time that evening—especially easy here as nobody dines before 9 o'clock if they can help it and later is better, as you know. Several times I have gone to restaurants here with friends, arriving about 8:30 at a roomful of empty tables. The Italian members of the party are always crushed with humiliation at being so countrified . . . . . Anyway at all, it is possible and even easy, and it might happen, if we can manage it . . . and it would be lovely, I think.

The newspaper cuttings you sent are delightful each in its own way. I used to know in Washington a relative of Speaker Rayburn's. I loved the dear Speaker, didn't you? the hidden romances of my later days, you might say, were two: Our Veep, Alben Barkley, and the Speaker; very pure and motiveless, no harm to anybody, I never saw either one of them![35] I just thought it gently miraculous that men, who spoil earlier and more utterly than women, should just the same produce these two seasoned old charmers! Well, this relative always called him Cud'n Sam, and told me that Cud'n told the funniest negro story in the world, but it was no good trying to describe it, you had to hear it! And now I am sure I have been reading it, and de good Lawd knows it is funny and sharper than a serpent's tooth! The Doris Peel story is a very touching kind of account of a way of feeling, a state of mind, that almost any rather sensitive, moderately intelligent person gets into about—well, it happens to be Germans now, but other times it was Russians, and sometimes Japanese, and of course, the very hardest nation in the world for Americans to come to terms with is England itself—a very fine country, but the natives do hate us so utterly and methodically and continuously it is nearly impossible to take a reasonable view of them in return. Now again in Europe, I have taken to reading European newspapers and it is astonishing the bitterness of the English newspapers against the Americans—North Americans, that is.

Yet I have several dear friends of that country; and what you say of the differences among Germans is true of every nation. The trouble is, mostly the kind of people we are likely to abhor, to mistrust, are the over-riding dangerous kind—the troublemakers; and that was true of Germany. Oh but it has all come to such incredible confusion it is a weariness of the soul to think of, especially when we remember what our hopes were!

You have always, I think, had a bent for friendship, for the love of just a few persons here and there, one at a time; never got this mixed with the perfectly good, natural social life of your time, which gives daily life a fillip of action and flavor. But it is not the important part. As I go, I sometimes wonder at the way my friendships and affections go on, and my friends stay friendly through dozens of years. One at a time we found each other, and one at a time I count them still, and not one of them can be replaced. Too many have disappeared from this world, and there is for me simply that blank and lonely place now that they, each one, occupied by himself. E. M. Forster, in his great novel <u>Passage to India</u>[36] just seemed to toss away in passing one of the really true things said on this subject. Dr. Aziz is looking at the photograph of his dead wife, missing her: "There had been no one in the least like her, and what is this uniqueness but love?" This looks perfectly right to me, but I am undoubtedly not quoting exactly. But it is what Forster meant, and I agree with him.

+++++++++

The Erna-Callie names are just right: and what a mutual admiration society we turned out to be! For you speak of my ways, and my curly black hair and gray eyes as if they had been beautiful to you; while <u>my</u> idea of beauty was <u>you</u>: tall and slender for your age always, thin shellpink skin, really live shining <u>long</u> golden hair, bright pure-blue eyes. I remember your hands and ears, no doubt because my own hands were always thin and flat and a little grubby, into garden dirt and every kind of out door climbing and picking and handling—animals, objects, all the fascinating natural world. My ears were, and are, too large: I wanted them small, rosy, discreet, like yours. But it is true, one thing—we were good friends, always interested in each other . . . we both had some quality of—I think it was of imagination and observingness—that did set us apart from any of the other children we knew, and both of us recognized this from the first. A friendship like ours does not just happen, nor is made out of thin air . . . How we did love to sing together! I am sure nobody rehearsed us: they just found out by listening that we could sing together, and made the most of it. I remember also the total conventionality of their taste—whoever They may have been one time and another—we always wore white dresses, dimity or lawn or some such blameless stuff, and your sash was invariably pale blue, (for blondes!) and mine was forever pink (for brunettes!) I wonder sometimes what would have happened, if we had just swapped sashes once, for the fun of it.

++++++

Here are some snapshots made a few days before Christmas here at the Toy Fair in Piazza Navona, a fine clear-cloudy soft day, like spring; that is a

blue linen suit I am wearing and an 8-ounce wool knit coat. In one I am holding the prizes I won at the Shooting Gallery.

****

Not that we would spend much time in shooting galleries; its just nice to
know we could do anything we pleased. I am in fine health and spirits, what I
needed was a little escape from all that senseless and ceaseless hurry, hurry—
for what!

Love to Rita and Glover[37] and to you as always
Callie

To: Abby Mann TLS 2pp. Maryland

Hotel Eden, Via Ludovisi Rome, Italy
1 May 1963

Dear Abby: Today begins my own special and personal month of the year, and
my spirits rise with the good weather; no matter where I am or what doing,
it always seems a festival sort of time, and I look forward to getting near the
sea where I can swim and go sailing. . . . Your letter from New York came
yesterday, just in time; May Day is a national holiday here, so the packers are
coming tomorrow to gather up all the books and papers—notes, unfinished
mss etc.—I have accumulated in five months here, and such smaller objects
I have not been able to resist buying, and I am really flying out by the 4th or
5th and I am going to Naples, Florence, Venice, over to Paris and over the
Pyrenees to Spain, that is to say San Sebastien and a short visit to Avila, Santa
Teresa's town—and I can't really say where else, but I'll be swarming over the
landscape here and there and yonder until the end of August. . . . Such are my
projects, anyway, and a travel agency will see that I catch the right planes and
trains and boats and outboard wheelbarrows. It all sounds charming except
when I stop really to think about it, and then it could easily be exhausting and
even a little boring. We'll see. If I get tired I'll just stop where ever I happen to
be . . and maybe write a little. That was what I intended to xxxxx do anyway. (I
can't manage a typewriter!)

You should, after our talks here on the subject, be pretty certain I am
not afraid you will ruin my book, or even harm it a little . . . far to the contrary, and I am leaving everything to you. Also you must have seen a few of
the really shockingly hostile reviews I have had—in England even worse
than the United States—with only a few extremely good ones from several

writers whose opinions I respect. But the book has generally been turned over to the second-and third-stringers, and I have been astonished not only at the personal malevolence of their tone, but the fact that they never have found out what the book is <u>about</u>; there is one man, Robert Heilman,[38] whom I knew slightly years ago when he was a professor in the University of Louisiana, and who had, so far as I knew, never showed the slightest interest in my work. Lately La Salle College in Philadelphia got out a little special KAP number, and I am sending you the article.[39] Glenway Wescott did a good job in his essay about my life and works, you might say, a personal kind of bouquet from a dear friend, but still, he is a first-rate critic, too, and I find his analysis very reassuring. I am also sending you, just for the hell of it, a letter I received a few days ago. It nearly MUST be a woman writing, and yet I cannot quite tell. Maybe you can. At any rate, what is there in the human mind that causes quite millions of people to swallow whole Mailer's <u>The Naked and the Dead</u>, or Miller's <u>Tropic of Cancer</u>, or even Lawrence's detestable <u>Lady Chatterley's Lover</u>, or the truly dreadful <u>Little Tin Drum</u> by Grass, <u>Naked Lunch</u> (a man named Burroughs, I believe) and one of the most awful—frightening really—things I ever read by a man named Hawkes (Or Hawke?) about a stolen race horse, more or less if it is really about anything, of which the high point is a man beating a woman to death with a sand bag, the whole scene being conveyed in sexual terms . .[40] I have read endless comments on all these books by critics who have seemed at least partially responsible, and some of them really thoughtful, and I have never seen any shock at all at the authors' peculiar views of human nature or any resentment of the characters or their acts . . . No, no, just all litera-ture and therefore not to be confused with Life. Yet in all these books there are such hatred, such contempt, such fear, and such brutality of—well, the writer himself towards his characters and indeed, his world. . . . WHY did they choose my simple, plain, extremely conservative novel of everyday conduct and motives for this special attack? Compare my characters, and my view of them, with almost any novels going the rounds, some old clas-sic ones too, and look around at the lives of many persons you know, and how can you help seeing that they—none of them—are really so bad! And I do not hate them really, though some I do dislike a little for good cause, I hope—but there is not one life on that boat that sooner or later is not shown in a softened, human light, even absurd Denny: even the Captain . . . even wretched Frau Rittersdorf . . even anybody you like. So, dear Abby, I hope you will believe me, or see this for yourself as you work, and bring out a little as you feel to do something of the gentle and loving passages of that book, for I am overwhelmed at the lack of understanding of so many readers—and yet, my private mail is full of letters from all sorts of people who seem to understand it so much better than the reviewers!

Well, I didn't mean to go on like this. It is just I am intensely concerned with the next phase of this book, which is in your hands, and good hands too, I believe without question.

When you were here, we did touch lightly on the possibility of my coming to California—to visit you, yes, but also maybe as a—well, I don't know what my title might be, but as a paid assistant of some kind on the picture? My feeling has been rather that beyond just discussing the way we did, and taking up points that you might find of interest, I have not a great deal to contribute. On the other hand, I have been thinking about settling somewhere, I must buy a house: I know where I want it to be—in a good climate where I can grow the kind of trees and flowers I love, and it must be near the sea. . . . I could I suppose stay in Italy, but I shall always be a stranger here, no matter how pleasant the place and the people are; still I must go home, if I can find out where it is. . . . I keep remembering Santa Barbara where I looked out of my windows on blue water and white sails, and yet great camellia trees and roses and azaleas and gardenias grew wonderfully and there were fig trees and apricots and peaches and almonds in the back garden . . Even Santa Monica, where I lived for about four years, in a pleasant house within sight of the sea, was lovely. And letters from an old friend who is there now, started the entire series of pleasant memories up in my mind, and I thought—why not find a place in Santa Barbara, far enough from Los Angeles, but not isolated, God knows—

Now mind you, dear Abby, this is not meant as blackmail, or bribery or any form of mental or moral turpitudes: but if you did hire me for wages for a while—if you can decide what you would like me to do! I could come out there and buy a house, something I simply can't get round to with the Publishers on one hand and the Revenooers on the other sitting on my beautiful sacks of gold, accumulating and gathering dust so far as I know in Fort Knox. . . . The fact is, I love great cities and always live in a world capital when I am in a city at all; but I'm a born country woman, its in my veins, we've been on the land in every branch of my family I know for 500 years, and its just too late to change now! Everything we had came from the land, and it was literally the foothold from which any of us through centuries made any other career. . . . you just can't know how bored I am with unmodified city mice who have no notion in the world what the love of the earth and its fruits can give of warmth and satisfaction the whole year round—land, near the sea—that is what I am looking for now, and once I find it, nothing in this world short of a bomb—I don't know the name of the one they'll be making next—shall get me out of it!

And my decision is going to be made within the next few months. It gives life in the immediate future a very nice shape, somehow; and it will happen, somewhere. Meantime, I'm off on a little fling. Just a few minutes ago I stopped writing this and was looking at an Italian weekly magazine full of pictures and personal notices, and saw this: "Katherine Anne Porter, who wrote 'Ship of Fools' has been for five months in Rome, in a state of almost absolute self-retirement, to write a romance about the Southern States of the US." Well, my translating is about to give out, but it goes on to say in effect that I am rarely seen and then only with two or three friends, and I am not to be found in literary circles. . . .

Well, I have been given a big evening at the American Academy, have been invited to some fine literary cocktail parties—I went to two of them! and have lunch now and again in princely palazzos with princes and other titled folk, who seem to know more about literature than some of the literati, and I walk about Rome by myself staying off the Via Veneto except to buy my lovely intarsia table top from a shop up near the wall with three great arches—or are they two? I'll have to look again—but this kind of stuffy little note reminds me of my favorite Hollywood notice, by Hedda Hopper, I think: about Shelley Winters,[41] a good many years ago; it seemed her friends were very uneasy about her, they feared she was having a nervous breakdown; she had shut herself up at home for three days and would not even answer the telephone! For me a perfectly private life, not just for days or weeks but for months and years, seems entirely normal and a wonderful way to live. But it is a fact, unless one lives on the sidewalk or a birdcage, one is suspected of being a little funny, to put it mildly. Well, I'll settle for it.

If you ever finish reading this, or get round to sending me a word, address as below. I'll send you postcards if I am not moving too fast. Good luck with that Ship, and bless you.

Yours
Katherine Anne

Atlantic Monthly Press
8 Arlington Street
Boston, 16, Massachusetts
Please get a copy of the latest Paris Review with Barbara Thompson's Interview!

To: Abby Mann TLS 3pp. Maryland

10 July 1963
Address until further notice! as follows:
KAP Villa Adrienne 19 Avenue du Géneral Leclerc Paris XIV, France

Dear Abby: You must be in Moscow this minute, for some reason a place as far away and inaccessible to me as the other side of the moon. We may get to the other side of the moon any day now and I may go to Moscow sometime, but I think not. So you must tell me about the festival and what goes on there. I used to delight in the Russian refugees and emigrés in Mexico when the Bolsheviks first chased them out, they were such a beautiful aristocratic high-steppin' lot, merry and mad and up to anything: I knew some more later on in Paris, and I never knew people I got on with better, before or since; and they gave all Bolsheviks and later Communists a very bad start with me: if these were the people <u>They</u> were trying to exterminate in Russia, I was all against them. For other and later, if no better reasons, I still am agin 'em. I don't mean the people. I mean the Gummint, as Pogo calls it.[42] I hope you are enjoying the festival—will the Russians ever again make such pictures as they did—well, God help us, twenty five and thirty years ago! But then, will the French ever do anything better than The Italian Straw Hat, or Carnival in Flanders? (La Kermesse Heroic. My favorite picture of ALL time: have seen it at least twenty times since I saw it five evenings running the first week it appeared in Paris in I think 1934. And when I see it announced again anywhere near me, I'll see it again!)[43]

My little scamper for freedom from Rome to Naples to Florence to Venice to Paris was lovely, lovely, and now its over. Here in Paris, I ran full tilt into reporters and interviewers and photographers and publishers and translators and literary persons (and a few dear good old friends who happened in, or who happen to be here already:) and you know I have no grudge against my estate in life, this is what I must expect now and then, its the seamy side of being an artist, and I have made up my mind not to be dramatic about it: but I do get very tired, I feel very lonely, after a kind of siege of this sort of thing I get something like melancholy, it all does seem so very pointless: that is, I know I am unreasonable, but I expected to enjoy my life a little, and I don't really enjoy the strange gritty world of publicity and "celebrity." It simply does not seem to have much to do with what I am doing, or what I have in mind, or my real life. . . . .

+++++++

I am going to change the subject. Let's talk about moneymoneymoney—
that is, my prospects of getting invited to Hollywood at a perfectly criminal
wage—I mean really enough to have something left over after taxes . . . So, I
welcome with huzzas your suggestion that there may be one or two things
out there I could work on: but you will have to tell me, I know nothing at all
of what is happening there now, and I must wait to hear. One thing from the
first I have had a feeling against being associated with the actual making of
the picture of Ship of Fools. Or the scenario, your job. . . . . I should so like
to talk to you more about all kinds of things and questions as you brought
up in Rome about all sorts of details—simply to clarify your own view of a
character, to fix a scene—but for your own use, to take or leave as you need it:
You know how much material as sheer background we need: we may throw
half of it away, but just the same we couldn't have done the other half without
it! So in this way I could help: not by specific advice but simply by talking on
the subject so that you may find here or there some stipulation that sets your
own mind to work in its own track—I know the value of this from experience.
So if you feel that this would be useful, I'll be delighted to come out and say
whatever is in my mind on our current subject, as well as everything else we
may think of. . . .

Meantime, yes of course, I'd love to work on a couple of projects, and I
want your advice which I shall keep as a sacred confidence: but it is true that I
must have a paid errand, or I can't get there, and of course I want a nice outra-
geous one. Who doesn't? So let's just see what I'm worth in that field, for once.

Now then, it looks as if I have exhausted that subject for the moment. My
friend Cyrilly Abels writes me that certain magazines are asking for things,
at $5000 a throw (woops! moneymoneymoney!) and of course they would
like a short story, something like Flowering Judas or Holiday. But they will
take articles, and the Saturday Post would like one about Fellini! All I know
about Fellini (besides what I read in the news papers) is his picture 8½ which
I found very entertaining except a little too noisy, but who does he think he's
fooling? Not this old timer, who started out with the Cabinet of Dr. Caligari
and wore right on through the Blood of a Poet, Beauty and the Beast, Alexander Nevsky (was that the title?) and such. . . . I've seen Alfred Hitchcock
films that offered me more real psychological interest, if that isn't too serious
a word. But just the same, I enjoyed it thoroughly, and I wish Fellini wouldn't
take himself so seriously, and his work perhaps <u>more</u> so. I loved Divorce Italian Style, which I saw before I left Washington, and I thought that dealt with
the technique of projecting phantasy and daydreams into real life scenes even
better than 8½ did—[44]

Are you tired of this? I am just idling along because I have found a little hiding place down here, I don't know how long it will last; but it is a small tacky furnished floor of a pavilion between two fine old gardens; it couldn't be more petit-bourgeois than it is, in an old fashioned working kind of neighborhood full of markets and children and no telephone, and the concierge receives all messages and mail and packages and will fend off visitors; and suddenly I have time, and quiet and I sleep better, and I have better food than in my luxury hotels—this, naturally, because I cook it myself, or go to a brasserie where they give me fresh hot <u>French</u> food, and I bring home cherries and little melons and dark-red peaches and sweet apricots and fresh asparagus and the sweetest oranges I have tasted since my childhood, and where do they come from? Corsica! D' you suppose I ought to go to live there? We don't grow such fruit any more in our country—why, I wonder? I get my favorite coffee from Columbia—at Josephine Bonaparte's old coffee company, still going in Paris! Did you know where she got her money? Well, not from Napoleon, as we all know, nor from any body or any where except her own coffee business, which I think has been founded by her first husband. Well, anyway, I can get Columbia coffee there, and it is the best in the world, I think ..

Goodbye for the moment . . . Do keep me in mind for one of those preposterous grand picture assignments you mention!

Yours
Katherine Anne

To: Abby Mann TLS 2pp. Maryland

8 December 1963

Dear Abby: I never wonder why I don't get answers to letters because I know what lives most of the people I know live, and some of them are just strong-minded enough to refuse to answer letters unless they bring news of a life-and-death emergency. I can't remember that I said anything worth answering in that letter. Also, I had a maid in Georgetown who decided to tidy up my workroom. She took a bushel basket of unanswered letters—I do not exaggerate—down three flights of stairs and emptied them into TWO ashcans in the areaway, and it was totally by accident that I came in from the sidewalk—I realize I should never have started this, you'd have to know the typical Georgetown house to get the scene straight—and happened to glance into the ground floor entrance and saw them stacked up there, with no lids on:

not only my private life and public affairs for the past three months but those of several hundred trusting persons who had written to me freely about all sorts of things. The maid was gone by then, and I had to go up stairs and get the basket and go down again, and I did this three times before I got all those letters back in the workroom. The next day I told her what she had done, and offered her three weeks pay and a fond farewell with the hope that I should never see her face again: and she wept and said, "Whah, Honey—how did I know?" And it was true, I had never told her. So she stayed on until I left for Europe, raising hell in every department of my life, sowing disaster and disorder like dragon's teeth hither and yon, and always with that sad parrot cry, "Whah, honey—you nevah tole me!" And she was right, I hadn't. . . . Get in that fix sometime if you want to feel really licked to a standstill.

Just before I left Paris I was told that Marlene Dietrich[45] wanted to see me, or write me a note, but she left for London the next day and I have not heard. But I still get letters with suggested casts for the Ship of Fools, and she is the leading contender for La Condesa. I like her for that role—I wonder if she would care for it.

I haven't been working, and I am terribly swamped with unfinished promised things, my preface for the anthology, my memoir of Sylvia Beach, and two or three other things that may probably interest only me, but still, I want to write them. And in February or March perhaps—well they are talking about asking me to do a little tour of duty in Mexico with the USIS—it always costs me money, and always knocks me out, and why I even consider doing it I can't say: and I am looking for a house, it MUST be over salt water, in Cape Ann, Maine, Delaware and Connecticut. I am going to have a house, and one I like in a place I like where I can fend off people and get a little writing done. A large order, and it will no doubt be expensive but I am not discouraged. Now then, have you something in mind for me about Ship of Fools, and what do you suggest? I couldn't take on more than one thing at a time, if that, so if I come to Ship of Fools I can't go to any other company. Do think it over and let me know and suggest something, with the time I should expect to stay there, what expected to do, salary,—all, in fact. I am in a most floating sort of state at the moment, now really is the time to make a plan or program, for in a little while I'll decide on something and will not be movable!

Think of it and let me know. The "press" for Mad, Mad, Mad, Mad—is quite wonderful, what I have seen of it . . . That, and Tom Jones seem to be the best of the season.[46]

I feel I can't wait to see them—both—but I shall wait just the same, because I am in Washington, and things get around here as a sort of last resort—but they do get here, and I do see them. Through the long ages, I remember as my very loved comedies, The Italian Straw Hat, Carnival in Flanders, On Approval, Kind Hearts and Coronets, Man about Town (Chevalier, old) Murder She Said and Divorce Italian Style.[47] I am sure there are others but these are the ones that come first.

Others, like King Henry VIII and Chaplin's Klondyke . . .[48] It is going to be simply wonderful to see TWO fine ones in the same season—it never happened before. I'm speaking only of comedies, which I love.

Now don't let anything happen to this letter, because I am saying something I hope you will read and answer. I shall be here at my favorite little "theatrical" hotel where I always stay in Washington when I haven't a house, and I'll be here until I decide what to do next. So write me here directly, as soon as you have something in mind. . . .

Yours
Katherine Anne

To: Russell Lynes TLS 3pp. Maryland

[Letterhead: The Jefferson Hotel
1200 Sixteenth Street, N.W.
Washington 6, D.C.]
20 March 1964

Dear Russell:

It was really a comeuppance, this round of pneumonia, my ninth, unless I have lost count: my doctors say it was a very narrow squeak, and the next time I'd better look out: but I have lived with this, if we can call it living, since the Great Plague of 1918, and I can reasonably expect to die with it, but not necessarily this year or even the next, and of course, it could be tomorrow—but never, of course, today.

I had a charming little tour arranged, University of Alabama, where I stayed three days, arriving feeling very well, and leaving feeling very exhausted, naturally. Then to Dallas, and then to Puerto Rico for two weeks, and back to Louisville Kentucky to University there; and a visit with my good friend Barbara Anderson and a week-end with the Barry Binghams,[49] which would have been this week-end . . Instead, I got off the plane at Dallas with 104 fever, walked into a battery of cameras and reporters surrounding the plane, into an interview in the hotel and a welcome party until 11 P.M. myself all the time saying I was very tired and should like to go to bed, as the next day was my big job . . . I was told how wonderful I looked and in what spirits

I so obviously was, and next morning half-delirious I called the Desk and asked for a doctor, who came with the nurse, and in half an hour I was on a stretcher being wheeled to the ambulance and so to the earthly paradise of St Paul's hospital with angels wearing Normandy peasant bonnets surrounding and bearing me up. My doctor says at this point I nearly died, and on the whole, it might have been the right moment; for I was quite untroubled and could have drifted away in sleep, and now I am working my way back through the tedium of a long convalescence, with no real interest in the process. But I take my medicines and keep my hours and do as I'm bid and remember that this is the first day of another spring and I hope to enjoy it. I would like to be near the sea in a garden, no doubt looking for that heaven I saw in my euthanasia all those years ago: but that vision was only what I should like to have on earth, and every time I have managed to come anywhere near it, a country garden near water alone in a pleasant house—it has happened three times!—I always work well and live well. I shall begin looking for this again I hope in a few weeks more.

+++++++

About Miss Vliet's wanting to see my letters.[50] Of course, anybody can see them who wants. They aren't private anymore, are they, in the Yale University library? Good heavens, my dear old friend, I have already lamented the tendency of the young to try to embalm me while I am still walking around, but when my own, or approximate, generation, give or take 10 or fifteen years— begins to give my letters to various public libraries while we are both still alive, and that without even notifying me of the transfer, combined with a nearly total ceasing of letters from every direction—well, this sentence has got away from me, and I am too tired to try to organize it, but I don't doubt my meaning is clear. It makes me feel funny—funny peculiar. Am I really dead, and just haven't the presence of mind to lie down? Norman Holmes Pearson[51] bought a sheaf of my letters from my dear friend Bob McAlmon when he was dying of tb I think in New Mexico or Arizona; when I heard of it and wrote to ask him for copies or photostats, he sent three, but by various means I discovered he has <u>Twenty</u> Three, in his private collection, but I suppose they will go to Yale eventually. Genevieve Taggard's husband[52] notified me after her death that my letters to her were impounded for fifty years in the N.Y. Public Library. Well, well. . . . . Our dear Glenway is thinking of publishing a collection, and I hope he does. I have thousands of letters to hundreds of persons for at least fifty years floating around—I know I keep all letters received, and so does everybody else, apparently,—and it heartens me to think what a lovely bonfire they would make, or laid end to end would encircle the globe at least three times . . . Never mind, my dear. Its not a question I ever dreamed would arise, and I am bound to conclude that, since I can do nothing whatever about it, this is all none of my affair. Two huge Libraries and three universities have asked for my remains—on paper, that is—and I suppose one day I shall be bundling my friends' and enemies' and husbands' and lovers' letters off to some cultural mausoleum like anybody else.

What else can we do, really? I have always wished for a private life while I lived, it seems to me the most rudimentary decency, the primary human right: but if one's work has roused curiosity as to one's daily life, I see no harm in letting the records be freely available. I have no notion what the inquirers could possibly make of my written records, and though I must say I shouldn't like to be infamous in death any more than I should in life, what the future does with me or my work is of very little concern to me . . . I dare say I average one-a-day of the serious researching students, but most of them ask me to write a few hundred well-chosen words telling them just what I meant and how I did it; adding that I was "assigned" to them by their teacher. I am tempted to write a piece about these teachers, too lazy or too ignorant to teach their students how to read and study and perceive or even surmise what a writer meant by what they see on the pages before them.

But it would be too dull, I'm afraid.

Your news about your fine children—and I remember them as so good looking and spirited and bright, really shimmering in the mind—is good. And give my love to Mildred and the hopes that she keeps well. There is no earthly prison like sickness, God keep us from it. Tomorrow a friend is coming to take me to see Dr. Strangelove[53]. . . and we will have dinner here in my apartment—from the kitchen downstairs, of course. Except for the jet-flight from Dallas, it will be the first time I have been out since February 14. I was supposed to be at a lunch at the White House yesterday, Mrs. Johnson entertaining a lot of ladies described as "doers"—I missed it, of course, and the account in this morning's paper makes me think I was much better entertained at home with The Sot-Weed Factor,[54] a lively parody of an 18th century Picaresque novel, only bawdier, and with a real look at the seamy side of founding a great nation!

Must Stop. Your same old friend
Katherine Anne

To: Abby Mann TLS 3pp. Maryland

Still here, but not for long. Please see P.S. and Nota Bene, thank you!

11 May 1964
[Letterhead: Jefferson Hotel
1200 Sixteenth Street, N.W.
Washington 6. D.C.]

Dear Abby: All your news is wonderful and I am happy to see a name or two
I hadn't found in the newspapers.. I don't read them much, but friends send
me little notices. Oskar Werner?[55] Several years ago Camera Three dramatized
some scenes from Ship of Fools, one of them being the scene on deck between
La Condesa and the Doctor. A fine French actress from the Comédie Fran-
çaise played La Condesa beautifully, and a splendid German actor played Dr
Schumann. I wonder if this could be Werner? Anyway they were a fine pair,
and I saw for the first time how at least parts of that book could be done as a
picture....
    The cast is pretty overwhelming, isn't it? Heavens, Olivier[56] would have
been too much. I believe he is the best actor in the world, and has been for at
least thirty years; he has had, and has, some great runners-up, but nobody has
passed him yet. But he is for Oedipus Rex, and Lear and Othello and Hamlet
and Henry Vth and classical comedy—leave him in his glory! I'll settle for
Oskar Werner.
    Now at this fairly late moment, I have some things to suggest to you, and I
will put them on separate pages so you may find them easily and refer to them
if you like. They are merely practical details, but I think important.
    As to what you make of the story as a whole or the individual characters,
we agreed in Rome, didn't we? that this would be your affair. The two mediums are simply too different and cannot be ruled by the same laws. Very well.
I read in the papers,—as Will Rogers[57] used to say—that Vivien Leigh[58] would
play Mrs. Treadwell, the she-wolf who tries to murder somebody! Good God,
says I to myself, no woman could be further from she-wolfishness than Mary
Treadwell. She is exactly what I say she is: a woman brought up tenderly who
makes a bad marriage, gets shocks of cruelty which frighten her into retreat
from life, a fear of people, of experience; yet her heart is tender and easily
moved. Her first impulse is to a kind of impersonal friendliness—her second
a drawing away with a kind of cynical remembrance of her past entangle-
ments. When she is attacked with threats of rape and bone-breaking by a
drunken thug, she defends herself with an accumulated rage against such

brutalities in all life, not just her own. Yet some of the reviewers resented loudly her resentment of the insult offered her, and called her names I shan't repeat. There was never one word against Denny for his conduct to her. This is shocking to me, and I can only say, that if I had ever found myself in Mrs. Treadwell's situation, I hope I might have had a more effective weapon. That's all.

First, about the Music for the picture.

Wagner and Schubert for the Sunday morning music, if you use that A Mighty Fortress is Our God, for Lutheran Services if you have any. Strauss Waltzes, with Tales From The Vienna Woods mostly. Be sure the band plays Adieu, Mein Kleiner Garde-Offizier, adieu etc

And for Hans, Das Gibt Nur Einmal which he sings or whistles on his way to Concha . . .
Remember also, Marlene Dietrich's Ich Bin Die Fesche Lola—all three of these were popular tunes at the time, it should be easy to find them, on records or in sheet music. Cucaracha of course, for the Havana students, and also The Peanut Vendor, both ragingly popular then.

José Greco's troupe[59] will no doubt have its own music, so I suppose you will leave that choice to them.

It is odd: Noon Wine has been made into more Tv and Radio plays than I like to think about, all of them incurably awful, and not one time has any one made the faintest attempt to find out the tune of the song which is a leit-motif in the whole story . . It really exists, it is really a Scandinavian drinking song, it is a most touchingly beautiful tune, and though I cannot tell them the name I could sing it for them, or play them the notes on a piano so they could "arrange" it. But no—nothing at all.

(Afterthought. Maybe I shan't need two pages.)
Second: About dress: I wore slacks and riding britches in Mexico in 1923 on, and have pictures to prove it . . . Backless sun dresses as well as evening frocks in high style at same time. 1930 those ugly hermaphrodite skirt-pants came in and I was fool enough to wear them, too. Great wide sunhats—also berets falling off one side of the head. . . . . get the dress authentic and not exaggerated. La Condesa's dress is always romantic, graceful, expensively simple. . . . .

When Jenny goes on board at Vera Cruz, she should be wearing a pair of plain tight fitting dark blue denim pants, with a light limp short-sleeved shirt, light blue. Item, NO DARK GLASSES EVER She can be carrying a wide straw hat, and must have Mexican huaraches (sandals) In fact her outfit is an offense to God and man of that time in Mexico, and anywhere else; but Jenny is not a bitch or an evil woman, and I hope Miss Ashley[60] will be allowed to play her the way she is: honest and frank and hopelessly friendly and aspiring and confused and suffering and joyous—she is not going to have the usual kind of luck, nor the conventional future, but she is not as whipped as she seems when she gets to Germany. She is just starting! I hope this will get over in the general mix-up!

Now I think this will do! Please pay attention, I shall not write again about this ... I know you are doing wonderfully well; you can't imagine how eager I am to see that picture, if there are any festivities when it comes out I want to be there. Meantime, I'll be here, and from now on you will not be puzzled about my address. I have leased a house here in a pretty gardenish sort of part of town, a good big house I can't outgrow as I do most of them and my address in full is below. I need my books and papers badly. After June 1st next address me as follows:

Miss Katherine Anne Porter
3601 49th Street, N.W.
Washington D.C 20016.

That's it until April 1969, and maybe, maybe 1970.... That seems pretty far off, doesn't it? What if it never came at all?

Affections and remembrances, Rome seems far away and the fall seems very near—when do you think the picture will really be shown? The very notion is exciting. Bless you, and all good fortune .. I have a birthday on this May 15, and I'm glad of it! I never expected to have it!

Katherine Anne

To: Margaret Harvey TLS 2pp. Maryland

3601 49th Street, N.W.
Washington D.C. 20016
15 September 1964

Dear Margaret:

What a lovely anniversary sort of letter to drop out of the blue September sky, for it is just 47 long improbable years this September since I was given a job on the Rocky Mountain News by dear good ever-remembered Bill Shanklin,[61] who took me on in the sheer generosity of his heart. I told in Pale Horse Pale Rider what he did for me during the plague, I didn't even bother to change his first name. I didn't tell that the Rocky Mountain News paid my little wages—$15 a week, all the time I was sick and believe it or not, I lived on that, then! Three dollars a week for a room with steam heat, and twenty five cents for lunch, and so on. And then, when I came out of the hospital, crippled from phlebitis in my left leg, bald as an egg and wearing turbans, with my right arm in a sling, after having been in a cast, with a cracked elbow,—due to the nurses trying to stand me up too soon—Bill took me back and I went right on, typing with one hand. Ask Helen if she doesn't remember any of this? And did she recognize the story, in Pale Horse, Pale Rider, of Miranda and Mary being sent to report an elopement scandal, and we suppressed most of it because the victims wept and begged so hard to be spared further disgrace—and that villainous Post printed all the sordid details next day. I've forgotten what happened to Helen, but I was demoted to theatre and music.

I remember you, and yes, Thomas Hornsby Ferril,[62] then a beginning young poet, very good looking; I saw him long after, in 1942: he was still good looking as ever, but a much better poet! Please tell the younger generation of newspaper gals that "Pale Horse, Pale Rider" is set in Denver, and is based on my own little love story there with a young soldier who died in the plague, after having taken care of me, who survived it.

Now then, I didn't have pneumonia in St. Louis, I got it there and wore it out in Charlottesville, Virginia and that was in February 1959. I had pneumonia again this spring, February again, but in Dallas this time. All hang-over from that 1918 disaster. I went to Europe for a year after the Ship came out, October 1962, to November 1963—now have settled in Washington for good, have a big house in an edge of Washington like a great park: I have squirrels and chipmunks, and rabbits, and the neighbors' cats, and birds of numerous feathers—robins and orioles and cardinals and wrens and doves and thrushes and so on . . . And old roses, still blooming like mad. I have a life lease with option to buy, and am in no hurry to do anything, except get a little more writing done.

Now then, about that hand-lettered scroll, I would dearly love to have it. I shall frame it and hang it in my liberry, as it was sometimes pronounced in southern dialect of my childhood—the only thing being, though, that every family had one and knew what it was even if they didn't pronounce it properly. I am honored and delighted, and lets just agree that it is never too late to give thanks for a charming deed, or to make up for lost time in friendship.

So please, at your next meeting, give all those present my greetings and read my letter to them, and wish them well for me. I remember those Denver days, those days of living on $15 a week, during war time, in the great plague and surrounded by death and every sort of human disaster, through that "golden haze" that Henry James remembered his childhood.[63] Because I never have seen since more friendly and generous young people than I knew on that newspaper; and I never saw better behavior nor courage under pressure than I did in that hospital where I nearly died, on the part of every doctor, nurse, orderly and attendant in the place—the County Hospital. It was the only place Bill Shanklin could find that had a bed for me . . .

So you see, dear Margaret, how living that past is for me, too, and how, though I suppose none of us would live over a day of it,—certainly I would not—yet I wouldn't have missed it for anything! It was tremendous, but once is enough! I am glad you all remember me so delightfully, I didn't feel in the least glamorous or mysterious, I would never have known I was beautiful if I hadn't been told, but I do know I was naturally merry-hearted and loved gayety and loved to sing and act and recite poetry . . . That part is right, is a fact, and the other I'm sure is just an illustration of Plato's lovely theory that Beauty is in the eye of the beholder, and love is in the lovers, not the beloved, who may be quite unconscious of the whole business!

Thank you for your letters. Let's keep a little in touch, not a régime but a being in each others' minds and memories. I love to be remembered by those I remember with affection. . . . . . If I can manage it I'll come to Denver again and see your Press Club. Boy! Who could forget Mrs. Crawford Hill?[64]

My love and best wishes to you and the whole Press Club, though of course specially to those of you I knew when—we Old-Timers must stick together!

Katherine Anne

To: Caroline Gordon TLS 3pp. Princeton

3601 49th Street, N. W
Washington D C
5 November 1964

Caroline darling: it is pretty late in the day for me to be telling you how I rejoiced in your rebuke to Brer Nance about his silly presumptuous book[65]— such a perfect blend of good temper, wit, and a shattering blow to his flimsy little International Critical Machine: O, sancta simplicitus!

"Any one with a feeling for machinery must pity the plight of Professor Nance's ICM. . . ." and onward, what delicious fun-making. And I wish all Freudians could have their attention called to Freud's own statement which you quote, and remind them that he never attempted to criticise literature, music or painting by his own methods. (After all he misunderstands the whole Oedipal episode, even by his own themes!)

It was a heroic act of friendship for you to take the immense trouble to smack that hovering insect, and I am grateful, for I have had a swarm of them. . . . I understand your weariness, your refusal any longer to read anything about your work. It is appalling to see how these reviewers, you cannot call them critics, apparently can read every word, or at least every line of a work and not understand one idea or emotion it contains. What you know so well by nature, that one "grows by what one rejects" (I wish I could remember who said that) that every rejection implies the choice of something else, that the whole art of life itself is the weeding out of the irrelevant, the superfluous, the <u>not-needed</u>, to make room for the things we recognize as ours which we cannot deny or reject or let be crowded out except at our mortal risk. . . . It is so strange they cannot see the difference between flight and a going <u>towards</u>; between adventure and a pilgrimage. How clearly and purely you have said this: I wonder if the poor little limited soul can take it in! The way you understand Harry, and the place, the pre-eminently lordly detached, above-the-battle place of the southern male, especially of that generation <u>and before</u>. My grandmother remarked on hearing of the Emancipation Proclamation, "I hope it works both ways," but she was disappointed. The slaves were freed, more or less, but her bondage of moral, spiritual, practical, material responsibility ended only with her death; and her two old left-over slaves who refused to leave her followed her to the grave side and wept because they had lost their last true friend. There is just something about the south of the past these Johnny-come-latelies will never be able even to imagine . . .

I wish they could be persuaded to read <u>Alex Maury</u>[66] before they go casting their half-baked opinions about, mostly based on the researches of the Brooklyn intellectuals in a Yiddish accent. If ever there was a man who was not only the head of his own house, but the head of his society: (power consists in being about to thwart, frustrate, and confound all attempts made upon your liberty and your human rights,) and if he didn't practise this as a fine art, I don't know of any one who ever did. He was somewhat baffled by the younger generation, but not confused—not derailed. . . .

Yes angel, I do have a principle of rejection. I reject Brer Nance and his combination of Cambric tea and arsenic: I prefer an honest hatchet job such as some of the muscle boys of the quarterly reviews did. I resent him calling my family "genteel"—or that we were like Lizardi's family,[67] panic-stricken for fear of slipping into the lower-class on account of poverty. We were never afraid of our society, and if there was any judging to be done, or choosing of company, we did it. Poverty was honorable when it came for honorable reasons, and that is something else these funny people can't understand: that we loved an ample life with luxuries and comforts and pleasures and had as much of them as we could pay for: but when we couldn't have them, we did not lose our self-respect or identity on that account.... We were, as I have said somewhere before, in the best of company.

Oh my dear, my good friend from so many years back, why am I writing all this to you who know it in your blood stream, except for the joy of talking to you about things we know and love, and just now, when we are on the eve of a great change, to set down what we felt and thought about certain things in this time of our life.

++++++++++

I am trying to write something about Flannery: and about Ford. I have been asked to do this, and I want to: I grew to know Ford very well at a certain late point in his life, when he seemed to decide to forgive me for not being a disciple, but I think he could never read my stories: I didn't mind, and our friendship was a kind of scramble from day to day trying to find food and raise a little money now and then—it couldn't have been a more all-four-feet-on-the-ground sort of life! But I remember it with a kind of laughter, and so does Janice—or did when I saw her last in Paris in 1952. Flannery I saw on exactly three days, rather spaced if I remember, and the impression she made on me is all I can tell about. I have really no idea what she thought or felt about me, except it was courteous and gentle, as she was in everything she did that I saw: and I believe and have always believed that she was a genius if ever I saw one, and the profundity of her vision of this world and its relation to eternity is mysterious and almost appalling . . . (I had some trouble writing the word mysterious, I have a slightly crippled right hand, and one finger is especially rebellious, loves to hit the key NEXT to the one I aim for—oh the years! They do catch up, don't they?)

++++++++++

You did know once if you have forgotten now that I think your novel NONE SHALL LOOK BACK[68] is the one true inarguably great novel about the War[69] and I have a copy of the original edition, but I can't find copies to lend or give to students. Is it out of print? And why? Please let me know. You said more in that book than has been said in all these four years on that Subject.

+++++++++

I have a good house now, not the house I would build, or even choose to buy, but I haven't built or bought it; leased it for life, and I am IN—every book, scrap of paper, object, I possess now under one roof for good and all, and I am planting mock-orange and anemones and lilies of the valley and pink Magnolias—the kind that bloom before they leaf out—and crocus—besides of course, roses in an already prepared rose bed full of old persistent sturdy sweet smelling roses that aren't even in the catalogues any more, and they were blooming right up to the moment when the gardener came and cut them off short for the winter ... Never mind. The place is full of azaleas, which seem to thrive here, and other stuff that I don't take much interest in, except there is a bank at the back covered with tiny wild roses and honeysuckle, all tangled with ivy and weeds. I am going to have it cleared out and have nothing but wild roses and honeysuckle there. I send you snapshots, not very good, of the house with my sweet lovely niece Ann in the front, and the hall with my Orpheus I brought from Naples last year, and my Taormina Virgin. I put her out in the walk against green in the sunshine, and forgot to use the close-up lens, But its a dear love of a thing, isn't it?

Now I must stop—but I am cherishing the magazine with your reply to our poor misguided man—he is not good enough, for your attention, but I'm glad you did it, just the same; (selfish me,) and I hope to hear from you when you have a free minute you don't need to garden with your desperately needing-money grandsons—or lying down to rest some afternoon. Goodbye, darling, bless you.

Katherine Anne

To: Malcolm Cowley DTLS 2 pp. Newberry

3601 - 49th Street, N.W.
Washington, D.C.
March 16, 1965

Dear Malcolm:
Your nice, long letter came, and I sort of liked having the news from you. I don't need my memory refreshed about the passage in Exile's Return as I have a copy of the first edition.[70] You will think I am hard to please, but I was never a "newspaper woman." I went to Denver with my insipient bronchitis and asthma looking for climate and had to have some kind of job to subsist. Like many romantic young women who "want to write," I was a victim to the idea that a newspaper job was the place to learn one's craft. It isn't so, of course, and it only took me about eight months to discover this fact of life. I was never any good at it. They kept shifting me around from spot to spot trying to find

where I would fit in. If I am really a newspaper woman, I wonder what those real old professionals on that paper in my time would call themselves. I think you wouldn't call me a newspaper woman because it is simply not true.

All I ever said was that Mexico City was not my Paris; it was my beloved Mexico City. As you know, I never saw Taxco until we went there that time. Our ex voto is still in the church I am told by friends who have seen it; I have never been back, and I was never in exile as I have said in print by now. I always knew where I was, who I was, and what I was doing. You must remember that in my childhood in Texas I heard as much Spanish spoken as I did English. My father took me on a trip to Mexico before I was ten years old. I was used to the atmosphere of San Antonio, Texas. I went to Mexico because I was not going into exile, but I was going back to a place I knew and loved; so you can see I might question even that short reference to me in your delightful book. I wish I had a true place in it, but, of course, I haven't.

What does astound me is that within four lines and a fraction you could make three mistakes in my history, and we had known each other quite a while by then. Don't let it worry you; I know what changes in plates will do. I had a perfect nightmare with Ship of Fools. It took me eight printings to work the typos out of the hard cover edition. The ninth printing was paperback, and I went over it again and got it clean. In the last round they thought up ten or fifteen new ones of their own. Nothing really serious I suppose unless you count two pretty obvious slips in grammar as serious—not my slips either.

I suppose it is the common fate to have busy friends on the margin of our efforts at literature who want to get in the act in the latter rounds. I see that Frances Steloff[71] is more or less claiming credit for the Ship of Fools being finished at last because she gave moral support to Seymour Lawrence while he was giving me moral support in my job; so I said to him not long ago it was news to me that all that time I thought I was leaning on him I seemed to really be leaning on Frances Steloff. Well, my dear, this is just gossip. I never knew Frances at all, except she sent me books on account wherever I was—

I am taking time off from all kinds of silly and stupid things about income tax and insurance and people who don't know how to hang curtains to write you a letter.

I think you are very brave to go back to Stanford year after year. Once was enough for me, but I suppose one year of me was enough for them too.

Please give my remembrances and greetings to Muriel and also to Dick and Lucy Jones[72] with my warmest Texas regards right back. How I remember Lucille's mother on one of her birthdays. I think her eightieth or more and she said something to me that was a revelation and a fine, charming lesson to me which I had never heard said before and which I still tell about her. I simply said to her, "I congratulate you on your birthday, and you look wonderful and happy." She said very sweetly, "I enjoy my age." It was like a flash of light through my imagination. I had been a victim of the notion that old age was a kind of walking death. Now I am old, and I find she was right. I enjoy my age.

Aff'ly, aff'ly as Allen used to say
Katherine Anne

KAP/lcm

To: Monroe Wheeler TLS 2pp. Maryland

3601 49th Street N W
Washington D C 20016
7 July 1965

Monroe darling: I shall dash off hastily the true history of that Mexican Ballet for Pavlowa:

Early in 1920, February or March, I met Adolfo Best-Maugard in New York, where he had come as a young painter with a system of design he had invented himself based on ancient Mexico designs from buried cities, mostly Mayan. Though Aztec and other tribes contributed motifs.

I found it fascinating, Best and I spent long days talking about this, he proposed that I help him get out a text-book on the subject in English . . I undertook it, but was as then so sunk in my own projects, I got him finally to turn it over to some one else. It appeared and I don't know its history here. But it was adopted as textbook in all the primary schools in Mexico and at least a whole generation of Mexican children learned to draw and paint by his method. Even Diego Rivera and above all, Miguel Covarrubias and the younger ones of his time were formed on Adolfo Best's system, and it shows even in the work of the latest comers today.

However, in those times we were all ballet mad. I had seen the Diag-ileff Ballet with its great galaxy of stars—in 1916—a new world to us—and Adolfo adored Pavlowa, and somehow managed to get near her with his idea for A Mexican Ballet.[73] Castro Padilla, (who later was to write my little per-sonal song, La Norteña (Girl From the North) and I don't know who wrote La Pelegrina (The Pilgrim) for Alma Reed;[74] but it would be nice if people would get this little thing straightened out, if they refuse to forget it altogether.

And if it is going to go on being remembered, Here is the story of Best's Ballet for Pavlowa: He asked me to do the libretto, making it perhaps a simple romance with a background of Xochimilco, and working in three of the most attractive Mexican dances. I did this. I gave him the manuscript. Castro Padilla in Mexico started doing the music—based of course on the dance tunes already popular and a few things of his own. Best started painting the scenery—this was spring and summer of 1920, in a big loft somewhere over near Broadway in the theatrical district, a magnified and fantasified vision of the Floating Gardens. I used to go over now and then to sit and watch. You should have seen Adolfo in all his Hildago elegance on a step ladder with a dirty paint stained shirt tied around his waist by the arms, surrounded by buckets of paints and brushes, pale and exhausted, working with such concentration and singlemindedness as I have not seen too often in this world. The designs and colors were quite simply magnificent. Well—Pavlowa accepted the whole thing, studied the Mexican dances with a teacher, adapted them to her own school, and they were announced for the fall or early winter of 1920. It must have been no later, for I was in Mexico by December 21 of that year. And I went to the opening night of the ballet in New York, having invited friends, to see the new Ballet for which I had written the libretto such as it was, and had been promised that my name would be on the program and behold, the ballet itself was never danced in New York so far as I know. Well, Adolfo, who was crushed, told me why. Nobody had told him better—and all sorts of theatre people who must have known, Norman Bel-Geddes, Lee Simonson[75] I remember well as coming to watch the work, never hinted to him that paper scenery was not allowed in New York Theatres—a fire hazard. . . . So there was not time to do other scenery, the whole thing was simply put aside in this country: but Pavlowa danced that ballet where ever she was for the next three years, except in the USA, and the great triumphal performance given in Mexico took place in 1923, probably with a new libretto, or arrangement of mine by a Mexican to keep it 100% castiza;[76] I was not in Mexico that year, for it was the year after the disastrous episode of our great Mexican Exhibition of Mexican popular Arts, the story of which I told to Henry Lopez[77] when I was last in Mexico and he printed in his magazine Dialogos.

I wrote the monograph to go with the show and a copy of it is here in the Library of Congress. I haven't a copy. But I was very embittered about the political skullduggery that had nearly destroyed that show, and I mean to tell it in every detail before I die. Just the other day in my old papers I found the cable notifying me that President Obregon was appointing me American Organizer of the show, naming the fee and asking me to return to Mexico at once . . I have come across letters from many who took part, and Guerrero's final gloomy report from Los Angeles, and a comic outburst from our camera man saying what he thought of all the scoundrels who had interfered . . .

So darling, I should most certainly be doing something else than writing this: but no, it is useful to me, for I have a copy and it will be an aid to memory when I get all the fragments of this little history put together.

Adolfo died suddenly in Athens as you know, and was buried in Mexico City just about three days before I got there last November. But there are many old-timers, still going on, who knew me WHEN, and they all turned out in force to hear me speak, and I told the story of that show for the first time, and they crowded around me to tell me they remembered, and that what I said was true. And I am going to get them as witnesses, because more and more I am appalled at the utter carelessness and inaccuracy of people who give long accounts of something they know nothing about, repeating gossip, rumors: and I am going to leave documented statements of certain things in which I took part and I know what happened. I do not want credit, if I had wanted to make a career of anything, I could have done it, as you know. I had no motive then except a fascinated interest with what we were doing, and I am glad we did it, and I am happy to have taken part, but it was all an incident which closed for me because I had something quite other of my own to do, and could not spend my time assisting at other peoples' projects for ever.

But there are always those greedy, grabby birds, the crows that swarm to the planted corn field—the biophages,—as Motherlanty called them according to Julian Green[78]—and I have seen them at work in every situation of life for half a century and I just think I shall enjoy tripping them up a little. . . . I wrote a libretto for Pavlowa in 1920. I never saw her perform it. I was appointed by President Obregon spring of 1922 to help gather and organize that first great and beautiful show, and I did—and I never saw the show except as it was set up in Mexico for the government officials and the public to see . . . This is all I can say now.

****

Monroe, Personal note - Please give me the date of your coming with Glenway. William Humphrey and his wife are spending July 24–25 with me here in the house. You said, end of July. Let me know darling. Same faithful believing love

Katherine Anne

To: Barbara Harrison Wescott TLS 1p. Maryland

3601 49th Street, N W
Washington D C 20016
January 4, 1966

Dearest Barbara: It is disappointing, need I say, that you and Glenway cannot
be here. I invited Stephen Spender because he is Poetry Consultant here, but
he doesn't get back from London until tomorrow. So I don't know. Eleanor
and Red Warren will be here, and William Humphrey and Dorothy, and Seymour and Merloyd Lawrence, and other littery friends you may or may not
know, I should say about twenty if everybody gets here—That is, twenty now
that you and Glenway will be absent. Pity, pity—but maybe some time you
will come and stop with me a while all by yourself.

Day before yesterday I left my bed all day, the first time in a month. Yesterday I went to my doctors, shopped for the party, and today early I went to
the hairdresser and he turned me out nicely. I am holding up and believe I
shall go on getting better now. It has been a great bore.

I hope your cold has run its course by now—it can be as miserable an
affliction as any I know.

Your Christmas, merry with children, sounds lovely. I spent that day and
New Year's by myself in bed, reading—Barbara Tuchman's The Proud Tower—
simply wonderful—Truman Capote's In Cold Blood – gruesome, a companion piece to the Tuchman book, because the infinite and infernal brotherhood
of the lowest criminals and the highest statesmen begins seeping into one's
mind like brimstone from hell coming through cracks in the earth. Thomas
Berger's Little Big Man is comic relief, yet another sort of scoundrelism.[79] It is
a fairly wicked world, Barbara, in spots, and I wonder why people got so mad
at my Ship and resented my views—

Well, these books and stacks of magazines and newspapers got me nicely
through the season, and both on Christmas Eve, and New Year's Eve, I opened
a little bottle of your wonderful Moét et Chandon and sat up in my golden
bed reading and sipping in great good cheer and contentment. Deborah[80] sent
me the most delightful card, a photograph of her family, all smiles and beauty
and each parent holding a baby . . . It is lovely.

It is amusing isn't it, to think of that little old song I translated so long ago
having this wild run, just thirty three years after—What fine, warm memories
I have of the whole Harrison of Paris episode, what a world, what a time, where
did it go? Yet, look, here we are, and I suppose none of us wish to be anywhere
else, or have life very different from what we have, after all, made it. . . .

Do be well, darling. I love you dearly and devotedly and always have, and wish you health and joy for many years, to come. Specifically, Happy New Year, 1966.

Katherine Anne

For food, I am going to have capon simmered in chicken broth, A Smith-field Ham, already cooked in Virginia, and roast filet of beef, Hot rolls, green salad, Fruit tarts—cherry and strawberry. Vosne Romanée with the meats, champagne with the tarts. Fresh things with the cocktails—you would have had sherry—and endive, radishes, celery hearts, carrot strips. A lot of things you could eat!

Love again
K.A.

To: Barbara Harrison Wescott TLS 2pp. Maryland

3601 49th Street, N W
Washington D C 20016
26 January 1966

Dearest Barbara: Your letter of the 24th reached me this morning, through our first real snowdrifts here, too. Winter was a little late this year, happily. And I have the bad news that you were not coming to see me on Tuesday just twenty four hours later. Frustration works every which way there is, don't you find? I believe the only way to baffle these incidents and do something once in a while that we want to do for a change, maybe, is to pick up and come down on your lone, whatever day you can spare—I expect you can't really spare any, but in that case, just confiscate one, let me know a little before so I have a supply of croissants on hand—beef steaks and Belgian endive I have—and the rest will be repose and doing anything you like: Let's just up and do this some day. Don't wait on Lloyd or Glenway: I have never seen two men more up to their eyes in their own projects than they—well, so have we projects, and let's get on with them.

Peter Seeger sent me that record,[81] and I thought it was pretty nice, but a little toneless: Uh, uh, uh, is not really an improvement on Oh, Oh Oh, or even, this being a protesting girl, Ah. Ah. Ah—he could give a funny little imitation of her voice and manner—but then, there he is, and very popular too: I am a little past my folk song period, though. I made myself a medieval gown, long sleeves, long train, tight-waisted, of red wool jersey: wore with it a henequen—two-horned, mine, with a great gauzy stiffened white organdy veil: and I trouped a local Louisiana-Texas-Arkansas circuit singing ballads from Percy's Reliques and old Negro songs—Pale horse, Pale Rider; He Never Said a Mumblin Word: Swing Low, Sweet Chariot: Water Boy: oh a list of them: This was in the terrible winter of 1914. So you see my folksong era is far away. A most terrible winter it was, in every way I can mention: yet I would not take anything for that year. Everything in it put me to the grim test of whether I could survive or not, without shame and without compromise. I could.

There was in every little country town—I played in churches, Elks Halls, school houses,—an eager young girl happy to play the piano for me: I carried my music with me: one rehearsal and we were ready. . . . I hope I live to write that story. I can hardly expect it to be believed, yet it all happened—to me. I wish I had had time—and money, no doubt—to have paused and had my photograph taken in that outfit. Too late now.

****

I had roundabout echos of Pauline's party at Mouton: I should like to see that museum—Stephen Spender was there for a time with the others, then showed up here at my party, and gave delightful little scraps of news. He is one of the most omnipresent persons in the world: every time I see or hear of him he is just setting off for somewhere far away, or is just back, and setting out again in three hours. Such capacity for absorbing everything in sight simply overwhelms me. And he does take everything in, and acts on situation positively; and with intention. It's a gift.

****

Our letter book is going to be fascinating to US if no one else can imagine that round of letters among you, Glenway, Monroe, me, Giorgio,[82] Russell and Mildred? The last two with only a few, but still belonging there. I did not realize how outward-looking we all were, really living in our world at a pretty good speed, each from his own stance and territory, but a genuine example of what everybody is now trying to say is impossible—communication, that desolate abused word. We did it without even trying. And are still getting on with it pretty well.

Love again and always
Katherine Anne

To: Dayton Kohler TLS 1p. VPI

3601 49th Street, N W
Washington D C 20016
29 April 1966

Dayton Kohler, Esquire
Virginia Polytechnic Institute
Department of English and Foreign Languages
Blacksburg, Virginia 24061

Dear Mr. Kohler:

Your review of <u>Ship of Fools</u> in your annual Review is one of the best, clearest, most understanding ones I have seen:[83] I have been amazed at some of the interpretations, bad guesses at motives, total misunderstanding, and above all, the tone of <u>personal</u> rancor that seeped like dirty water through some of the "critical" estimates. The most common mistake of these run-of-the-mill reviewers is to ascribe the views and behavior of the author's characters, to the author himself: the question most often asked me by students and random readers is: (after "Where do you get your ideas?") Where are you in the book? which character do you represent?" My answer is considered either flippant and evasive or just downright deception: I tell them that I am everybody on board ship from the sea-sick bull dog to the Captain on the bridge, the fat man in the cherry-colored shirt who sang and made mischief, the deported sugar workers in the steerage—in fact, I am the ship, too, and I suspect, even the ocean and the islands in the sea—for I wrote the book, and all of my living substance is in it—all I had to give at the time. And this mere simple fact of what working in an art means is incredible to them, they cannot grasp even the margins of this central principle. I wonder sometimes why they insist on invading territories that will be strange to them always; and yet it never seems to occur to them that they have missed a point, or failed to see the meaning, of the work they abuse.

Thank you profoundly for your essay, and for sending me the Annual. I hope to see more of your work, I wish you well in a long life of good work. Sincerely yours,

Katherine Anne Porter

To: Eudora Welty TLS 3pp. Mississippi

3601 49th Street N W
Washington, D C 20016
19 January 1967

Dear remembering Eudora:

Spring came into the house with your note and flowers just ahead of a snow storm, which it has baffled and frustrated entirely. Think of it—anemones, carnations, tulips, white and pink snap dragons, yellow snapdragons, too, and small purple irises—a true great lovely bouquet, the kind I love. Bless you; and I hope you will be coming back here soon, and will come to stop with me! I still have the biggish house and my guest rooms are empty, for the dear ones I would love to stay in them are in London or France or Connecticut or New York or Mississippi—and one is even in South Africa, I forget why. Few, but a bouquet I should love to gather again all at once.

Please tell me something about yourself. You were looking so wonderful the last time I saw you—you have never looked anything but well in your special Eudora way but there was just a nimbus of light around you that day which I do not forget. I want real news of you—what are you doing; how do you feel; have you new plans? Going anywhere soon? Or later? And—yes, I know this is a question angels know better than to ask—what are you writing now? And so on, darling, you see that I miss you and want to fill in these spaces of absence and silence.

The last three, now nearly four, years have been for me a fairly trying time, near-fatal pneumonia three times in something less than three years, until at last I have to take the hint that I had to get off the merry-go-round which had become a treadmill for me. But it has been tiresome. I haven't been able to work, or indeed live at all: so the past months, since October, have been spent in and out of hospitals, taking tests—and that is the right word for those exasperating trials of patience and endurance of soul and body—but my doctors think now they have got to the root of my trouble, which is merely long continued exhaustion. So I am being treated head to foot day in, day out, for that: and something is working nearly like magic. I have been out of hospital eleven days today, this is the first letter I have written, I am staying up half a day at a time now, and the endless bottomless fatigue is little by little going, or at least for part of the time ... I have managed to do a few necessary things— my will, my gift of papers and library to the University of Maryland, the establishment of my little Foundation to give money to good writers who need it: Eudora, I'll have to send you the papers on this very soon, but first I will ask you—would you consent to help me choose candidates, would you be part of it to that extent? William Humphrey has agreed, but of course, the other officers are secretary and treasurer, executors of the will, my lawyers, and soon what we need and must have are writers capable of judging excellence and who ever could be better for that than you? But just the same, this is no attempt to kidnap you or appeal to friendship, or anything but just what it says: if you can find time or inclination to help, I will be always grateful; if not, please just let me know; I have thought of you from the first, but all the practical things have been arranged by half a dozen very practical men who know their business, and I have not been able to get in touch with you about this.

Don't be troubled, please: I will send you the little constitution in a few days.

It has been a rather wonderful help to my mind to have these things, important to me, all arranged so well.

Here is a photograph made by the university photographer a few days before I went to hospital last December. He has smoothed me out much too much, but at my time of life—a phrase I never expected to use but which now seems to come quite naturally—no woman can complain of a little flattery in her pictures. So I send this to be taken with a grain of salt, and my perpetual loving wishes for your health and joyful going forward in your writing. Nobody I know has kept every performance on such a high level as you have: that is your way, but from the outside it looks like magic.

Happy New Year
Katherine Anne

To: Marianne Moore TLS 2pp. Maryland

3601 49th Street, N W
Washington, D C
16 January, 1968

Marianne Darling:
This typewriter has been so long neglected the ribbon is dried out, so I am being very careful and sending you a carbon copy: dear George Platt Lynes once asked me years ago why I never kept copies of my letters. He said, "How can you remember what you said to Who?" and I said, "I never get my

friends mixed up." That is one way of remembering. But your delicate handwriting is easy to read, and mine is just such a shattered line I can hardly read myself when it is cold.

I came out of the hospital in Baltimore just seventeen days ago, much improved from that odd fracture of two vertebrae which happened spontaneously just seven years after a fall down stairs in Georgetown. But I am up and about for most of the day, a little disciplined or something of the sort after two months in hospital, but I shall go on walking and standing straight, so I suppose I should be grateful and not complain. Alas, Marianne, I have very little martyr-spirit in me—I suffer in silence at the top of my voice and this episode has been no different. But I can tell you something that may be of some value to you—doctors pay good attention to a howling patient.

Your letter and card when I was in Baltimore, and your blessed card this morning have made my days happy and good, too. I think it is high time and I hope you will not mind if I tell you now that I have loved you and what you are—THAT IS, YOUR POETRY, YOUR BEING, BECAUSE YOU ARE JUST ONE element or substance, since I first knew of you, when you were a golden-haired young athlete with amber pins in your hair, knocking the ribs out of a tennis ball—do you remember those pictures? These, and your poetry and your stiletto wit seemed nearly too much endowment for one woman, but the rest of us had to put up with it as gracefully as we could. No, my dear, my admiration for you was a world away from envy—it was very pure, I do believe, and is now.

Your notes about my story about Mary Alice[84] are dear to me, and the things you choose to write about—I love so much the Early medieval stories and songs about the Child and the Blessed Virgin when they were still pictured and sculptured, as laughing together, she feeding Him with fruit and giving him her milk—I used to stand and stare through the iron fence of the Cluny at that lovely Being with her Baby, in the garden of one of my favorite museums—both laughing and happy. It was later that He became suffering and streaming with blood and She was broken to bits at the foot of the Cross. I wonder what became of the early joy of Christianity.

Little personal note: I was taken on a stretcher in an ambulance to the Baltimore hospital on your birthday which is why you didn't get a telegram from me: I shall be 77 my next birthday, the 15th of next May, which makes us exactly across the calendar from each other, and in astrology this opposition has great meaning. I forget what, but it is a happy omen. And in spite of all, everything that has happened, every grief and disaster we must have known, every evil, every disappointment, and God, it HAS been a long war, hasn't it?

I still say it was rather a triumph to be born at all, and a great victory to have held out so long, and the Old Chinese were right to wish long life to those they loved and wished well.

Marianne, your notes have made me very happy, and I wish we could see each other, and I remember your face so vividly, and will never forget the time you and Monroe out of the bluest sky imaginable came rolling up that steep hill on Roxbury Road to visit with me. Remember? Bless you, Poet. With my love

K.A.

Part Six

1970–1979

By the time Katherine Anne Porter turned eighty in 1970 her letter writing was considerably reduced. The conversations her earlier letters represented now took place for the most part on the telephone. The letters she did write, however, gradually began to change in character as she hired persons as amanuenses. Gone were the phonetic spellings, the eccentric punctuation and running series of points and dashes, the stringing together of clauses separated by commas—missing was much of the informality and spontaneity.

The last decade of letters nevertheless reveals the subjects on Porter's mind as she assessed and redefined what she sometimes called her "mis-spent life." To be sure, she had regrets and disappointments, some of which she was willing to admit. First, she wished she had completed more books, confiding to Raymond Roseliep that she had "a horrible sense of guilt at how I wasted my life on so many things which seemed right and fruitful at the time." And she regretted she had not remained a landowner, a status that distinguished social classes in her youth. "I feel this terrible lack, this absence of life-source, always," she wrote Peter Taylor.

The subject that still rankled her was the critical reception and analyses of *Ship of Fools*, which she described to Carl Griffin as her "much belaboured novel that half a dozen Johnny-Jump-Ups have attacked with forks or with hope but not much intelligence or imagination." "Most of the critics," she said, "have made all their guesses and almost everyone is wrong." She also complained about the "fashionable" attitude of critics who "take for granted that the author is the last person to consult on what he meant by what he said," a principle of the New Criticism with which she disagreed.

But she had satisfactions. She had stopped apologizing for writing the best-selling *Ship of Fools*. "I like it," she declared to James T. Farrell, referring to the money the novel earned. "It has kept me from the one thing that made me nervous since the days when I realized that my strength and energy would come to an end—that I should have to sleep under a bridge." She was able to say, "I am living simply in the modest but pleasant lap of luxury." She also had the "lovely tranquility of long assured friendships, the kind of love that does really last a life time, the kind I treasure with all my heart."

Her greatest contentment, however, lay in her certainty that she had per-severingly adhered to her artistic principles. She told James T. Farrell, "I am sure you must have known all this time that I began my life as an artist with exactly your code and I have observed it without one misstep ever since just as you have." Although she admired his commitment, she was careful not to tell him she liked his work, preserving her lifelong principle of being honest about art.

Neither had the iron will that had sustained her through eight decades weakened. When she was seventy-two years old she accepted an assignment from *Playboy* to accompany a group of scientists and other writers on a cruise ship who would watch from a close vantage point the launching of the twen-tieth century's last spaceship to the moon, after which she was to write an article about it. The article was never finished, but she had another good story to tell. That experience, her return to her homeland in 1976, and the publica-tion in 1977 of her memoir of the Sacco-Vanzetti affair were the high points of the last decade of her life.

But there is no question that death was on her mind. She told Peter Tay-lor, "I have been so often so near to death, I know now there is nothing to fear in it," and, indeed, her mood was not one of fear as much as weariness and waiting. She told Raymond Roseliep, "I am simply sitting on a raft in the middle of the ocean with the tide carrying me out" and "I am very slowly mil-limeter by millimeter leaving this world." She told Red Warren in March of 1979, "I am really dying now and do not quite know when." She had a year and a half more of "rolling this stone uphill every day," as she had described her life to Peter Taylor eight years earlier.

To: Peter Taylor and Eleanor Ross Taylor ALS 2pp. Vanderbilt

[Sligo Gardens Nursing Home
Takoma Park, Maryland]
18 May 1970—

Dear Eleanor and Peter—
Here it is already the 18th of May and I am 72 hours older than I was on the 15th—80 years old at last, my dears, and I thought I would never arrive at it!
I fractured my left hip-bone a few days after Barrett's party in the F Street Club[1]—a classically conservative, granny-kind of trick—and had a fierce long operation in a state of total oblivion followed by a blissful state of nit-wittedness, I spent nearly five weeks in Hospital, screeching like a banshee every time I was touched and am now in a Rest-Home trying to learn to walk again—
It was a joyous open-house sort of birthday party, champagne and all—and now the discipline of recovery is lightened a little, and I am happy to be alive; and happy that you-all (alle Beide, Tout les deux) are in the world in my time. Suppose I had missed you? Not to be <u>thought</u> of—
Eudora's book[2] is my delight. I read a word at a time, or I'll miss something—a merry, sinister, tragic book, comic with desperate knowledge of life, slapstick comedy with undertones to bring tears—a reconciliation with the terrors of life, a battle that <u>nobody</u> wins, ever!
I don't know how long I'll be here, in this Convalescent Home, but I have a new address on the first of June—
6100 Westchester Park Drive, apartments 1517–1518, College Park, Maryland
I hope you are well and merry!

Love—Katherine Anne

To: Peter Taylor ALS 3pp. Vanderbilt

[6100 Westchester Park Drive, apartments 1517–1518
College Park, Maryland]
Friday March ? [c. 11] 1971

Dear Peter—It is fine news that you and Eleanor are collecting land again—the good old Southern land-hunger led to the best things about us. One of my ancestors on my father's side—or rather on his mother my grandmother's side, helped his elder brother, Daniel Boone to survey Kentucky, which was divided into Kentucky, Missouri, Indiana and I forget what else. He was paid in land—Daniel, I mean—by the government, 90,000 acres of good land in what is now Missouri (I <u>think</u>) but what became of it I don't know—This same grandmother had from her father 6000 acres of a Texas land grant when Texas was still Mexico—By some legal sleight of hand, a man named Burleson swindled her out of this long, long ago. A descendant of that Burleson became Postmaster General in my time, and another became the lawyer in my story "Old Mortality" though nobody but me ever knew this, until now. I never told anybody before—You will both, separately or as one, think of something very good to do with that land with such appropriate country names—

I am a country woman by birth, tradition and a town-country upbringing, and my best memories are of the country—(see Notes on Sources, Noon Wine, and the story itself) but I do not own one inch of land, and I feel this terrible lack, this absence of life-source, always. Just leave it to the children! They'll be glad of it.

XXXX

Your family difficulties even seem so southern, so familiar—I will not now tell you mine, mere echos of your own, but going over thirty years just past, with the long complications of four long hard deaths of my father, my only brother, my sister and my brother's widow,[3] happily put away in peace four weeks ago; her devoted children, the four of them, have wept as if hers was the first death in this world . . . I have been so often so near to death, I know now there is nothing to fear in it. Only We—Southerners—seem so tough, so hardy—we die long and hard—and now—in my age, 81, next May 15, it troubles me to think how much I have endured and survived, <u>What</u> can it take to kill me? It is not that I am tired of living, or tired of the world; my friends are dear to me as ever, I wouldn't have missed living for anything—but yes, I am tired of rolling this stone uphill every day, sitting by it at the foot of the hill all night, to take it up again at every sunrise—

Dear Peter and Eleanor—

It is now the 25th of March. I began this letter at least two weeks ago—was interrupted, closed the tablet, and opened it again this morning: off it goes, now—Please come to see me! Love and hope –

Katherine Anne

To: John Malcolm Brinnin ALS 5pp. Delaware

[6100 Westchester Drive, Apartments 1517–1518
College Park, Maryland]
27 November, 1971

John Malcolm, my dear!

Your note to me about your wonderful party on the S.S. Peter Stuyvesant is most surely the loveliest ever I received in my long lifetime, and I bless you for it, with my love and faith—to be <u>seen</u> so in the eyes of a poet, does not happen to every woman! It is my happy fortune to have known and believed in you with all affection and tenderness—in your eyes I am beautiful, and that is crown enough for me!

I have been reading your book[4]—and I want words to say what a miracle of knowledge, gleaned and experienced, it is—I counted your bibliography to persuade myself that you were not—could not have been—present at every incident you describe, every speech you made us <u>hear</u>—no! not in 1837, let's say—and yet, you <u>were</u> there—in the same sense that I have a way of saying, when asked how long my family—or families, some sixty known—have been in this country—"I have been here since 1648—" and very truly, without being able to explain, I do feel that I was really here, even then!

------------------December 11, same year—a little nearer to Christmas—
Twelfth Night, January 6, 1972

It has not been a time of parties and visitors and all such celebrations of the season—No—just a weariness and silence—<u>within</u>, and very few friends dropping in, and myself sitting up in bed working on my Cotton Mather book I began to write in 1929, after two years research—a research that has never ended—but I have a part time secretary who is typing the <u>last</u> copy as I edit it a little, really very little, but I have three or four more chapters in first draft which I must finish. Then I want to finish a few essays long since begun, and my ancient French murder trial—<u>then</u> [three lines underline] I shall be free, and hope to have a little time of sweet idleness, full of music and books and friends and conversation in some pleasant climate near the sea—

What a dream! But it helps to keep me alive until I can get a little more work finished.

Tonight at midnight I shall turn out the lights on the two Christmas trees at either side of the flats standing at the glass walls overlooking the balconies, strewn with colored lights . . . Blow out the candles, and face another year—

XXXX

And so to your matchless book, like no other in the world—I read and read again in it, all through, not skipping about even, because the swaying is not in the grand saloon, but in the sea itself. The whole strange eerie history is a long—an endless—voyage that cannot not be broken—for me—except by a safe coming to harbor,—but think what the floors of all the ocean must be! Malcolm, I believe that all great works of any art are done in that state of rapturous sustained attention which among people who "teach" others to write, for example, call "self indulgence." You said to me that this book was something you had always wanted to do, you did it for the pure pleasure it gave you; and this warmth and breathing life—this so-strangely innocent pleasure is given in turn to the reader. Bless you for writing it. I wish we could see each other to talk about it!

With my love and remembrance
Happy New Year!
Katherine Anne

To: Monroe Wheeler DTLS 1p. Maryland

[6100 Westchester Park Drive, apartments 1517–1518
College Park, Maryland]
18 November 1972

Darling,

I am enjoying a luxury, having help from a friend in writing letters and catching up with the correspondence that I have neglected all these years. I am being selfish and letting her write on the typewriter, but I am tired.

Please let me know how your slow convalescence is coming along. I know a lot about slow convalescences. I have been working at it 24 hours a day for 3 years! It might even be fun if it weren't for the pain pills.

Your wonderful flight through the world was for me like a flight for myself, but in a dream. Is it by miracle that you do so much, know so many people, having so many interests? It <u>seems</u> so varied, yet I know the secret of your life has been that it has never left a certain deep line of interest and that you have played 10,000 variations on one theme. Happy, blessed you.

Please let me know how you are, news of Barbara, news of Glenway, and come to see me—not just for a day but for 2 or 3 days if you can. I should love it.

On December 3 I am going to Cape Canaveral to see the last manned moonshot and on to a 10-day cruise in the Caribbean on a ship full of strangers—scientists reporters and so forth—for PLAYBOY. I am to write a story for them. Wish you were going to be with me. I only tell you this because I think it might surprise you; or maybe you will respond as I say I do to unusual news—I can still be shocked but I dare you to try to surprise me.

Love and kisses.
As ever, and evermore—
Katherine Anne

[Typed by Maria Gower, secretary to E. Barrett Prettyman Jr.]

To: John Malcolm Brinnin ALS 1p. Delaware

16 May 1974

Dear John Malcolm—
Your dear greetings for my 84th round in this wild wooly world brings me the lovely tranquility of long assured friendship, the kind of love that does really last a life time, the kind I treasure with all my heart. Bless you—

I wish you had been here for the sailing party in Annapolis, with lunch at the yacht club, and a roam-around in that most enchanting city—I rather wish I had followed my impulse to live there years ago. But I do know better now than to regret <u>anything</u> that cannot be done <u>again</u>, even maybe done better—I wish I could see you <u>again</u> . .

Love <u>again</u>, as always—
Katherine Anne

Picture [enclosed] made May 10, 1974
Dear Malcolm, I'm setting the table for supper. Wish you were here! KAP.

To: Carl H. Griffin DTLS 2pp. Maryland

Apartment 1517–1518
6100 Westchester Park Drive
College Park, Maryland 20740
October 21, 1974

Mr. Carl H. Griffin
404 N.W. 25th Street
Gainesville, Florida 32607

Dear Mr. Griffin:

Your letter of this early summer was lost. I have never received it. It is not the kind of letter I would have overlooked if it had reached me. I am so glad that you sent it again because I think this is very important, the thing you have in mind. Without going into any details, because everything can be talked over clearly when we see each other, I shall be very glad to see you at 2 o'clock in the afternoon on Saturday, the second of November. I shall like very much for you to stay for supper with me and, if you are able, to stay over for Sunday. I could put you up at the University of Maryland; they have guest rooms there. Or, I could even put you up here in my apartment. I have plenty of room and plenty of help and we might go very well to the finish of this discussion which would be all the things that you need for your purposes. It is a great relief to me to find at last someone who has discovered what this book "is about." I remember Mr. Forster one time saying that a piece by Virginia Woolf about having a tooth pulled[5] was much the same as saying that Melville's novel was about catching a whale. Most of the critics have made all their guesses and almost everyone is wrong. So, you manage your time so that you can come here and we can talk it out once and for all because we may never have another chance and I would like awfully to be able to get it straight that you will be able to say that this is what I said about my intention in this book. It is fashionable among "critics" now to take for granted that the author is the last person to consult on what he meant by what he said; this could be true at times, but not always and no matter how much he is mistaken, he still knows more than the next person.

Mr. Liberman's calling my novel an "apologue"[6] is his own business and has nothing to do with the case, he made some very good guesses but that is not one of them.

I did not see Jon Spence's article in manuscript; I have not seen the Spring one he reviewed but as I subscribe I think they will be sending it to me.[7] The book is a novel and I have no doubt this will be discovered and cleared up in the next fifty years.

I shall not go on with this; I shall wait until you come and we can talk it out. I have a feeling that this is a very good thing we're beginning.

Sincerely yours,
Katherine Anne Porter

KAP:gw

To: Carl H. Griffin DTLS 2pp. Maryland

Apartment 1517–1518
6100 Westchester Park Drive
College Park, Maryland 20740
January 17, 1975

Carl Griffin, Esquire
404 NW 25th Street
Gainesville, Florida 32607

Dear Carl:

Perhaps we may as well get on the first name basis since our work getting my mis-spent life set in order in proper chronology will probably last my lifetime and through much of yours. I should first tell you that I got your wonderful bushel, at least it looked like that, of oranges and grapefruit and they were heavenly. Along with almost everything else, the orange crop had seemed to have failed this year. I bought some little thin-skinned dried up things, it took five oranges to make four ounces of juice and it looked as if I was going to have to give up my morning orange juice but the temple oranges and yours have come in and I am swimming in my favorite liquor. Thank you for your marvelous Christmas present.

I have been struggling trying to get ahead of not only just my letters but of my work, the rest of the things that I would like to do during what is left of my life, but I have all kinds of drawbacks that I shan't bore you with details, but I do believe I am getting a little bit back on the track and I am going to get some writing done now. Meantime, I think a great deal of you working on Ship of Fools and I don't mind telling you that I would like very much for you to give me a kind of outline of what your basic understandings and feelings are and just how you are going about correcting those foolish fellows who have been giving me marvelous associations and accusing me of symbolisms and of religious motives that I assure you I never had, or at least not consciously, and I cannot agree with T. S. Eliot who said that quite often people had found meanings and associations in his poetry that he had not put there at all but they had made it a better poem by this generous view.

So far, I cannot agree with my group which more than once has reminded me of a pack of hounds in pursuit of a fox who can after all do nothing but go to earth for that day. The run isn't over though until the next time he puts his nose out into the fresh air. I think the most extreme use of this was someone who accused me that when I named my heroine of "Flowering Judas" Laura I must have had Petrarch's Laura in mind, and overlooked for years as many did that the one thing I had consciously taken, the only thing I had consciously borrowed from that story was the title, "Flowering Judas" filched from Eliot's great poem.[8] I can't tell you how fascinated I am about the idea that you are working on that much belaboured novel that half a dozen Johnny-Jump-Ups have attacked with forks or with hope but not much intelligence or imagination and I admit that I have been waiting patiently for someone who really knew what he was talking about to attack that book; and by attack you know I don't mean always with hostility. I am given to attacking the subjects I love best for fear they will get away from me when I'm not looking.

While I'm writing this rather rambling letter, I am looking at your snapshot of Carl Christopher, age two, he must be now about age two and a half and I'm sure he's as happy and as healthy and as beautiful as he was then with only just a six months' advantage added. It is the most charming and ingratiating smile, and what I really love about the atmosphere of it is the expression of his face which shows him to be so confident of being altogether adored. Please forgive my slowness, I am having a dreadful time working my way out from under this stack of paper, there are only probably a hundred papers in the whole lot worth rescuing but we have to go through ten thousand papers to get to them. Please know that I wish for you and your wife and your baby a wonderful good year and health and prosperity and the nice joy that can come with all those things. You remember my favorite toast which begins, "Health and Money . . ."—well, it is still a good foundation.

Sincerely,
Katherine Anne Porter

KAP:gw

To: Carl H. Griffin DTLS 2pp. Maryland

[6100 Westchester Park Drive, apartments 1517–1518
College Park, Maryland]
Second Day of Spring [March 22], 1975

If you don't mind, I'll begin this letter, or rather manuscript as we keep calling typescript, for this correspondence could go on for a lifetime whatever that turns out to be, for both. Hence—

Dear Carl: A motto is again floating around—I heard it first about fifty years ago, but it has returned, by way of a Ford who gave the name a bad name even before a headfull of cold flapjacks finally got the name into the White House: "Never complain, never explain," says he.[9] This is not only bad manners, but bad morals, based on bad intentions to conceal or disguise bad behavior of all kinds and sizes from drunken driving with a lady-friend while one's wife is far absent on a social occasion, to: let us say, Watergate in all its preposterous deathly farce; yet I want to say to you, please never explain or apologise for not answering my letters promptly—I am pleased and astonished if you find a breathing moment to answer at all. Of course, I hope we can make a bargain: I really CAN'T explain why I am fifty-odd letters in arrears this minute, except that Life, capital L, is in such a hell of a fix I hardly know morning from evening, much less what time of day it is. I see from my old window now and then that the sun is setting, or a moon in many phases is drifting by—in spite of the darkness, morning is coming in, again. . . . . .

I find nothing to complain of in this: and does it need to be explained? I'm all for letting well enough alone, if we can find out what that is. There are times when I feel absent from the place I live in, and your letter this morning is like a letter from that region, where ever it is.

Slight pause due to Time being a hare, and I am tortoise in what seems to be a premature re-incarnation. . . .

15th day of spring . . . Now where was I?

My dear Colleague its no good my trying to finish this letter. I am trying to write another fragment of my memories of a largely wasted life—I try to console myself with Henry James' father who carried the doctrine of waste of education to the point where he was the only one who could understand what education he meant, but his son Henry, decided that taken individually waste was education.[10] If that is so, I would be one of the most educated people in the world. Enough of this. I am sending you in this big envelope a manuscript that I think might amuse and interest you. I am not going to take time to tell what it is or what it is about, I just think you might find it very useful if the time ever comes for you to write about my life. I am now going to try to get to work on a little memoir which I intend for Esquire. Deadline May 1 or as soon as I can manage.

Sincerely
Katherine Anne Porter

KAP:gw

To: Robert Penn Warren ALS 4pp. Yale

[6100 Westchester Park Drive, apartments 1517–1518
College Park, Maryland]
Telephone (not listed) 301-345-8768
Tuesday 15 September 1975
18¼ minutes after 8 o'clock in the morning—

Red darling it is a foggy gray cool morning, and a voice like battered tin has just brought me up to the second what time it is in the world outside—what nation is threatening what nation, which people are starving, who kidnapped who when and where, who got murdered last night, first internationally, then in our beloved country, and finally, local—The dead ones were found in jail, or lying around in alleys, or in their own bedrooms, or driveways,—and no policeman was anywhere near, nobody witnessed anything, no one has the faintest notion <u>who</u> did the trick—so on and on. . . . . . every day every night, every 8 minutes in Prince George's County, where I live on the 15th floor of my condominium in two joined apartments, where Barrett[11] a few days ago warned me to keep all doors locked in my double apartment, to walk the long way round rather than have 2 unlocked doors to cross the hall between them. I do, usually. But I was brought up in a time and a region where we never locked a door even when nobody was at home, and in the country in summer we each took a sheet and pillow and slept in the grass in the front of the house, surrounded by rose bushes, china berries, irises, honeysuckle, mulberries, cedars,—who can remember all that greenery?—so I am now sitting in bed with my morning coffee, a beautiful bowl of roses a friend brought me yesterday, listening, until now, to the light dancing kind of Hayden music. That is just right for waking up, and I shut off the raucous voice telling me the careless, endless, monotonous horrors of this world when I am sitting among silk blankets from Italy and linen from Ireland and silver from Boston and

Philadelphia 1810–20 and George III coffee pot and Queen Anne Bowl full of peaches Barrett brought me, and writing to you while looking at <u>Poetry and Democracy</u>[12] with your words written in your own hand—really somewhat stunned with life as it seems absolutely to <u>be</u> [underlined three times] against every reason I am able to round up trying to give some possible shape and meaning to—well, <u>anything</u>—I believe Calderon hit a kind of <u>fact</u>—"La vida es sueno," he said once in a moment of having hit his head against the stone of pure mystery.[13]

By God, some measureless absolute merciless Power owes us an explanation. Please don't take me for the village atheist—I believe totally in something I have never heard or read or thought in words—I don't fright, or weep. I just wait, hoping to <u>see</u>—someday.

I can't even tell you how I got started on this letter to you except I longed to see you, to hear <u>you</u> speak and I revelled in being quite fearless that I should be called wander-witted—my wits are wandering easily and happily—It is your book, my hopes still of getting a copy of <u>Or Else</u>[14]—It is ordered <u>again</u>—and my joy that you have found my work more than once worth believing in. Bless you. We live in the head, don't we? How else could we endure to live? "The heart has its reasons that reason does not know." I translated that for my own mouth thirty years ago—"Le Coeur à de raison que la raison ne connais pas"[15]—Probably messy French by now, but a great truth in any language. I hope my bundle of notes reach you soon. I wish I had your telephone number—

Love to all the triumphant household—
Katherine Anne

To: Roger L. Brooks DTLS 2pp. Texas State University

Apartment 1517–1518
6100 Westchester Park Drive
College Park, Maryland 20740
October 7, 1975

Dr. Roger L. Brooks, President
Howard Payne University
Brownwood, Texas 76801

Dear Dr. Brooks:

I am delighted with the mementos you sent me from Indian Creek and I want to tell you what a strange and happy surprise to learn from you about the inscription on the blue marble tombstone above my mother's grave. I visited once nearly forty-one years ago for the last time until now and we sat there beside her for a long time and we planted flowers around her grave and none of us saw or mentioned the poetic inscription of which you have made a rubbing and sent me and typed for me. My mother died there of childbirth and my father sold the land we had there to some friends who were living on the place running it as a rather good and pleasant farm when my father, sister, and I made our visit together in 1934. They were old friends of my father and the rest of the family there and were awfully good simple people yet gentle with really good English speech which I remember impressed me very deeply. I am shocked at myself not to remember the name of these lovely people, but I would like very much if I could see that place again and I wish to ask you if it might be possible since I am going to be in Austin, Texas, at the University to speak on the 28th of December, Sunday. I will arrive in Austin on Saturday, make my speech on Sunday and leave on Monday morning and I wonder if you can suggest a simple way of my getting to Indian Creek to visit your school and to visit my mother's grave and if possible to see the old house that I saw twice in my life, once when I was 2½ years old when my father took me back when he went to raise that tombstone over my mother and later when, many years later, we went back again to visit there.

The farm still had its pecan grove and its little vineyard of small purple grapes and a good orchard of peaches and plums and they told me the woods around were full of blackberries. There was a lovely, deep lively creek running right through the yard, deep and clear and full of beautifully colored pebbles on the bottom and my sister and I rolled up our skirts past discretion I suppose and took off our shoes and stockings and borrowed some milk pails from the friends in the house and went in and collected pails of those colored stones to take back to put in her garden in Houston. Every member of my family that I saw then after my long residence in Mexico and Europe and New York is dead and I am 85 years old, so I have a great feeling that it is time for me to gather up a great many of these scattered memories and all the mementos I can find to leave as a part of a possible biography; I am sure of at least one and there might be more and I should like to have the small, apparently unimportant details right. I am so tired of the misstatements and the rash guesses that people make about one's life, knowing nothing about it at all. I would be so delighted if you could tell me what would be the simplest way from Austin, Texas, to make my visit there. I wish that you would help me make a plan and if you say you would like, I would be pleased to visit your school or give a public speech in any place you find appropriate.

I happen to be the first native of Texas in its whole history to be a professional writer. That is to say, one who had the vocation and practiced only that and lived by and for it all of my life. We have had a good many lately in the last quarter century perhaps and we have had many people who wrote memoirs and saved many valuable stories and have written immensely interesting and valuable things about Texas; and they are to be valued and understood. But, I am very pleased that I am the first who ever was born to the practice of literature and though it never gave me a living until I was 72 years old, I had to lecture and teach and to write criticisms and reviews and when I was younger I had all kinds of strange jobs, but they never had any meaning for me except as a way to earn my slice of bread, maybe with a little butter, for that day so that after I finished my little chore I could get back to my writing.

I am writing much too much of a letter, but I am fascinated with these pictures you have sent me and the various little incidents that I begin to remember just from seeing these pictures that you have sent and the letter you have written and I hope I shall hear from you about this soon and we can really make a plan and I will bring copies of my books if I can collect them to go in your school library if you like. Thank you so much for your kindness in sending me these things. I hope you are well and I am glad you think that part of the country is delightful; I think so. It has that wonderful black land soil which caused people to say you had only to plant your walking stick in it, and it would sprout. I am quite sure this is a plain fact, aren't you?

Sincerely yours,
Katherine Anne Porter

KAP:gw

To: Roger L. Brooks DTLS 1p. Texas State University

Apartment 1517–1518
6100 Westchester Park Drive
College Park, Maryland 20740
October 21, 1975

Dr. Roger L. Brooks, President
Howard Payne University
Brownwood, Texas 76801

Dear Dr. Brooks:

My sister and other members of the family have told me what a lovely country Indian Creek is and I am very glad that I shan't be there in December but in May with you to visit Howard Payne University and the old places where my life began. I think it makes me happy beyond any way of telling you how happy I will be to spend my 86th birthday, May 15, next year in Indian Creek where my life began very hopefully as I have always been told by people who remember that day I was born. It seems marvelously lucky for me that I am going to come to visit that lovely place much in the role of "Local Girl Makes Good," even if it did take her more than three-quarters of a century to achieve that grandeur. And please don't think I am being ironical. I am not trying to be funny, for as happy as I feel, I have always smiled at these big public parties and parades for the local girl or boy, but I find when my time comes, it is never too late and if I laugh, it's for joy.

I am also looking forward to a doctoral degree from your University. Someday, maybe when we meet, I shall be able to express to you really the happiness I have in knowing that my native country, the spot where I was born, is going to celebrate my existence a little there—this is entirely too unexpected and emotional an occasion for me to be quite coherent on the subject just now; but, I must warn you that I do not lack for words very long.

Thank you for your lovely letters.

Sincerely yours,
Katherine Anne Porter

KAP:gw

To: Raymond Roseliep DTLS 2pp. Maryland

Apartment 1517–1518
6100 Westchester Park Drive
College Park, Maryland 20740
June 11, 1976

Dear Ray:

Your beautiful envelope with its lovely stamps and bouquet of forget me nots contained a very charming "Little Poem"[16] still in your style as always even with the smallest number of words and some nice witty little things by other poets mostly unknown to me, so that I was really shocked by two poems belonging to those hidden retreats known as rest rooms in our strange argot which I am sure I need not quote to you but I have crossed them out with a quote under one "How does this get in here?" and under the second quotation: "A louse is biting Rilke, bring the spray"; and a note to David Ray— "Your poetry belongs on the walls of any pissoir!" I find this the strangest thing in the world about certain kinds of minds like Roth, for example, who in his best selling book has I'm afraid rather properly estimated the level of mind for which he is writing by taking for granted and catering to their private toilet habits.[17]

I suppose this is enough of that. I have put the "Little Book"—apparently it's a monthly magazine for it is marked July, 1976—back into its elegant envelope and putting it with your other letter as a keepsake for your poem and its lovely inscription for me. I have something else in mind. Did I ever send you a print of the photograph made of me last summer sitting on my balcony wearing a large straw hat? It is a good human photograph and I would as soon be remembered like that as in any other photograph I am likely to have taken. I intended to send it, but if not, please let me know and it will be on its way at once. You are making a wonderful record for yourself by writing as you are and being published freely. This makes me happy and I hope to be able to send you something of mine shortly—prose, of course and not fiction but it might interest you.

You are a dear friend and a happy memory and I don't forget the first visit of yours to that tall house in Spring Valley. How many years ago I can't say now when we sat up and talked sitting at that long table in the library very cheerfully until two o'clock in the morning over a bottle of whiskey. I think bourbon—does it matter? I hope you remember this as pleasantly as I do.

I have just completed my 86th year and am putting up with life as patiently as I am able which is not very patient. I am trying to finish one book, but two of the books on which I had staked my life as an artist are not finished; both of them at the halfway stage which haunts me with a horrible sense of guilt at how I wasted my life on so many things which seemed right and fruitful at the time. I am very slowly millimeter by millimeter leaving this world, or maybe it is like a friend said to me in rebuke: "why are you leaving this world so determinedly?" and I said in inspiration "I am not leaving this world, this world is leaving me," and really that is the way I feel about it. I am simply sitting on a raft in the middle of the ocean with the tide carrying me out. Don't think this is sad or melancholy, I am only concerned that I have done so little with my life that I believe was worth more than I realized. Henry James' father used to preach the doctrine of the volume of waste in life. He insisted that 90% of it was material wasted in order to perfect the use of that 10% which made the whole thing precious and eternal. Well he was an old dear and I hope he was right.

Please let me know that you are well and that you are in good health. I know that you are in good mind and if you were here I would talk your ear off but I must stop writing as I am dictating to a friend this wandering sort of manuscript and I hope you can read it in serenity.

With my love,
Katherine Anne

KAP:wrw

To: Lon Tinkle DTLS 5pp. Maryland

Apartment 1517–1518
6100 Westchester Park Drive
College Park, Maryland 20740
August 19, 1976

Dear Lon:
Dr. Joan Givner's essay on my stories and novel happened along with another event that was almost as exciting and very closely related and the two of them have opened up a fine smooth looking road we can take off on when I have finished with the Sacco and Vanzetti book. The second critic and essayist is named Miss Joan Flanders and I think a PhD who has spent many years collecting my published works, as she calls them, which as I remember it consists of random reviews of all sorts of books and all sorts of

magazines with occasional attempts at essays on subjects that captured my roving attention.[18]

Naturally she expects to make a book of this and I am delighted she has it in mind and would be glad to give her permission if she is willing for me to edit her choices and correct any errors that are in the original pieces. Also she seems to feel that her main and most important discovery about my work is its rather bold feminist tone. For me feminism is a dirty word and I take it as a personal affront almost as bitterly as I do the phrase "Southern Belle". I do not really know what self-named feminists think of that word, it must have special meaning to them which I can't grasp. It is this interpretation of hers that is so entirely wrong that I must head it off before such a thing creeps into some book that will remain to create such an awful impression of me when I am no longer here to correct it.

But her letter and plans have given me a certain courage to look about where there have been stories published about me which I hope to be able to find and add to this history if it is to be written. A most important one occurred in Dallas I should say around 1915 or maybe 1916. I never kept any clippings and never had a copy of anything I ever wrote and it is obvious that I missed many stories that I have forgotten. One time in Dallas I was looking for a job and I went to the Dallas News having been advised by a reporter on the staff to look there. I asked for a job and I didn't get it but somehow it became a story that I had worked for the Dallas News. I never did. But the good friend who had hoped I might be employed by the Dallas News as I badly needed a job took another step that brought on a fantastical episode and made such a great impression on me that it has lasted a lifetime. I had some troubles with my chest and it was pronounced tuberculosis. Of course I was penniless, unable to go to the hospital, unable to pay a doctor's bill and the Dallas News, led by this young man took steps to get me admitted to a charity hospital for the poor and helpless sick suffering from different diseases. I was not to go as a patient although I was to receive some care and attention and what treatment was necessary but I was classed as an assistant to take care of the afflicted children there.

It was a fearful place shockingly badly managed by the most lazy sodden people—fat men and women in their late middle life who simply sat about, in the winter especially near the fireplace and obviously overate all year long. I was in a women's ward where the pathetic, shrivelled bodies of women were dying slowly almost silently with almost no care at all. I who thought I couldn't start a day without a good strong cup of coffee was shocked to find that here the people were given no tea or coffee. They had no fruit and ate mostly a thin kind of soup with dry bread and really, I remember it so bitterly, all of it, that I don't want to say that that was all they had. They had just enough to survive a while—to help them to die more slowly. I spent the day taking care of the children, in a kind of shack some distance from the wards where we all lived. They were starved and neglected but full of life, lovable, mischievous and most certainly worth saving but certainly doomed. I took all the care I could of them, guiding them a little in their play. We lived out of doors as much as we could in the summer and fall but as the cold weather came, I asked for clothing for them and there wasn't any. I asked for their diet to be changed so that they could have meat or chicken. I didn't get any. Talking to my friend on the Dallas News, I said that the children needed help and everybody helped. One of the reporters wrote a story which created a marvelous commotion and the people of Dallas sent a burst of food, fruit and toys, and pleasant and excited people drove out to see for themselves how it was at this beautiful warm time and it was real. I had given them sizes and ages so that clothing could be provided for the children and there was plenty for all of them—warm wool sweaters and clean cotton underwear and solid shoes. I had all these things delivered and with the help of some people who came I began to get things together so that the children could have some of it at once. Then, people came up from the headquarters building and began to take things away from us. They picked out the best of the clothing for their own children and those we never saw again. Crates of oranges had been sent, which I took for God's blessing. These people were starved for fruits and vegetables. The oranges disappeared so I went to the main office to consult and to ask where things had gone. I wanted to ask that I be allowed to handle these things for the children and there they were—four or five big fat people sitting in wicker arm chairs with glasses in their hands in front of a blazing fire. On the table there was a gallon glass pitcher of orange juice. There had been several bags of candy such as lemon drops, caramels, marshmallows and I asked what became of these. They said the children were not supposed to have sweets. I said they needed a little sugar, some fat and milk and that we had to have some up there. The townspeople kept bringing things and I told the reporters it was not feeding the children and that some were slowly dying in the wards. I had asked especially for coffee and tea and we had twenty pounds of coffee and two or three of tea. It was picked up and we never saw it again. At this point I gave up. There was a scandal. I don't remember all of what was said that people were very indignant. I remember that there was a very good story in the Dallas News and they published a picture of me with a little mulatto baby or two or three in my arms, surrounded by other small children, all smiling, full of life.[19] I was given one copy of the picture which I have treasured all these years and I am reasonably certain that I still have it. I seem to remember that I had seen it when I shuffled through the hundreds of pictures I had in three baskets. They have been reorganized, picked over and classified a little and I am afraid that that picture is lost or at least that I shan't be able to find it.

Dear Lon, by now you have decided what I am up to. I am going to ask you to do me this great favor. This is one thing when my little story is written I would like to have included with that picture because this was one of the most unbelievable wretched times in my whole life. I do not know how I survived or how I didn't lose my nerve completely but I remember that episode in spite of the horror of gruesome people in charge of helpless dying creatures and I know the state provided for them well—that is they had the means to provide and the others stole and gobbled everything and yet it is strange how happy I was with those children. We played and I managed to snatch toys and socks and sweaters enough to give each something to wear. That's all, there was no change left for them. They got out, the little boys and girls and started to dig at one end of the yard where there was a bump in the earth and they dug a tunnel ten or twelve feet long and wide enough for them—even the large ones were not very large—to crawl through to the little round door of daylight at the other end and one by one they all crawled through and challenged me. I said I was too big and that I would get stuck. They said they would make it bigger for me. The fact is, of course, that I am terrified of tight corners and dark places. Nothing could have persuaded me to have gone through that tunnel if it had been five feet in circumference. The children insisted on start-ing to dig the tunnel wide enough to fit me and I had an embarrassing time getting out of that predicament. I realize now how many false excuses and reasons I made to get out of that. They considered it a promise that if they made the tunnel wide enough, I'd go through it. I was wearing a little watch so I looked at it and announced that it was time for lunch. It wasn't. The children all looked and said "no, it is not".

Dear Lon, I want a copy of that story and the picture if they are still in the morgue. I know you have had an illness and I have a little twinge of guilt for fear I might distress you in some way or ask you to act more than is good for you and yet if you can manage to find them I shall be so grateful and if you can't, after all it is not necessary but just something I would like to have in the record. It has taken me nearly all my life to realize that I have a record that several people feel is worth keeping and publishing and for the first time in my life I am self conscious about the reporting of my history. You know perfectly well that I don't want it to be flattering or too pleasing. I just want a story that is, after all true but working just from the material that exists and can be gathered and sifted for the facts of the case. Maybe all of this is a wild vain hope but here among my vanishing days, I suddenly have a deep personal interest in something that never touched me before and that is, what kind of little historical record I am going to leave, in spite of myself and at the mercy of anybody who will go through the pages and baskets and boxes and papers with printing on them about my life and work. Nonsense, what. But I'll begin to feel that it is someone else's story I'm leaving, just as now when I read through my novel or stories, two or three pages at a time, I feel distant and impersonal as if they were written by someone else, someone I don't know very well.

Bless you, my dear friend. I would so like to see you and Maria[20] again— here or there. I promise that this is the last thing I shall ever ask you to do, except to remember me and let me have news from you from time to time and I hope that sometime we may see each other.

In the meantime, my friendly love to you both.

Katherine Anne

KAP:wrw

To: Charlotte Laughlin DTLS 2pp. Private

September 2, 1976

Dear Charlotte:

Bill[21] read me part of your letter in which you said that you didn't want to write and trouble me with letters which I would feel obliged to answer. My dear, you have seen the situation very clearly. I don't like it at all but the situation has become so difficult it is very annoying to find every day that I am a little less able to do even one half of the things I had planned or hoped to do, or which need to be done and it does seem ironical that the first things that have to be limited are letters and telephone calls and the various enjoyments of society and all those things which take time and energy and I am singularly limited in my time for work. But just the same I hope to be able to finish that plan we have made about the books and some of my belongings; but I have first to destroy my present will and make another and this is going to take a little time. Then I hope to be able to send a box of books which I promised to you and which promise I mean to keep as soon as I can. That too takes a little time, simply to make the list and get them packed and on their way.

My dear, I suppose it would be hard for you to imagine how charmed I was to find you there in that place which is so dear to me—such a lovable person that I should like to have your correspondence without any limitations but just running along pleasantly in the normal way of life—well, I suppose the life we are living is normal, considering our ages and our histories. It is true that I am not able to write letters to anybody except necessary messages. I meant this to be about three lines and I have quite a number of notes that must be sent pretty soon. So, bless your gentle and good heart and I beg you to take care of yourself. Try not to harm your health and try to live as long as you can. You are too precious a sort of person to be wasted or to waste yourself.

With my love,
Katherine Anne

KAP: wrw

To: James T. Farrell DTLS 2pp. Newberry

October 7, 1976

Dear Jim:

In my age at the very time when dear old friends have accumulated years enough to warrant a birthday celebration, I have been for seven years recovering from a series of broken bones and two or three indispositions that have been pronounced chronic and incurable, so I have been more or less housebound for this time. It was an immense surprise to a person who got around as much and as far as I did and when at last I had a double cataract operation that has interfered a great deal with my work and my eyesight, it was rather a problem to concede that I had better try to improve my health and start to do a little writing again.

I don't tell you this to make you sad, or to convey a sense of weariness or oppression here. This is only to tell you why I have not produced the three books that I have at hand, hoping to finish them, why I have not been able to attend pleasant exciting birthday parties that good old friends (none of them as old as I am) have been giving, because as I have said before if you are going to have conversation and champagne and dancing I was to be invited even if I can't get there.

So it was lovely to have your letter this morning with the merry news about the big party and your going straight on with the life you elected to live—well, it comes to more than 50 years now. I am sure you must have known all this time that I began my life as an artist with exactly your code and I have observed it without one misstep ever since just as you have; and I have not taken kindly from some of my old friends with whom I spent my early life in their same poverty and incertitude and all the trouble that comes from trying to do one's best in a work that depends upon a money making trade to publish our writing that most of these friends and a great deal of my friendly readers have never forgiven me for writing a best seller. I didn't write a best seller. I wrote the best book I was able. Don't ask me to explain how it became a best seller. It was not my fault. But I feel about it as you did about your big birthday celebration at the St. Regis of which you formally disapproved—I like it. It has kept me from the one thing that made me nervous since the days when I realized that my strength and energy would come to an end—that I should have to sleep under a bridge. SHIP OF FOOLS which cost me 20 years of uncertainty working on the margin of my effort to make a living by teaching and lecturing saved me from all that and I hope you'll be happy to know that I think it is the best thing I ever did and I don't take back one word of it. Dear Jim, I have never written or said this publicly to anyone all these years. I say it to you now in this private letter because I am somewhat astonished at the attitudes of some of my friends who one example of their honest work didn't hit the jackpot, for that's what it is. When they give you a big party at the St. Regis, I know you are not starving, thank God and I am sure you are as happy to know that I am living simply in the modest but pleasant lap of luxury and I intend to keep it up as long as the money lasts. Just think Jim how almost penniless we were all those hard years and to end up like this.

Alleluia—let us praise God together.

Affectionately,
Katherine Anne

KAP: wrw

To: Robert Penn Warren DTLS 1p. Yale

December 7, 1976

Dear Red:
   I have for a long time needed some real examinations and diagnoses of my many afflictions and lately they have all piled up to the extent that I can no

longer believe that a round of vitamins and a good night's sleep is all I need. I am very seriously in need of help. I have been wondering if it would not be a good thing for me to apply at Johns Hopkins for examinations on three things—the condition of both of my eyes which are seriously painful and two oculists have failed to get glasses made to Dr. Moretti's prescription that really fit so that I am suffering from eye strain. I don't know whether it is my heart or my emphysema that is gradually closing in on me and I need work on at least one wisdom tooth. Dear Red, you can see that I am really in a corner at last and it is a good sign that people say no longer "Oh, you're going to live to be 100"; it must be plain to anybody that that is not possible and it is not just breathing I want to do. I see no point to being here unless I can work. Please advise me as to what step I should take—where should I apply—what doctors should I apply to to get into Johns Hopkins for a going over and for some diagnoses that they would confide to me as well as each other and the records.

I have started my little history of the medieval murder trial and am so joyously excited over the prospect of really finishing another book. I feel like trying to live a little longer till I finish. THE NEVER-ENDING WRONG has been received and accepted joyously by everybody and the Owen Laster[22] Divine Providence in your shape sent to me is the best thing that has happened to me in a great number of years.

Tell me about Eleanor, how she is. She looked so well and so beautiful when I saw her last and her eyes hadn't changed with her trouble. I was so happy to see you both. I hope somebody at Johns Hopkins knows exactly what to do for her. I love you dearly—all of you—and I look forward to your coming here to work with my little history—well, really just to see you and to enjoy your company.

Bless You,
Katherine Anne

KAP: wrw

To: Robert Penn Warren 2pp. DALS Yale

[6100 Westchester Park Drive, apartments 1517–1518
College Park, Maryland]
April 28, 1979

Dear Red darling,

You and Eudora in that marvelous so charmingly merry strange place, which I never saw you before, gave me so much joy when a young friend of mine brought me the picture of you.[23]

I have been longing to see you for I have so many changes to make and things to tell you. All the things we have known all these years.

I wish you could come to see me even if only for a day or two. For my heart's sake.

I need in my day, now short and difficult, to hear you one time and let me tell you what my life has been in all these years we have not seen each other. I wait with love the bringing on of your new book.

Oh what a happy day it would be if you could bring it to me. But please be sure of one thing, that I am really dying now and do not quite know when. But hope to see you just once more.

With All My Hopes and Memories,
K.A.P.

Notes

1. Mary Alice (Baby) Porter Hillendahl, whom KAP referred to variously as "Mary," "Alice," or "Baby."

2. KAP habitually omitted names of lovers when writing to her family. This letter, however, may have been copied from a handwritten original to obscure her lover's name. "Himself" may have been Carl Clinton von Pless (1892–1954), to whom KAP was briefly married in 1917.

3. "What One Woman Is Doing," *Dallas Morning News*, 16 December 1916.

4. KAP was not well enough to accept a job, if it was in fact offered, but she did publish a children's story, "How Baby Talked to the Fairies," in the *Dallas Morning News*, 18 March 1917, when she was a patient at the J. B. McKnight tuberculosis sanatorium in Carlsbad, TX.

5. Gay's children, Mary Alice Holloway and Thomas Holloway Jr., whom KAP insisted on calling "Paul" after her and Gay's brother, Harrison Paul Porter.

6. Breckenridge Porter (1914–1999) was the son of Mary Alice Porter and Herbert Townsend, who died shortly before Breckenridge's birth. He was later adopted by his uncle, Harrison Paul Porter Sr.

7. KAP's brother, Harrison Paul Porter Sr., married Constance (Connie or Concha) Eve Ingalls (1882–1971) in 1916.

8. The managing editor at the *Dallas Morning News* at the time was Prescott Twoomey.

9. Toosey is Thomas H. Holloway Jr., and Toddles is Mary Alice Holloway.

10. Kuno is Julius Arnold Hillendahl, the husband of Mary Alice Porter Townsend Hillendahl.

11. Mary Alice Holloway, born 8 December 1912, died of spinal meningitis 19 July 1919.

12. Lute, or Loute, was a young African American girl who helped Gay with the children.

13. Dorothy Ray Porter, the first child of Paul and Connie Porter, was born in 1918.

14. Olive Thomas (1894–1920), Elaine Hammerstein (1897–1948), Eugene O'Brien (1882–1966), and Owen Moore (1886–1939) were silent film actors who worked at the Selznick Studio.

15. Bessie Beatty (1886–1947), leftist writer, journalist, and editor.

16. Eva Chappel (c. 1893–1983), left-leaning journalist on the staff of the *Rocky Mountain News* and subsequently a member of Porter's Greenwich Village circle.

17. Berta Hoerner (1891–1976) and Elmer Stanley Hader (1889–1973), husband-and-wife writers and illustrators of children's books and stories.

18. Whether this article ever appeared or whether under Porter's name is uncertain.

19. KAP is referring to John Koontz's failure to pay her promised alimony.

20. KAP was writing the libretto for a ballet featuring Anna Pavlova.

21. Charles Ray (1891–1943), silent film actor.

22. KAP is quoting from Gilbert Murray's translation (1915).

23. George Arliss [George Augustus Andrews] (1868–1946), English actor, playwright, and author, who was the first British actor to win an Academy Award (for *Disraeli*, in 1929).

24. Lily Cahill (1885–1955), KAP's second cousin and a successful stage and film actress, married the Irish actor James William Brandon Tynon (1875–1967) 9 June 1920.

25. In the fall of 1920 *El Heraldo* was owned by General Salvador Alvarado (1880–1924), military governor of Yucatán 1915–1917.

26. Robert Haberman (1884–1962), Romanian-American socialist lawyer, educator, and labor leader, and his wife, Thorborg Brundin Haberman, a Swedish journalist.

27. Only two issues of the *Magazine of Mexico* were published.

28. Adolfo Best-Maugard (1892–1965), Mexican painter and art theorist.

29. Popocatepl is an active volcano, about forty miles southeast of Mexico City, and the second highest point in Mexico.

30. Without the aid of a doctor or midwife KAP assisted at the difficult birth of Gay's second child.

31. KAP's brother, Harrison Paul Porter Sr.

32. KAP's father and brother were terribly disappointed in her scandalous divorces and let her know. She spent the rest of her life trying to elicit from them expressions of love and forgiveness.

33. At that time the presidential palace.

34. General Álvaro Obregón (1880–1928) was elected president of Mexico in September 1920; KAP attended his December inauguration.

35. Luis Napoleón Morones (1890–1946), head of the Confederación Regional Obrera Mexicana (CROM: Regional Confederation of Mexican Workers).

36. KAP is referring to "My Chinese Marriage," which she ghostwrote for Mae Tiam Franking.

37. Felipe Carrillo Puerto (1874–1924), governor of Yucatán 1922–1924.

38. Natasha Michaelova, a Russian agent in Mexico.

39. Rabindranath Tagore (1861–1941), Bengali author, painter, and musician, who won the Nobel Prize for Literature in 1913.

40. Antonio Díaz Soto y Gama (1880–1967), revolutionary, politician, and educator.

41. *Diputado*: a member of parliament.

42. Arthur Brisbane (1864–1936), American newspaper editor.

43. José Doroteo Arango Arámbula [Francisco or Pancho Villa] (1878–1923), revolutionary leader and advocate for agrarian reform.

44. W. D. Outman (b. 1877) was the publisher of the magazine.

45. In a previous letter Hanna apologizes for not writing to tell her all he knows about Retinger's situation.

46. Joseph Jerome Heronimum [Józef Hieronim] Retinger (1880–1960), Polish diplomat and political activist.

47. Félix Palavicina (1881–1952), founder of influential newspaper *El Universal.*

48. *Pelados*: Spanish for poor, uneducated workers.

49. Gilbert Vivian Seldes (1893–1970), American author and social critic.

50. A reference to KAP's friend Kitty Barry Crawford (1887–1982) and Crawford's friend Jane Anderson (1888–1972), who had affairs with both Seldes and Retinger.

51. Diego Rivera (1886–1957), leader of the Mexican Mural Renaissance.

52. KAP's essay "Where Presidents Have No Friends," in which she describes a story told her by a young Mexican about the Carranza presidency that illustrates her point that a president of Mexico can trust no one.

53. KAP's hair turned white, or gray, during her serious bout of influenza in the 1918 epidemic.

54. Her cat.

55. The poem was written in 1921 after KAP had undergone a life–threatening abortion.

56. Anna Gay Holloway [Ann Holloway Hemmerly Heintze] (1921–1987).

57. KAP was at a Connecticut farm rented for the summer by her friends Liza and John Dallett.

58. Burton Egbert Stevenson (1872–1962), author and librarian, published four volumes of *The Home Book of Verse* (1918).

59. Genevieve Taggard was married to Robert Wolf at the time. Their daughter, Marcia Sarah, was born in 1922.

60. British painter Ernest Stock.

61. *The Making of Americans: Being a History of a Family's Progress*, by Gertrude Stein (1874–1946), was published in a limited edition in 1925.

62. Josephine Herbst and John Herrmann, who lived in a nearby farmhouse.

63. KAP reviewed Taggard's *Words for the Chisel.*

64. Kenneth Durant (1889–1972), American journalist and director of the American office of the Soviet press agency TASS.

65. Ernestine Evans (1889–1967), journalist and author, married to Durant at the time. As editor at various times for the *Century*, the *New York Herald Tribune*, the *Nation*, the *Christian Science Monitor*, and the *New Republic*, she often assigned KAP book reviews and articles.

66. Mary Louis Doherty (1896–1995), left-leaning American expatriate teacher and journalist and the primary model for Laura in KAP's story "Flowering Judas."

67. Xavier Guerrero (1896–1974), Mexican communist painter and engraver, assistant to Rivera 1922–1924.

68. A biography of Cotton Mather for which she had signed a contract with Boni & Liveright.

69. KAP is exaggerating; she will not become a celebrated cook until the mid-1930s in Paris.

70. Virginia (Jinny) Myers Cahill, Harrison Boone Porter's first cousin, was an amateur genealogist.

71. Marcellus Elliot Foster (1870–1941) was the founder and editor of the *Houston Chronicle.*

72. Constance Patricia Porter, daughter of Paul and Connie Porter, was born 9 June 1925.

73. KAP is referring to Thomas H. Holloway, Gay's husband.

74. KAP shared the house with Dorothy and Delafield Day and Dorothy's young daughter, Tamar. They and other boarders called the dilapidated house "Caligari Corners" or "Casa Caligari," after the silent horror movie *The Cabinet of Dr. Caligari* (1920).

75. Rebecca and John Crawford's house in Brooklyn.

76. Margery Latimer (1899–1932), feminist writer, had recently published her first novel, *We Are Incredible,* which KAP reviewed for the *New York Herald Tribune Books.* The hostess for the party, held at the apartment of Liza and John Dallett, was likely Joan Foley.

77. Caroline Gordon and Allen Tate, their daughter, Nancy (1925–2007), and James Rorty (1890–1973), poet and journalist.

78. Edgar Holger Cahill (1887–1960), early supporter of American folk art and later national director of the Federal Art Project of the WPA.

79. Eliza Jane Skaggs Myers (1858–1939), sister of KAP's grandmother Catharine Ann Skaggs Porter.

80. KAP would sublet the house from Thorborg Haberman and her new husband, Basil Ellison. Delafield and Franklin Spier were visiting also.

81. The Crawfords' young daughter.

82. "Thieves Market" was the current working title of a long novel KAP was writing about Mexico.

83. Bill is William Rollins Jr. (1897–1950), best known for his proletarian novel *The Shadow Before* (1934).

84. Eric is Josephson's firstborn son.

85. Mike Gold, the pseudonym of Itzok Isaac Granich (1894–1967), leftist novelist, literary critic, and founding editor of the *New Masses.*

86. Floyd Dell (1887–1969), poet, journalist, and critic affiliated with the Chicago Renaissance and bohemian radicals of Greenwich Village.

87. Rose Wilder Lane (1886–1968) was a prominent author in Greenwich Village at the time.

88. Alexander S. Gumberg (1887–1939), businessman, Trotskyite, presidential advisor.

89. Armando Zegri (c.1899–?), Chilean writer.

90. Malcolm and Peggy Cowley.

91. An allusion to 1 Kings 17: 4–6, in which Elijah is fed by ravens as commanded by God.

92. Delafield's sister, Dorothy Day.

93. Probably the working title of an in-progress semiautobiographical work by Day. KAP later chose it as the title for her long novel but finally selected "Ship of Fools" instead and settled on "For here we have no continuing city" as an epigraph for the third part.

94. KAP collaborated with William R. Doyle on the play *Carnival*. She incorporated the experience in her story "Theft."

95. The *New York Daily News*.

96. Liza Dallett.

PART TWO

1. KAP reviewed *Wedding Day and Other Stories* (1930) and *Plagued by the Nightingale* (1931) under the title "Example to the Young" for the *New Republic*.

2. Luis Vicente Cabrera Lobato (1876–1954), Mexican lawyer and politician who was exiled to Guatemala by his political opponent President Pascual Ortiz Rubio (1877–1963).

3. Plutarco Elías Calles (1877–1955), president of Mexico 1924–1928.

4. Moisés Sáenz (1888–1941), Mexican educator, minister of education in the Calles administration.

5. KAP was referring to articles published in the *New Republic* by Edmund (Bunny) Wilson (1895–1972), influential author and critic who was also associate editor of the *New Republic* 1926–1931.

6. Sonora, the native district of four Mexican presidents between 1920 and the early 1930s, was a center of rebellion.

7. Pascual Ortiz Rubio (1877–1963) was president of Mexico from February 1930 to September 1932.

8. John George Eugene Jolas (1894–1952), influential modernist writer, editor, critic, translator, and founder of the Parisian literary magazine *transition*, where KAP's stories "Magic" and "The Jilting of Granny Weatherall" were published.

9. Harold Hart Crane (1899–1932), modernist American poet whom KAP met in Greenwich Village in 1920s and who lived in Mexico near KAP in 1931–1932.

10. Natalie Vivian Scott (1890–1957), New Orleans playwright, journalist, social worker, and educator, was a member of the expatriate community in Mexico.

11. Marguerite Frances (Peggy) Baird (1890–1970), American landscape painter, was married to Malcolm Cowley from 1819 to 1931, when he left her to marry Muriel Mauer.

12. KAP is making a joking reference to Wilson's *Axel's Castle: A Study in the Imaginative Literature of 1870–1930* and a straightforward reference to *Savage Messiah*, a biography of the sculptor Henri Gaudier-Brzeska, by art collector and author Harold Stanley (Jim) Ede (1895–1990).

13. Editor and author Susan Jenkins Brown (1896–1982) and author William Slater Brown (1896–1996).

14. Achilles Holt (1911–1993), poet, fiction writer, and Winters' student at Stanford.

15. Dwight Whitney Morrow (1873–1931), ambassador to Mexico 1927–1930; Ivy Ledbetter Lee (1877–1934), public relations and propaganda expert; Charles Lyon Chandler (1883–1961), historian and U. S. foreign service officer; Hubert Clinton Herring (1899–1967), Secretary of the Department of Social Relations of the Congregational Education Society and expert on American-Mexican relations.

16. Burke's *Towards a Better Life: Being a Series of Epistles, or Declamations* (1932).

17. Eugene Pressly and expatriate American journalist Mary Louis Doherty (1896–1995), with whom KAP shared a house in Mixcoac in 1931. Pressly would become KAP's fourth husband, and Doherty was one of the primary models for Laura in KAP's "Flowering Judas."

18. *The Confessions*, Book 6.

19. Liza Dallett.

20. Sally Calkins Wood Kohn (1897–1985), American author, friend of Gordon and Tate.

21. KAP is referring to the group of twelve known as the Southern Agrarians: John Crowe Ransom (1881–1974); John Gould Fletcher (1886–1950); Henry Blue Kline (1905–1951); Lyle H. Lanier (1903–1988); Andrew Nelson Lytle (1902–1995); Herman Clarence Nixon (1886–1967); Frank Lawrence Owsley (1890–1957); Tate; John Donald Wade (1892–1963); Robert Penn Warren; and Stark Young (1881–1963). Centered at Vanderbilt University, in Nashville, TN, the group evolved from the Fugitive Group of Poets at Vanderbilt that included Ransom and Tate as well as Merrill Moore (1903–1957) and Donald Davidson (1893–1968).

22. *I'll Take My Stand: The South and the Agrarian Tradition* (1930) includes essays by the twelve Agrarians.

23. KAP is talking about living in a primitive cabin on the property of Gordon and Tate's estate Benfolly in Clarksville, TN.

24. Stringfellow Barr (1897–1982), historian, author, and editor of the *Virginia Quarterly Review*, 1931–1937, during which time he published KAP's "Hacienda" (shorter, largely nonfiction version), "That Tree," "The Grave," and "Two Plantation Portraits" ("The Witness" and "The Last Leaf").

25. Elizabeth Madox Roberts (1881–1941), Kentucky novelist and poet who had a marked influence on the Southern Renaissance of the 1920s and 1930s.

26. Paul Higgins Stevenson, better known in Mexico as Pablo Estaban O'Higgins (1904–1983), Communist muralist and pianist whom KAP met in the early 1920s when he was assistant to Diego Rivera. He stopped by to see her in Berlin on his way to Russia in 1931.

27. Hunt Stromberg (1894–1968), Hollywood movie producer who joined MGM in 1925.

28. Park McKee French (1881–1974), Denver (and later Los Angeles) architect with interest in theater; KAP's fiancé for a few months in 1919.

29. Grace Graham Wilson Vanderbilt (1870–1953), wife of Cornelius Vanderbilt III.

30. "Theft," originally published in 1929 in *Gyroscope*.

31. Burke's article "Boring from Within" appeared in a February issue of the *New Republic* as a counter to Wilson's "Appeal to Progressives," which had appeared in the *New Republic* in January.

32. Mixcoac.

33. "Válgame Dios!" translates idiomatically as "Bless me!"

34. Otto Kahn.

35. *Starry Adventure* (1931), by Mary Hunter Austin (1868–1934), author focusing on the American Southwest and California.

36. *The Waves* (1931), Woolf's experimental novel KAP had agreed to review for the *New Republic* but never completed.

37. Cowley rejected KAP's "Parvenu," her review of Stuart Chase's *Mexico: A Study of Two Americas* (1931), on grounds that it was too harsh.

38. Gottfried Benn (1886–1956), German physician and writer sympathetic to socialism, which he later renounced.

39. KAP is referring to their separation necessitated by their mutual decision for Pressly to try to find work in Spain, where he was fluent in the language.

40. From *Poems 1926–1930*, by English poet, novelist, and translator Robert von Ranke Graves (1895–1985).

41. Rosa Reichl, the landlady of the boardinghouse, fictionalized in KAP's "The Leaning Tower."

42. KAP was taking German lessons.

43. Emma Goldman (1869–1940), Russian-born writer, lecturer, and anarchist KAP met in Greenwich Village in the fall of 1919 before Goldman was deported in December.

44. Maria MacDonald Jolas (1893–1987), an editor with her husband, Eugene, of *transition*.

45. KAP is referring to Janice Biala, who was Ford's companion through the 1930s but never legally married to him.

46. Sylvia (Nancy Woodbridge) Beach (1887–1962), American patron of writers and founder of English-language Paris bookshop Shakespeare and Company in Paris that was the hub for expatriate writers, including KAP; Beach is remembered for publishing James Joyce's *Ulysses* (1922).

47. Caresse (Mary Phelps Jacob Peabody) Crosby (1891–1970), American poet and patron of the arts who with husband Harry Crosby (1898–1929) founded the influential Black Sun Press.

48. Stories by Robert McAlmon, Hale's friend who introduced him and KAP.

49. KAP is referring to the color philosophy proposed by Oswald Manuel Arnold Gottfried Spengler (1880–1936), German historian who in codifying colors in his *The Decline of the West* (1917) associated red and yellow with commoners, women, children, and savages.

50. Camelots du Roi: a royalist youth group founded in 1908 to promote French integral nationalism, which defended social differentiation and hierarchy while encouraging cooperation among social groups.

51. Peggy Cowley and Hart Crane had formed a romantic alliance in Mexico.

52. Angel Flores (1900–1992), prolific Puerto Rican writer, publisher, translator, and educator who compiled and edited numerous anthologies of Spanish and English essays and stories. KAP wrote the introduction to *Fiesta in November—Stories from Latin America* (1942), edited by Flores and Dudley Poore.

53. Manuel de Falla y Matheu (1876–1946), twentieth-century Spanish composer who promoted the work of French composer Claude-Achille Debussy (1862–1918).

54. Gordon's first novel, *Penhally*, was published in 1931.

55. KAP's story "The Cracked Looking-Glass" was published in the May 1932 issue of *Scribner's Magazine* and was eligible for the Scribner's short novel prize of $5,000. Herrmann's story was a co-winner with Thomas Wolfe's "A Portrait of Bascom Hawke," both published in the August issue of the magazine.

56. "The Cracked Mirror" was an earlier title for the story published as "The Cracked Looking-Glass."

57. Charles Boone (Sonny) Porter (1933–).

58. Johannes Enschedé en Zonen, Haarlem, Holland.

59. KAP and Pressly were subletting Ford's apartment while Ford and Biala were living in Toulon; Pressly also was typing Ford's manuscript "It Was the Nightingale" in exchange for partial rent.

60. Donald Clifford Brace (1881–1955), a founder of Harcourt, Brace and KAP's publisher until his death.

61. Philippe Soupault (1897–1990), French Dadaist writer, critic, translator, political activist, and one of the founders of surrealism.

62. Henry Allen Moe (1894–1975), administrator, humanist, secretary and then president of the John Simon Guggenheim Foundation.

63. *The Autobiography of Alice B. Toklas* (1933); Alice Babette Toklas (1877–1967) was Gertrude Stein's companion and lover.

64. KAP is referring to Ford's argument in his *Henry James: A Critical Study* (1915).

65. Alfred North Whitehead (1861–1947), British mathematician and philosopher.

66. Carl Van Vechten (1880–1964), American writer, photographer, and Stein's literary executor.

67. The Katzenjammer Kids, title characters in a comic strip created in 1897 by Rudolph Dirks (1877–1968) and Harold Knerr (1882–1949); *Krazy Kat*, a comic strip created in 1913 by American cartoonist George Herriman (1880–1944); Paw Perkins is a character in the comic strip *Polly and Her Pals*, created in 1912 by American cartoonist Cliff Sterrett (Paw is the high-strung father of Polly, a suffragette and forerunner of the 1920s flapper).

68. Joseph Delteil (1894–1978), French writer active in the early surrealist movement.

69. *Pity Is Not Enough*, a semiautobiographical novel and the first in Herbst's Trexler trilogy.

70. Lincoln Edward Kirstein (1907–1996), American writer, founder of the *Hound & Horn*, one of the founders of the New York City Ballet, and a member of KAP's circle in the 1930s and 1940s.

71. Hermann Wilhelm Goering (1893–1946), German politician and a leader of the Nazi Party. When KAP met him early in 1932, he was Hitler's representative in Berlin and the leader of the Nazi Party Reichstag delegation.

72. Louis Graveure (1888–1965), British opera singer and actor.

73. Erhard Milch (1892–1972), German field marshal and founding director of the Deutsche Luft Hansa following World War I.

74. German for "landlady."

75. Lewis Christian Bentzley (c. 1895–1977) was president of the communist United Farmers Protective Association; in 1933 he was ailing, and other sympathetic communists sent contributions for the support of his wife and three children.

76. Aldous Huxley (1894–1963), English modernist writer best known for his novel *Brave New World* (1932); Catherine Roxburgh Carswell (1879–1946), Scottish author whose biography of Lawrence, *The Savage Pilgrimage*, was published in 1932.

77. Mabel Evans Dodge Luhan (1879–1962), American patron of the arts who established a literary colony in Taos, NM, and published a memoir about Lawrence, *Lorenzo in Taos* (1932); Lady Dorothy Brett (1883–1977), painter and part of the Bloomsbury circle; John Middleton Murry (1889–1957), English critic.

78. Frieda Frelin von Richthofen (1879–1956) married Lawrence in 1914.

79. *Thunder Over Mexico* was one of three films (including *Eisenstein in Mexico* and *Death Day*) produced by American muckraking writer Upton Beall Sinclair (1878–1968) and his wife, Mary Craig Kimbrough Sinclair (1882–1961), and created from the original footage shot in Mexico by Russian avant-garde director Sergei Eisenstein (1898–1948) for the film intended to be titled *¡Qué viva México!* In 1931 KAP visited the Hacienda Tetlapayac, where Eisenstein was directing the film. Her slightly fictionalized account was published as "Hacienda," and the longer, fictionalized version was published as a separate book by Harrison of Paris.

80. Eduard Kazimirovich Tissé (1897–1961), Soviet cinematographer, and Grigori Vasilyevich Alexandrov (1903–1983), Soviet film director, both of whom collaborated with Eisenstein on a number of films; the parenthetical names are the fictional names KAP assigned them in *Hacienda*.

81. At the beginning of his memoir, *Goodbye to All That* (1929), Graves quotes the verse from *Biography for Beginners* (1905), by English novelist and humorist Edmund Clerihew Bentley (1875–1956).

82. James's *A Small Boy and Others* was published in 1913.

83. *Aleck Maury, Sportsman* (1934).

84. The *Hound & Horn*, where KAP's "Flowering Judas" was published in 1930, had ceased publication in 1934.

85. *The Executioner Waits* (1934), the second book in Herbst's Trexler trilogy but her fourth published novel.

86. Gordon's short story "Old Red" was published in *Scribner's Magazine* in 1934 and won a second-place O. Henry prize.

87. *Provence* (1935) was Ford's celebration of the history and qualities of the French region.

88. KAP gave a talk at the American Women's Club in Paris; the title of her talk was the working title of her three-part novel-in-progress that had supplanted the Mexican novel she worked on in the 1920s.

89. *Flowering Judas and Other Stories* (1935), an expansion by four stories of the 1930 *Flowering Judas*.

90. English playwright and fiction writer William Somerset Maugham (1874–1965); *Of Human Bondage* (1915); "Rain" (1921) was adapted in 1928 as a musical silent film called *Sadie Thompson* and as a talking film by the title *Rain* in 1932.

91. The magazine *Story* was founded in 1931 by Whit Burnett (1900–1972) and his first wife, Martha Foley.

92. KAP reviewed Gordon's *None Shall Look Back* (1937) for the *New Republic*.

93. Andrew Lytle.

94. The working title of a short novel intended to be part of a collection of short novels Harcourt, Brace planned to publish. It evolved, however, into a long novel, titled "No Safe Harbor" and eventually "Ship of Fools."

95. *Everybody's Autobiography* (1937).

96. Meraud Guiness Guevara (1904–1993), Anglo-Irish painter in Stein's Paris circle.

97. Elizabeth Barrett Browning (1806–1861), English romantic poet best known for her collection of love lyrics *Sonnets from the Portuguese* (1850).

98. An ordinary bar.

99. Emma (Cinina) Brescia [Gardner] (1898–1996), Warren's first wife.

100. Nearby land KAP bought with plans to build a house there.

101. An allusion to *The Way of the World* (1700), by English playwright William Congreve (1670–1729), in which the character Millamant says, "If I continue to endure you a little longer, I may by degrees dwindle into a wife" (IV.v).

102. *Night Rider* (1939).

103. The Olivet Writers' Conference at Olivet College in Olivet, MI, established by president Joseph Hillyer Brewer (1898–1990), who brought to the summer workshop some of the most influential writers at the time, including, in addition to KAP, Gordon, and Tate, such persons as Ford, Ezra Pound, Sherwood Anderson, and Gertrude Stein.

104. Edmund Wilson and his first wife, Mary Blair Wilson; *I Thought of Daisy* (1929); Mary McCarthy (1912–1989), author and critic, was Wilson's third wife.

105. *Bouvard et Pécuchet* (1880) unfinished satirical work by Gustave Flaubert (1821–1880) that was published posthumously; *Madame Bovary* (1857), his most influential work.

106. *Wuthering Heights*, by Emily Jane Brontë (1818–1848), was published in 1847.

107. Bibi Fellow and Vili Von Istanthal, a tiny high-strung dachshund, were dogs owned by Gordon and Tate.

108. Edith Amy (Tinkum) Brooks (1911–1986), wife of Cleanth Brooks; Jean Albrizio (1915–2008); *The World's Body* (1938), by poet and critic John Crowe Ransom (1888–1974); *Voyage au Congo* (1927), by French poet André Paul Guillaume Gide (1869–1951).

109. Both KAP's *Pale Horse, Pale Rider: Three Short Novels* and Herbst's *Rope of Gold* were in the Harcourt, Brace 1939 catalog.

110. Édouard Daladier (1884–1970), French radical who served as prime minister in 1933, 1934, and 1936, and was elected again in 1938.

111. *Seasoned Timber* (1939), by American author, educator, and social activist Dorothy Frances Canfield Fisher (1879–1958).

112. Duncan Ferguson (1901–1974), political activist, sculptor, and LSU faculty member.

113. The better known among the guests were critic and biographer Carl van Doren (1885–1950); Louis Henri Jean Charlot (1898–1979), French painter KAP met in Mexico; journalist and music critic Paul Rosenfeld (1890–1946); and surrealist painters Jared French (1905–1988) and Paul Cadmus (1904–1999).

114. Henry McBride (1867–1962), American art critic.

115. Margaret Frances (Peggy) Bacon (1895–1977), American painter; William Gropper (1897–1977), radical cartoonist, painter, and political activist; Constantin Brancusi (1867–1957), Romanian-born sculptor.

116. Wysten Hugh Auden (1907–1973), British poet with whom KAP became friends in 1938.

117. Mildred Akin Lynes (1909–1999) was also affiliated with the Museum of Modern Art.

118. Erika Julia Hedwig Mann (1905–1969) and Klaus Mann (1906–1949) were the daughter and son of the German writer Thomas Mann.

119. Monteagle, TN, where Tate and Gordon had a summer home.

120. Harcourt, Brace, and Company.

121. Siegfried Sassoon (1886–1967), English World War I soldier and antiwar poet.

122. KAP is confusing persons who interviewed her in Denver in 1918 under the Sedition Act of 1918 with the Lusk Committee (The Joint Legislative Committee to Investigate Seditious Activities), formed in 1919 by the New York State Legislature to investigate persons in the state of New York suspected of seditious activities.

123. Although Adam in "Pale Horse, Pale Rider" was identified by KAP as a soldier named "Alexander" whom she loved, there is considerable evidence that he was completely fictional.

PART THREE

1. Paris fell to the German army 14 June 1940.

2. Erskine's mother and sister.

3. René Karl Wilhelm Johann Josef Maria Rilke (1875–1926); *Wartime Letters of Rainer Maria Rilke, 1914–1921* (1940).

4. Erskine was editing Kenneth Burke's *Philosophy of Literary Form* (1941) for the LSU Press.

5. David Leo Diamond (1915–2005), American composer of classical music who became KAP's good friend at Yaddo.

6. The Bread Loaf Writers' Conference at Middlebury College in Middlebury, Vermont.

7. Lev Davidovich Bronstein (Leon) Trotsky (1879–1940), Russian Marxist revolutionary and founder of the Red Army, died exiled in Mexico 21 August 1940, a day after an assassination attack.

8. German White Paper, a compilation of archives from the Polish Foreign Office.

9. Rivera was unjustly implicated in the Trotsky assassination owing to a well-publicized dispute between them.

10. The subject is Erskine's self-description for his draft papers; KAP's description of him is almost identical to that of her fictional character Adam in "Pale Horse, Pale Rider."

11. Oscar Levant (1906–1972), American musician, author, comedian, and actor.

12. KAP is suggesting any surreal character that might be found in a fictional work by German writer Franz Kafka (1883–1924).

13. Norman Mattoon Thomas (1884–1968), American socialist leader and six-times candidate of the Socialist Party of America for president of the United States.

14. In the presidential election of 1940, FDR defeated Republican candidate Wendell Lewis Wilkie (1892–1944).

15. Eugene Victor Debs (1855–1926), a founder of the International Labor Union and the Industrial Workers of the World and several times candidate of the Socialist Party of America for president of the United States. KAP saw him in San Antonio in 1904 during the Presidential campaign.

16. Elizabeth Ames (1885–1977), the first executive director of Yaddo.

17. Several radio manufacturers, including General Electric, produced Model One tabletop radios.

18. KAP was working on a story called "Season of Fear" (uncompleted).

19. "The Leaning Tower" was published in the autumn 1941 issue of the *Southern Review*. Since the only pieces of fiction KAP published between 1941 and 1960 were excerpts from the long novel-in-progress (*Ship of Fools*), one of those excerpts might be the "third story."

20. *Open House* (1941).

21. Richard P. Blackmur (1904–1965), critic and educator.

22. Henry Bernstein (1876–1953); Maurice Maeterlinck (1862–1949); Marc Chadournes (1895–1975); and Maurice Dekobras (1885–1973).

23. Ambroise-Paul Toussaint-Jules Valéry (1871–1945); André Paul Guillaume Gide (1869–1951); Louis Aragon (1897–1982); Valery Larbaud (1881–1957); George Duhamel (1884–1966).

24. Bravig Imbs (1904–1944), writer, journalist, and radio announcer, his wife, Valeska, and their daughter, Jane; friends of Stein and Toklas in Paris.

25. Marjory Peabody Waite (1884–1944), adopted daughter of George Peabody, second husband of Katrina Trask, who with her first husband founded Yaddo.

26. Publication of the *Southern Review* was suspended in 1942 by the administration of LSU; it was not resumed until 1965.

27. KAP is referring to the title "Ship of Fools"; the working title of the long novel was first "Promised Land," then "No Safe Harbor." At one time, she seemed to be calling it "The Land That Is Nowhere."

28. Van Wyck Brooks (1886–1963), critic and biographer.

29. First two lines of "I Am of Ireland" (1933), by William Butler Yeats (1865–1939).

30. Saint Augustine of Hippo (354–430); Saint Francis of Assisi (c. 1181/1182–1226); Saint Joan of Arc (c.1412–1431); Saint Thomas More (1478–1535); Dr. Samuel Johnson (1709–1784); Dean Jonathan Swift (1667–1745), the title referring to his receiving the deanery of St. Patrick's in Dublin.

31. General Courtney Hicks Hodges (1887–1966), commander of the First U.S. Army in northwest Europe in World War II.

32. A small harpsichord KAP had bought in Paris and was storing with George Platt Lynes.

33. "Lord Zouche's Masque," a march composed by Giles Farnaby (b.1560); "Wolsey's Wilde," composed by William Byrd (c. 1539–1623).

34. Prescott's review of "The Leaning Tower" appeared in the *New York Times* 18 September 1944.

35. Henry Seidel Canby (1878–1961), critic and Yale professor.

36. From James's short novel *The Figure in the Carpet* (1896), reflecting both James's and KAP's concept of art.

37. *Chin P'ing Mei* (or *Jin P'ing Mei*), first translated as *The Plum of the Golden Vase*, a four-volume sixteenth-century Chinese vernacular novel considered pornographic by many Chinese but hailed by modern western scholars as a great novel in the tradition of *Don Quixote*. The four volumes were : (1) *The Gathering*; (2) *The Rivals*; (3) *The Aphrodisiac*; and (4) *The Climax*. KAP and Schaumann were no doubt reading Clement Egerton's 1938 English translation published as *The Golden Lotus*.

38. *Journey to the West* (known simply as *Monkey*), by Wú Cheng'en (c.1500–1582), an important Chinese classical novel.

39. The Latin *Satyricon*, believed to be written by Gaius Petronius (27 BCE–65 CE), recounts the escapades of the narrator, Encolpius, and his sixteen-year-old lover, Giton; KAP favored the lyric poetry of Quintus Horatius Flaccus (65 BCE–8 BCE).

40. Greek philosopher Heraclitus of Ephesus (c.540–480 BCE) and Athenian orator Pericles (c.493–429 BCE).

41. Director and producer Sidney Franklin (1893–1972).

42. KAP's nephew, Harrison Paul Porter Jr.

43. Katherine Mary Dunham (1909–2006), American choreographer, dancer, author, and founder of the Katherine Dunham Dance Company; known as the "matriarch and Queen Mother of Black Dance."

44. Marcella Comès Winslow (1905–2000) hosted a birthday party for KAP the year before when KAP was boarding with her in Georgetown. Schaumann was one of the guests at the party, probably brought there by Lincoln Kirstein.

45. Wescott's novel *Apartment in Athens* (1945) was a best-selling novel and critically acclaimed. Although KAP praised it in her *Herald Tribune* review, she had some reservations owing to its propagandistic bent.

46. Tony Duquette (1914–1999), popular Hollywood interior designer and jewelry maker.

47. Atwater Kent (1873–1949), inventor and radio manufacturer.

48. Baroness (Marie Rose Antoinette) Catherine d'Erlanger (1874–1959), Hollywood hostess and owner of Café Gala, a nightclub popular with Hollywood celebrities, especially gays and lesbians because of featured gay singer Johnny Walsh.

49. Robert Lewis (1909–1997), American actor, director, author, and cofounder of the Actors' Studio in New York in 1947; KAP was living in his house while he was away.

50. Dorothy Parker (1893–1967), American writer and satirist.

51. Screenwriter Alan K. Campbell (1904–1963).

52. Harriet de Onis was a prolific author and translator.

53. American artist Paul Cadmus (1904–1999), best known for his drawings of male nudes, drew KAP's portrait.

54. Screenwriters and producers American Charles William Brackett (1892–1969) and Austro-Hungarian Billy Wilder (1906–2002).

55. *Madame Sans-Gêne*, adapted from the 1893 play by Victorien Sardou and Émile Moreau, had been produced before, in 1924 as a silent film starring Gloria Swanson and in

1941 starring French actress Léonie Marie Julie Bathiat (1898–1992). It eventually would be produced again in 1962, starring Sophia Loren.

56. Elizabeth Ruth (Betty) Grable (1916–1973), American actress and dancer.

57. Charles Spencer "Charlie" Chaplin (1899–1977), English actor, producer, screenwriter, and legendary star of silent film era.

58. Oona O'Neill Chaplin (1925–1991), daughter of playwright Eugene O'Neill, married Chaplin in 1943.

59. Paul Green (1894–1981), Pulitzer Prize–winning American playwright.

60. Frances Ethel Gumm, professionally "Judy Garland" (1922–1969), American singer and actress.

61. *Selected Short Stories of Katherine Anne Porter*, the Armed Services Edition (1945), was the twenty-first of the 3½-by-5½-inch paperback volumes to be published by Editions for the Armed Services, Inc., a nonprofit organization established by the Council on Books in Wartime.

62. *The Short Novels of Dostoevsky* with Mann's introduction (1946) includes "The Gambler," "The Double," "The Friend of the Family," "The Eternal Husband," "Uncle's Dream," and "Notes from Underground."

63. Mann's *A Man and His Dog* was published in 1918.

64. KAP is objecting to various forms of mysticism in vogue.

65. Lockeed's *Constellation* aircraft was used primarily for military transport, but civilians could sometimes book a seat on it, too.

66. Persons who had held previous fellowships at the Library of Congress constituted the "Fellows" who met annually to award prizes and fellowships.

67. Since Wolfe used the words *desolation* and *desolate* repeatedly in a number of works, it's not clear whether KAP was referring to *Of Time and the River* (1935) or *You Can't Go Home Again* (1940).

68. Martin Niemöller (1892–1984), German Lutheran theologian.

69. *The German Talks Back* (1945), by Heinrich Hauser (1901–1955).

70. Stephen Harold Spender (1909–1995), English writer and Poet Laureate Consultant in Poetry to the United States Library of Congress in 1965. He frequently addressed social issues of the day.

71. French mathematician and philosopher Blaise Pascal (1623–1662); comment about fear of the spaces between the stars recorded in his *Pensées*, a title given posthumously to his notes.

72. *Under the Volcano* (1947), by English writer Malcolm Lowry (1909–1957); *All the King's Men* (1946), by Robert Penn Warren.

73. Huey Pierce Long (1893–1935), governor of Louisiana, U. S. senator, and the model for the character Willie Stark in Warren's novel.

74. Generally attributed to Pascal.

75. William Lyon Mackenzie King (1874–1950), prime minister of Canada.

76. Farrell's social-protest novel *Bernard Clare* (1946) was considered inflammatory by Canadian authorities and many conservative Americans as well.

77. Sonya Michell.

78. In "Gertrude Stein: A Self Portrait" KAP harshly criticizes Stein, an article with which Herbst expressed mild and affectionate disagreement, but a few months later she published a riposte ("Miss Porter and Miss Stein") in the *Partisan Review*, in which she attacked KAP. It ended the friendship.

79. Victor Sawdon Pritchett (1900–1997), British writer and critic; Arthur Koestler (1905–1983), Hungarian author who early embraced communism and later renounced it; Pritchett's essay is "Koestler: A Guilty Figure" (January 1948).

80. Milton Crane mentioned KAP in his article "Experimental Writings of the Last Decade" (21 December 1947).

81. Cockrell at one time lived in Dallas, TX, where two forks of the Trinity River meet.

82. *The Circus in the Attic and Other Stories* (1947).

83. William Hazlitt (1778–1830), English writer and critic; "On the Want of Money" (1827).

84. Oliver Goldsmith (1730–1774), Anglo-Irish writer and physician.

85. A reference to *The Crock of Gold* (1912), by Irish writer James Stephens (1882–1950), in which the Philosopher complains about lumps in his porridge and beats his wife as punishment.

86. Walter Van Tilburg Clark (1909–1971), western American writer and educator.

87. George Davis (1906–1957), influential American fiction editor at *Harper's Bazaar* and *Mademoiselle*.

88. *The Robe* (1942), a best-selling historical novel by American Lutheran minister and author Lloyd Cassel Douglas (1877–1951).

89. Thomas Edmund Dewey (1902–1971), governor of New York and in 1944 and 1948 Republican candidate for president of the United States.

90. Frederick Nims (1913–1999), American poet and educator.

91. Erskine Caldwell (1903–1987), American author who focused on the social problems of the South.

92. KAP had been keeping copies of her letters since the late 1920s.

93. In *Notes on Poems and Reviews* (1868) Algernon Charles Swinburne (1837–1948) wrote, "I have never been able to see what should attract men to the profession of criticism but the noble pleasure of praising."

PART FOUR

1. KAP's satiric name for Truman Capote (1924–1984), American writer she met at Yaddo.

2. *The Analysis of Beauty* (1753), by English artist and critic William Hogarth (1697–1764).

3. Capote's southern gothic best-selling novel published in 1948.

4. *Tropic of Cancer* (1934), by American writer and painter Henry Miller (1891–1980).

5. *The Grass Harp* (1951), by Capote.

6. Bennett Alfred Cerf (1898–1971), publisher and cofounder of Random House; and Robert Linscott (1888–1964), editor with Houghton-Mifflin and Random House.

7. Carson (Lula Carson Smith) McCullers (1917–1967), American fiction writer who apparently pursued KAP at Yaddo.

8. Kay Boyle (1902–1992), American writer and social activist KAP met in Paris.

9. Jean Stafford (1915–1979), American Pulitzer Prize–winning fiction writer.

10. *Mademoiselle* magazine.

11. Guinelda Archibald, KAP's maid.

12. Cyrilly Abels (1903–1975), managing editor of *Mademoiselle* 1945–1960, after which she opened her own literary agency and became KAP's agent.

13. Left-wing friends of KAP in Greenwich Village in the 1920s.

14. Roland Hays (1887–1977), internationally acclaimed African American lyric tenor who traveled with McAlmon in the 1930s.

15. *Being Geniuses Together* (1938).

16. Anglo-Irish writer and translator James Stern (1904–93) and his German wife, Tania Kurella Stern (1906–1995), physical therapist and translator.

17. Norman Holmes Pearson (1909–1975), American author, editor, and Yale professor.

18. Robert Wetterau was a Los Angeles bookseller and collector.

19. Pauline Potter (1908–1976), American writer and fashion designer who married Baron Philippe de Rothschild in 1954.

20. Janet Flanner (1892–1978), American writer and journalist who wrote under the pen name Genet; Virgil Thomson (1896–1989), American composer and critic; Cyrill Vernon Connolly (1903–1974), English writer and editor; and Philippe (Philip) de Rothshild (1902–1988), banker and writer.

21. Calvin Kentfield (1924–1975), American fiction writer KAP knew at Yaddo. His most celebrated publications lay in the future, especially his *All Men Are Mariners* (1963).

22. *Four Saints in Three Acts*, an opera by American composer Thomson with libretto by Gertrude Stein (1874–1946).

23. Jean Prouvost (1885–1975).

24. Ernst Robert Curtius (1886–1956), scholar who translated into German Goyen's *The House of Breath* (1950).

25. KAP is mocking Spender's pronunciation of the name of his wife, the English pianist and author Natasha Litvin Spender (1919–2010).

26. Frederick Louis MacNiece (1907–1963), Irish writer; Antoinette Millicent Hedli Anderson (1907–1990), English singer and actor.

27. Darsie Rutherford Gillie (1903–1972), British journalist who also reported for *The Guardian* and the BBC.

28. Marcelle Sibon, KAP's translator.

29. *They Had a Glory* (1952), by Davenport Steward.

30. Sidonie-Gabrielle Colette (1873–1954), French writer and performer.

31. Suzy Mante-Proust (1903–1986), niece of Marcel Proust (1871–1922), who had entrusted to her his corrected and annotated typescript of the sixth volume of *À la recherche du temps perdu* discovered after her death.

32. Laurance Page Roberts (1907–2002) was director of the American Academy in Rome from 1946 to 1960.

33. *Life with Father* was a Broadway play (1939–1946) by Howard Lindsay (1889–1968) and Russel Crouse (1893–1966) based on the stories by Clarence Day Jr. (1874–1935).

34. For many years Gertrude had been working on a critical analysis of *Hamlet*, which was never published.

35. Charles Henry Ford (1913–2002), a Mississippi-born surrealist writer, editor, and filmmaker who was a friend of Glenway Wescott and George Platt Lynes and part of Gertrude Stein's Paris salon.

36. KAP's grandnieces, the granddaughters of her brother, Harrison Paul Porter Sr.

37. John Melville, the close friend of Harrison Paul Porter Jr.

38. English writers Edith Louisa Sitwell (1887–1964) and her brother Osbert Sitwell (1892–1969).

39. Sacheverell Sitwell (1897–1988), brother of Edith and Osbert, and his Canadian-born wife, Georgia Doble Sitwell (1905–1980).

40. The letter to his daughter "Patsy," dated December 22, 1783, has been widely quoted.

41. "The Overcoat" (1842), a story by Russian author Nikolai Vasilievich Gogol (1809–1852).

42. KAP often quoted the motto Mary Stuart, Queen of Scots (1542–1587), embroidered on her cloth of estate while confined to prison awaiting her beheading. KAP's nephew, Harrison Paul Porter Jr., chose the motto to be engraved on her tombstone.

43. Caroline Lee Frost Jones (1835–1914), KAP's maternal grandmother.

44. Mary McAden was a younger member of the McAden family, who were Indian Creek neighbors of KAP's parents.

45. Sally Jones, the widow of KAP's uncle Alonzo Jones.

46. KAP was referring to Osbert Sitwell's five-volume autobiography: *Left Hand, Right Hand* (1945), *The Scarlet Tree* (1946), *Great Morning* (1948), *Laughter in the Next Room* (1949), and *Noble Essences* (1950).

47. Ben Hecht (1894–1964), American screenwriter and fiction writer; and American novelists Solomon (Saul) Bellow (1909–1981) and Nelson Algren (1909–1981).

48. Joseph Leon Edel (1907–1997), critic and biographer best known for his five-volume *Henry James: A Biography* (1953–1971), the first volume of which, *The Untried Years 1843–1870*, was the only one KAP could have read; Frederick Wilcox Dupee (1904–1979), professor, editor of left-wing journals, and author of the highly acclaimed *Henry James* (1951).

49. Edward Godfree (Richard) Aldington (1892–1961), poet, novelist, and biographer.

50. Sigismund Schlomo Freud (1856–1939) and Alfred Adler (1870–1937) were founders of the psychoanalytic movement, which eventually included Carl Gustav Jung (1875–1961).

51. *The Last Word* was an informational television series that ran in 1957 and 1958, the format of which was a panel hosted by lexicographer and professor Bergen Baldwin Evans (1904–1978).

52. KAP is referring to prayer said on a rosary while contemplating the Joyful Mysteries (five decades of five mysteries each) of Mary and Christ.

53. *Sanctuary* (1931) by William Faulkner.

54. Harry Lillis (Bing) Crosby (1903–1977), American singer and actor with a renowned enthusiasm for golf.

55. One of KAP's writing students at the University of Michigan.

56. American writers Thomas Lanier (Tennessee) Williams (1911–1983) and William Saroyan (1908–1981).

57. William Humphrey (1924–1997); James Otis Purdy (1914–2009); George Palmer Garrett (1929–2008).

58. Mary Flannery O'Connor (1925–1964).

59. In the summer of 1924 KAP and McGuire were guests at a Connecticut farm when she was pregnant. Although she decided to carry the child to term, she apparently discussed abortion with McGuire.

60. KAP read these lines in Cotton Mather's diary when she was doing research for her (unfinished) biography of Mather.

61. Katharane Edson Mershon McGuire (1892–1986), dancer and author who was in Bali with José Miguel Covarrubias Duclaud (1904–1957), Mexican painter and caricaturist whom KAP met in Mexico in the early 1920s.

62. David Locher.

63. Seymour Lawrence (1927–1994), editor and publisher.

64. The End, Praise be to God.

65. *Selected Poems* (1955), by Randall Jarrell (1914–1965), American writer and Poet Laureate Consultant in Poetry at the Library of Congress.

66. "Rothschild's Fiddle" (1894), a story by Anton Pavlovich Chekhov (1860–1904).

67. Both *La Maison de Claudine* (1922) and *Sido* (1929) were translated into English in 1953 by Enid McLeod and Una Troubridge, the first as *In My Mother's House*, which had been translated into English in 1937 as *The Mother of Claudine*. *L'étoile Vesper* was translated into English as *The Evening Star: Recollections* in 1973.

PART FIVE

1. Lowell has been combating mental illness.

2. *The Linen Bands* (1961).

3. James Laughlin (1914–1997), founding editor of New Directions publishing house.

4. James Otis Purdy (1914–2009).

5. *Color of Darkness* (1957), a collection of eleven short stories and a novella.

6. Persons selected for induction into the American Academy of Arts and Letters.

7. "Up Hill," by English poet Christina Rosetti (1830–1894) begins, "Does the road wind up-hill all the way? / Yes, to the very end. / Will the day's journey take the whole long day? / From morn to night, my friend."

8. Locher's poem "Sister Bumblebee" appeared in *Sponsa Regis*.

9. Locher sent Hemingway a rosary he had crafted and a poem he wrote about him ("The Mountain Man: For Ernest Hemingway"). Hemingway responded with a letter of thanks.

10. Locher's poem "Along the Trace: For Katherine Anne Porter" was published in the *Beloit Poetry Journal*.

11. The passage appears in "The Mountain Man: For Ernest Hemingway."

12. Columnist David McDonald is cited in the *New York Times* article "Intellectual Lag Laid to Catholics" (2 February 1961); Eugene McCarthy (1916–2005), U.S. senator from Minnesota 1959–1971; Philip Scharper (1919–1985), journalist, screenwriter, editor of *Commonweal*, and editor-in-chief of Sheed & Ward, a Catholic publishing house; Francis J. (Frank) Sheed (1897–1981), theologian and founder of Sheed & Ward; the Reverend Gustave A. Weigel (1906–1964), Catholic theologian; the Right Reverend Monsignor John Tracy Ellis (1905–1992), author and professor.

13. James Farl Powers (1917–1999), American writer with a focus on Catholic issues and clergy.

14. Felicia Geffin (1904–1995), director of the American Academy of Arts and Sciences.

15. Norman Kingsley Mailer (1923–2007), American writer known especially for his innovations in creative nonfiction.

16. At this point KAP admired Philip Milton Roth (1933–) and his short novel *Goodbye, Columbus* (1959). She later rejected his work.

17. "Dicthung und Wahrheit: An Unwritten Poem," a prose work by Anglo-American poet Wystan Hugh Auden (1907–1973) included in his collection *Homage to Clio* (1960).

18. *The Best American Short Stories*, ed. Edward J. O'Brien (1892–1941) and Martha Foley (1897–1977), began appearing in 1915.

19. Amos Bronson Alcott (1799–1888), American transcendental educator, writer, and reformer.

20. Voltaire, pen name of French Enlightenment writer François-Marie Arouet (1694–1778); Denis Diderot (1713–1784), French Enlightenment writer; Jean-Jacques Rousseau (1712–1784), Swiss romantic writer; Helmut Richard Niebuhr (1894–1962), American theologian.

21. Percy Brand Blanshard (1892–1987), American philosopher; Orestes Augustus Brownson (1802–1876), American transcendentalist who converted to Roman Catholicism; Rudolph Carnap (1891–1970), German-born philosopher; Morris Cohen (1910–1995), American communist convicted of spying for the Soviet Union; Herbert Feigl (1902–1988), Austrian philosopher; James McCosh (1811–1894), Scottish philosopher; George Gordon Meade (1815–1872), Civil War Union general; Samuel Miller (1769–1883), theologian and author; Charles Sanders Peirce (1839–1914), American philosopher; George Ripley (1802–1880), American philosopher and founder of utopian community Brook Farm; Paul Johannes Tillich (1886–1965), German-American existential philosopher; John Witherspoon (1723–1794), clergyman and signer of the Declaration of Independence; John Woolman (1720–1772), American Quaker abolitionist; Chauncey Wright (1830–1875), American philosopher.

22. Knight apparently took note of this point because Henry David Thoreau (1817–1862) was the subject of one of the four books published in the series.

23. Horace Mann (1796–1859), American educator and congressman; William James (1842–1910), American philosopher and psychologist.

24. Rosanna Phelps Warren (b. 1953), KAP's godchild; and Gabriel Penn Warren (b. 1955).

25. Herman Wouk (1915–), best-selling American author whose novel *Youngblood Hawke* was on the *New York Times* best-selling list for twenty-six weeks in 1962; *Ship of Fools* was on the list for twenty-eight weeks.

26. John James Ellis Palmer (1913–2009) was editor of the *Yale Review*; the review ("Yes, But Are They Really Novels?") was written by Wayne Clayson Booth (1921–2005), American critic and University of Chicago professor.

27. *The Guns of August* (1962), by American historian Barbara Wertheim Tuchman (1912–1989); *George* (1962), by Welsh playwright George Emlyn Williams (1905–1987).

28. John Prince (1922–), caterer and real-estate broker, and his wife, Catherine, were friends of KAP's from the early 1940s until 1964.

29. Mario Einaudi (1905–1994), scholar and president of the Republic of Italy 1948–1955.

30. Denis Devlin (1908–1959), Irish diplomat and poet; Alberto Moravia (1907–1990), Italian novelist; Ignazio Silone, pseudonym of Secondino Tranquilli (1906–1978), Italian author.

31. Roseliep's title *The Small Rain* (1963) was taken from the anonymous sixteenth-century poem: "O Western wind, when wilt thou blow / That the small rain down can rain? / Christ, that my love were in my arms / And I in my bed again."

32. *The Reivers* (1962).

33. William Dean Howells (1837–1920) was an early supporter of Twain, but he was restrained in the realism he advocated ("reticent realism"). Twain's wife, Olivia (Livy) Langdon Clemens (1845–1904), was also cautious about realism.

34. "Raid" (1934) was one of the long stories in *The Unvanquished* (1938); and "Spotted Horses" (1931) was incorporated into *The Hamlet* (1940).

35. Samuel Taliaferro Rayburn (1886–1961) Democratic Texas congressman, speaker of the House; Alben W. Barkley (1877–1956), Democratic vice president with President Harry S. Truman (1884–1972).

36. *Passage to India* (1924).

37. Erna's son Glover Johns Jr. (1912–1976) and his wife, Rita LeCoyer Johns (1916–2002).

38. Robert Heilman (1906–2004), American academic and critic.

39. The quarterly journal produced by La Salle College was *Four Quarters*. The issue devoted to KAP appeared in 1971.

40. *The Naked and the Dead* (1948), by Mailer; *Tropic of Cancer*, by American writer and painter Henry Valentine Miller (1891–1980); *Lady Chatterley's Lover* (1928), by Lawrence; *Little Tin Drum*, by German Pulitzer Prize–winning novelist and SS member (revealed in 2006) Günter Wilhelm Grass (1927–); *Naked Lunch* (1959), by postmodern Beat writer William Seward Burroughs II (1914–1997); *The Lime Twig* (1961), by John Clendennin Talbot Hawkes (1925–1998).

41. Hedda Hopper [b. Elda Furry] (1885–1966), American actress and gossip columnist; and Shelley Winters [b. Shirley Schrift] (1920–2006), Academy Award–winning American actress.

42. The comic strip *Pogo*, created by American cartoonist Walter Crawford Kelly Jr. (1913–1973).

43. *The Italian Straw Hat* (1927), silent comedy; *Carnival in Flanders* [*La Kermesse Heroic*] (1935), French historical romance.

44. Federico Fellini (1920–1993), Italian film director and script writer (*8½* [1963], his avant-garde Academy Award–winning film); *The Blood of a Poet* (1930), directed by Jean Cocteau; *Beauty and the Beast* [*La Belle et la Bête*] (1946); *Alexander Nevsky* (1938), historical drama directed by Eisenstein; Alfred Joseph Hitchcock (1899–1980), English film director and producer; *Divorce Italian Style* [*Divorzio all'italiana*] (1961), Italian comedy.

45. Marlene Dietrich (1901–1992), German actress and singer.

46. *It's a Mad Mad Mad Mad World* (1963), produced by Stanley Kramer; and *Tom Jones* (1963), a British comedy that won four Academy Awards.

47. *On Approval*, produced as a film in 1930 and 1944, based on a 1926 play by English dramatist Lionel Frederick Lonsdale (1881–1954); *Kind Hearts and Coronets* (1949), a British black comedy; *Man About Town* (1947), starring French actor, singer, and vaudeville star Maurice Auguste Chevalier (1888–1972); *Murder She Said* (1961), mystery film based on novel by Agatha Christie.

48. *The Private Life of Henry VIII* (1933); *The Gold Rush* (1925).

49. George Barry Bingham Sr. (1906–1988), Kentucky media mogul.

50. Vida Ann Rutherford Vliet (1931–) was working on her doctoral dissertation "The Shape of Meaning: A Study of the Development of Katherine Anne Porter's Fictional Form" at the Pennsylvania State University.

51. Norman Holmes Pearson (1909–1975), American academic and archivist at Yale.

52. Kenneth Durant.

53. *Dr. Strangelove or: How I Learned to Stop Worrying and Love the Bomb* (1964), satiric black comedy starring British actor Richard Henry (Peter) Sellers (1925–1980).

54. *The Sot-Weed Factor* (1960), a novel by John Simmons Barth (1930–).

55. Oskar Werner (1922–1984), Austrian actor.

56. Laurence Kerr Olivier (1907–1989), English actor, director, and producer.

57. William Penn Adair (Will) Rogers (1879–1935), American cowboy, comedian, and vaudeville performer.

58. Vivien Leigh (1913–1967), English actress.

59. The flamenco dance troupe founded in 1949 by dancer and choreographer José Greco (1918–2000).

60. Elizabeth Ashley (1939–), American actress who was best known as a Broadway actress before becoming a movie actress, was cast as Jenny Brown in the movie *Ship of Fools*.

61. William ("Wild Bill") Shanklin was the city editor of the *Rocky Mountain News* and reportedly had a soft spot for recovering tuberculosis patients.

62. Thomas Hornsby Ferril (1896–1988), Colorado poet and journalist.

63. James uses this phrase to refer to his childhood in his autobiography *A Small Boy and Others* (1913).

64. Louise Bethell Hill (c.1896–1955), Denver society matron who established the "sacred 36," a socially elite group of women who met regularly at her mansion.

65. *Katherine Anne Porter and the Art of Rejection* (1964), by William L. Nance (1933–1976); Gordon's review ("Katherine Anne Porter and the ICM") appeared in the November 1964 issue of *Harper's* magazine.

66. Gordon's 1934 novel, *Aleck Maury, Sportsman*.

67. José Joaquín Fernández de Lizardi (1776–1827), Mexican author of *El Periquillo Sarniento* (1816), which KAP translated as *The Itching Parrot* (1942)

68. *None Shall Look Back* (1937).

69. The Civil War.

70. Cowley's original work was *Exile's Return: A Narrative of Ideas* (1934); it was reprinted as *Exile's Return: Literary Odyssey of the 1920s* (1951). Cowley had written: "Katherine Anne Porter worked for a newspaper in Denver before she went to Mexico City, where she lived and worked for most of the decade. At no time did she think of herself as being expatriated." Because Cowley chose to ignore KAP's critically acclaimed fiction, especially *Flowering Judas* (1930), she considered his statement a reduction of her to a "newspaper woman."

71. Frances Steloff (c.1888–1989), founder of the Gotham Book Mart in New York City.

72. Texan Richard Foster Jones (1886–1965), author and head of the Stanford English Department when KAP was writer-in-residence, and his wife, Lucille Jones.

73. Sergei Pavlovich Diaghilev (1872–1929), Russian art critic and founder of Ballets Russes; Anna Pavlova [alt. Pavlowa] (1881–1931), Russian ballerina.

74. Alma Marie Sullivan Reed (1889–1966), American journalist who wrote about Mexican art and moved in KAP's circle in Mexico in the 1920s.

75. American set designers Norman Melancton Bel-Geddes (1893–1958) and Lee Simonson (1888–1967).

76. *Castiza* here translates as "pure."

77. Enrique Henry (Hank) Lopez (1920–1985), Mexican lawyer, editor, and author.

78. French writer Henry de Montherlant (1895–1972); Julien Green (1900–1998), American dramatist who wrote mostly in French.

79. Tuchman's *The Proud Tower: A Portrait of the World Before the War, 1890–1914* (1966); Capote's *In Cold Blood* (1966); *Little Big Man*, by Thomas Berger (1924–).

80. Barbara and Lloyd Wescott's daughter, Deborah.

81. The album *Strangers and Cousins: Songs from His World Tour*, by American folk singer Peter (Pete) Seeger (1919–); one of the songs on it is "Uh, Uh, Uh."

82. KAP often called George Platt Lynes "Georgio."

83. Kohler's original review, "Miss Porter Writes of Allegorical Voyage," was published in the *Louisville Courier-Journal*, 1 April 1962; it was reprinted in the Richmond *News Leader*.

84. "A Christmas Story" was published by *Mademoiselle* in the December 1946 issue and as a separate illustrated hardback book in 1958.

PART SIX

1. KAP's friend and attorney, E. Barrett Prettyman Jr. (1925–), hosted a party in her honor to celebrate the publication of her *Collected Essays and Occasional Writings of Katherine Anne Porter*, which she dedicated to him.

2. *Losing Battles* (1970).

3. Constance (Connie) Porter, wife of Harrison Paul Porter Sr.

4. *Skin Diving in the Virgins, and Other Poems* (1970).

5. Woolf's essay was "On Being Ill" (1926).

6. A reference to "The Responsibility of the Novelist: The Critical Reception of *Ship of Fools*," by Myron Mandell Liberman (1921–1995), who argued that critics had failed to recognize the novel as a medieval apologue.

7. Jon Spence's article "Looking-Glass Reflections: Satirical Elements in *Ship of Fools*" appeared in the *Sewanee Review* in the spring 1974 issue.

8. "Gerontion" (1920).

9. Attributed to Henry Ford II (1917–1987) and repeated by Gerald Rudolph Ford Jr. [born Leslie Lynch King Jr.] (1913–2006), president of the United States 1974–1977.

10. James wrote in *Notes of a Son and Brother* (1914) that his family "breathed somehow an air in which waste, for us at least, couldn't and didn't live"; in his essay "Is There a Life After Death?" (1910) James wrote, "The probability is, in fact, that what we dimly discern as waste the wisdom of the universe may know as a very different matter."

11. E. Barrett Prettyman Jr.

12. Warren's book was *Democracy and Poetry* (1975), based on his 1974 Jefferson lecture "Poetry and Dermocracy."

13. *La Vida es Sueño* [*Life is a Dream*] (1635), play by Spanish playwright Pedro Calderón de la Barca (1600–1681).

14. Warren's *Or Else—Poem/Poems 1968–74* (1974).

15. "Le coeur a ses raisons que la raison ne connaît point," attributed to Blaise Pascal (1623–1662), French mathematician and philosopher.

16. KAP is referring either to "You Did a Poet's Legwork" or "After the Portrait by Armand Thibault de Navarre," both poems by Roseliep and dedicated to KAP in the chapbook *A Beautiful Woman Moves with Grace* (1976), which he edited.

17. *Portnoy's Complaint* (1969), by Philip Milton Roth (1933–).

18. Joan Mary Givner (1936–), author of numerous articles on Porter and her works and the first full biography; KAP might have been referring to "Her Great Art, Her Sober Craft: Katherine Anne Porter's Creative Process," published in the *Southwest Review* in 1977. Joan Flanders likely sent KAP a draft of her article "Katherine Anne Porter's Feminist Criticism: Book Reviews from the 1920s," which would be published in 1979.

19. "What One Woman Is Doing to Help Children," by Gordon Shearer, *Dallas Morning News*, 16 December 1916.

20. Maria Ofelia Garza Tinkle, Lon Tinkle's wife.

21. Bill Wilkins.

22. Owen Laster of the William Morris Agency was KAP's agent for a while.

23. Both Warren and Eudora Welty received the Presidential Medal of Freedom at the White House in 1980.

Index

on "Indian Revolution," 81–82
influences on, 143
interwar period observed by, 66
on Irish revolutionists, 152
iron will of, 320
jewelry of, 282
jokes told by, 69, 150–51, 156
as landless, 322
as lecturer, 40
on legend and memory as sources of
    literature, 129
letters: attitudes toward, xxi–xxii, 209–
    10; copies kept by, 359n93; as poor
    keepers of secrets, 28; writing of, 151,
    199, 259, 319
on Life, capital L, 226, 231, 257, 329
on limited editions, 105
as Local Girl Makes Good, 334
on love, 44, 54–56, 198, 231; illusion of, 34,
    61, 80, 104, 190–91
love affairs of, xiv, xv, xxv, xxxi, xxxv,
    4, 5–6, 34, 61, 79–80, 153, 217, 261;
    with Aguilera, 30–32; with Goyen,
    221–22, 231; with Hidalgo, 44, 45; with
    Josephson, 54–55
on love and hate, 47–48
love from family sought by, 20
luxury loved by, 80, 107–8
magazine and editing work of, 49
maids employed by, 75, 81–82, 146, 151,
    221, 294–95
on marriage, 104, 198
marriages of, xiv, xv, xvi, xxviii, 66, 108,
    142, 257; abuse suffered in, 3, 104
Mather family researched by, xv, 42
melancholy of, 237, 292
on men, 79–80, 139
as Mexico friend and critic, 79
on midwesterners, 130–31
on modern novel, 218, 244
as modern woman, xxii
modernist movement embraced by, xxiii
on money, 44, 82, 207–8, 257

on moral force, 209
on morality in politics, 210
movie work by, xiv, xvii
on music, 248
music studied by, 77, 109
name changed by, xiii, xiv
on name "Miranda," 56
on naming children, 56–57
near-death of, 322
on negro art, 175
in the news, 5, 147, 204, 273, 291
"newspaper woman" label rejected by,
    306–7
newspaper work of, 29
on old age, 308
on Old South and New South, 85
older literature preferred by, xxii
outspokenness of, 154
as pacifist, 137
papers of, 247, 253, 255–56, 298, 315–16
perfumes favored by, 5
on perverted people, 97
photographs of, 18, 29, 34, 179, 262, 267,
    287–88, 306, 316, 325, 335; on Atlantic
    cover, 248; Cadmus's drawing of, 179;
    in Harcourt, Brace catalog, 165
piano lessons and playing by, 77, 86, 109,
    177
on place in American literature, 253
on poetry, 32, 272; love poetry, 275; lyric
    poetry, 275
political positions of, 153
on politics and public affairs, 129
poverty of, 79, 82
on poverty and misery, 244
pregnancies of, 35, 362n59; miscarriages
    of, 3; stillbirth of son, 36
on privacy, 119, 147, 218, 252, 298
private life of, 263
as professional writer, 333
on "proletariat" as term, 203
property owned by, 153, 163–64, 187,
    189–90